AQA Mathematics

Book 1
Higher (Linear)

New GCSE

Series Editor
Paul Metcalf

Series Advisor
Andy Darbourne

Lead Authors
Sandra Burns
Shaun Procter-Green
Margaret Thornton

Authors
Tony Fisher
June Haighton
Anne Haworth
Gill Hewlett
Andrew Manning
Ginette McManus
Howard Prior
David Pritchard
Dave Ridgway
Paul Winters

Nelson Thornes

Text © Sandra Burns, Tony Fisher, June Haighton, Anne Haworth, Gill Hewlett, Andrew Manning, Paul Metcalf, Ginette McManus, Howard Prior, David Pritchard, Shaun Procter-Green, Dave Ridgway, Margaret Thornton and Paul Winters 2012
Original illustrations © Nelson Thornes Ltd 2010, 2012

The right of Sandra Burns, Tony Fisher, June Haighton, Anne Haworth, Gill Hewlett, Andrew Manning, Ginette McManus, Paul Metcalf, Howard Prior, David Pritchard, Shaun Procter-Green, Dave Ridgway, Margaret Thornton and Paul Winters to be identified as authors of this work has been asserted by them in accordance with the Copyright, Designs and Patents Act 1988.

All rights reserved. No part of this publication may be reproduced or transmitted in any form or by any means, electronic or mechanical, including photocopy, recording or any information storage and retrieval system, without permission in writing from the publisher or under licence from the Copyright Licensing Agency Limited, of Saffron House, 6–10 Kirby Street, London, EC1N 8TS.

Any person who commits any unauthorised act in relation to this publication may be liable to criminal prosecution and civil claims for damages.

This edition published in 2012 by:
Nelson Thornes Ltd
Delta Place
27 Bath Road
CHELTENHAM
GL53 7TH
United Kingdom

12 13 14 15 16 / 10 9 8 7 6 5 4 3 2 1

A catalogue record for this book is available from the British Library

ISBN 978 1 4085 1850 2

Cover photograph: Steve Debenport/Getty Images

Illustrations by Rupert Besley, Roger Penwill, Angela Knowles and Tech-Set Limited

Page make-up by Tech-Set Limited, Gateshead

Printed and bound in Spain by GraphyCems

Photo acknowledgements
Alamy: p19
Fotolia: p7, p33, p60, p67, p104, p114, p122, p136, p179, p221, p267, p281
Getty Images/AFP: p36
iStockphoto: p25, p28, p34, p55, p81, p93, p100, p111, p117, p128, p157, p181, p205, p210, p254, p272, p277
NASA: p106, p143
Science Photo Library: p146

Contents

Introduction 5

Chapter 1 Angles and areas 7

1.1 Angles and parallel lines 8
1.2 Bearings 11
1.3 Area of parallelograms, trapeziums and triangles 13
1.4 Circumference and area of a circle 17
1.5 Compound shapes 20
Chapter 1 Assess 22

Chapter 2 Prime factors 25

2.1 Factors and multiples 26
2.2 Prime numbers and prime factors 29
Chapter 2 Assess 32

Chapter 3 Collecting data 34

3.1 Types of data 35
3.2 Data collection methods 38
3.3 Organising data 41
3.4 Sampling methods 43
Chapter 3 Assess 48

Chapter 4 Fractions and decimals 50

4.1 Adding and subtracting fractions 51
4.2 Multiplying and dividing fractions 53
4.3 One quantity as a fraction of another 56
4.4 Fractions as decimals 57
4.5 Dividing quantities in given ratios 59
4.6 Rounding 60
4.7 Decimal calculations 63
Chapter 4 Assess 65

Chapter 5 Graphs of linear functions 67

5.1 Drawing straight-line graphs 68
5.2 Gradients of straight-line graphs 70
5.3 The midpoint of a line segment 74
5.4 Lines through two given points and parallel lines 76
Chapter 5 Assess 79

Chapter 6 Working with symbols 81

6.1 Expanding brackets and collecting like terms 82
6.2 Factorising expressions 86
6.3 Multiplying two brackets together 89
6.4 Simplifying algebraic fractions 90
Chapter 6 Assess 91

Chapter 7 Percentages 93

7.1 Percentages, fractions and decimals 94
7.2 Increasing or decreasing an amount by a percentage 97
7.3 Successive percentages 100
7.4 Compound interest 102
7.5 Writing one quantity as a percentage of another 105
7.6 Finding a percentage increase or decrease 107
7.7 Reverse percentages 110
Chapter 7 Assess 112

Chapter 8 Statistical measures 114

8.1 Frequency distributions 115
8.2 Grouped frequency distributions 120
Chapter 8 Assess 124

Chapter 9 Sequences 128

9.1 The nth term of a sequence 129
Chapter 9 Assess 133

Chapter 10 Ratio and proportion 135

10.1 Finding and simplifying ratios 136
10.2 Using ratios to find quantities 139
10.3 The unitary method 141
Chapter 10 Assess 144

Chapter 11 Area and volume 1 — 146

| 11.1 | Volume of a prism | 147 | Chapter 11 Assess | 155 |
| 11.2 | Surface area of a prism | 152 | | |

Chapter 12 Real-life graphs — 157

| 12.1 | Distance–time graphs | 158 | Chapter 12 Assess | 167 |
| 12.2 | Other real-life graphs | 162 | | |

Chapter 13 Indices and standard index form — 171

| 13.1 | Rules of indices | 172 | Chapter 13 Assess | 179 |
| 13.2 | Standard index form | 175 | | |

Chapter 14 Properties of polygons — 181

| 14.1 | Properties of quadrilaterals | 182 | Chapter 14 Assess | 188 |
| 14.2 | Angle properties of polygons | 185 | | |

Chapter 15 Equations and inequalities — 192

15.1	Equations where the unknown (x) appears on both sides	193	15.4	Inequalities and the number line	198
15.2	Equations with brackets	194	15.5	Solving inequalities	199
15.3	Equations with fractions	196	15.6	Inequalities and graphs	200
				Chapter 15 Assess	204

Chapter 16 Trial and improvement — 205

| 16.1 | Trial and improvement | 206 | Chapter 16 Assess | 208 |

Chapter 17 Scatter graphs — 210

| 17.1 | Interpreting scatter graphs | 211 | Chapter 17 Assess | 218 |
| 17.2 | Lines of best fit | 214 | | |

Chapter 18 Reflections, rotations and translations — 221

18.1	Reflection	222	18.4	Transformation and congruence	239
18.2	Rotation	227		Chapter 18 Assess	244
18.3	Translation	235			

Chapter 19 Measures — 247

| 19.1 | Accuracy of measurement | 248 | Chapter 19 Assess | 253 |
| 19.2 | Compound measures | 249 | | |

Chapter 20 3-D shapes, coordinates and graphs — 254

| 20.1 | Plans and elevations | 255 | 20.3 | Graphs | 262 |
| 20.2 | Coordinates in 3-D | 260 | | Chapter 20 Assess | 269 |

Chapter 21 Pythagoras' theorem — 272

| 21.1 | Pythagoras' theorem | 273 | Chapter 21 Assess | 281 |
| 21.2 | Pythagoras' theorem in three dimensions | 278 | | |

Chapter 22 Surds — 284

| 22.1 | Simplifying surds | 285 | Chapter 22 Assess | 289 |
| 22.2 | Rationalising the denominator | 287 | | |

Glossary — 290
Index — 295

Nelson Thornes and AQA

Nelson Thornes has worked in partnership with AQA to ensure that this book and the accompanying online resources offer you the best support for your GCSE course.

Nelson Thornes has a thorough quality assurance process to ensure that their contents closely match the AQA specification. You can be confident that the content of these materials have been written, checked and approved by AQA senior examiners, in order to provide the best possible support.

The print and online resources together unlock blended learning; this means that the links between the activities in the book and the activities online blend together to maximise your understanding of a topic and help you achieve your potential.

These online resources are available on kerboodle Secondary which can be accessed via the internet at www.kerboodle.com/live, anytime, anywhere.

If your school or college subscribes to kerboodle Secondary you will be provided with your own personal login details. Once logged in, access your course and locate the required activity.

For more information and help on how to use kerboodle Secondary visit www.kerboodle.com.

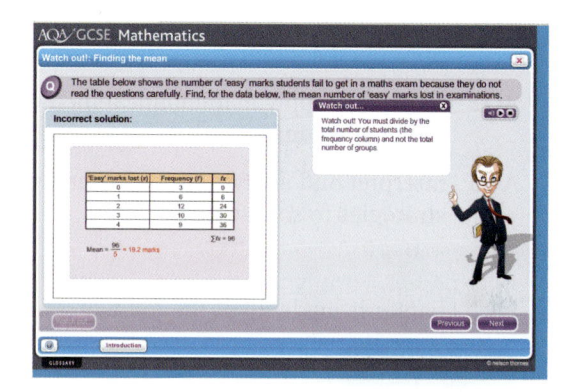

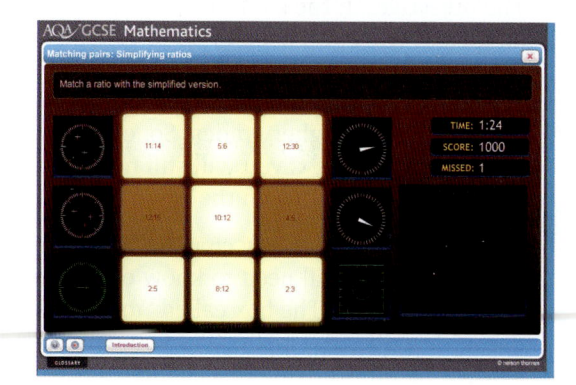

How to use this book

To help you unlock blended learning, we have referenced the activities in this book that have additional online coverage in Kerboodle by using this icon:

The icons in this book show you the online resources available from the start of the new specification and will always be relevant.

In addition, to keep the blend up-to-date and engaging, we review customer feedback and may add new content onto Kerboodle after publication!

Welcome to GCSE Mathematics

This book has been written by teachers and examiners who not only want you to get the best grade you can in your GCSE exam, but also to enjoy maths. Together with Book 2 it covers all the material you will need to know for AQA GCSE Mathematics Higher (Linear). Look out for calculator or non-calculator symbols (shown below) which tell you whether to use a calculator or not.

In the exam, you will be tested on the Assessment Objectives (AOs) below. Ask your teacher if you need help to understand what these mean.

- **AO1** recall and use your knowledge of the prescribed content
- **AO2** select and apply mathematical methods in a range of contexts
- **AO3** interpret and analyse problems and generate strategies to solve them.

Each chapter is made up of the following features:

Objectives

The objectives at the start of the chapter give you an idea of what you need to do to get each grade. Remember that the examiners expect you to do well at the lower grade questions on the exam paper in order to get the higher grades. So, even if you are aiming for a Grade C you will still need to do well on the Grade G questions on the exam paper.

On the first page of every chapter, there are also words that you will need to know or understand, called Key Terms. The box called 'You should already know' describes the maths that you will have learned before studying this chapter. There is also an interesting fact at the beginning of each chapter which tells you about maths in real life.

Learn...

The Learn sections give you the key information and examples to show how to do each topic. There are several Learn sections in each chapter.

Practise...

Questions that allow you to practise what you have just learned.

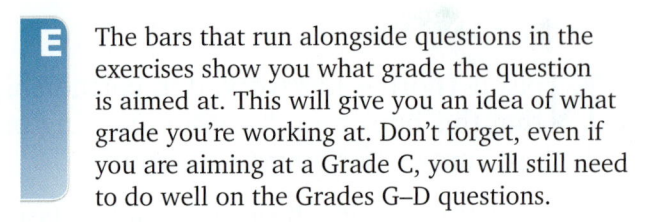

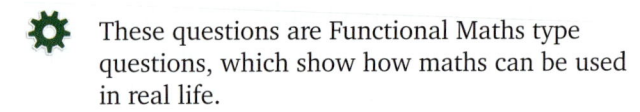

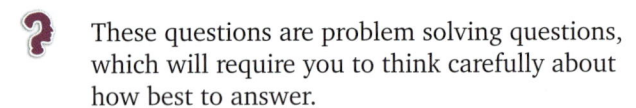

E The bars that run alongside questions in the exercises show you what grade the question is aimed at. This will give you an idea of what grade you're working at. Don't forget, even if you are aiming at a Grade C, you will still need to do well on the Grades G–D questions.

These questions are Functional Maths type questions, which show how maths can be used in real life.

These questions are problem solving questions, which will require you to think carefully about how best to answer.

These questions are harder questions.

These questions should be attempted **with** a calculator.

These questions should be attempted **without** using a calculator.

Assess

End of chapter questions written by examiners. Some chapters feature additional questions taken from real past papers to further your understanding.

Hint

These are tips for you to remember whilst learning the maths or answering questions.

AQA Examiner's tip

These are tips from the people who will mark your exams, giving you advice on things to remember and watch out for.

Bump up your grade

These are tips from the people who will mark your exams, giving you help on how to boost your grade, especially aimed at getting a Grade C.

1 Angles and areas

Objectives

Examiners would normally expect students who get these grades to be able to:

D

recognise corresponding, alternate and interior angles on parallel lines

understand and use three-figure bearings

find the area of a triangle, trapezium and parallelogram

find the area and perimeter of shapes made from triangles and rectangles

calculate the circumference and area of a circle

C

work out the perimeter and area of a semicircle and compound shapes made from parts of a circle.

Key terms

vertically opposite
parallel
transversal
alternate angle
corresponding angle
interior (allied) angles
bearing
base
perpendicular height

Did you know?

Wind and sails

If you want to sail a boat, you need to understand how the area of the sails and the angle the boat travels relative to the wind direction affect the boat's progress. If a sailor wants to travel 'upwind' (towards the wind), it's best to travel about 45° from the direction that the wind is coming from. This is called 'close-hauled' or 'on a beat'. In a storm sailors would minimise their sail area to prevent the sudden strong gusts of wind capsizing the boat. They would 'ride out the storm'!

You should already know:

✓ the terms clockwise and anticlockwise
✓ how to distinguish between acute, obtuse, reflex and right angles
✓ that angles at a point add up to 360°
✓ that angles on a straight line add up to 180°
✓ that vertically opposite angles are equal
✓ that angles in a triangle add up to 180°
✓ how to find the perimeter and area of rectangles
✓ the definition of a parallelogram and a trapezium
✓ the names of basic parts of a circle: centre, diameter, radius and circumference.

Learn... 1.1 Angles and parallel lines

Angles at a point add up to 360°.

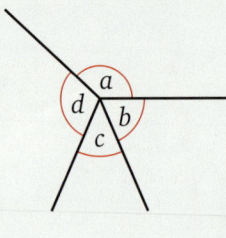

Angles on a straight line add up to 180°.

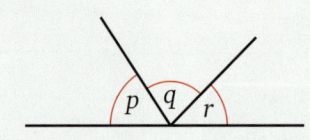

$a + b + c + d = 360°$

$p + q + r = 180°$

Where two lines cross, the **vertically opposite** angles are equal.

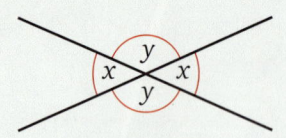

Two lines which stay the same perpendicular distance apart are called **parallel** lines.

The arrows show that the lines are parallel.

A line through the two parallel lines is called a **transversal**.

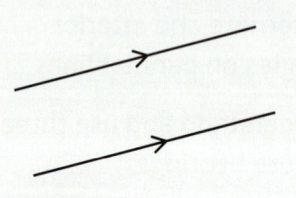

Several pairs of equal angles are formed between the parallel lines and the transversal.

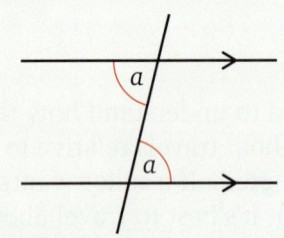

The angles marked a are **alternate angles**.

They are equal.

The angles are on opposite sides of the transversal.

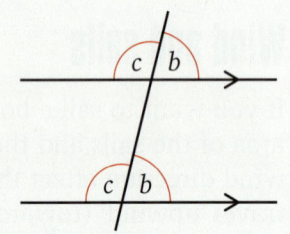

The angles marked b are **corresponding angles**.

They are equal.

The angles are in similar positions on the same side of the transversal.

The angles marked c are another pair of corresponding angles.

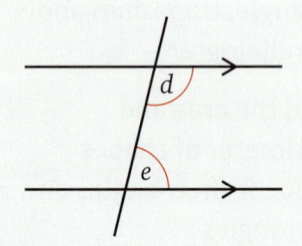

Angles d and e are **interior** (or **allied**) angles.

They always add up to 180°.

So $d + e = 180°$

Example: Work out x.

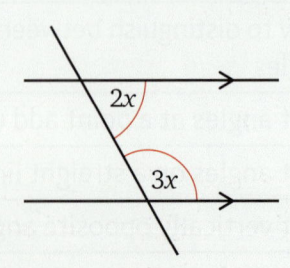

Solution: $2x$ and $3x$ are both interior angles and add up to 180°.

$2x + 3x = 180°$
$5x = 180°$
$x = 36°$

Chapter 1 Angles and areas

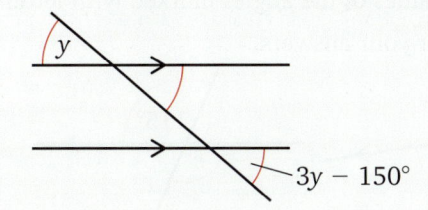

Example: Work out y.

Solution: y and the marked angle are vertically opposite angles. Therefore they are equal.

The marked angle and $3y - 150°$ are corresponding angles. Therefore they are equal.

So y and $3y - 150°$ are equal.

$3y - 150° = y$
$2y - 150° = 0$
$2y = 150°$
$y = 75°$

It is often possible to find angles by more than one method.

Practise... 1.1 Angles and parallel lines   D C B A A*

In this exercise the diagrams are not drawn accurately.

1 Work out the values of angles x, z, q, r and s.
Give reasons for your answers.

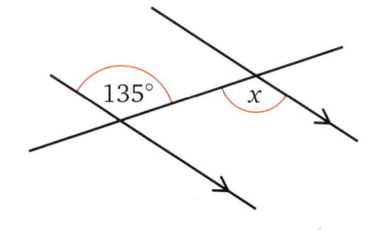

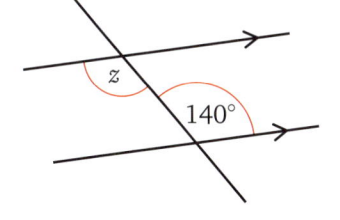

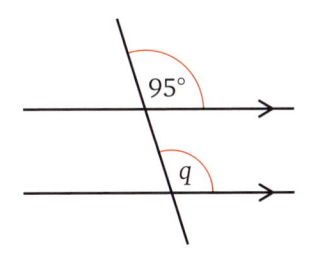

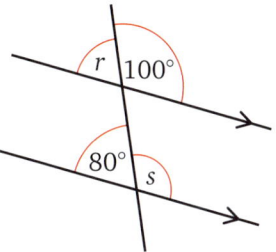

135°, x

z, 140°

95°, q

r, 100°, 80°, s

2 Work out the values of angles x, y and z.
Give reasons for your answers.

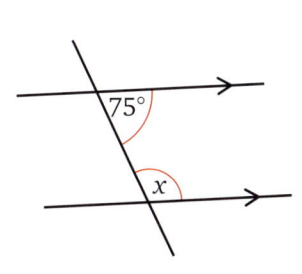

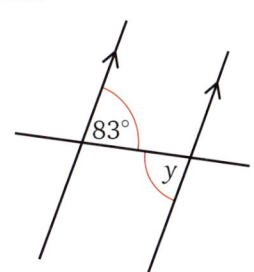

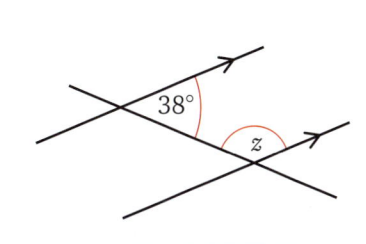

75°, x

83°, y

38°, z

Hint
Remember that you can use facts about angles at a point or on a line as well as angle properties of parallel lines.

10 AQA GCSE Mathematics

D

3 Work out the values of the angles marked with letters.
Give reasons for your answers.

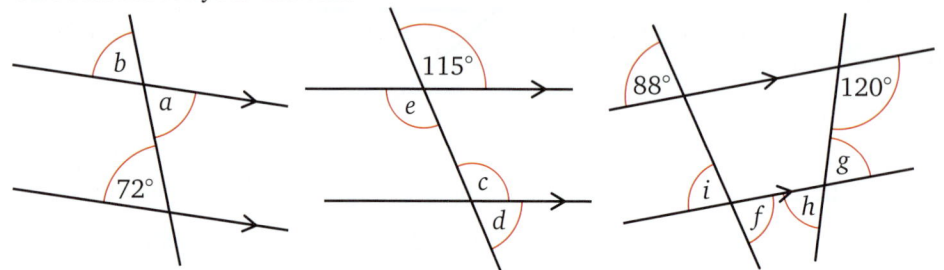

C

4 a Are lines AB and CD parallel?
Give a reason for your answer.

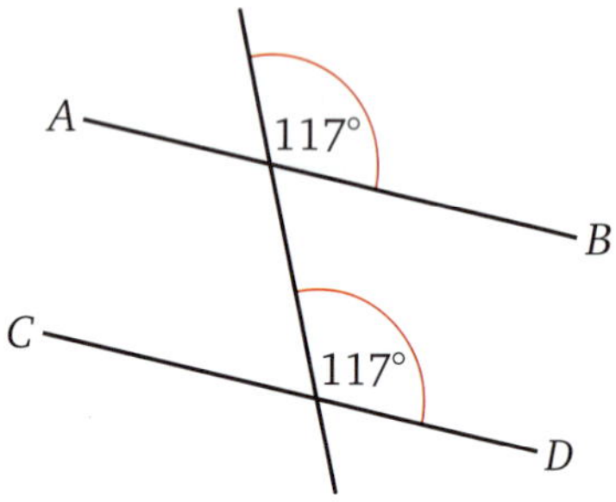

b Are lines EF and GH parallel?
Give a reason for your answer.

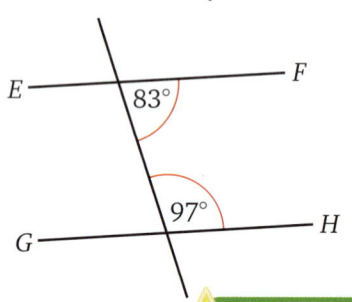

> **Bump up your grade**
> To get a Grade C you need to be able to prove that lines are parallel.

5 Calculate the size of the angles marked with letters.

a

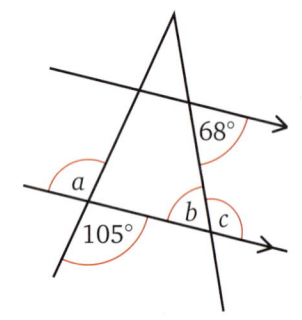

b

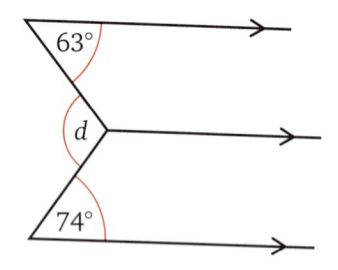

c

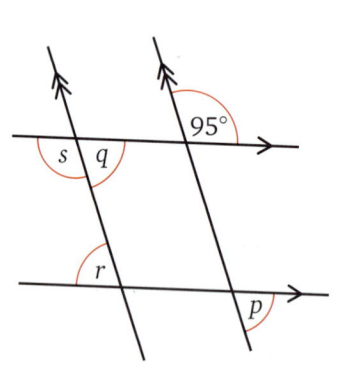

⚠ 6 a Work out x and y.

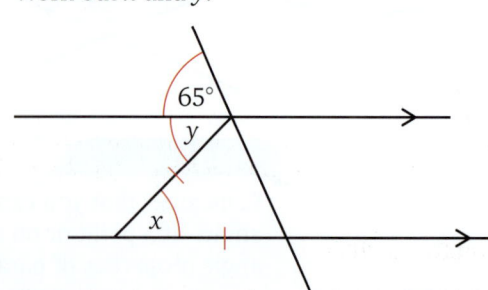

b Work out x and y.

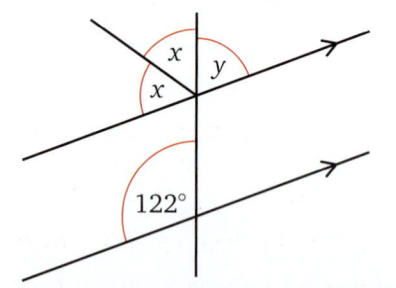

Chapter 1 Angles and areas

Learn... 1.2 Bearings

Directions can be described using the points of the compass such as south, north-west and so on.

Directions can also be described using **three-figure bearings**.

A three-figure bearing gives the angle measured in a clockwise direction from the north line.

Angles of less than 100° need a zero placed in front to make them three figures.

So south has a bearing of 180°, east has a bearing of 090° and west has a bearing of 270°.

Other directions can all be described using bearings.

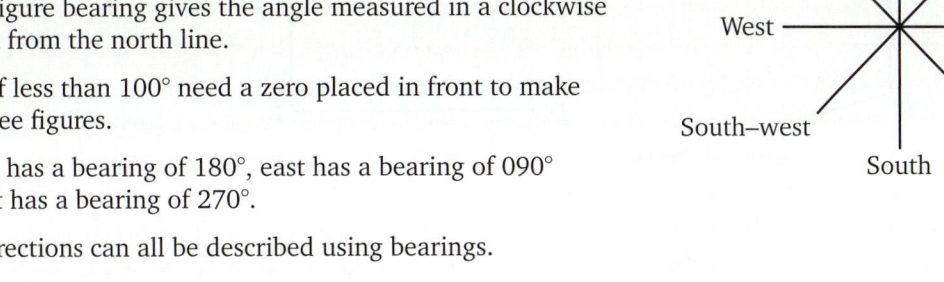

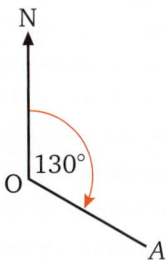

Bearing of 130°   Bearing of 325°   Bearing of 075°

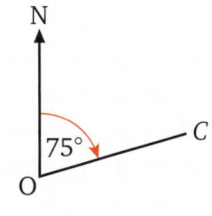

Bearings **from** one place to another can be found by measurement or by calculation.

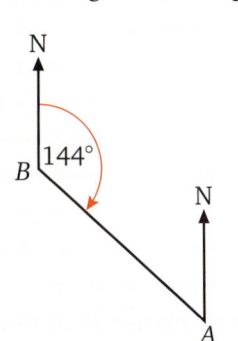

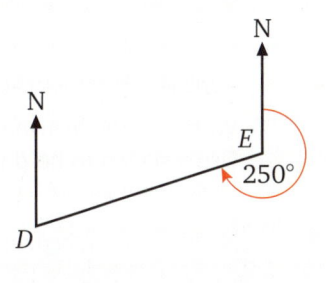

The bearing of A **from** B is 144°.   The bearing of P **from** Q is 055°.   The bearing of D **from** E is 250°.

Example: Branton is on a bearing of 105° from Averby.

Work out the bearing of Averby from Branton.

Solution: Draw a sketch.

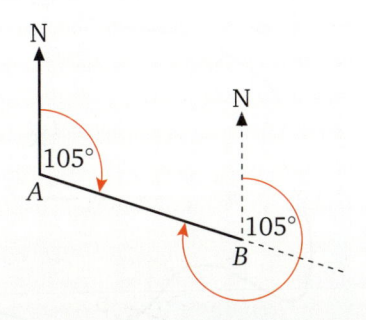

AQA Examiner's tip

Remember to put the north line at the place you are working the bearing out '**from**'.

Face towards Averby **from** Branton, so the north line is drawn at Branton, then the angle is measured clockwise from north around to the line joining B to A (as shown by the arrow). The angle measured clockwise from north is 105° + 180° = 285°.

So the bearing of Averby **from** Branton is 285°.

Practise... 1.2 Bearings

1 For each diagram, write down the three-figure bearing of D from E.

a) 115° (angle from N at E to D)

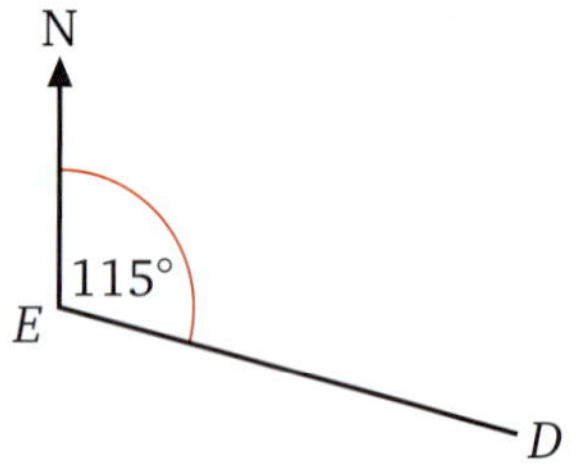

b) 29° (angle from N at E to D)

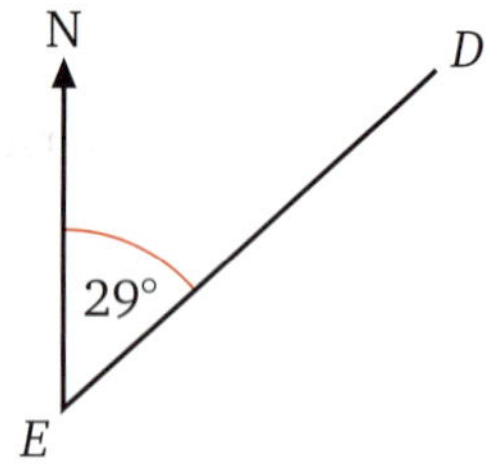

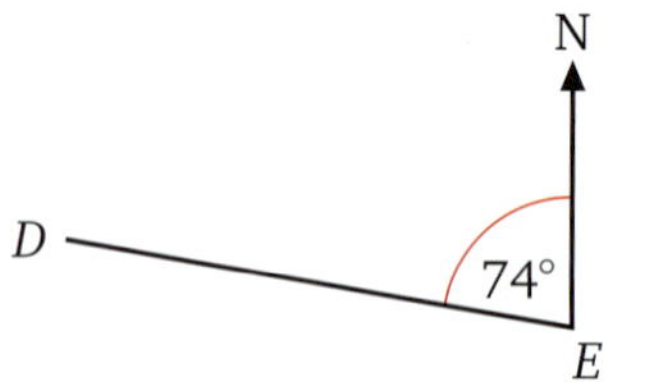

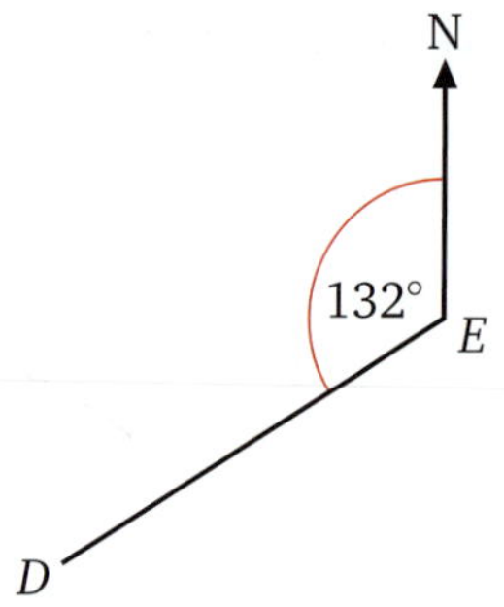

c) 90° (right angle from N at E to D; D is west of E)

d) 74° (angle at E from N to D, with D to the west)

e) 132° (angle from N at E to D)

f) 9° (angle from N at E to D)

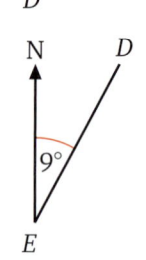

2 Use a protractor to draw accurate diagrams to represent these bearings.

a 140°   c 210°   e 85°   g 163°
b 045°   d 320°   f 108°   h 258°

3 Thatham is on a bearing of 78° from Benton.

Work out the bearing of Benton from Thatham.
Use a sketch to help you.

4 Newby is on a bearing of 250° from Reddington.

Work out the bearing of Reddington from Newby.

5 Jake leaves home and cycles for 6 kilometres on a bearing of 070°. He then cycles for 5 kilometres on a bearing of 140°.

Make an accurate drawing of his route and use it to find the bearing and distance he needs to travel to return directly to his home.

6 Here is a map of an island.

P is a port. H_1 and H_2 are hotels.
T is a town and B is a beach.

a Which hotel is on a bearing of 055° from the port?

b Measure and write down the bearing of the beach from the port.

c Measure and write down the bearing of the port from the town.

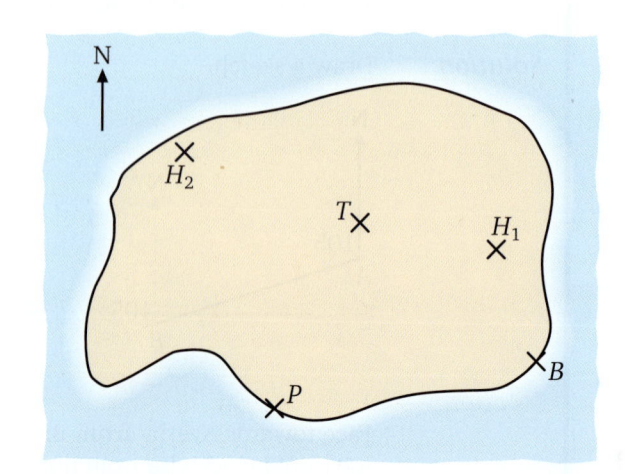

7 Bridgetown is 80 miles north and 50 miles east of Archway.

By making an accurate scale drawing, calculate the bearing of Archway from Bridgetown.

Chapter 1 Angles and areas 13

Learn... 1.3 Area of parallelograms, trapeziums and triangles

Here is a parallelogram drawn on squared paper.

If the shaded triangle is cut from one end of the parallelogram and put onto the other end, the shape becomes a rectangle.

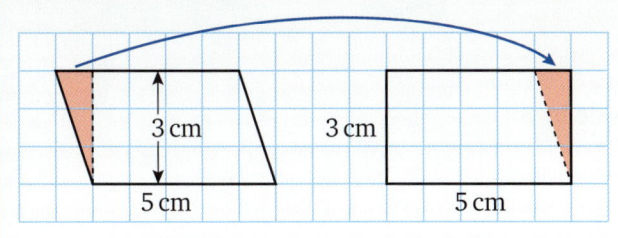

3 cm   3 cm
5 cm   5 cm

Not drawn accurately

The area of the parallelogram is the same as the area of the rectangle.

The **base** of the parallelogram is the same as the length of the rectangle.

The **perpendicular height** (at right angles to the base) of the parallelogram is the same as the width of the rectangle.

Area of rectangle = length × width = 5 × 3 = 15 cm²

Area of parallelogram = 5 × 3 = 15 cm²

The area of any parallelogram can be calculated using the formula:

   area = base × perpendicular height

AQA Examiner's tip
Be careful that you do not use the sloped height. Examiners often put three measurements on a parallelogram.

A diagonal has now been drawn on the parallelogram.

The diagonal divides the parallelogram into two equal triangles.

The area of each triangle is half the area of the parallelogram.

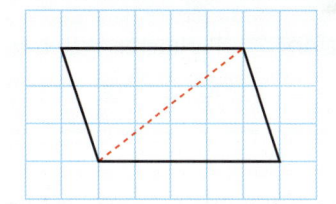

This gives the formula for the area of a **triangle**:

   area = $\frac{1}{2}$ × base × perpendicular height

The shape in the example below is a **trapezium**.

The area of a trapezium can also be found by using the formula:

   area = $\frac{1}{2}(a + b)h$

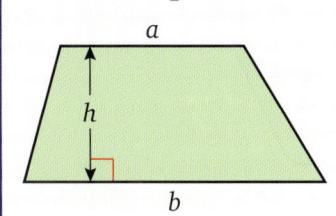

a
h
b

Example:
Calculate the area of this triangle.

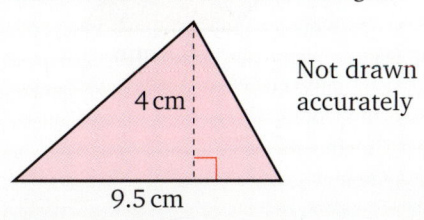

4 cm
9.5 cm

Not drawn accurately

Solution:
Base = 9.5 cm

Perpendicular height = 4 cm

Area = $\frac{1}{2}$ × base × perpendicular height

Area = $\frac{1}{2}$ × 9.5 × 4 = 19 cm²

Example: A parallelogram has an area of 51 cm².

The perpendicular height of the parallelogram is 3 cm.

Work out the base of the parallelogram.

Solution: Area = base × perpendicular height

51 = base × 3

$\frac{51}{3}$ = base   *Divide each side by 3*

17 = base

The base of the parallelogram is 17 cm.

Example: For this trapezium work out:

a the perimeter   **b** the area.

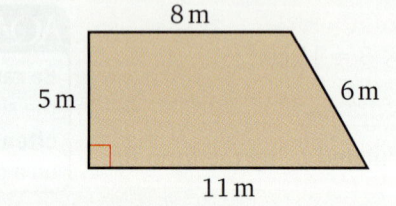

8 m
5 m   6 m   Not drawn accurately
11 m

Solution: Perimeter = 8 + 6 + 11 + 5 = 30 m

Area = $\frac{1}{2}$(8 + 11) × 5 = $\frac{1}{2}$ × 19 × 5 = 47.5 m²

Practise... 1.3 Area of parallelograms, trapeziums and triangles   D C B A A*

The shapes in this exercise are not drawn accurately.

1 Work out the area of each parallelogram.

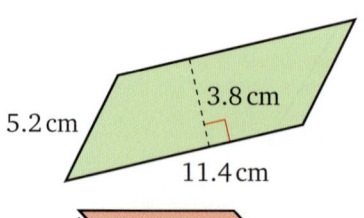

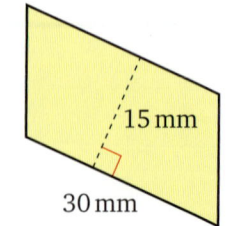

a 8 cm, 12 cm

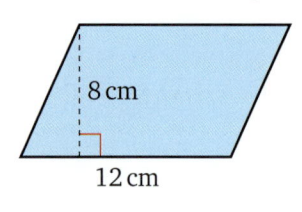

b 15 mm, 30 mm

c 5.2 cm, 3.8 cm, 11.4 cm

d 4 mm, 5.8 mm, 6.5 mm

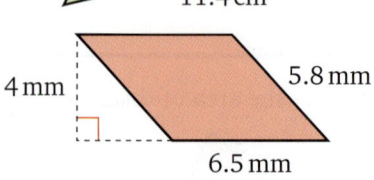

2 Work out the area of each triangle.

a 6 cm, 8 cm

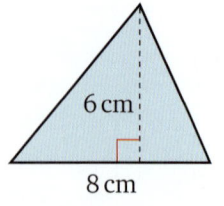

b 9.6 m, 2.4 m

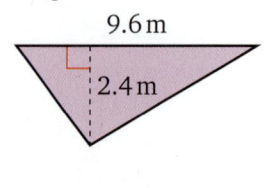

c 14 cm, 3 cm

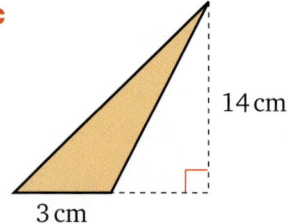

d 18 cm, 5 cm

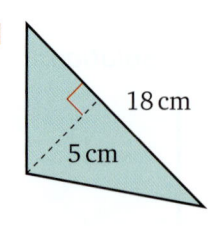

Chapter 1 Angles and areas

3 Which of the following shapes has the largest area?
Show your working.

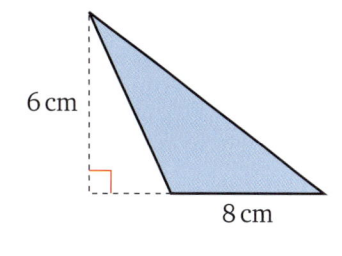

a 9 cm × 4 cm rectangle

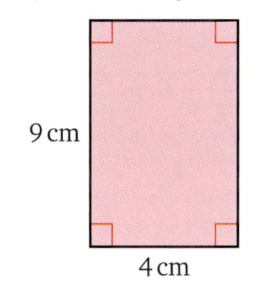

b triangle with 6 cm height and 8 cm base

c parallelogram with 5 cm height and 8 cm base

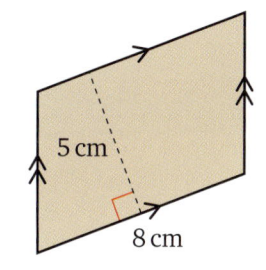

4 A parallelogram of base 7.2 cm has an area of 97.2 cm².

Work out the height of the parallelogram.

5 Four students are trying to find the area of this triangle.

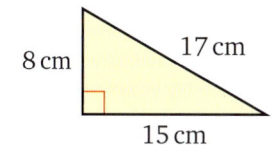

Javed thinks the answer is 40 cm² because 8 + 15 + 17 = 40
Kieran thinks the answer is 120 cm² because 8 × 15 = 120
Leanne thinks the answer is 60 cm² because $\frac{1}{2}$ × 15 × 8 = 60
Megan thinks the answer is 127.5 cm² because $\frac{1}{2}$ × 15 × 17 = 127.5

Who is correct?

What mistakes have the other students made?

Triangle: 8 cm, 17 cm, 15 cm

6 For these parallelograms, work out:

a the perimeter   b the area.

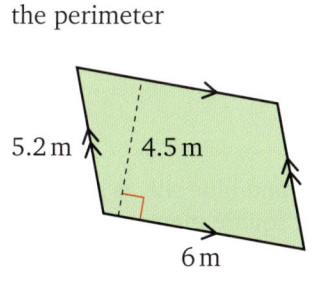

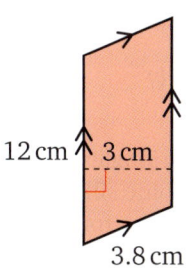

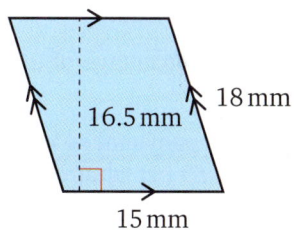

Parallelogram 1: 5.2 m, 4.5 m, 6 m
Parallelogram 2: 12 cm, 3 cm, 3.8 cm
Parallelogram 3: 16.5 mm, 18 mm, 15 mm

7 A triangle has a perpendicular height of 22 cm. The area of the triangle is 308 cm².

Work out the length of the base of the triangle.

8 Each of these shapes is a trapezium.

Work out the area of each shape.

a 8.4 mm (top), 6 mm (height), 11.2 mm (bottom)

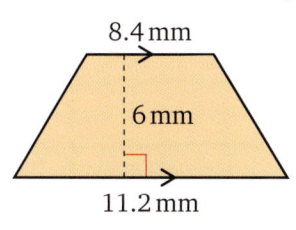

c 76 mm (top), 54 mm (height), 42 mm (bottom)

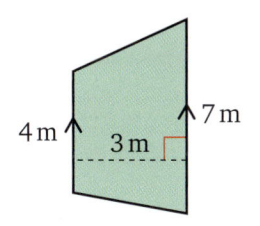

b 4 m, 3 m, 7 m

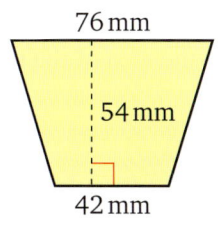

d 3.7 cm (top), 2.8 cm (height), 4.9 cm (bottom)

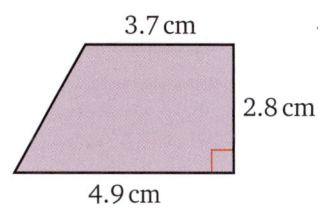

9 Work out the area of each of these shapes.

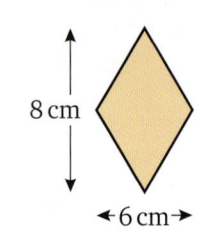

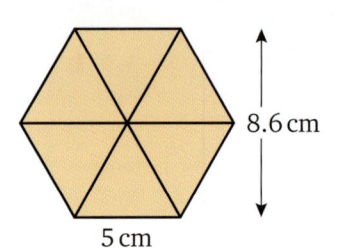

a 8 cm, 6 cm (rhombus)

b 8.6 cm, 5 cm (hexagon)

10 The triangle has the same area as the parallelogram. Work out h.

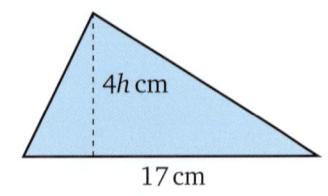

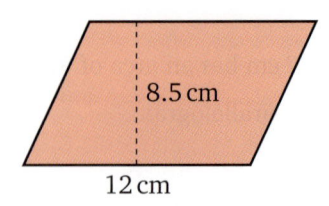

Triangle: 4h cm (height), 17 cm (base)

Parallelogram: 8.5 cm (height), 12 cm (base)

Bump up your grade
To get a Grade C you need to be able to find the height or base of a shape given the area.

11 A club logo is to be made out of metal.

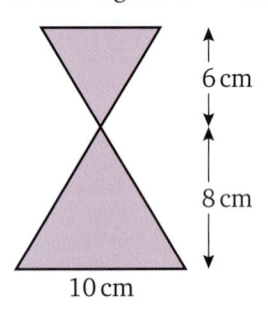

6 cm, 8 cm, 10 cm

Work out the dimensions of the smallest rectangle that can be used to cut out a logo.

What percentage of metal is wasted?

12 A company makes kites. They cut triangles from yellow and blue silk as shown. The yellow silk costs £5 per square metre and the blue silk costs £7 per square metre. Find the cost of material used for each kite. Assume that the triangles for several kites can be cut from the material without wastage.

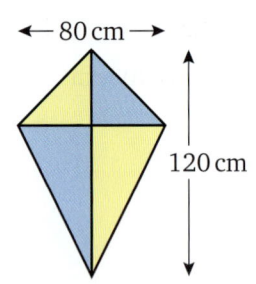

80 cm, 120 cm

13 This trapezium is twice the area of the triangle. Work out x.

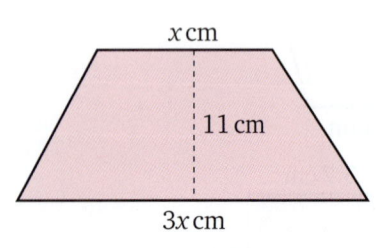

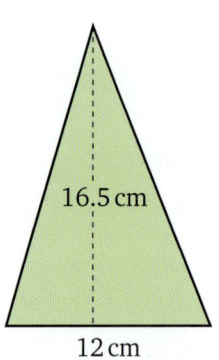

Trapezium: x cm (top), 11 cm (height), $3x$ cm (bottom)

Triangle: 16.5 cm (height), 12 cm (base)

Chapter 1 Angles and areas

Learn... 1.4 Circumference and area of a circle

Parts of a circle

Remember the following parts of a circle.

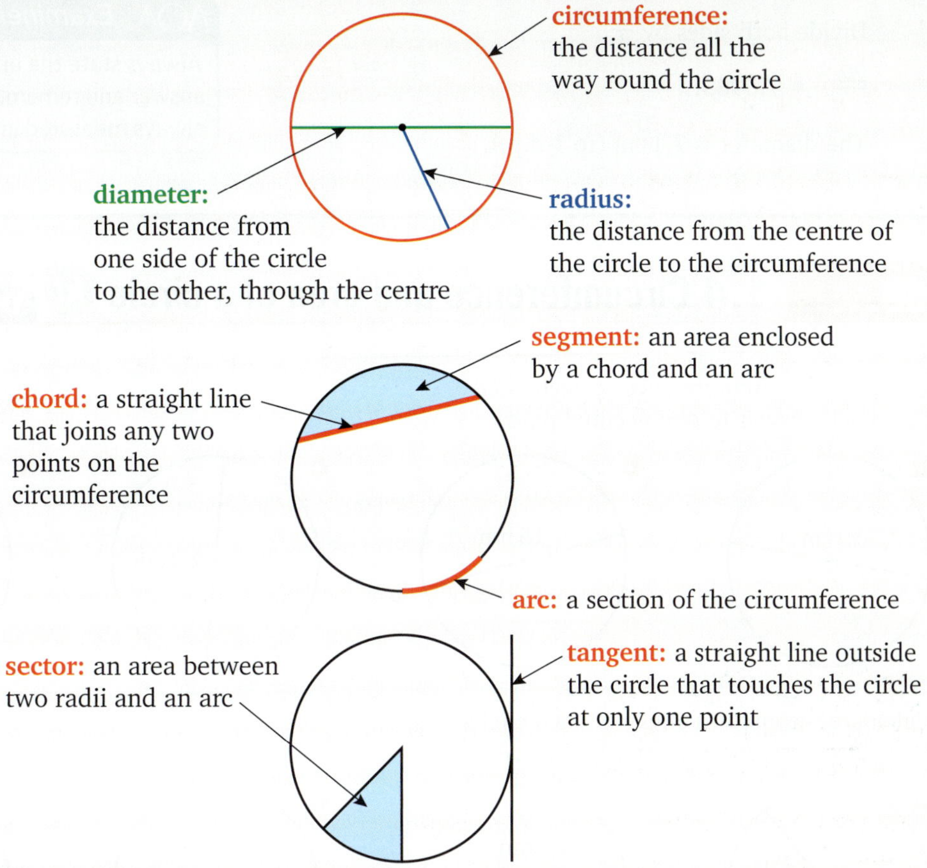

circumference: the distance all the way round the circle

diameter: the distance from one side of the circle to the other, through the centre

radius: the distance from the centre of the circle to the circumference

segment: an area enclosed by a chord and an arc

chord: a straight line that joins any two points on the circumference

arc: a section of the circumference

sector: an area between two radii and an arc

tangent: a straight line outside the circle that touches the circle at only one point

Circumference of a circle

The circumference, C, of a circle can be calculated using $C = \pi d$

where d is the diameter of the circle and π is the Greek letter pi, and represents a value of 3.1415... (Look for the π button on your calculator.)

Area of a circle

The area, A, of a circle can be calculated using the formula $A = \pi r^2$ where r is the radius of the circle.

Example: Find the circumference and area of a circle of diameter 12 cm.

Give your answers to one decimal place.

12 cm

Solution: $C = \pi d$ so $C = \pi \times 12$

Using the π button on a calculator gives $C = 37.69911...$

So the circumference of the circle is 37.7 cm (to 1 d.p.).

To find the area we must use the radius. If the diameter is 12 cm the radius is $\frac{12}{2} = 6$ cm

$A = \pi r^2$ so $A = \pi \times 6^2$ or $\pi \times 6 \times 6$

Using the π button on a calculator gives $A = 113.0973...$

So the area of the circle is 113.1 cm² (to 1 d.p.).

(Remember that area is always measured in square units.)

18 AQA GCSE Mathematics

Example: Find the diameter of a circle of circumference 22.3 cm.

Give your answer to one decimal place.

Solution: $C = \pi d$ so $22.3 = \pi \times d$

Divide both sides by π.

$\dfrac{22.3}{\pi} = 7.0983\ldots$

The diameter is 7.1 cm (to 1 d.p.).

AQA Examiner's tip
Always state the units of your answer and remember that area is always measured in square units.

Practise... 1.4 Circumference and area of a circle D C B A A*

1 Calculate the circumference of each circle.
Give each answer to one decimal place.

a 10 cm   b 15 mm   c 2.4 cm   d 19.5 cm

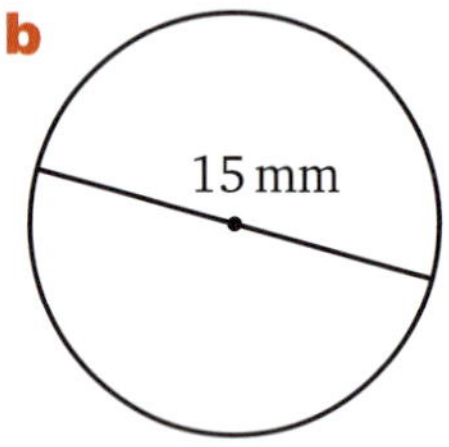

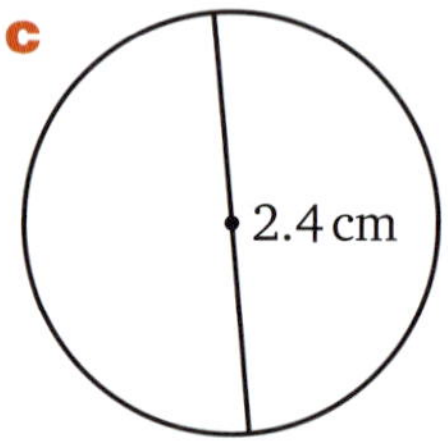

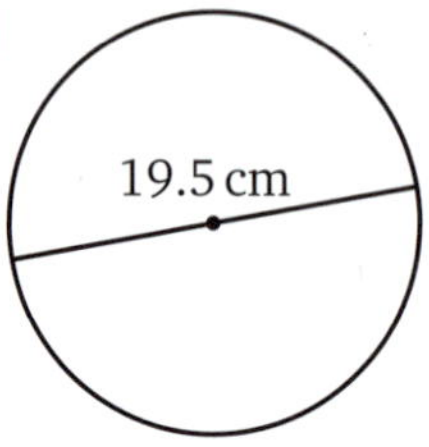

2 Calculate the circumference of each circle.
Give each answer to one decimal place.

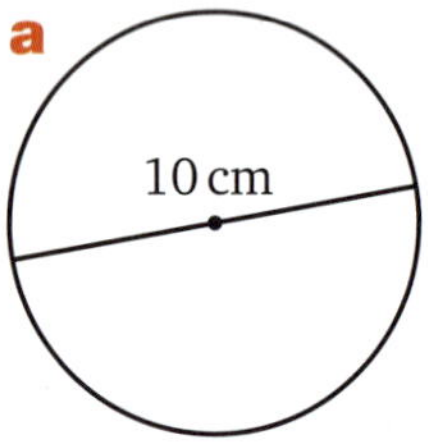

a 4 m   b 32 mm   c 17.4 cm   d 8.6 cm

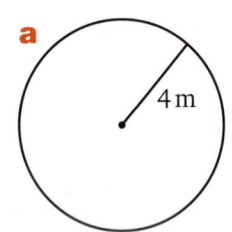

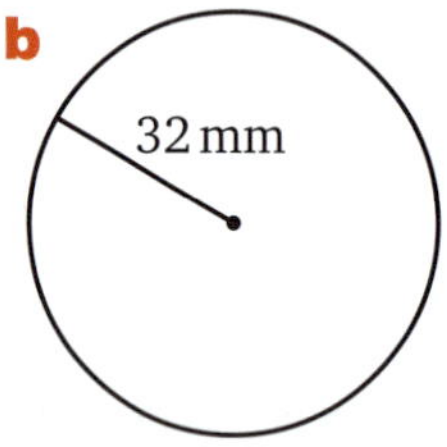

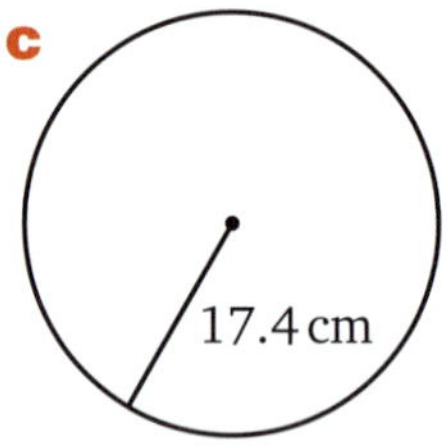

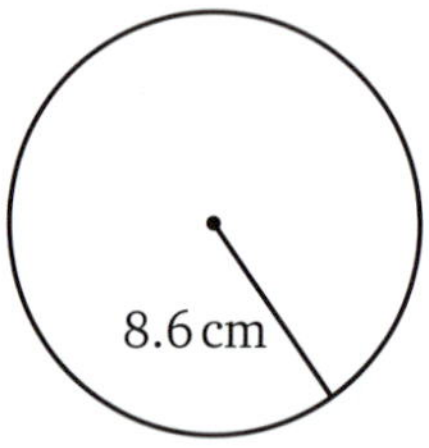

3 A circle has a circumference of 62.8 cm.

Work out the diameter of this circle.
Give your answer to the nearest whole number.

4 Calculate the area of each circle.
Give each answer to two decimal places.

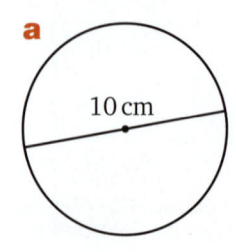

a 4 m   b 32 mm   c 17.4 cm   d 8.6 cm

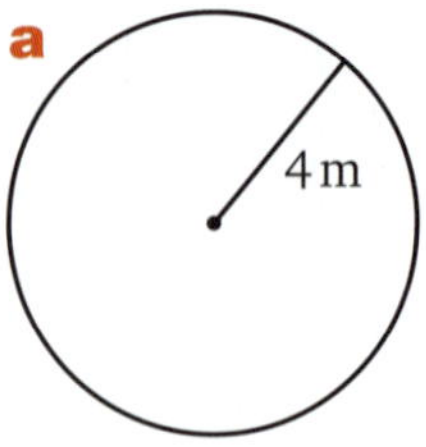

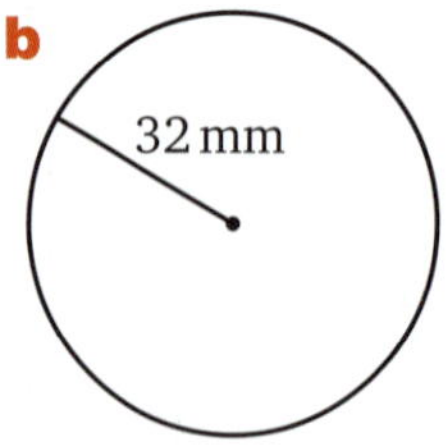

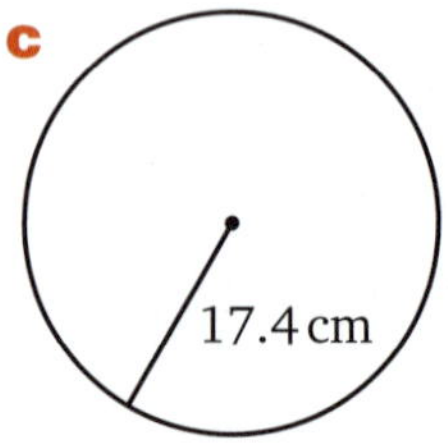

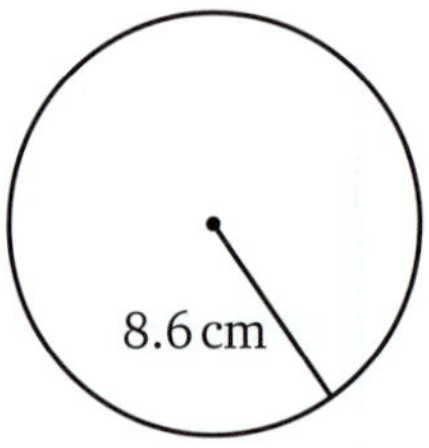

5 Calculate the area of each circle.
Give each answer to two decimal places.

a 10 cm   b 15 mm   c 2.4 cm   d 19.5 cm

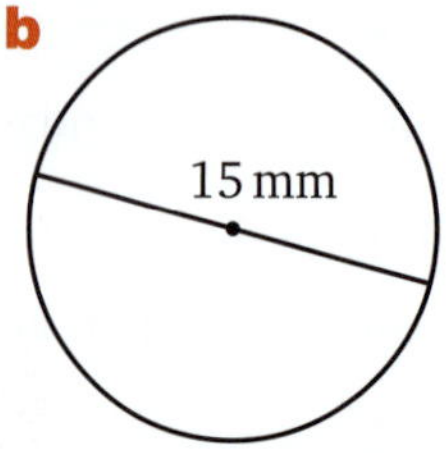

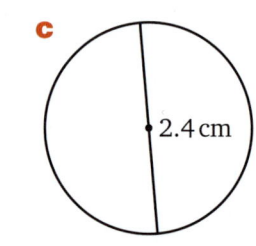

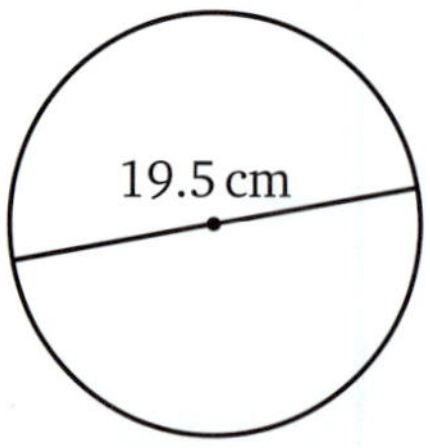

6 Find the perimeter and area of each semicircle.
Give each answer to one decimal place.

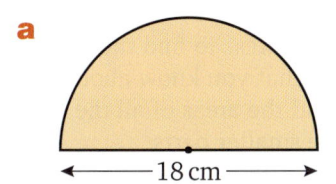

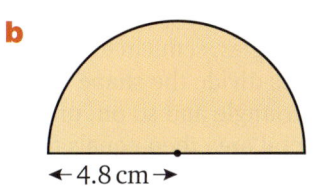

a ← 18 cm →

b ← 4.8 cm →

7 A semicircular rug has a diameter of 75 cm.
It is edged with fringing.

Calculate the length of fringing needed to go all the way round the rug.

> **Bump up your grade**
> To get a Grade C you need to be able to find areas and perimeters of semicircles.

⚠ 8 A circle has an area of 201 mm².

Calculate the radius of the circle giving your answer to the nearest whole number.

⚠ 9 Calculate the perimeter and area of each of these shapes.

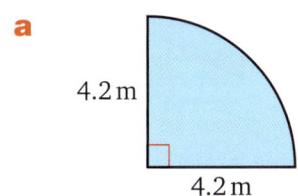

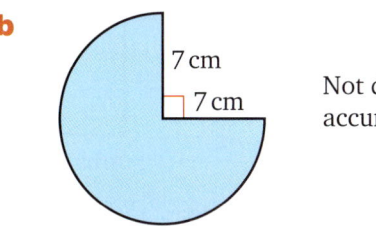

a 4.2 m, 4.2 m

b 7 cm, 7 cm Not drawn accurately

⚙ 10 Teri is training for a fun run.
She needs to run 10 000 m each week during her training.
The diagram shows the running track where she trains.
Teri says 'If I run five times round this track each day from Monday to Friday I will have run more than 10 000 m in a week.'

Is she correct?
Show your working.

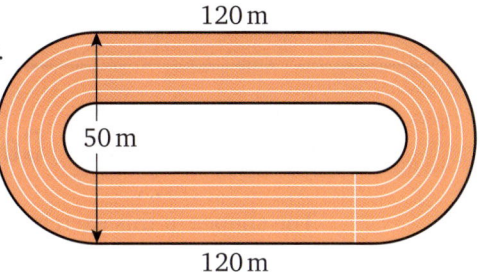

120 m
50 m
120 m

⚙ 11 A circular cake tin has a diameter of 22.5 cm.
The lid is sealed with tape.

The ends of the tape overlap by 1.5 cm.

Calculate the length of tape needed to seal the tin.

❓ 12 The London Eye has a diameter of 135 m and takes approximately 30 minutes to complete one revolution.

How far does the base of a capsule travel every 5 minutes?

Learn... 1.5 Compound shapes

Many shapes are made up of triangles, semicircles and rectangles or squares. To find the area of more complicated or compound shapes divide the shape up into the shapes that you know about. Then find the area of the rectangle, then the triangle and so on, until you have found the areas of all the parts that make up the compound shape. The total area then equals the sum of all the smaller parts.

Example: Find the area of this shape.

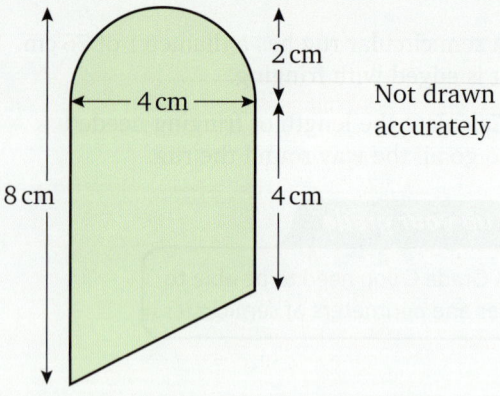

2 cm
4 cm
Not drawn accurately
8 cm
4 cm

Solution: Divide the shape into a semicircle, a square and a triangle and work out the area of these smaller shapes.

Not drawn accurately

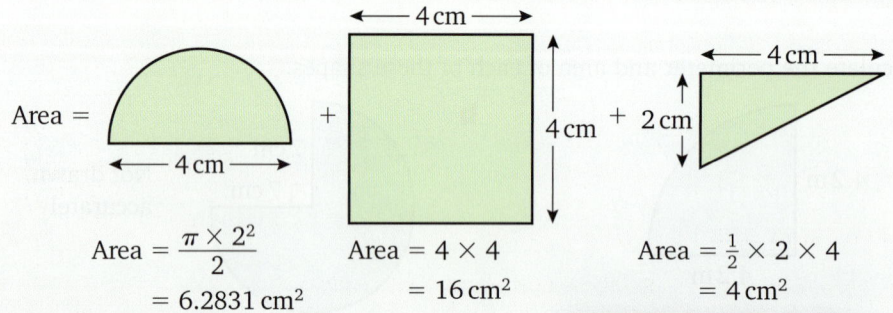

Area = [semicircle, 4 cm] + [square, 4 cm × 4 cm] + [triangle, 4 cm × 2 cm]

Area = $\frac{\pi \times 2^2}{2}$ Area = 4×4 Area = $\frac{1}{2} \times 2 \times 4$
     = 6.2831 cm²   = 16 cm²   = 4 cm²

Total area = 4 + 16 + 6.2831 = 26.28 cm² to 2 d.p.

AQA Examiner's tip
Remember to state the units of your answer.

Practise... 1.5 Compound shapes   D C B A A*

The shapes in this exercise are not drawn accurately.

1 Work out the area of each shape.

a 4 cm, 10 cm, 5 cm

b 3.2 m, 5.8 m, 7.4 m

c 18 mm, 7 mm, 24 mm, 9 mm

d 4 m, 2 m, 6 m

e 7 cm, 4 cm, 9 cm, 4 cm, 2 cm

f 12 m, 8 m, 4 m, 1 m

2 For each of these shapes find:

  i the perimeter
  ii the area.

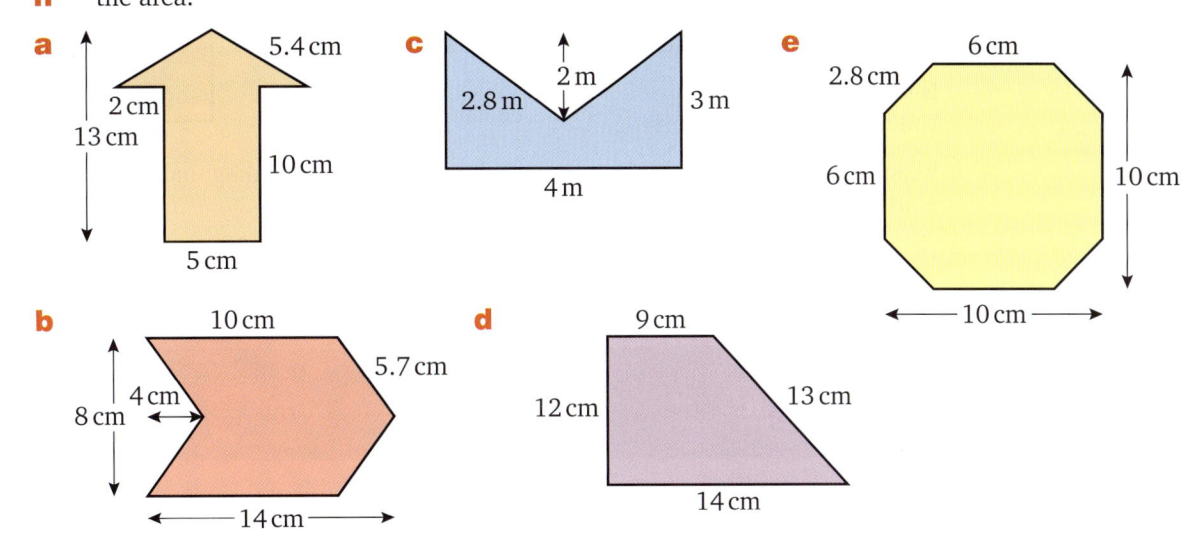

a 5.4 cm, 2 cm, 13 cm, 10 cm, 5 cm

c 2 m, 2.8 m, 3 m, 4 m

e 6 cm, 2.8 cm, 6 cm, 10 cm, 10 cm

b 10 cm, 5.7 cm, 4 cm, 8 cm, 14 cm

d 9 cm, 12 cm, 13 cm, 14 cm

3 Alex is making badges out of card.

Bump up your grade
To get a Grade C you need to be able to find areas of compound shapes made from parts of a circle.

She takes a square of side 6 cm and cuts quarter circles of radius 1.5 cm from each corner as shown.
Calculate the area of the badge.
Give your answer to one decimal place.

4 Work out the area of the coloured part of each shape.

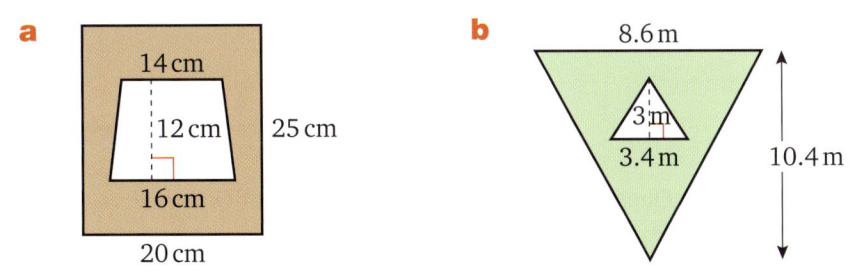

a 14 cm, 12 cm, 25 cm, 16 cm, 20 cm

b 8.6 m, 3 m, 3.4 m, 10.4 m

5 Sam is making badges to the design shown. Sam uses silver foil for the surround of the white centre shape. He has 45 cm² of silver foil left.
Does Sam have enough foil to complete the badge?
Show your working.

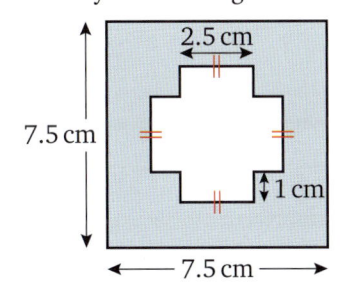

2.5 cm, 7.5 cm, 1 cm, 7.5 cm

6 This is a sketch of Vikki's dining room.

  a Vikki wants to paint the floorboards which cover the whole of the floor.
  One tin of floorboard paint will cover 9.5 m² of floor.
  Vikki thinks that two tins will cover all her floor.

  Is she correct?
  You must show your working.

  b Vikki fits new skirting board around all the room except the diagonal corner.
  Skirting board is sold in 2.4 m lengths costing £7.99 each.

  Work out the total cost of the skirting board.

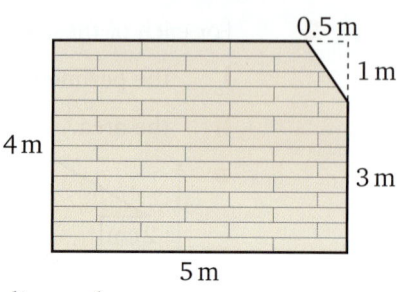

Assess

1 Work out the size of each of the marked angles.
Give a reason for each answer.

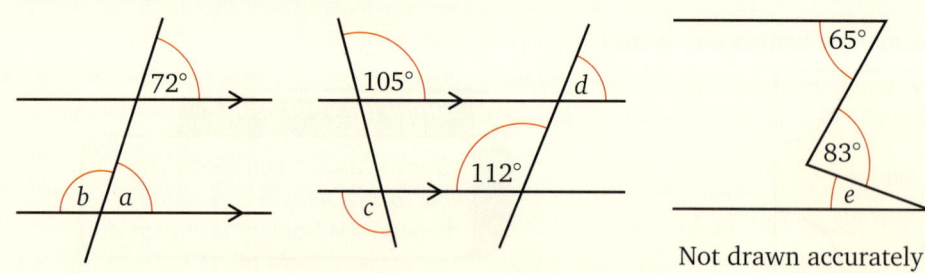

Not drawn accurately

2 For each diagram write down the three-figure bearing of P from Q.

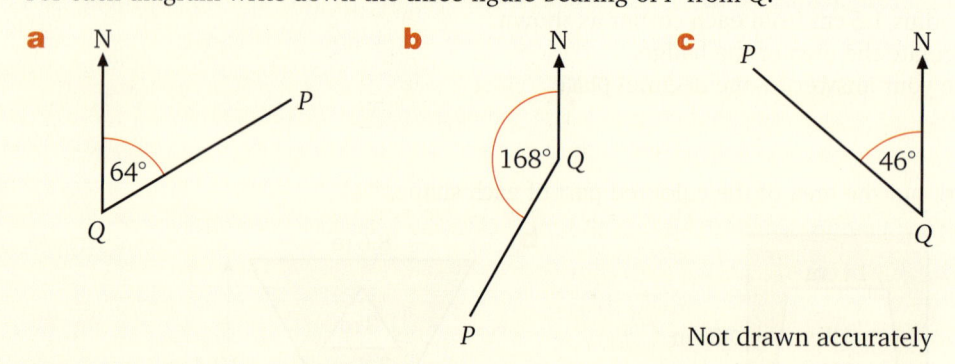

Not drawn accurately

3 For each of the diagrams in Question 2, write down the bearing of Q from P.

4 The diagram shows the positions of three buoys A, B and C.

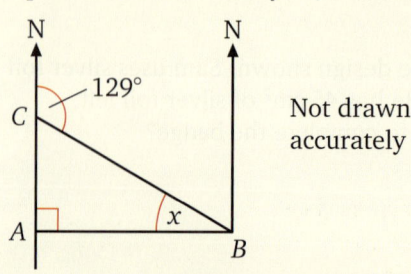

Not drawn accurately

B is due east of A and C is due north of A.

The bearing of B from C is 129°.

Work out angle x.

What is the bearing of C from B?

5 Find the area of each parallelogram.

a 3 cm, 8 cm

b 6.3 cm, 6 cm, 10 cm
Not drawn accurately

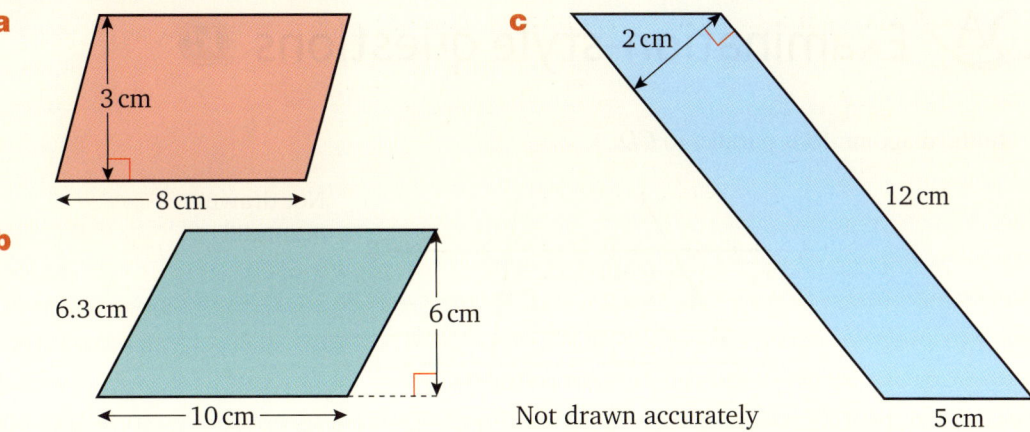

c 2 cm, 12 cm, 5 cm

6 Find: **i** the circumference **ii** the area of each circle.

a 7.8 m

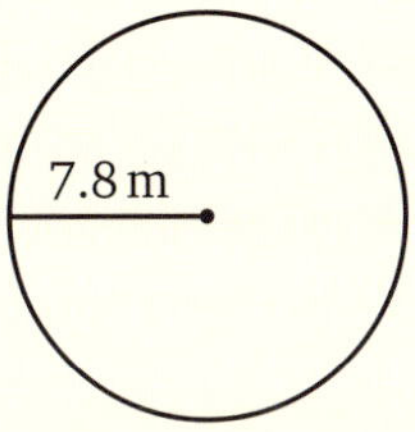

b 8.6 cm

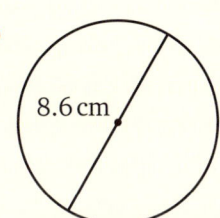

c 15 mm

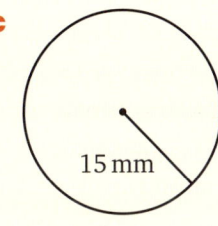

d 33 cm

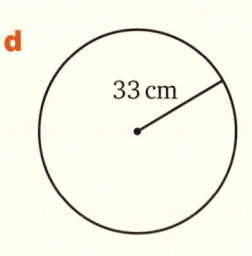

Not drawn accurately

7 A circle of diameter 45 cm is cut out of a square of side 50 cm.

Calculate the shaded area.

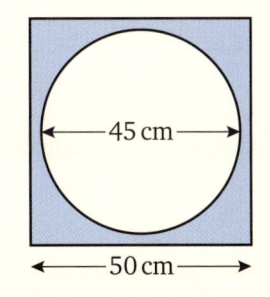

45 cm, 50 cm

Not drawn accurately

8 Are lines AB and CD parallel? Give a reason for your answer.

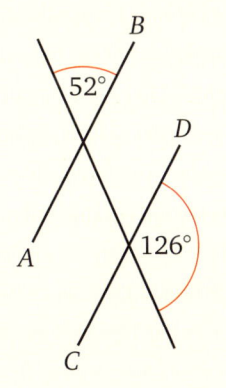

52°, 126°

Not drawn accurately

9 The groundsman at the local sports field wants to spread lawn feed.
The field is the shape opposite.
One sack of lawn feed is enough to cover 100 m². He has bought 80 sacks.

Will he have enough lawn feed to cover the whole area?
Show your working.

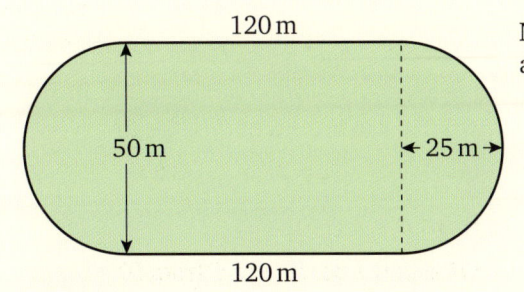

120 m, 50 m, 25 m, 120 m

Not drawn accurately

AQA Examination-style questions

1 In the diagram AB is parallel to CD.

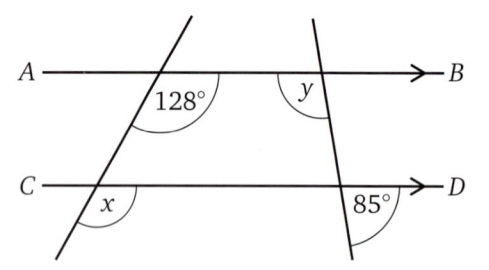

Not drawn accurately

a Write down the value of x. Give a reason for your answer. *(2 marks)*

b Work out the value of y. *(2 marks)*

AQA 2008

2 The radius of the semicircle is 10 cm.

Work out the area of the semicircle.
State the units of your answer.

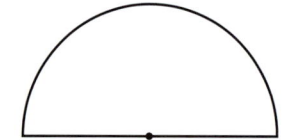

Not drawn accurately

(3 marks)

AQA 2008

3 The shaded shape below is cut from a piece of rectangular card measuring 10 cm by 15 cm.

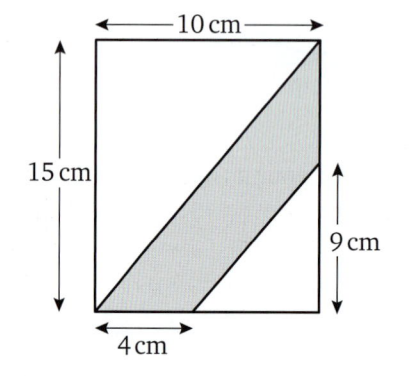

Not drawn accurately

a The larger right-angled triangle has two sides of 15 cm and 10 cm, as shown. Show that the area of this triangle is 75 cm². *(1 mark)*

b Calculate the area of the shaded shape. State the units of your answer. You must show all your working. *(4 marks)*

AQA 2008

2 Prime factors

Objectives

Examiners would normally expect students who get these grades to be able to:

C

find the least common multiple (LCM) of two simple numbers

find the highest common factor (HCF) of two simple numbers

write a number as a product of prime factors

B

find the least common multiple (LCM) of two or more numbers

find the highest common factor (HCF) of two or more numbers.

Key terms

prime number
product
factor
common factor
highest common factor (HCF)
multiple
least common multiple (LCM)
index

Did you know?

Padlocked

Did you know that **prime numbers** are used to keep credit card numbers secret when people buy things on the internet?

The system works a bit like a padlock and key. The seller sends the buyer a 'padlock' (the product of two very large prime numbers), but keeps the 'key' (the two prime numbers themselves). The buyer uses the padlock to 'lock up' their credit card number and send it to the seller. The seller is the only person who has the key to unlock the padlock. This system is very safe because it is extremely difficult to find two large prime numbers that multiply to give a particular product. Can you find two prime numbers whose product is 817?

The **product** is the result when you multiply numbers.

Those used for internet shopping are much larger than 817.

You should already know:

✔ how to apply the four rules, +, −, × and ÷, to integers
✔ about place value
✔ how to recognise even and odd numbers
✔ the meaning of 'sum', 'difference' and 'product'

Learn... 2.1 Factors and multiples

A **factor** is a positive whole number that divides exactly into another number.
For example, the factors of 16 are: 1   2   4   8   16

Factors usually occur in pairs:
$1 \times 16 = 16$, $2 \times 8 = 16$, $4 \times 4 = 16$

A factor is sometimes called a divisor.

To find all the factors of a number, look for factor pairs.

For example, $20 = 1 \times 20$ so 1 and 20 are factors of 20
              $20 = 2 \times 10$ so 2 and 10 are factors of 20
              $20 = 4 \times 5$ so 4 and 5 are factors of 20

AQA Examiner's tip
Be systematic so you don't lose any factors.

The factors of 20 are 1, 2, 4, 5, 10, 20.

The **common factors** of two or more numbers are the factors that are the same for all the numbers.

The **highest common factor (HCF)** of two or more numbers is the highest factor that is the same for all the numbers.

The **multiples** of a number are the products in its multiplication table.
For example, $1 \times 3 = 3$, $2 \times 3 = 6$, $3 \times 3 = 9$, ... The answers 3, 6, 9, ... are the multiples of 3.
So the multiples of 3 are   3   6   9   12   15   18   21, ... (goes on forever)

The **least common multiple (LCM)** of two or more numbers is the least multiple that is the same for all the numbers.

Example: Find the highest common factor (HCF) of 20 and 24.

Solution: A factor of a number is something that divides exactly into the number.

AQA Examiner's tip
Remember 1 is a factor of all numbers.

             The factors of 20 are **1, 2, 4**, 5, 10, 20
             The factors of 24 are **1, 2**, 3, **4**, 6, 8, 12, 24

             The common factors are the numbers that are in both lists.

             The common factors are **1, 2, 4**.
             The highest common factor is **4**.

Example: Find the least common multiple (LCM) of 6, 8 and 12.

Solution: A multiple of a number is something that the number divides into.

             The multiples of 6 are   6, 12, 18, **24**, 30, 36, 42, **48**, 54, 60, 66, **72**, ...
             The multiples of 8 are   8, 16, **24**, 32, 40, **48**, 56, 64, **72**, ...
             The multiples of 12 are 12, **24**, 36, **48**, 60, **72**, ...

             The common multiples are the numbers that are in all lists.

             The common multiples are **24, 48, 72**, ...
             The least common multiple is **24**.

Bump up your grade
For a Grade C, you must be able to find the highest common factor and the least common multiple.

Chapter 2 Prime factors

Practise... 2.1 Factors and multiples

D C B A A*

1
- **a** Write down the first 12 multiples of 9. Then find their digit sums. What do you notice?
- **b** Here is a list of numbers.
  153   207   378   452   574   3789
  Which of these do you think are multiples of 9?
- **c** Check your answers to part **b** by dividing by 9.
- **d** How can you tell whether a number is a multiple of 9?
- **e** How can you tell whether a number is a multiple of 18? Explain your answer.

2 Sam is finding factors of 627.
Here are his results so far.

627 ÷	1	3		
gives	627	209		

- **a** Explain why Sam does not need to try dividing by 4 and 5.
- **b** Sam works out 627 ÷ 7 and gets 89.5…
  How does this show that 7 is not a factor?
- **c** Copy and complete Sam's table of factors.
- **d** Explain how you know that there are no other factors.

3 Find the common factors of the following pairs of numbers.
- **a** 9 and 12
- **b** 8 and 28
- **c** 14 and 35
- **d** 24 and 36
- **e** 15 and 35
- **f** 12 and 30

4 Which of these statements are true? Which are false? Explain your answers.
- **a** 16 is a common factor of 32 and 80.
- **b** 16 is a common multiple of 32 and 80.
- **c** The smallest common factor of 12 and 20 is 2.
- **d** The highest common factor of 12 and 20 is 4.

5 Find the common factors of 42 and 70 and write down the highest common factor.

6 Find the factors then the highest common factors of the following sets of numbers.
- **a** 12 and 18
- **b** 24 and 32
- **c** 48 and 60
- **d** 75 and 100
- **e** 8, 10 and 12

7
- **a** The highest common factor of two numbers is 7. Give a possible pair of numbers.
- **b** The highest common factor of three numbers is 15. Give a possible set of three numbers.

8 Find the least common multiple of the following sets of numbers.
- **a** 6 and 8
- **b** 5 and 9
- **c** 12 and 20
- **d** 2, 3 and 5
- **e** 6, 18 and 24
- **f** 3, 4 and 7

9 Tracy says that the least common multiple of 24 and 60 is 12.

Is she correct? Explain your answer.

10 Find the least common multiple of the following sets of numbers.

a 6, 8 and 32

b 15, 20 and 25

c 50, 75 and 100

11 Ahmed says that the least common multiple of any two numbers is the same as their product.

He gives the example that the least common multiple of 4 and 5 is $4 \times 5 = 20$

Give an example to shows that Ahmed is not correct.

12 Find the highest common factor of:

a 36, 45 and 54

b 14, 56 and 84

c 60, 75 and 90.

13 a Find the least common multiple of:

  i   12 and 13

  ii 12 and 14.

b Explain why the LCM of 12 and 13 is the same as their product, but the LCM of 12 and 14 is not the same as their product.

14 a One common factor of 48 and 60 is an odd number. What is it?

b A common multiple of 2 and 7 lies between 30 and 50. What is it?

15 John sets his watch using the kitchen clock. But the kitchen clock loses one hour a day.

How long will it be until John's watch next shows the same time as the kitchen clock?

16 Mark is trying to find 'perfect' numbers.

	Definition	Example
Perfect	A number whose factors (not including itself) have a sum that is **equal** to the number itself.	6 (factors 1, 2, 3, 6) because $1 + 2 + 3 = 6$
Deficient	A number whose factors (not including itself) have a sum that is **smaller than** the number itself.	9 (factors 1, 3, 9) because $1 + 3 = 4$ which is smaller than 9
Abundant	A number whose factors (not including itself) have a sum that is **greater than** the number itself.	12 (factors 1, 2, 3, 4, 6, 12) because $1 + 2 + 3 + 4 + 6 = 16$ which is greater than 12

a Find the next perfect number after 6.

b List the deficient and abundant numbers that lie between 6 and your answer to part **a**.

c Explain why all prime numbers are deficient.

Learn... 2.2 Prime numbers and prime factors

A prime number is a positive whole number that has **exactly two factors**.

The first seven prime numbers are:

2	3	5	7	11	13	17
Factors	Factors	Factors	Factors	Factors	Factors	Factors
1 & 2	1 & 3	1 & 5	1 & 7	1 & 11	1 & 13	1 & 17

1 is not a prime number because it has only one factor.

2 is the only even prime number. All other even numbers have 1, themselves and 2 as factors, and may have other factors as well.

All the missing odd numbers have three or more factors.
For example, the factors of 15 are 1, 3, 5 and 15.

Index form

Prime numbers are the 'building blocks' of mathematics. All other numbers can be written as products of prime numbers.

For example, $12 = 2 \times 2 \times 3 = 2^2 \times 3$ ← index

This is called index form or **index** notation.

and $81 = 9 \times 9 = 3 \times 3 \times 3 \times 3 = 3^4$ ← index

Sometimes the **prime factor decomposition** of more difficult numbers can be found from that of easier numbers.

For example, $120 = 12 \times 10 = 2^2 \times 3 \times 2 \times 5 = 2^3 \times 3 \times 5$

Multiplying by 10 raises the power of 2 by 1 and gives an extra factor 5.

The following example shows another way of finding prime factors, called the **tree method**.

Example: Write 280 as a product of its prime factors in index form.

Solution: Two 'trees' are shown below. The first starts by splitting 280 into 28×10.

The numbers are then split again and again until you get to prime numbers.

The second tree starts by splitting 280 into 2×140.

This shows that whichever tree you use, you end with three 2s, a 5 and a 7.

This is sometimes called prime factor decomposition.

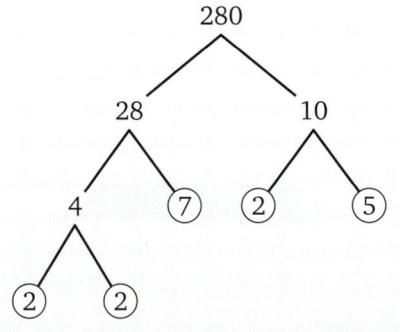

Keep splitting up until you reach prime numbers.

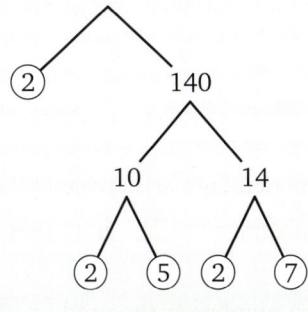

Can you see why you stop when you get prime numbers?

280 written as a product of its prime factors is $2 \times 2 \times 2 \times 5 \times 7$

In index form, $280 = \mathbf{2^3 \times 5 \times 7}$

$2^3 = 2 \times 2 \times 2$

Bump up your grade

For a Grade C, you must be able to write a number as a product of its prime factors.

Example: **a** Write each of these numbers as a product of prime factors in index form.

   i 280   **ii** 300

b Find the highest common factor (HCF) of 280 and 300.

c Find the least common multiple (LCM) of 280 and 300.

Solution: **a** The ladder method is a systematic way of writing a number as a product of its prime factors.

> **AQA Examiner's tip**
> Remember 1 is NOT a prime number.

2	280
2	140
2	70
5	35
7	7
	1

Try the next prime number to see if it is a factor:
2 then 3, 5, 7, 11, …
Sometimes you can divide by a factor more than once.

2	300
2	150
3	75
5	25
5	5
	1

280 written as a product of its prime factors is $2 \times 2 \times 2 \times 5 \times 7$

$300 = 2 \times 2 \times 3 \times 5 \times 5$
$= 2^2 \times 3 \times 5^2$

In index form, $280 = \mathbf{2^3 \times 5 \times 7}$

b Compare $280 = 2 \times 2 \times 2 \times 5 \times 7$
with $300 = 2 \times 2 \times 3 \times 5 \times 5$

To find the HCF of 280 and 300, multiply all the factors they have in common.
The HCF of 280 and 300 = $2 \times 2 \times 5 = \mathbf{20}$

c The LCM must contain all the factors of both numbers.
The LCM of 280 and 300 = $2 \times 2 \times 2 \times 3 \times 5 \times 5 \times 7$
This has the same factors as 300 with an extra 2 and 7.
So the LCM of 280 and 300 is $300 \times 14 = \mathbf{4200}$

Practise… 2.2 Prime numbers and prime factors   D C B A A*

1 Write down all the prime numbers between 20 and 40.

2 Which of these numbers are **not** prime numbers?

51   53   55   57   59

Explain your answers.

3 Two prime numbers lie between 80 and 90. Find:

a their sum   **b** their difference.

> **Hint**
> Add to find the sum.
> Subtract to find the difference.

4 Write each number as the product of two prime factors.

a 14   **b** 33   **c** 65   **d** 91

5 Write each number as a product of prime factors. Use index notation.

a 24   **c** 84   **e** 132   **g** 216

b 36   **d** 96   **f** 144   **h** 520

6 **a** Write 30 as a product of prime factors.

    b Use your answer to part **a** to write these numbers as products of prime factors in index form.

        i 60   **ii** 90   **iii** 210   **iv** 300   **v** 750

7 **a** Write each number as a product of prime factors, using index notation.

        i 270   **ii** 450

    b Use your answers to part **a** to find:

        i the highest common factor of 270 and 450

        ii the least common multiple of 270 and 450.

8 **a** Write each number as a product of prime factors, using index notation.

        i 42   **ii** 60   **iii** 72

    b Use your answers to part **a** to find:

        i the highest common factor of 42, 60 and 72

        ii the least common multiple of 42, 60 and 72.

9 A Mersenne number is one less than a power of 2. This can be written as $2^n - 1$.

For example, when n is 3, $2^3 - 1 = 8 - 1 = 7$. So 7 is a Mersenne number.

    a Copy and complete this table of Mersenne numbers.

n	1	2	3	4	5	6	7	8	9	10
$2^n - 1$			7							

    b Which of these Mersenne numbers are prime?

10 Which of these numbers **cannot** be prime?

    1895   2356   3457   5739

Give a reason for your answers.

11 **a** Write each of these numbers in the form $2^a \times 3^b \times 5^c$.

        i 1080   **ii** 1800   **iii** 8100

    b Write the HCF and LCM of these three numbers in the form $2^a \times 3^b \times 5^c$.

12 The prime factorisation of a number is $2^3 \times 3^2$. What is the number?

13 The product of two prime numbers is sometimes used as a security device. To 'break the code' you need to find two prime numbers that give a particular product.

    a Find two prime numbers that multiply to give:

        i 111   **ii** 221   **iii** 319   **iv** 437   **v** 767

    b Why are even numbers not very useful in this situation?

    c What advice can you give someone who is trying to find two prime numbers that multiply to give a particular product?

14 Work out what each number is.

  a It is a prime number. It is a factor of 35. It is not a factor of 25.

  b It is less than 50. It is a multiple of 3. It is also a multiple of 5.
         The sum of its digits is a prime number.

  c It is a prime number less than 100.
         It is one more than a multiple of 8 and its digits add up to 10.

  d Make up number descriptions of your own. Ask a friend to find the numbers.

15 Any even number greater than 4 can be written as the sum of two odd prime numbers, sometimes in more than one way.

For example, 22 = 3 + 19 or 5 + 17 or 11 + 11

  a Find two odd prime numbers that add up to:

    i 8   **ii** 20   **iii** 42   **iv** 60

  b Any number greater than 7 can be written as the sum of three prime numbers.
         Find three prime numbers that add up to:

    i 12   **ii** 25   **iii** 48   **iv** 99

Can you explain why this is true?

2 Assess

1 Write down all the factors of 36 which are also factors of 48.

2
  a Write down a 2-digit number that is a factor of 105 and a multiple of 7.
  b What is the next prime number after 89?

3 Find:
  a the highest common factor of 16 and 24
  b the least common multiple of 16 and 24.

4 Write 392 as a product of its prime factors in index form.

5 Here are three numbers.

    36   42   49

Give a reason why each number could be the odd one out.

6
  a Express 120 as the product of its prime factors.
         Write your answer in index form.
  b Find the highest common factor of 84 and 120.

7 Helen is training for a triathlon.
She plans to run every 2 days, swim every 4 days and cycle every 5 days.
Today she ran, swam and cycled.

How many days will it be before she next runs, swims and cycles on the same day?

Chapter 2 Prime factors 33

8 James races two model cars around a track.
The first car takes 42 seconds to complete each circuit.
The second car takes 1 minute to complete each circuit.
The cars start together from the starting line.

How long will it be before they are together on the starting line again?

9
  a You are given that $54 = 2 \times 3^3$
  Write each of the following as the product of prime factors in index form.
  i 108 **ii** 216 **iii** 540

  b What is the highest common factor of 54 and 84?

  c What is the least common multiple of 54 and 84?

10 Sara says that the value of the expression $n^2 + n + 41$, where $n = 0, 1, 2, 3, \ldots$ always gives prime numbers.

  a Show this is true for $n = 0$ to 6.

  b Without any calculation, name one value of n that disproves Sara's theory.

AQA Examination-style questions

1 Polly Parrot squawks every 12 seconds. Mr Toad croaks every 21 seconds.
They both make a noise at the same time.
After how many seconds will they next make a noise at the same time? *(2 marks)*
AQA 2007

2 Work out the highest common factor (HCF) of 63 and 105. *(2 marks)*
AQA 2008

3 $N = a^2b$ is a formula where a and b are prime numbers.
  a Find N when $a = 5$ and $b = 3$ *(1 mark)*
  b When $a = b$, what sort of number is N? Choose from the options below.
  PRIME   SQUARE   CUBE *(1 mark)*
  c Find the values of a and b when $N = 2009$ *(3 marks)*
AQA 2009

3 Collecting data

Objectives

Examiners would normally expect students who get these grades to be able to:

D
understand and name different types of data

design and use data collection sheets, surveys and questionnaires

design and use two-way tables for discrete and grouped data

understand and name other types of data collection methods

C
identify possible sources of bias

understand the data handling cycle

understand that increasing sample size generally leads to better estimates

A
select and justify a sampling scheme and a method to investigate a population

use sampling methods including random and stratified sampling.

Did you know?

The Great Fire of London

Q: How do you know what has happened in the past and what is happening now?

A: This is because someone has recorded it. They have then written about it, talked about it, filmed it or collected data about it.

This has always been the case. You may have heard of the Great Fire of London from 1666. This is probably due to a man called Samuel Pepys. He kept a diary for many decades about life in London. Below is an extract from 2 September 1666.

'So down [I went], with my heart full of trouble, to the Lieutenant of the Tower, who tells me that it begun this morning in the King's baker's house in Pudding Lane, and that it hath burned St. Magnus's Church and most part of Fish Street already. So I [went] down to the waterside, … and there saw a lamentable fire. … Everybody endeavouring to remove their goods, and flinging into the river or bringing them into lighters that layoff; poor people staying in their houses as long as till the very fire touched them, and then running into boats, or clambering from one pair of stairs by the waterside to another. And among other things, the poor pigeons, I perceive, were loth to leave their houses, but hovered about the windows and balconies, till they some of them burned their wings and fell down.'

(The Diary of Samuel Pepys, 1666)

When producing statistics you need to think about how data can be collected, recorded and sorted.

You should already know:

✓ how to calculate with fractions

✓ how to use five bar gates for tallying

✓ how to design and use tally charts and frequency tables for discrete and grouped data.

Key terms

hypothesis
raw data
primary data
secondary data
qualitative data
quantitative data

discrete data
continuous data
population
sample
sample size
questionnaire

survey
open questions
closed questions
pilot survey
observation

controlled experiment
data logging
data collection sheet
observation sheet
two-way table

census
random sampling
stratified (random) sampling

Learn... 3.1 Types of data

The data handling cycle is the framework for work in statistics. It has four stages.

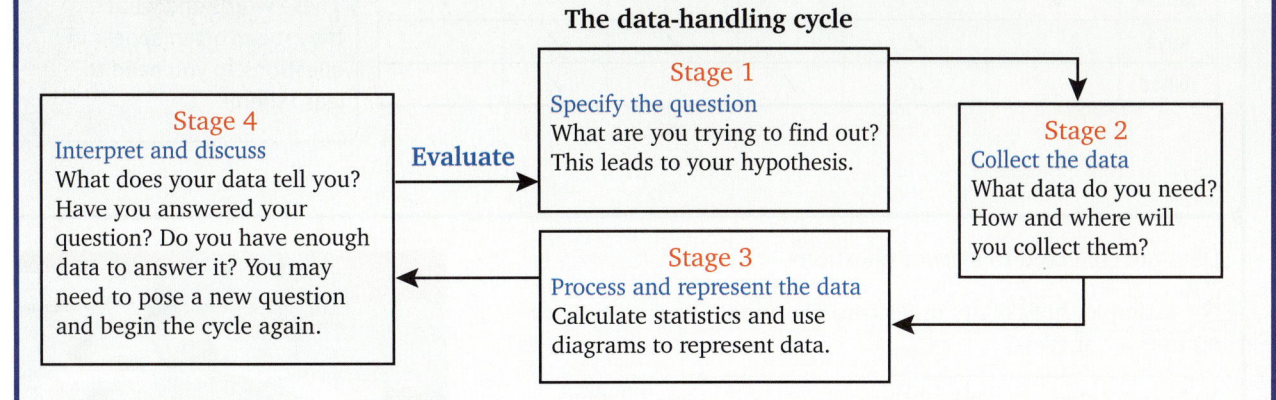

The data-handling cycle

Stage 1 — Specify the question
What are you trying to find out? This leads to your hypothesis.

Stage 2 — Collect the data
What data do you need? How and where will you collect them?

Stage 3 — Process and represent the data
Calculate statistics and use diagrams to represent data.

Stage 4 — Interpret and discuss
What does your data tell you? Have you answered your question? Do you have enough data to answer it? You may need to pose a new question and begin the cycle again.

Evaluate

In any statistical project it is usual to go through the data handling cycle at least once.

The first stage is to decide on what you are trying to find out. This leads to the **hypothesis**, a statement that you want to investigate.

The second stage is to think about what data you need and how to collect it.

The third stage is to make calculations and summarise the collected data using tables and diagrams.

The fourth stage involves interpreting the diagrams and calculations you have produced. This should lead to an indication of whether the hypothesis has been supported or not.

After completing the full cycle, it may be necessary to refine the original hypothesis and begin the cycle again.

The way you collect the data, and how you represent them, may depend on the type of data you want.

When data are first collected they are called **raw data**. Raw data are data before they have been sorted.

Data can be **primary data** or **secondary data**.
Primary data are data that are collected to investigate the hypothesis.
Secondary data are data that have already been collected, usually for another purpose.

Data can be **qualitative** or **quantitative**.
Qualitative data are not numerical. These data measure a quality such as taste or colour.
Quantitative data involves numbers of some kind (a quantity).

Quantitative data can be **discrete** or **continuous**.
Discrete data means exact values such as the numbers of people in cars. They are numerical data that can only take certain values.
Continuous data are numerical data that can take any value.
They are always measurements, such as distance or time, which have to be rounded to be recorded.

Example: Draw a table and tick the correct boxes to show whether the following data are qualitative or quantitative, discrete or continuous, and primary or secondary.

a   Sammi collects information about hair colour from the internet.

b   Kaye measures the height of 100 people.

c   Ashad spots the numbers on the sides of trains in the station.

Solution:

Person	Qualitative	Quantitative	Discrete	Continuous	Primary	Secondary
Sammi	✓		✓			✓
Kaye		✓		✓	✓	
Ashad		✓	✓		✓	

AQA Examiner's tip

These words and what they mean often appear in questions so you need to learn them!

Data are collected to answer questions.

For example, how many miles can a Formula 1 racing car run on one set of tyres?

You do not need to wait and see, others will have collected data on this.

All the tyres of the same type should run for about the same number of miles.

The **population** of tyres is all the tyres that are the same type.

At some point a **sample** of the tyres will have been tested.

A sample is a small part of the population.

Information about the sample should be true for the population.

Populations are not always this large. For example, you might be collecting data just in your own school. In this case, the population would be much smaller.

The **sample size** is important.
This is the number of people or items in the sample.

It is important to think carefully about a sample size.

The bigger the sample then the more reliable the information.

So, the more tyres in the sample the more reliable the information.

However, it can be expensive or time consuming to collect data on a very large sample.
You can't sell tyres you have used for testing!

Example: Ellie is investigating the question 'What is the average height of a Year 10 girl?'

a What is the population for her question?

b Give an advantage of a large sample.

c Give a disadvantage of a large sample.

Solution: **a** All Year 10 girls (in the world).

b The larger the sample the more reliable the results.

c It would be almost impossible to include all the Year 10 girls across the world. Trying to get too many results will be very time consuming.

Chapter 3 Collecting data 37

Practise… 3.1 Types of data

1 Copy the table and tick the correct boxes for these data.
   a Nat finds out the cost of a cruise holiday in the newspaper.
   b Prita counts the number of red jelly babies in 100 bags.
   c Niles records the weather at his home every day for one month.

Person	Qualitative	Quantitative	Discrete	Continuous	Primary	Secondary
Nat						
Prita						
Niles						

2 For each of the following say whether the data are discrete or continuous.
   a The number of votes for a party at a general election
   b The number of beans in a tin
   c The weight of recycling each household produces each week
   d How many people watch the ten o'clock news
   e How long it takes to walk to school
   f The number of sheep Farmer Angus has
   g The weights of Farmer Angus' sheep
   h The heights of Year 10 students in your school
   i The number of eggs laid by a hen

3 a What is a sample?
   b Why are samples taken rather than looking at the whole population?
   c Give **two** reasons why a sample should not be too large.

4 Write down some:
   a qualitative data about a jumper someone has knitted for you
   b quantitative discrete data about a local football team
   c quantitative continuous data about the launch of a space rocket
   d primary data you might collect about your maths homework
   e secondary data you might collect about keeping a pet rat.

5 Find a copy of a newspaper or use the internet.
   Find 10 facts and figures given in the newspaper or on websites.
   List the type of data involved each time.
   Use as many words which describe data as possible.
   Your choices must include data which uses each word below at least once.

   Qualitative   Quantitative   Discrete   Continuous   Primary   Secondary

6 A company produces energy-saving light bulbs.
   They claim each bulb uses 90% less energy in its lifetime than ordinary bulbs.
   Explain how and why sampling will have been used in testing this claim.

Learn... 3.2 Data collection methods

Writing a good questionnaire

One method of obtaining data is to ask people questions using a **questionnaire**.

Surveys often use questionnaires to find out information.

Questions can be **open** or **closed**.

Open questions allow for any response to be made (see Q1 in the example below).

Closed questions control the responses by using options (see Q2 in the example below).

It is important that questionnaires:
- ✔ are easy to understand
- ✔ are short and do not ask for irrelevant information
- ✔ give option boxes where possible
- ✔ do not have overlap or omissions in them where options boxes are used
- ✔ are not biased (such as 'Do you agree that …?')
- ✔ avoid asking for personal information unless vital to the survey
- ✔ are tested before being used to show up errors or problems (this is called a **pilot survey**).

Example: A shop manager wants to know the age of his customers.

He considers using one of these questions in a questionnaire.

Q1. How old are you?   Answer_____

or

Q2. Tick the box that contains your age.

20 or under   20–40   over 50
☐   ☐   ☐

a What problems might there be with these questions?

b Write an improved question.

Solution: **a** Q1 is an open question so all kinds of different responses (answers) could be given.

e.g. $18\frac{1}{2}$, 45, not telling you, over 50.

This would make the data very difficult to organise.

Also people may not wish to give their exact age.

Q2 is a closed question so people are more likely to answer it. However, the option boxes are badly designed.

For example:

The groups overlap. If you are 20 which box do you tick? Some ages are missing. There is no box for people in their 40s.

The groups are quite wide so details are vague about the ages.

b Tick the box that contains your age.

☐   ☐   ☐   ☐
under 20   20–39   40–59   60 or over

AQA Examiner's tip

Always make sure you have covered all possible responses. Here this is done using an open-ended final group of 60 or over.

Other methods of collecting data

Surveys (and questionnaires) can be carried out in many ways.

Here are the most common.

Each method has advantages and disadvantages.

Method	Description	Advantages	Disadvantages
Face to face interviews/ telephone surveys	This is the most common method of collecting data and involves asking questions of the interviewee.	Can explain more complex questions if necessary. The interviewer is likely to be more consistent when they record the responses. More likely to get responses than with postal or email surveys.	Takes a lot of time and can be expensive. The interviewer may cause bias by influencing answers. The interviewee is more likely to lie or to refuse to answer a question.
Postal or email surveys	These surveys involve people being selected and sent a questionnaire.	The interviewee can take their time answering and give more thought to the answer. Interviewer bias is avoided. The cost is usually low.	Low response rates which may cause bias. Can take a long time. Different people might interpret questions in different ways.
Observation	This means observing the situation directly. For example, counting cars at a motorway junction or observing someone to see what shopping they buy. It can take place over a short or a long period of time.	Usually can be relied upon as those being watched do not know they are being observed and so act naturally. Often has little cost involved.	The interviewee may react differently because they are being observed. Takes a lot of time. Outside influences can affect the observations. Different observers can view the same thing but record it differently.
Controlled experiment	An experiment is more general than you might think and is not just for science. For example, timing cars along a particular piece of road is an experiment. A controlled experiment is where the conditions are stated and are not normally changed.	Results should be reliable. Repeats of the same experiment are possible if more data is needed.	Getting the right conditions for the experiment may be difficult, costly or time consuming. The experiment may need special equipment or expertise.
Data logging	A 'dumb' machine collects data automatically. For example in a shop or car park entrance. The machine could then prevent more cars trying to enter an already full car park.	Once set up, machines can work without needing human resources. Data collection is continued for as long as required.	The machines can break down. The data are basic, e.g. you cannot tell if people entering a shop are male, female, adults or children just by using the logged data.

Practise... 3.2 Data collection methods

1 The following questions are taken from different surveys.

Write down one criticism of each question.

Rewrite the question in a more suitable form.

   a How many hours of TV do you watch each week?

      Less than one hour ☐   More than one hour ☐

   b What is your favourite football team?

      Real Madrid ☐   Luton Town ☐

   c How do you spend your leisure time? (You can only tick one box.)

      Doing homework ☐   Playing sport ☐   Reading ☐

      Computer games ☐   On the internet ☐   Sleeping ☐

   d You do like football, don't you?

      Yes ☐   No ☐

   e How much do you earn each year?

      Less than £10 000 ☐   £10 000 to £20 000 ☐   More than £20 000 ☐

   f How often do you go to the cinema?

      Rarely ☐   Sometimes ☐   Often ☐

   g Do you or do you not travel by taxi?

      Yes ☐   No ☐

   h I hate dogs. What do you think?

      So do I ☐   They are OK ☐   Not sure ☐

2 Write down the data collection method in each of these situations.

   a A machine counts entry to a nightclub to prevent it becoming overcrowded.

   b Jez fills in some questions on his PC about his mobile phone contract.

   c Doctor Jekyll records blood pressure rates of people watching horror films.

   d Annie is stopped by a person with a clipboard on the High Street asking about perfume.

   e Iona records where students sit in a classroom the first time they enter it.

3 Look again at each of the situations in Question 2.

   a For each, give one advantage of collecting data in the given way.

   b For each, give one disadvantage of collecting data in the given way.

4 Give **two** reasons why a pilot survey might be carried out.

5 For each of the following situations write a short questionnaire (of up to four questions) using:

   a closed questions only   **b** open questions only.

      i To find out whether an adult is married or not

      ii To find out the favourite holiday destination of families

      iii To find out how many hours sleep the average person gets

      iv To find the most popular pet for pensioners.

   c Explain, for each situation, whether your open or closed questions are better for finding out the desired information.

Chapter 3 Collecting data 41

6 Write a questionnaire which could be used to find out:

    a where students have been on holiday in the last two years

    b who likes Wayne Rooney

    c the cost of newspapers bought by students' families.

> **AQA Examiner's tip**
> Make sure you consider all possible responses when writing questions for a questionnaire.

Learn... 3.3 Organising data

Sometimes when collecting data you need to design a **data collection sheet** or **observation sheet**. These can be very simple. The key issue is that any possible item seen can be recorded.

Example: Quinlan is collecting data about the types of vehicles passing his house.
He wants to see if there are differences between weekdays and weekends.
Design an observation sheet that Quinlan could use.

Solution: Here is one possible answer.

	Car	Bus	Lorry	Bicycle	Other
Weekday					
Weekend					

> **AQA Examiner's tip**
> Data collection sheets must allow for all possible outcomes for any situation. Remember to include a section for 'other'. This is often forgotten in examinations.

The table in the example above is an example of a **two-way table**.

Two-way tables are used to show more than one aspect of the data at the same time (time of week and type of vehicle).

Two-way tables can show lots of information at once.

Example: Students in a school were asked whether they had school dinners or packed lunches.
Their results are shown in the table.

Write down nine facts that can be obtained from this two-way table.

	Boys	Girls
School dinner	24	16
Packed lunch	12	32

Solution:
1. 24 boys have school dinner.
2. 16 girls have school dinner.
3. 12 boys have packed lunch.
4. 32 girls have packed lunch.
5. 40 (24 + 16) students have school dinner.
6. 44 (12 + 32) students have packed lunch.
7. 36 (24 + 12) boys have either school dinner or packed lunch.
8. 48 (16 + 32) girls have either school dinner or packed lunch.
9. 84 (24 + 16 + 12 + 32) students have either school dinner or packed lunch.

Practise... 3.3 Organising data

1 The two-way table shows information about gender and wearing glasses.

	Boys	Girls
Glasses	8	17
No glasses	15	24

Use the table to answer the following questions.

a How many people wear glasses?
b How many girls were in the survey?
c How many boys do not wear glasses?
d What method of data collection could have been used to obtain this data?

2 The table shows the different animals on a farm.

	Sheep	Cattle	Pigs
Male	80		90
Female		70	

The farmer has:
- 130 sheep in total
- 340 male animals
- 600 animals in total.

Copy and complete the table.

3 a Design an observation sheet to collect data in each of the following situations.
   i The favourite fruit of Year 10 girls and Year 10 boys
   ii The hair colour of males and females entering a club
   iii How full buses are in the morning and evening rush hours
b What would be the difficulties in actually recording these data in each of the situations above?

4 Mike thinks the weather is often better in the morning than the afternoon.

Design an observation sheet to collect data to investigate this.

5 The two-way table shows the price of holidays.

Prices per person per week for Costa Packet

	7th April to 5th June	6th June to 21st July	22nd July to 5th Sept
Adult	£124	£168	£215
Child (6–16 years)	£89	£120	£199
Child (0–5 years)	Free	£12	£50

The Brown family consists of two adults and two children aged 3 and 12 years.

They have a maximum of £500 to spend on a one week holiday at Costa Packet.

a On which dates could they go on their holiday?
b Mr Brown says that if they save up another £200 they could have a two week holiday at Costa Packet. Is he correct?

Learn... 3.4 Sampling methods

Whatever method you use to collect data you need to consider sampling.
Sampling is obtaining data from part of a population rather than all of it.

Collecting data from the whole population is called a **census**. This can be very expensive and time consuming.

There are a number of different ways to choose a sample.

Random sampling

For a **random sample** to be taken, every member of the population must have an equal chance of being included in the sample.

The two most common ways of obtaining random samples are:

Use of random numbers
1. Number everyone in the population.
2. Obtain random numbers from a list or a calculator.
3. Match the people on the list with the numbers ignoring repeats.

Use of a 'hat'
1. Write everyone in the population on a separate piece of paper.
2. Put them all in a 'hat'.
3. Draw the required number out without replacing them.

Example: Paul and Sally decide to have a holiday by choosing two destinations at random from a list of places they like.

Their list is:

Aberdeen	France	London	Tenerife
Blackpool	Germany	Majorca	USA
Chester	Holland	Newquay	
Durham	Italy	Portugal	
Edinburgh	Jamaica	Spain	

The list does not need to be in alphabetical order like this, but it can help.

a Describe two different methods of obtaining the random sample.

b Which is the easier method to use? Explain your answer.

Solution: **a** Paul and Sally could use random numbers or a 'hat'.

Random numbers: Number the places, e.g. 01 Aberdeen 02 Blackpool 03 Chester and so on ... up to 17 USA

They need to get 2-digit random numbers as there are more than 10 items.

e.g. 34 76 12 78 32 19 12 55 06

Matching the numbers to the places their random selection would be:

34 Number too large so ignored
76 Number too large so ignored
12 Choose Majorca
78 Number too large so ignored
32 Number too large so ignored

19 Number too large so ignored
12 Number is a repeat so ignored
55 Number too large so ignored
06 Choose France

Paul and Sally would holiday in Majorca and France.

Use of a 'hat': Write each place name on a separate piece of paper.

They could then put the pieces of paper in a container.

Two pieces of paper could then be drawn out.

The names on the two pieces would be the destinations for their holiday.

b In this case as the 'population' was so small it was far easier to use pieces of paper.

If there are hundreds or thousands of items you should use random numbers.

Stratified random sampling

Most data have some natural groups or strata within them.

For example, people are either men or women.

To get the best possible sample it is often useful to reflect any strata within the population.

So if a college is 70% male students, a sample should be 70% male to be as representative as possible.

For a **stratified random sample**:

- each group is represented by the same proportion as in the population. This allows you to calculate the *number* of items or people
- each item or person should be chosen at random from the group.

Example: Three quarters of a cricket club are non-playing members. The rest are playing members.

How would a stratified random sample of 40 members be chosen?

Solution: The sample of 40 should have the same proportion of playng members and non-playing members as the population.

There should be $\frac{3}{4} \times 40 = 30$ non-playing members in the sample.

There should be $\frac{1}{4} \times 40 = 10$ playing members (or $40 - 30$) in the sample.

The 30 non-playing members should then be chosen at random from all the non-playing members.

The 10 playing members should be chosen at random from all the playing members.

Example: The table shows the number of students in a school by year group.

Year	7	8	9	10	11
Number	200	200	240	220	140

a In a sample of 50 students from this school, stratified by year group, how many of each year group is there?

b Explain how you would then choose the students from Year 7.

Solution: **a** The proportion in each year group in the sample must be the same as in the population.

Step 1 Add up to find the total $200 + 200 + 240 + 220 + 140 = 1000$

Step 2 Find the fraction of this total for each year e.g. for Year 7 $= \frac{200}{1000}$

Step 3 Calculate the correct fraction of the sample for each year

e.g. for Year 7 $\quad \dfrac{200 \text{ (number in Y7)}}{1000 \text{ (total population)}} \times 50 \text{ (required sample size)} = 10$

So, 10 Year 7 students would be in the sample.

The table shows the remainder of the calculations.

Year	7	8	9	10	11
Number	200	200	240	220	140
Fraction	$\frac{200}{1000}$	$\frac{200}{1000}$	$\frac{240}{1000}$	$\frac{220}{1000}$	$\frac{140}{1000}$
For a sample size of 50	$\frac{200}{1000} \times 50$ = 10 students	$\frac{200}{1000} \times 50$ = 10 students	$\frac{240}{1000} \times 50$ = 12 students	$\frac{220}{1000} \times 50$ = 11 students	$\frac{140}{1000} \times 50$ = 7 students

Alternative solution to part a

The population is 200 + 200 + 240 + 220 + 140 = 1000

The sample required is 50.

The sample fraction is $\frac{50}{1000} = \frac{1}{20}$

This means you just need $\frac{1}{20}$ (5%) of each year total for your sample.

For Year 7, 5% of 200 = 10   For Year 9, 5% of 240 = 12   For Year 11, 5% of 140 = 7
For Year 8, 5% of 200 = 10   For Year 10, 5% of 220 = 11

b Each set of students should now be chosen by random sampling. For Year 7, number the students from 000 to 199 (or 001 to 200). Calculators can give 3-digit random numbers or tables can be used.

Here is a set of 3-digit random numbers from a random number table.

    546   322   108   232   081   002   826 and so on

So far students numbered 108, 081 and 002 are chosen.

The system is continued until 10 students have been chosen.

Remember all numbers too large and any repeats are ignored.

Example: In a company there are:

426 workers on the shop floor

49 supervisors

11 managers.

In a sample of 37 workers, stratified by worker type, how many workers from each type are there?

Solution: Sometimes the numbers for the final sample do not work out nicely.

Step 1 Find the total 426 + 49 + 11 = 486

Step 2 Fractions of each worker type are:

    Shop floor = $\frac{426}{486}$ Supervisors = $\frac{49}{486}$ Managers = $\frac{11}{486}$

Step 3 Calculate the correct fraction of the sample for each group.

    Shop floor = $\frac{426}{486} \times 37 = 32.432...$

    Supervisors = $\frac{49}{486} \times 37 = 3.730...$

    Managers = $\frac{11}{486} \times 37 = 0.837...$

Step 4 Round each value to the nearest integer.

    Shop Floor = 32 workers in sample

    Supervisors = 4 workers in sample

    Managers = 1 worker in sample

Now check the total sample is the correct size. 32 + 4 + 1 = 37 which is correct.

Sometimes the total sample is one out. In this case it is necessary to round, but not to the nearest integer.

For example a stratified random sample of 116 for a population split as below.

Type	A	B	C	D
Number of type	204	396	185	743

This would give sample sizes before rounding of:

A = 15.48...   B = 30.06...   C = 14.04...   D = 56.40...

Which, after rounding to the nearest integer gives:

A = 15   B = 30   C = 14   D = 56

Now, 15 + 30 + 14 + 56 = 115 which is 1 short of the desired sample size of 116.

Looking at the decimals, you might round A up to 16.

This is because the decimal for A was closest to being rounded up initially.

The final sample sizes are A = 16, B = 30, C = 14, D = 56

Practise... 3.4 Sampling methods

Where necessary in this exercise use the random number button on your calculator.

AQA Examiner's tip
In an exam you would never be asked to produce your own random numbers. You will be given a list.

1 Use random numbers to obtain a random sample of five from these towns and cities.

Arbroath, Bangor, Coventry, Derby, Eastbourne, Fishguard, Glasgow, Holyhead, Immingham, Jarrow, Kingston, Liverpool, Manchester, Norwich, Oxford, Plymouth, Queenshead, Reading, Scunthorpe, Tamworth, Uxbridge, Ventnor, Watford, Exeter, Yeovil.

2 The table shows the number of students in each year group of a college.

Year	10	11	12	13
Number	300	300	220	180

a How many would be in each year group of a sample of 50 stratified by year group?

b How would these students then be chosen?

3 The table shows the number of people employed in a department store.

Occupation	Management	Sales	Security	Office
Number	10	130	25	35

a How many would be from each section for a sample of 40 stratified by occupation?

b Explain in detail how the office staff could then be chosen.

Chapter 3 Collecting data   47

4 Tanya wants a panel of 20 people to represent the views of students at her university.

She wants the panel to be stratified by area of study.

The areas students study at her university are given in the table.

Area of study	Social science	The arts	Science	Sport and leisure
Number	3127	1087	2432	976

Calculate the number from each area who should appear on the panel.

5 James is investigating the hypothesis 'children prefer to play on a computer rather than to play in a park'.

He asks a sample of 100 children from his town.

The age distribution of children from his town is given in the table.

Age group	5–7	8–10	11–13	14–16
Number in age group	77	105	133	111

a Why is it a good idea to stratify the sample?

b How else could he have stratified the sample apart from by age?

c How many from each age group should be in James' sample?

6 Look at the Premier League table either online or in a newspaper.

Use random numbers to obtain a random sample of five football teams from the Premier League.

7 The number of students in each year of a large comprehensive school is given below.

Year	7	8	9	10	11
Number in year	244	221	201	195	182

A sample of 100, stratified by year group, is to be taken.

Calculate the number of students from each year to be in the sample.

8 In a car factory, three machines A, B and C produce components.

Machine A produces 40%, Machine B produces 35% and Machine C produces the rest.

2000 components are to be sampled for checking.

Work out the most effective statistical sampling method to do this. Give all necessary details including how the sample should be obtained.

9 A leisure centre is considering changing its opening times.

The centre has 5894 members; 4004 of these are female.

$\frac{3}{4}$ of female members are adults, 70% of male members are adults.

A sample of 200 is to be taken to comment on these plans.

Complete this table for a sample stratified by gender and age.

	Adults	Children
Male		
Female		

3 Assess

D 1 In a survey, 40 adults are asked if they are left handed or right handed.

	Men	Women
Left handed	5	8
Right handed	19	8

Use the table above to answer the following questions.
 a How many men are in the survey?
 b How many of the 40 adults are right handed?
 c What fraction of those asked are right-handed men?
 d What percentage of women asked are left handed?

2 Some teachers are asked to choose their favourite snack, out of chocolate and sweets. Some of the results are shown in this table.

	Chocolate	Sweets
Male	24	
Female	16	

 a A total of 50 male teachers are asked and 30 teachers choose sweets. Copy and complete the table.
 b How many females are asked?
 c How many teachers are asked altogether?
 d What fraction of the teachers who prefer chocolate are female? Give your answer in its simplest form.
 e How many males who prefer chocolate should be in a sample of 10 stratified by gender and preference?

3 For each of the following say whether the data are discrete or continuous.
 a Ages of people
 b Goals scored in a school hockey match
 c Shoe sizes of people
 d The amount of water consumed by a household
 e The viewing figures for a TV programme
 f The time it takes to get home
 g The number of stars that can be seen in the sky

4 a Criticise each of the following questionnaire questions.
   i How many hours of television have you watched in the last two months?
   ii Do you or do you not watch news programmes?
 b Criticise each of the following questionnaire questions. Suggest alternatives to find out the required information.
   i What do you think about our new improved fruit juice?
   ii How much do you earn?
   iii Do you or do you not agree with the new bypass?
   iv Would you prefer to sit in a non-smoking area?
   v How often do you have a shower?

Chapter 3 Collecting data

5 Briefly explain a good method for collecting data in each of these situations.
   a The average weight of sheep on a farm with 1000 sheep
   b The favourite building of people in your town
   c The average amount of time spent on homework each week by students in your school
   d The average hand span of students in a school
   e The views of villagers on a new shopping centre
   f Information on voting intentions at a general election
   g The number of people entering a shop in the month of December

6 The owners of a small shop claim to have the cheapest prices for fruit and vegetables in a small town.

Discuss how this could be be tested by explaining how the full data handling cycle could be used in this investigation.

7 Use random numbers to obtain a random sample of three countries from this list.

Angola	Finland	Kazakhstan	Poland	Uganda
Brazil	Greece	Lebanon	Qatar	Venezuela
Colombia	Hungary	Mexico	Russia	Western Samoa
Denmark	Indonesia	New Zealand	Spain	Yemen
Egypt	Jordan	Oman	Tuvalu	Zambia

8 The table shows the number of people employed in a factory.

Occupation	Management	Office	Sales	Shop Floor
Number	10	15	30	145

   a Explain why a random sample of the employees might not be suitable for asking employees about working conditions.
   b Calculate the number of people from each section for the following sample sizes, stratified by occupation.
      i For a sample of 20
      ii For a sample of 35

AQA Examination-style questions

1 There are 600 members in a sports club.
A stratified sample, by age, is taken.
The table shows the age grouping of the members.
Some information is given in the table.

Age (years)	10–24	25–44	45–60	61+
Number of members	150			120
Number in sample			22	20

Copy and complete the table. *(4 marks)*

AQA 2007

4 Fractions and decimals

$$1 + \cfrac{1}{1 + \cfrac{1}{1 + \cfrac{1}{1+1}}}$$

Objectives

Examiners would normally expect students who get these grades to be able to:

D

find one quantity as a fraction of another

solve problems involving fractions

divide a quantity in a given ratio

solve simple ratio and proportion problems, such as finding the ratio of teachers to students in a school

add and subtract fractions and decimals

multiply and divide decimals

C

add and subtract mixed numbers

multiply and divide fractions and mixed numbers

find the reciprocal of a number

convert fractions to decimals

solve more complex ratio and proportion problems

solve ratio and proportion problems using the unitary method

round numbers to different degrees of accuracy, decimal places and significant figures

recognise that recurring decimals are exact fractions and that some exact fractions are recurring decimals

understand the effect of multiplying and dividing by numbers between 0 and 1

B

convert recurring decimals to fractions.

Key terms

denominator
improper fraction
mixed number
numerator
reciprocal
terminating decimal
recurring decimal
equivalent fraction
ratio
unitary method
significant figure

Did you know?

Continuing fractions

The word fraction comes from the Latin word *frangere* meaning 'to break into pieces'.

Here's an amazing fraction! $\cfrac{1}{1 + \cfrac{1}{1 + \cfrac{1}{1+1}}}$

It is part of a series of fractions that starts:

$1, \cfrac{1}{1+1}, \cfrac{1}{1 + \cfrac{1}{1+1}}, \cfrac{1}{1 + \cfrac{1}{1 + \cfrac{1}{1+1}}}, \cfrac{1}{1 + \cfrac{1}{1 + \cfrac{1}{1 + \cfrac{1}{1+1}}}}$

This is a sequence of what are called continuing fractions. Can you see how the sequence could continue?

The fractions in the sequence simplify to $1, \frac{1}{2}, \frac{2}{3}, \frac{3}{5}, \frac{5}{8}, \ldots$ Can you continue this sequence?

Have you seen these numbers before?

You may not be able to do hard fractions yet but by the end of the chapter perhaps you will!

You should already know:

✓ how to add, subtract, multiply and divide simple numbers without a calculator

✓ the meaning of 'sum', 'difference' and 'product'

✓ how to find equivalent fractions

✓ how to simplify ratios and fractions

✓ how to add and subtract simple fractions

✓ how to calculate fractions of quantities

✓ how to express simple decimals and percentages as fractions.

Chapter 4 Fractions and decimals 51

Learn... 4.1 Adding and subtracting fractions

To add fractions with different **denominators** you first have to change them so that they have the same denominator.

To find the sum of three-quarters and two-thirds you have to change the fractions to twelfths, because 12 is the smallest number that is a multiple of both 3 and 4.

$\frac{3}{4}$ is $\frac{9}{12}$

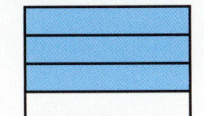

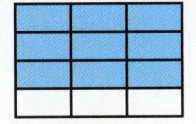

$\frac{2}{3}$ is $\frac{8}{12}$

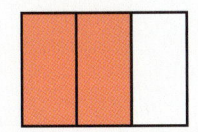

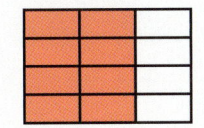

So $\frac{3}{4} + \frac{2}{3} = \frac{9}{12} + \frac{8}{12} = \frac{17}{12}$

This is an **improper** (top-heavy) fraction that can be expressed as a **mixed number**:

$\frac{17}{12} = \frac{12}{12} + \frac{5}{12} = 1 + \frac{5}{12} = 1\frac{5}{12}$

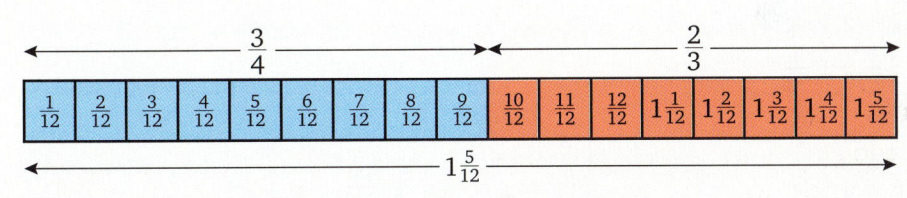

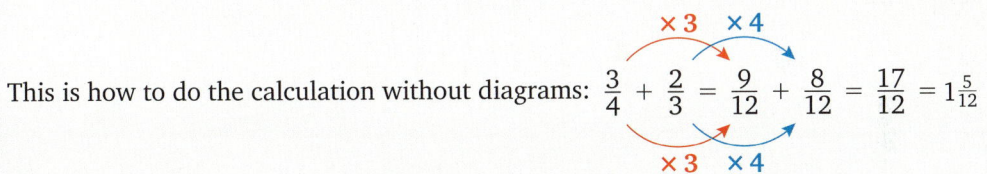

This is how to do the calculation without diagrams: $\frac{3}{4} + \frac{2}{3} = \frac{9}{12} + \frac{8}{12} = \frac{17}{12} = 1\frac{5}{12}$

×3 ×4
×3 ×4

Subtracting is just the same: $\frac{3}{4} - \frac{2}{3} = \frac{9}{12} - \frac{8}{12} = \frac{1}{12}$

Mixed numbers are numbers that contain an integer (whole number) and a fraction.
To add mixed numbers, first change them to improper (top-heavy) fractions:

$2\frac{2}{5} - 1\frac{2}{3} = \frac{12}{5} - \frac{5}{3}$

Then change to the same denominator and subtract: $\frac{12}{5} - \frac{36}{15} \quad \frac{5}{3} = \frac{25}{15}$

$\frac{36}{15} - \frac{25}{15} = \frac{11}{15}$

Example: Calculate $3\frac{2}{3} - 2\frac{5}{6}$

Solution: $3\frac{2}{3} - 2\frac{5}{6} = \frac{11}{3} - \frac{17}{6} = \frac{22}{6} - \frac{17}{6}$

$= \frac{5}{6}$

Bump up your grade

To get a Grade C you have to be able to add and subtract mixed numbers.

Practise... 4.1 Adding and subtracting fractions D C B A A*

1 Work out:

a $\frac{4}{5} + \frac{3}{4}$ b $\frac{4}{5} - \frac{3}{4}$ c $\frac{5}{8} + \frac{1}{3}$ d $\frac{5}{8} - \frac{1}{3}$

2 Fran says that:

$$\frac{1}{2} + \frac{1}{2} = \frac{1+1}{2+2} = \frac{2}{4} = \frac{1}{2}$$

What has Fran done wrong?

3 Two fractions add up to $\frac{9}{10}$. One fraction is $\frac{17}{20}$.

What is the other fraction?

4 Four of these calculations give the same answer and one gives a different answer.

Which is the odd one out?

A $\frac{1}{2} + \frac{1}{3} + \frac{1}{6}$

B $\frac{1}{2} + \frac{1}{2}$

C $\frac{2}{3} + \frac{1}{4} + \frac{1}{12}$

D $\frac{3}{4} + \frac{1}{8} + \frac{1}{16}$

E $\frac{3}{5} + \frac{1}{3} + \frac{1}{15}$

5 Work out:

a $\frac{3}{4} + \frac{3}{4}$ c $\frac{3}{4} + \frac{3}{4} + \frac{3}{4} + \frac{3}{4}$

b $\frac{3}{4} + \frac{3}{4} + \frac{3}{4}$ d $\frac{3}{4} + \frac{3}{4} + \frac{3}{4} + \frac{3}{4} + \frac{3}{4}$

6 Work out:

a $3\frac{3}{4} + 1\frac{4}{5}$

b $3\frac{3}{4} - 1\frac{4}{5}$

c $2\frac{2}{3} - 1\frac{5}{6}$

d $4\frac{1}{4} + 3\frac{1}{3}$

e $4\frac{3}{5} - 2\frac{3}{10}$

7 The fraction $\frac{1+3}{2+4}$ is between the fractions $\frac{1}{2}$ and $\frac{3}{4}$

Make other fractions like this from two others.
Is the result always between the two?

8 a   Anne's recipe needs $\frac{2}{3}$ of a cup of sugar. She has $\frac{3}{4}$ of a cup.
How much will she have left?

b   June's recipe needs $1\frac{1}{2}$ cups of sugar and $1\frac{2}{3}$ cups of sugar.
How much sugar does June need altogether?

9 A pair of trousers needs $1\frac{1}{2}$ yards of fabric and a jacket needs $2\frac{3}{8}$ yards.

How much fabric is needed in total?

Chapter 4 Fractions and decimals

Learn... 4.2 Multiplying and dividing fractions

Multiplying fractions

You can find the area of a rectangle by multiplying: $2 \times 3 = 6$

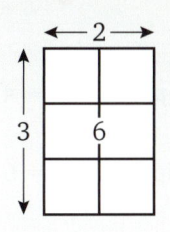

You can multiply fractions to find areas too.

The diagram shows that three-quarters times two-thirds is six-twelfths, which is a half: $\frac{3}{4} \times \frac{2}{3} = \frac{6}{12} = \frac{1}{2}$

The diagram shows why the answer is smaller than both three-quarters and two-thirds.

The 6 in the six-twelfths comes from the shaded area.
It is 3 units across and 2 units down, so contains 6 squares.

The 12 in the answer comes from the whole area.
It is 4 units across and 3 units down, so contains 12 squares.

6 out of 12 squares are shaded, so the answer is $\frac{6}{12}$, which simplifies to $\frac{1}{2}$

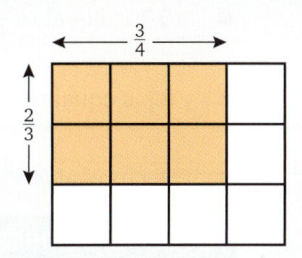

This is how to do it without the diagram: $\frac{3}{4} \times \frac{2}{3} = \frac{3 \times 2}{4 \times 3} = \frac{6}{12} = \frac{1}{2}$

multiply numerators
multiply denominators

AQA Examiner's tip
Be careful not to mix up the method for adding fractions with the method for multiplying them.

The working can be reduced by dividing the **numerator** and denominator of $\frac{3 \times 2}{4 \times 3}$ by 3 and by 2 to simplify the fraction: $\frac{3}{4} \times \frac{2}{3} = \frac{{}^1\cancel{3} \times \cancel{2}^1}{{}_2\cancel{4} \times \cancel{3}_1} = \frac{1 \times 1}{2 \times 1} = \frac{1}{2}$

What about calculations such as $1\frac{3}{4} \times 2\frac{2}{3}$?

To multiply mixed numbers you convert them to improper fractions:

$1\frac{3}{4} \times 2\frac{2}{3} = \frac{7}{4} \times \frac{8}{3}$

Then simplify if possible and multiply to get the answer.

$1\frac{3}{4} \times 2\frac{2}{3} = \frac{7}{\cancel{4}_1} \times \frac{\cancel{8}^2}{3} = \frac{7}{1} \times \frac{2}{3} = \frac{14}{3} = 4\frac{2}{3}$

Example: Work out $3\frac{1}{2} \times 2\frac{5}{6}$

Solution: Change the mixed numbers to improper fractions, then multiply numerators and denominators.

$3\frac{1}{2} \times 2\frac{5}{6} = \frac{7}{2} \times \frac{17}{6} = \frac{119}{12} = 9\frac{11}{12}$

Reciprocals and division of fractions

To divide by a fraction, you multiply by its **reciprocal**.

Any number multiplied by its reciprocal gives 1.
1 divided by a number gives the reciprocal of the number.
So the reciprocal of 2 is $\frac{1}{2}$ and the reciprocal of $\frac{1}{2}$ is 2.

Example: What are the reciprocals of these numbers?

    a 4   **b** $\frac{1}{6}$ **c** 0.7   **d** $2\frac{2}{3}$ **e** -2

Solution:

a Reciprocal is $1 \div 4 = \frac{1}{4}$

Hint
To find the reciprocal of a fraction, turn it upside down. This works because $\frac{a}{b} \times \frac{b}{a} = 1$

b Reciprocal is $\frac{6}{1} = 6$

c 0.7 is equal to $\frac{7}{10}$, so its reciprocal $= \frac{10}{7} = 1\frac{3}{7}$ ← Write a decimal as a fraction first.

d $2\frac{2}{3}$ is equal to $\frac{8}{3}$, so its reciprocal is $\frac{3}{8}$ ← Write a mixed number as an improper fraction first.

e Reciprocal is $\frac{1}{-2} = -\frac{1}{2}$

AQA Examiner's tip
You can check these by multiplying:
$4 \times \frac{1}{4} = 1$ $\frac{8}{3} \times \frac{3}{8} = 1$
$\frac{1}{6} \times 6 = 1$ $-2 \times -\frac{1}{2} = 1$
$\frac{7}{10} \times \frac{10}{7} = 1$

Bump up your grade
To get a Grade C you need to be able to find reciprocals.

Dividing fractions

To divide by $\frac{3}{4}$, multiply by the reciprocal of $\frac{3}{4}$, which is $\frac{4}{3}$:

$$\frac{2}{3} \div \frac{3}{4} = \frac{2}{3} \times \frac{4}{3} = \frac{8}{9}$$

For mixed numbers, change them to improper fractions first:

$$1\frac{3}{4} \div 2\frac{2}{3} = \frac{7}{4} \div \frac{8}{3} = \frac{7}{4} \times \frac{3}{8} = \frac{21}{32}$$

AQA Examiner's tip
Only the fraction you are dividing by gets turned upside down. The fraction you are dividing into does not change.

Bump up your grade
To get a Grade C you have to be able to multiply and divide mixed numbers.

Example: Work out $3\frac{1}{2} \div 2\frac{5}{6}$

Solution: Change the mixed numbers into improper fractions, change dividing to multiplying by the reciprocal, then multiply numerators and denominators.

$$3\frac{1}{2} \div 2\frac{5}{6} = \frac{7}{2} \div \frac{17}{6} = \frac{7}{2} \times \frac{6}{17} = \frac{42}{34} = 1\frac{4}{17}$$

Practise... 4.2 Multiplying and dividing fractions   D C B A A*

1 Work out:

a $\frac{4}{5} \times \frac{3}{4}$ **c** $\frac{5}{8} \times \frac{1}{3}$ **e** $12\frac{1}{2} \times \frac{3}{5}$ **g** $(2\frac{1}{2})^2$

b $\frac{4}{5} \div \frac{3}{4}$ **d** $\frac{5}{8} \div \frac{1}{3}$ **f** $12\frac{1}{2} \div \frac{3}{5}$ **h** $(1\frac{1}{2})^3$

2 These calculations can all be done very easily. How?

a $3\frac{2}{5} \div 3\frac{2}{5}$ **b** $1\frac{1}{2} \times \frac{2}{3} \div \frac{2}{3}$ **c** $1\frac{1}{2} \times \frac{2}{3} \times \frac{3}{2}$

3 Work out:

   a   **i** $\frac{2}{5} \div \frac{1}{3}$ **ii** $\frac{1}{3} \div \frac{2}{5}$

   b   What do you notice about the answers?

   c   Try another pair of fractions and compare answers.

   d   Does the same thing happen with 5 ÷ 3 and 3 ÷ 5?

4   **a**   Write down the reciprocal of: **i** 5   **ii** 8   **iii** 10   **iv** 20   **v** 100

      b   Write down the reciprocal of: **i** $\frac{1}{3}$ **ii** $\frac{1}{7}$ **iii** $\frac{1}{9}$ **iv** $\frac{1}{15}$ **v** $\frac{1}{50}$

      c   Write down the reciprocal of: **i** $\frac{2}{3}$ **ii** $\frac{4}{5}$ **iii** $\frac{5}{8}$ **iv** $\frac{3}{10}$ **v** $\frac{4}{25}$

      d   Find the reciprocal of: **i** 0.1   **ii** 0.6   **iii** 0.9   **iv** 0.03   **v** 0.15

      e   Find the reciprocal of: **i** $1\frac{1}{5}$ **ii** $2\frac{3}{5}$ **iii** $3\frac{5}{8}$ **iv** 1.2   **v** 2.8

      f   Find the reciprocal of: **i** −1   **ii** −3   **iii** $-\frac{1}{4}$ **iv** $-\frac{2}{5}$ **v** $-4\frac{2}{7}$

5 Work out:

    a $\left(1\frac{1}{4}\right)^2$ **b** $\frac{3}{4} + 2\frac{1}{2} \times 1\frac{1}{2}$ **c** $\left(\frac{3}{4} + 2\frac{1}{2}\right) \times 1\frac{1}{2}$

6   **a**   Which is bigger: $\frac{5}{6} \times \frac{2}{7}$ or $\frac{5}{6} + \frac{2}{7}$?   Explain how you got your answer.

      b   Which is bigger: $\frac{5}{6} \times \frac{2}{7}$ or $\frac{5}{6} \div \frac{2}{7}$?   Explain how you got your answer.

      c   Which is bigger: $2\frac{1}{2} \times 1\frac{1}{4}$ or $2\frac{1}{2} + 1\frac{1}{4}$? Explain how you got your answer.

      d   Which is bigger: $2\frac{1}{2} \times 1\frac{1}{4}$ or $2\frac{1}{2} \div 1\frac{1}{4}$? Explain how you got your answer.

7 A sequence of fractions starts $\frac{1}{2}$, $\frac{3}{4}$, …

Find the next term by adding 1 to the last term and dividing the result by the term before. Continue the sequence until you can see what has happened.

Do you get the same result with other starting numbers?

8 A recipe for 16 biscuits needs $\frac{2}{3}$ of a cup of flour.
How much flour is needed for 48 biscuits?

9 Jack fills three jugs with water.
Each jug contains $2\frac{3}{4}$ litres of water.

How much water is this altogether?

10 One kilogram is approximately $2\frac{1}{4}$ pounds.

How many pounds is 6 kilograms?

11 Seema makes tops for her friends.
Each top uses one and three quarter yards of fabric.

How many tops can she make from 6 yards of fabric and how much fabric is left?

12 Copy these calculations and find the missing numbers.

$\frac{1}{2} \times \boxed{} = 1$

$\frac{1}{2} \div \boxed{} = 1$

$2\frac{1}{2} \times \boxed{} = 4$

$\boxed{} \div \frac{3}{4} = 6$

Learn... 4.3 One quantity as a fraction of another

To work out one quantity as a fraction of another, change both quantities to the same units if necessary. Write the first quantity as the numerator and the second quantity as the denominator and then simplify the fraction.

Example: What fraction of £5 is 25p?

Solution: Change £5 to 500p.

The fraction is $\frac{25}{500}$.

The fraction in its simplified form is $\frac{1}{20}$.

Simplify the fraction by dividing the numerator and the denominator both by the common factor, 25.

Example: Some patients are taking part in a medical trial.
Drug A is given to 150 of them with a disease and 102 of them get better.
Drug B is given to 120 of them and 80 of them get better.

Find the fraction of patients who get better with each drug and simplify the fractions.

Solution: The fraction of patients who get better with Drug A is: $\frac{102}{150} = \frac{51}{75} = \frac{17}{25}$ ($\div 2$, $\div 3$)

The fraction of patients who get better with Drug B is: $\frac{80}{120} = \frac{8}{12} = \frac{2}{3}$ ($\div 10$, $\div 4$)

(Note: In real life, doctors need to compare the fractions to see which drug seems to be more effective. They would change the fractions to decimals or percentages.)

AQA Examiner's tip
Simplify your fractions whenever possible.

Practise... 4.3 One quantity as a fraction of another D C B A A*

Give all fractions in their simplest form.

1 Work out the first number or quantity as a fraction of the second.

a 150, 250
b 50p, £4.50
c 800 g, 2 kg
d 75 cm, 120 m
e 15 minutes, one hour
f 25 minutes, $2\frac{1}{2}$ hours

2 At a football match, the crowd was 15 000. There were 10 500 home supporters.

a What fraction of the crowd was this?
b What fraction of the crowd were not home supporters?

Chapter 4 Fractions and decimals 57

3 **a** Mr Howes is marking 35 Year 11 books.
What fraction has he still left to do when he has marked 14 books?

b Miss Jones has marked 12 books out of 32.
Who is further ahead with their marking, Miss Jones or Mr Howes?

4 Kate earns two and a half times as much as Andy.
What fraction is Andy's salary of Kate's salary?

⚠ 5 A rectangle has an area of bh cm² and a perimeter of $2(b + h)$ cm.
It is enlarged so that its area is $4bh$ cm² and its perimeter is $4(b + h)$ cm.

a What fraction is the old area of the new area?

b What fraction is the old perimeter of the new perimeter?

6 Sara's mark in one spelling test is 15 out of 20. In the next test, her mark is 20 out of 25.
Which mark is better?

7 In Class 9Y, 18 out of 20 passed a maths test. In Class 9X, 25 out of 30 passed the same test.
Which class did better?

8 In Kate's house, 16 of her 20 light bulbs are low-energy. In Jane's house, 20 out of her 24 bulbs are low-energy.

a Who has the higher fraction of low-energy bulbs?

b There are 30 bulbs in Dipak's house.
How many low-energy bulbs does Dipak need so that he has at least the same fraction as Jane?

Learn... 4.4 Fractions as decimals

To be able to convert fractions to decimals, remember that fractions are also divisions.

For example, if 7 pizzas are shared by 10 people each person would get $\frac{7}{10}$ of a pizza.
The fraction $\frac{7}{10}$ is the same as $7 \div 10$. You should already know that $7 \div 10$ is 0.7

To work out $\frac{5}{8}$ as a decimal, for example, calculate $5 \div 8$

$$8 \overline{)5.^50^20^40} \quad 0.625$$

AQA Examiner's tip
Make sure you divide 5 by 8 not the other way round!

$\frac{5}{8}$ is an example of a fraction that converts to a **terminating decimal**.

Not all fractions terminate. For example, $\frac{4}{11} = 4 \div 11 = 0.36363636...$ which is a **recurring decimal**.
This can be written as $0.\dot{3}\dot{6}$ showing that the number sequence 36 repeats forever.

For use in practical situations, recurring decimals have to be rounded to an appropriate degree of accuracy (see Learn 3.6).

Example: Here are some fractions: $\frac{1}{3}, \frac{2}{5}, \frac{5}{6}, \frac{7}{8}$

a Change the fractions to decimals.

b Which of these fractions convert to terminating decimals and which convert to recurring decimals?

Solution: **a** In each case, divide the numerator by the denominator until the division stops or recurs.
$1 \div 3 = 0.333333\ldots$ (or $0.\dot{3}$)
$2 \div 5 = 0.4$
$5 \div 6 = 0.83333\ldots$ (or $0.8\dot{3}$)
$7 \div 8 = 0.875$

b The fractions that terminate are $\frac{2}{5}$ and $\frac{7}{8}$.
The ones that recur are $\frac{1}{3}$ and $\frac{5}{6}$.

> **AQA Examiner's tip**
> If you have never learnt how to do division without a calculator now is the time to do so!

Expressing a terminating decimal as a fraction

Write the decimal as a fraction with a denominator of 1. Then change it to an **equivalent fraction** with a whole number numerator by multiplying numerator and denominator by 10, or 100, or 1000, … as necessary. Simplify the fraction if possible.

Example: Express 0.225 as a fraction.

Solution: $0.225 = \frac{0.225}{1} = \frac{225}{1000} = \frac{45}{200} = \frac{9}{40}$

$= \frac{9}{40}$

Expressing a recurring decimal as a fraction

This is done by using a clever mathematical method: multiply the recurring decimal by 10 or 100 or 1000, … so that the decimal part remains the same. Then subtract the original decimal from this number to leave an integer. The fraction can then be found by dividing in the usual way.

Example: Convert the recurring decimal $0.\dot{1}\dot{2}$ to a fraction.

Solution: Let $x = 0.\dot{1}\dot{2} = 0.121212\ldots$

Then $100x = 12.121212\ldots$
and $x = 0.121212\ldots$

Subtract x from $100x$
$99x = 12$

so $x = \frac{12}{99} = \frac{4}{33}$

Practise… 4.4 Fractions as decimals   D C B A A*

1 Which of these fractions will convert to terminating decimals?
 A $\frac{3}{5}$ B $\frac{4}{15}$ C $\frac{5}{12}$ D $\frac{4}{7}$ E $\frac{1}{6}$

2 By changing $\frac{5}{8}$ and $\frac{2}{3}$ to decimals, find out which fraction is bigger.

Chapter 4 Fractions and decimals

3 **a** Convert these fractions to decimals.

$\frac{1}{9}, \frac{2}{9}, \frac{3}{9}$

b Predict what the answers will be for $\frac{4}{9}, \frac{5}{9}$, etc. What about $\frac{9}{9}$?

4 Arrange these fractions in order by converting them to decimals.

$\frac{3}{4}, \frac{5}{8}, \frac{2}{3}, \frac{7}{9}, \frac{3}{5}$

5 Write these decimals as fractions in their lowest terms.

a 0.35   **c** 1.25   **e** 0.225
b 0.125   **d** 0.004   **f** 2.45

6 Express these recurring decimals as fractions in their lowest terms.

a 0.333…   **b** 0.181818…   **c** 0.999…   **d** 0.315315315…

7 **a** Write down the prime factors of the denominators of all the fractions you have seen so far that convert to:

i terminating decimals   **ii** recurring decimals.

What do you notice?

b Which of these denominators will produce terminating decimals?

i 25   **ii** 100   **iii** 18   **iv** 12   **v** 60

Learn… 4.5 Dividing quantities in given ratios

Suppose a college has £30 000 to be split between the Arts department and the Science department in the **ratio** of the number of students. If the Arts department has 250 students and the Science department has 350 students, the ratio of the numbers is 250 : 350 = 25 : 35 = 5 : 7

There are 12 parts altogether (5 + 7 = 12) so the money has to be split into twelfths. The Arts department is allocated $\frac{5}{12}$ and the Science department is allocated $\frac{7}{12}$.

$\frac{1}{12}$ of £30 000 = $\frac{£30\,000}{12}$ = £2500

$\frac{5}{12}$ of £30 000 = 5 × £2500 = £12 500

and

$\frac{7}{12}$ of £30 000 = 7 × £2500 = £17 500

The Arts department gets £12 500 and the Science department gets £17 500.

Finding one-twelfth first, then using that to find five-twelfths, is called the **unitary method**.

AQA Examiner's tip
Add the numbers in the ratio together to find out how many parts you have to calculate.

AQA Examiner's tip
Make sure that the shares add up to the original amount.

Bump up your grade
To get a Grade C you have to be able to use the unitary method.

Example: A mix of concrete is made from cement, sand and gravel in the ratio 2 : 3 : 5
What is the volume of cement in 500 litres of concrete?

Solution: The total number of parts required is 2 + 3 + 5 = 10

$\frac{1}{10}$ of 500 litres is 50 litres.

So the volume of cement is 2 × 50 litres = 100 litres

Practise... 4.5 Dividing quantities in given ratios

1 £5500 is shared between the Drama and Art departments in the ratio of the number of students who take GCSEs in each of those subjects.

45 students take GCSE drama and 65 take GCSE art.

Work out how much each subject receives.

2 **a** Split £100 in the following ratios.

  i 1 : 1 **iii** 1 : 3 **v** 1 : 5
  ii 1 : 2 **iv** 1 : 4

  Round your answers to the nearest penny if necessary.

  b Explain why some of these were easier to do than others.

3 Divide £100 in these ratios.

  a 2 : 3 : 5 **b** 1 : 4 : 5

4 What ratio, in its simplest form, is used to divide £150 to be split between two people so that the first person gets:

  a £20 **b** £13 **c** £x?

5 £6000 is shared between two people so that the first person receives twice as much as the second. How much does the second person receive?

6 A mix of concrete has cement, sand and gravel in the ratio 1 : 2 : 1

  a How much sand is needed for 30 kg of concrete?

  b A builder has only 20 kg of gravel, but plenty of cement and sand. How much concrete can he make?

7 In a typical group of people, the ratio of the number of right-handed people to the number of left-handed people is 9 : 1

  a How many left-handed students would you expect in a class of 30?

  b How many would you expect in a school of 1200 students?

  c Which of your answers is more likely to be correct (assuming you have worked out the numbers accurately)? Explain your answer.

Learn... 4.6 Rounding

If 9635 people were at a concert, it would be correct to say that the number attending was approximately 10 000. The number 9635 is rounded to the nearest thousand to give a good idea of the number of people at the concert.

Rounding to the nearest 10, 100, 1000

The number 9635 is between 9000 and 10 000 but nearer to 10 000 than to 9000.

```
9000          9635      10 000
```

So 9635 to the nearest 1000 is 10 000.

What is 9635 to the nearest hundred?

The number 9635 is between 9600 and 9700 but nearer to 9600.

```
|———————————|———————————————————————|
9600        ↑                      9700
           9635
```

So 9635 correct to the nearest hundred is 9600.

The number 9635 is exactly halfway between 9630 and 9640. The usual rule is that numbers exactly halfway are rounded upwards.

So 9635 to the nearest ten is 9640.

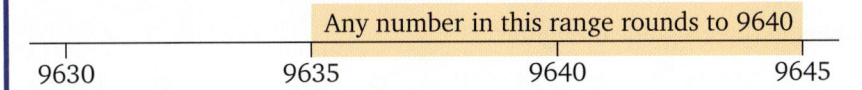

```
                 Any number in this range rounds to 9640
|————————————————|————————————————|————————————————|
9630            9635             9640             9645
```

The smallest number that rounds to 9640 is 9635.

The biggest integer that rounds to 9640 is 9644.

The biggest non-integer number that rounds to 9640 is 9644.9999…

So 9645 rounds up to 9650.   (Note: 9644.$\dot{9}$ = 9645, which rounds to 9650)

So, if n is a number that rounds to 9640 to the nearest ten, $9635 \leqslant n < 9645$. This means that 9635 is less than or equal to any number that rounds to 9640 ($9635 \leqslant n$) and any number that rounds to 9640 is less than 9645 ($n < 9645$).

If n is a number that rounds to 9600 to the nearest hundred, $9550 \leqslant n < 9650$

Example: Round these numbers to the nearest 100.

    a 77 530   **b** 48 967   **c** 145 235   **d** 398 684

Solution: **a** 77 500   **b** 49 000   **c** 145 200   **d** 398 700

Rounding to decimal places

Decimal numbers can be rounded to the nearest integer, to one decimal place, two decimal places and so on. You still have to consider numbers on either side.

Consider the number 9.635

```
|———————————|———————————————————————|
9.6         ↑                      9.7
           9.635
```

The number 9.635 is between 9.6 and 9.7 but nearer to 9.6 than to 9.7

So 9.635 correct to one decimal place is 9.6

When rounding 9635 to the nearest 100, you need zeros to show that the rounded answer is 9600 not 96. You do not need zeros to show that 9.635 to one decimal place is 9.6

So 9.635 correct to two decimal places is 9.64

> **Hint**
> For the numbers 12 000 and 13 000, zeros are needed to show the place value of the other digits. For 1.2 and 1.3 this is not necessary.

Example: **a** Round these numbers to two decimal places.

    i 7.3654   **ii** 35.689   **iii** 0.5637   **iv** 0.0673254

  b Round the same numbers to the nearest integer.

Solution: **a** **i** 7.37   **ii** 35.69   **iii** 0.56   **iv** 0.07

    b **i** 7   **ii** 36   **iii** 1   **iv** 0

Rounding to significant figures

You can also round to different numbers of **significant figures**.

The number 9635 rounds to 9600 and 9.635 rounds to 9.6

So 9600 is rounded to the nearest 100 and 9.6 to one decimal place, but they are both rounded to two significant figures. Each rounded answer has two significant figures, 9 and 6. (The zeros in 9600 indicate the place value of the 9 and the 6. They are not necessary in 9.6 and are not 'significant'.)

Zeros can be significant figures. 7.0235 rounded to two significant figures is 7.0; the zero is significant and shows that 7.0235 is nearer to 7.0 than it is to 7.1

Example: Round these numbers to three significant figures.

    a 9674   **b** 0.9674   **c** 342 960   **d** 0.3998   **e** 1.6784

Solution: **a** 9670   **b** 0.967   **c** 343 000   **d** 0.400   **e** 1.68

Note that zeros can sometimes be significant figures.

Bump up your grade
To get a Grade C you have to be able to round to different numbers of significant figures.

AQA Examiner's tip
Be sure you understand the difference between figures that are significant and those that are not.

Practise... 4.6 Rounding

1 Round these numbers to two decimal places.

    a 12.567   **c** 67.895   **e** 0.00482

    b 0.00385   **d** 0.568

2   **a** Vida says that 456 736 rounded to one significant figure is 5.
Is she correct? Explain your answer.

    b Arif says that 15.602 rounded to three significant figures is 15.60
Is he correct? Explain your answer.

3 Round these numbers to one significant figure.

    a 86   **c** 17.5   **e** 0.55

    b 950   **d** 0.175

4 Round these numbers to one significant figure and write down mental estimates of the answer to each calculation.

    a 56×4.45 **b** 0.55×124 **c** 27×956 **d** $12.9 \div 2.2$

5 Round these numbers to three significant figures.

    a 1946   **b** 24.567   **c** 129.25   **d** 0.00953

6 Round the numbers in Question 1 to two significant figures.
Which of the numbers is the same when rounded to two decimal places and two significant figures?

7 Find three numbers that are the same when rounded to one significant figure as when rounded to one decimal place.

Chapter 4 Fractions and decimals

8 To the nearest ten, a number rounds to 150.

a What is the biggest number it could be?

b What is the smallest number it could be?

9 Write down three different numbers that are 0.01 when rounded to one significant figure.

⚠ 10 Copy the diagram and then find one number to put in each of the three regions.

Numbers that are 0.4 to one significant figure

Numbers that are 0.44 to two decimal places

11 Think about the number 367.174

What would be sensible rounding of the number if it is:

a an amount of money in pounds

b the length of a field in metres

c the answer to a calculation where the numbers were correct to three significant figures?

Learn... 4.7 Decimal calculations

You should already know how to add, subtract, multiply and divide whole numbers without a calculator. Calculating with decimals is very similar.

Addition and subtraction of decimals

To add and subtract decimals, write the numbers in columns with the decimal points in line and add or subtract the numbers in the columns just as you do for whole numbers.

$$
\begin{array}{r}
5\,4^3.\,2^{11}\emptyset^1 \\
-\ \ 0.\,6\,7 \\
\hline
5\,3.\,5\,3
\end{array}
$$

Line up all the decimal points

Multiplying decimals

Any standard method of multiplying whole numbers, such as the grid method, works for decimals. The digits in the answer are just the same as for the whole number calculation. Use estimation to find where to place the decimal point in the answer.

So, if you need to multiply 0.63 by 4.7, remember that the digits in the answer will be the same as for the calculation 63 × 47.

So 63 × 47 = 2400 + 120 + 420 + 21 = 2961

Now estimate the answer to 0.63 × 4.7

0.63 × 4.7 is roughly $\frac{1}{2}$ × 5, which is 2.5

63 × 47 = 2961 so 0.63 × 4.7 = 2.961

×	60	3
40	2400	120
7	420	21

The decimal point is placed so that the answer is close to the estimate of 2.5

You can also find the position of the decimal point by finding the total number of figures after the decimal points in the question, then making the answer have the same total number. As there are two numbers after the decimal point in 0.63 and one in 4.7, there should be three numbers after the decimal point in the answer. So the answer is 2.961

Division

To divide by a decimal number, write the division as a fraction and change the fraction to an **equivalent fraction** with an integer denominator, then divide as normal.

$$135.2 \div 0.5 = \frac{135.2}{0.5} = \frac{135.2 \times 10}{0.5 \times 10} = \frac{1352}{5}$$

Multiply by 10 to change 0.5 to an integer

So $135.2 \div 0.5 = 1352 \div 5 = 270.4$

$$5 \overline{) 1\,1^13^35\,2.^20} \quad = 270.4$$

Example: Work out $15.3 \div 0.12$

Solution: $15.3 \div 0.12 = \frac{15.3}{0.12} = \frac{15.3 \times 100}{0.12 \times 100} = \frac{1530}{12} = 1530 \div 12 = 127.5$

$$12 \overline{)15^33^90.^60} \quad = 127.5$$

> **AQA Examiner's tip**
> Dividing a number by something less than 1 gives an answer bigger than the original number.

Practise... 4.7 Decimal calculations   D C B A A*

> **AQA Examiner's tip**
> Check that the answers you get are reasonable by estimating what they should be.

1 Work out:

   a 84×0.5 **b** $103.2 + 0.56$ **c** $15 \div 1.5$ **d** $67.5 - 29.8$

2 Work out:

   a 3.6×2.2 **b** 3.56×1.5 **c** $15 \div 2.5$ **d** $7.3 \div 25$

3   **a** Work out:

        i $150 \div 100$ **iii** $150 \div 1$ **v** $150 \div 0.01$

        ii $150 \div 10$ **iv** $150 \div 0.1$

   b What is happening to the divisors?

   c What is happening to the answers? Why?

4   **a** Work out:

        i 150×100 **iii** 150×1 **v** 150×0.01

        ii 150×10 **iv** 150×0.1

   b What is happening to the multipliers?

   c What is happening to the answers? Why?

5 82.1 × 5.6 = 459.76

Using the same digits in the same order, write down a multiplication sum with the answer:

 a 45.976   b 4.5976   c 0.45976   d 0.045976

6 42.6 ÷ 4 = 10.65

Using the same digits in the same order, write down a division sum with the answer:

 a 1.065   b 106.5   c 1065   d 10 650

7 Rob's employer pays him mileage expenses of 40p per mile.
He drives 15.2 miles one day and 17.9 miles the next.
How much will he be paid in total?

8 Sue is paid £1.50 for every exam paper she marks.
How many papers has she marked if she is paid £967.50?

9 Hafsa has £250 to spend on a carpet for her living room. She needs 17.6 square metres.
The carpet she likes costs £14.25 a square metre.
Does Hafsa have enough money to buy this carpet?

4 Assess

1 Work out the first quantity as a fraction of the second.

 a 24, 36   b £2, £4.50   c 10 cm, 1 m   d 150 g, 1.5 kg

2 Work out $\frac{7}{8} - \frac{3}{5}$

3 The reciprocal of a fraction is $3\frac{7}{8}$
What is the fraction?

4 Paula makes trousers for her twin toddlers.
Each pair of trousers needs three-eighths of a yard of fabric.
How much fabric is needed for four pairs of trousers?

5 Which is bigger, $2\frac{3}{5} \times 1\frac{1}{2}$ or $2\frac{3}{5} \div 1\frac{1}{2}$? Explain how you found the answer.

6 Convert these fractions to decimals and then arrange them in order of size, starting with the smallest.

$\frac{3}{4}, \frac{8}{9}, \frac{2}{3}, \frac{3}{5}, \frac{9}{10}$

7 Which of these fractions will convert to recurring decimals?

 A $\frac{4}{7}$ B $\frac{7}{20}$ C $\frac{1}{12}$ D $\frac{3}{11}$ E $\frac{7}{80}$

8 Find the reciprocal of:

 a 8   b −3   c $\frac{2}{5}$ d −0.5   e $2\frac{1}{4}$

9 One litre is approximately one and three quarter pints.
How many pints are there in 6.5 litres?

10 The ratio of the number of people with 'attached' earlobes to the number of people with 'unattached' earlobes is approximately 3 : 7
How many students with 'attached' earlobes would you expect in a school with 950 students?

11 A sum of money is divided between two people in the ratio 4 : 5
If the first person gets £18, what does the second person get?

12 A number is 0.05 correct to one significant figure.
Which of these numbers could it **not** be?

   A 0.045   **B** 0.0525   **C** 0.049999   **D** 0.055   **E** 0.0476

13 Manish drove for 3.5 hours and covered 215 miles.
Calculate how far he would go in one hour at the same rate, rounding your answer to an appropriate degree of accuracy.

14 Jane's car travels an average of 7.6 miles per litre of fuel.
How far can she travel if she has 22 litres of fuel?

15 Express these decimals as fractions in their lowest terms.

   a 0.245   **b** 1.205   **c** 2.795   **d** 5.572   **e** 17.4545

16 **a** What is the only number that is the same as its reciprocal?

     b What is the only number that does not have a reciprocal?

Explain your answers.

17 Say whether each of these statements is true or false.

   a $25 \div 0.35$ is less than 25

   b 25×0.35 is less than 25

   c $25 + 0.35$ is less than 25

   d $25 - 0.35$ is less than 25

   e $25 - -0.35$ is less than 25

18 Express these recurring decimals as fractions in their lowest terms.

   a 0.555…   **d** 1.272727…

   b 0.404040…   **e** 2.123123123…

   c 0.624624624…

AQA Examination-style questions

1 A box of coloured counters contains only red, white and blue counters.

   $\frac{1}{3}$ of the counters are red.

   $\frac{1}{4}$ of the counters are white.

   100 counters are blue.

   How many counters are in the box?   *(4 marks)*

AQA 2008

5 Graphs of linear functions

Objectives

Examiners would normally expect students who get these grades to be able to:

D

draw the graph of a line, such as $y = 3x - 5$, without being given a table of values

solve problems such as finding where the line $y = 3x - 5$ crosses the line $y = 4$

C

find the gradients of straight-line graphs

find the midpoint of a line segment such as the line from $A(1, 5)$ to $B(3, 7)$

B

find the gradient and equation of a line through two points such as $(0, 3)$ and $(5, 13)$

find the equation of a line parallel to another line, such as $y = 3x - 5$, passing through a given point.

Key terms

linear
gradient
variables
coefficient
intercept
constant

Did you know?

Rollercoaster

The design of a rollercoaster has to have a long slope with a chain lift to drag the rollercoaster car to the top. This gives it enough energy to reach the end of the track. The slope needs to be high enough so that the car will roll along to the end of the track. The designer has to choose a gradient for the first slope. If it is too steep, it could be unsafe. If it is too shallow, there may not be enough room within the area available for the rollercoaster in the theme park. Choosing the proper gradient is very important.

You should already know:

✔ how to plot points in all four quadrants
✔ how to recognise lines such as $y = 4$ or $x = -3$

Learn... 5.1 Drawing straight-line graphs

An equation such as $y = 3x - 5$ can be shown on a graph.

The graph will be a straight line and $y = 3x - 5$ is called a **linear** equation.

A linear equation does not contain any powers of x or y.

To draw the graph you need to work out the coordinates of three points on the line.

Choose any three values of x that lie within the range you have been given.

Work out the corresponding y-values, using the equation of the line.

Plot the points and then draw the line through them.

> **AQA Examiner's tip**
>
> It is a good idea to use zero as one of your x-values because it is easy to substitute.

Example: Draw the graph of $y = 3x - 5$ for values of x from -2 to 4.

Solution: Choose $x = -2, 0, 4$

Work out the y-values and put them in a table.

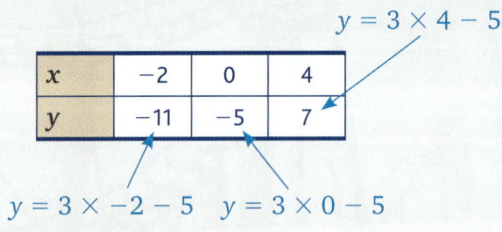

$y = 3 \times 4 - 5$

x	-2	0	4
y	-11	-5	7

$y = 3 \times -2 - 5$ $y = 3 \times 0 - 5$

Plot the points. (In the exam the axes will be drawn for you.)

Draw the line through your plots.

It must go all the way from $x = -2$ to $x = 4$

> **AQA Examiner's tip**
>
> Always use three plots, not just two. They should be in a straight line. If they are not, you have made a mistake in working out one of the y-values, so check and correct the values.

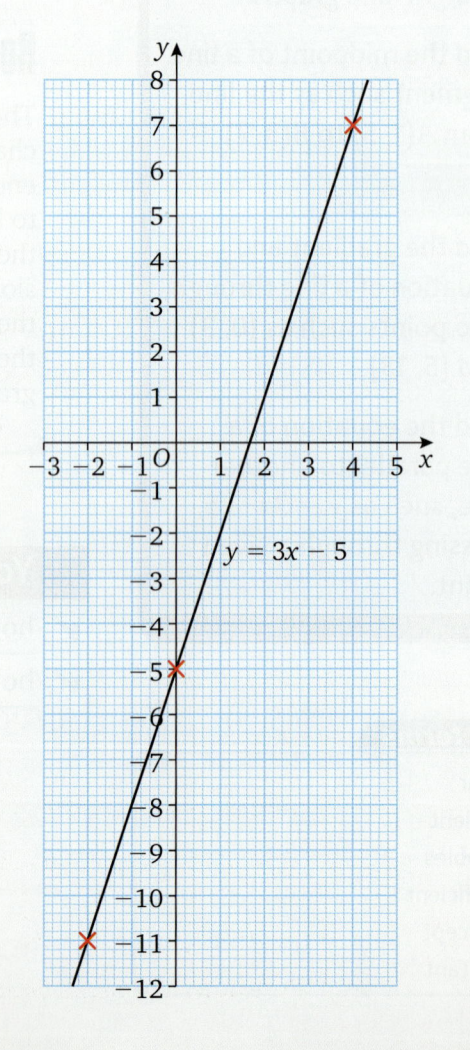

This straight-line graph has been drawn using the same scales on both axes.

This makes it easy to plot the points.

The range of y-values is large so the graph is tall and narrow.

Chapter 5   Graphs of linear functions   69

This is the same straight-line graph but using a different scale on the y-axis.

This makes it a little harder to plot the points, but the graph is not so tall.

You may be given axes with different scales to use in the exam, so you need to be able to plot against axes with different scales.

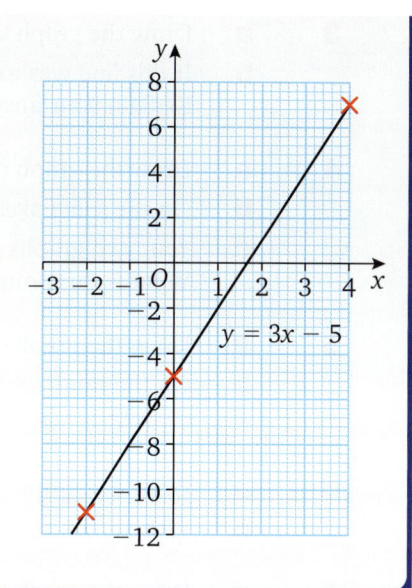

Example: a   Draw the graph of $x + y = 6$ for values of x from -1 to 6.

b   Write down the coordinates of the point where the graph crosses the line $y = 2$

Solution: a   Choose three values that are easy to substitute, for example: $x = 0$, $y = 0$, and one other value.

Work out the corresponding y-values and put them in a table.

x	0	2	6
y	6	4	0

$6 + 0 = 6$

Plot the points.

Draw the line through the plotted points, making sure it goes from $x = -1$ to $x = 6$

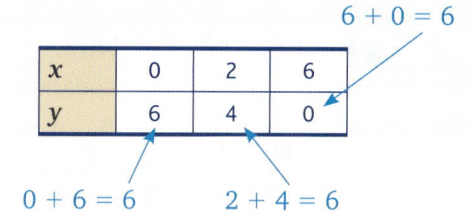

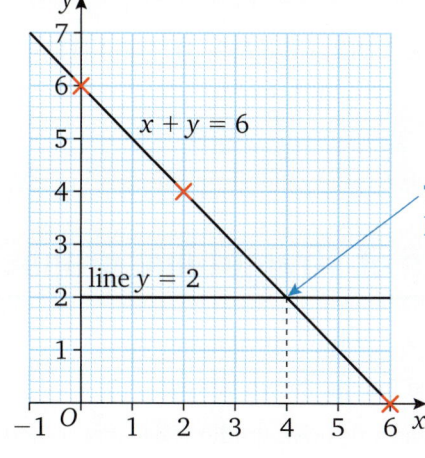

$0 + 6 = 6$ $2 + 4 = 6$

This is the point you have to find.

AQA Examiner's tip

Drawing in this dashed line will help you to read off the x-coordinate accurately.

b   Draw the line $y = 2$ on the same axes.

Read off the coordinates of the point where the two lines cross: (4, 2).

Practise... 5.1 Drawing straight-line graphs   D C B A A*

1   a   Draw the graph of $y = x + 2$ for values of x from -3 to 4.

b   Write down the coordinates of the point where this graph crosses the y-axis.

2   a   Draw the graph of $y = 3x - 1$ for values of x from -3 to 3.

b   Write down the coordinates of the point where this graph crosses the line $y = -3$

D

3 **a** Draw the graph of $y = \frac{1}{2}x$ for values of x from -4 to 4.
b If this line was extended, would it go through the point $(7, 4)$?
Explain your answer.

4 **a** Draw the graph of $y = 2x$ for values of x from -3 to 3.
b On the same axes, draw the graph of $y = x$ for values of x from -3 to 3.
c Your two graphs go through the same point.
What is this point?

5 **a** Draw the graph of $y = 2x + 1$ for values of x from -3 to 3.
b On the same axes, draw the graph of $y = 1 - 3x$ for values of x from -3 to 3.
c Write down the coordinates of the point where these two lines cross.

6 **a** Draw the graph of $x + 2y = 9$ for values of x from -2 to 5.
b Write down the coordinates of the point where your graph crosses the line $x = 4$

7 **a** Draw the graph of $x - 2y = 1$ for values of x from -3 to 3.
b Write down the coordinates of the point where your graph crosses the line $y = \frac{1}{2}$

8 Which of these points lie on the line $3x + 2y = 12$?
A $(0, 4)$ **B** $(2, 3)$ **C** $(3, 2)$ **D** $(1, 4\frac{1}{2})$ **E** $(0, 6)$ **F** $(6, -3)$ **G** $(-2, 8)$
Show how you found your answers.

9 $P(-3, 6)$, $Q(0, 0)$ and $R(2, -4)$ are three points on a straight line.
Which of these is the equation of the line?
$y = x + 9$ $x + y = 3$ $y + 2x = 0$
Show how you found your answer.

10 Each of the following points lies on one or more of the given lines.
Match the points to their lines.
Points: $A(-2, 7)$ $B(0, 0)$ $C(1, 4)$ $D(2, 5)$ $E(3, 3)$ $F(4, 1)$
Lines: $y = 4x$ $2x + y = 9$ $x + y = 5$ $y = 6x - 7$

Learn... 5.2 Gradients of straight-line graphs

The **gradient** of a straight-line graph is a measure of how steep it is.

The **gradient** can be found from the graph of the line as shown below.

A line that slopes from top right to bottom left has a positive gradient because y increases as x increases.

To find the gradient, draw a line parallel to the x-axis and a line parallel to the y-axis to make a right-angled triangle on the graph. The triangle can be anywhere on the graph.

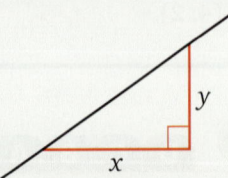

$$\text{gradient} = \frac{\text{increase in } y}{\text{increase in } x} = \frac{y}{x}$$

AQA Examiner's tip
Take a careful note of the scales on the graph. They might be different on the x- and the y-axes.

A line that slopes from top left to bottom right has a negative gradient because y decreases as x increases.

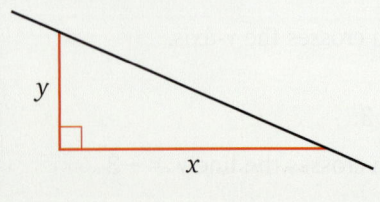

$$\text{gradient} = -\frac{y}{x}$$

Here is an example of finding the gradient from the graph:

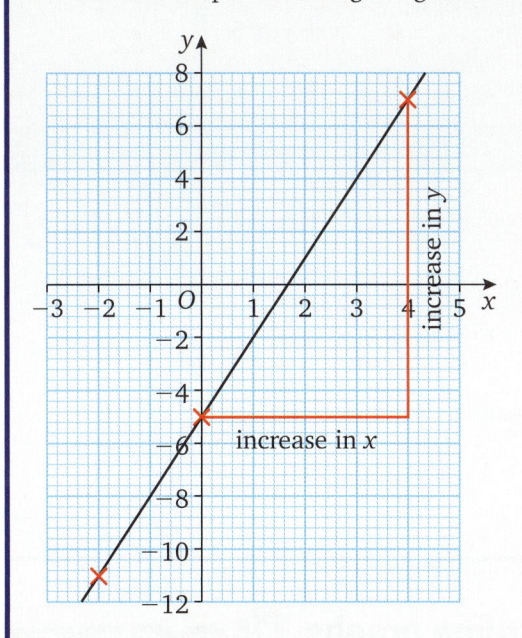

Bump up your grade

Being able to find the gradient of a graph is a good way to bump up your grade to a Grade C.

Increase in y from −5 to 7 = 12

Increase in x from 0 to 4 = 4

Gradient = $\frac{12}{4}$ = 3

The **gradient** can also be found from the equation of the line.
To find the gradient, write the equation of the line in the form $y = mx + c$
y and x are the **variables** in the equation.
m (the **coefficient** of x) is the **gradient** of the line.

The **intercept** is the point where the line crosses the y-axis.
In the form $y = mx + c$, c is the **constant** and the intercept is at (0, c).
For example:

The line $y = 2x - 1$ has a gradient equal to 2 and the intercept is at (0, −1).

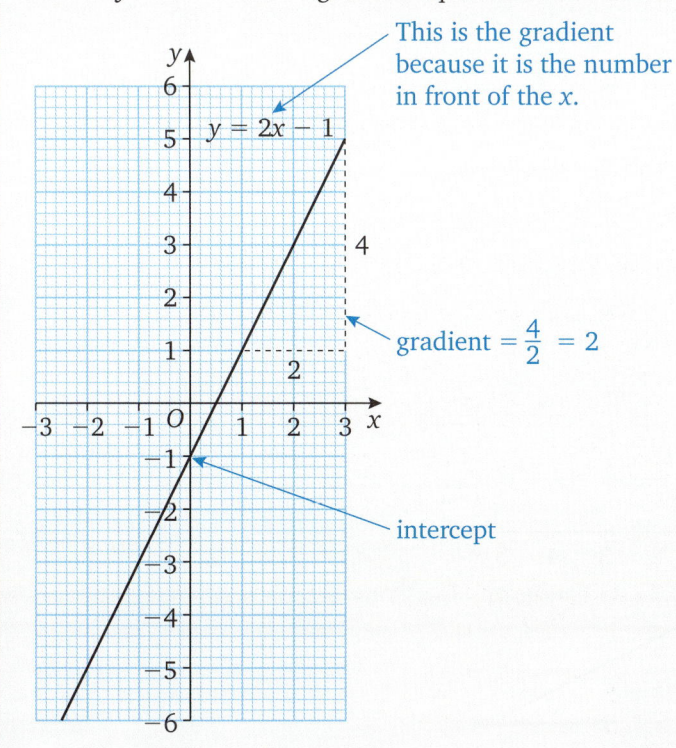

This is the gradient because it is the number in front of the x.

gradient = $\frac{4}{2}$ = 2

intercept

Example: Find the gradient and intercept of:

a $y = 5x - 2$
b $y = 3 - 2x$
c $x + y = 5$

Solution:

a $y = 5x - 2$
$m = 5$ so the gradient is 5
$c = -2$ so the intercept is at $(0, -2)$

b $y = 3 - 2x$
$m = -2$ so the gradient is -2
$c = 3$ so the intercept is at $(0, 3)$

c $x + y = 5$
You have to start rearranging the equation to read as $y = \ldots$
$x + y = 5$
$x + y - x = 5 - x$ Subtract x from both sides.
$y = 5 - x$

$m = -1$ so the gradient is -1
$c = 5$ so the intercept is at $(0, 5)$

Practise... 5.2 Gradients of straight-line graphs   D C B A A*

1 Write down the gradient and intercept of each line.

a

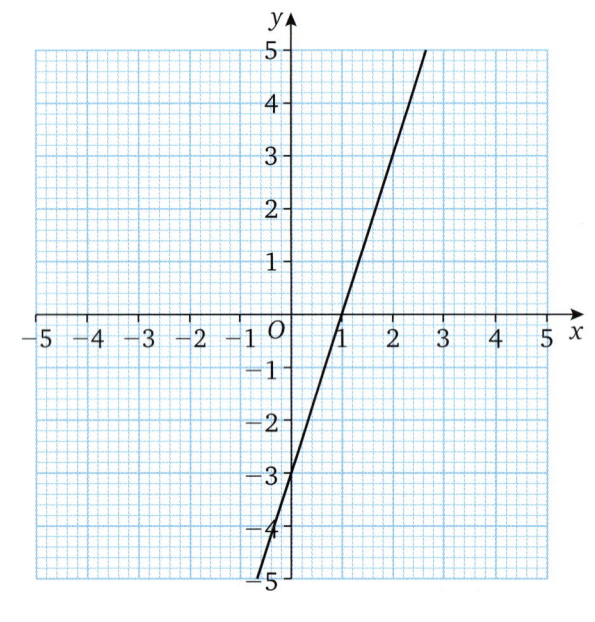

b

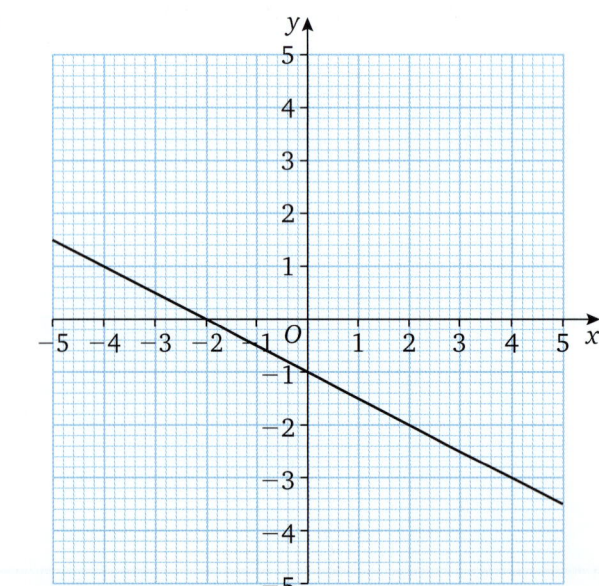

Chapter 5 Graphs of linear functions   73

2 Jo says that the lines whose equations are $y = 5 - 2x$ and $y = 5 - 4x$ have the same gradient. Explain why Jo is wrong.

3 Look at these lines.

   a Which line has a gradient of 2?
       How do you know?

   b Which line has a gradient of 1?
       How do you know?

   c Which line or lines have a negative gradient?
       How do you know?

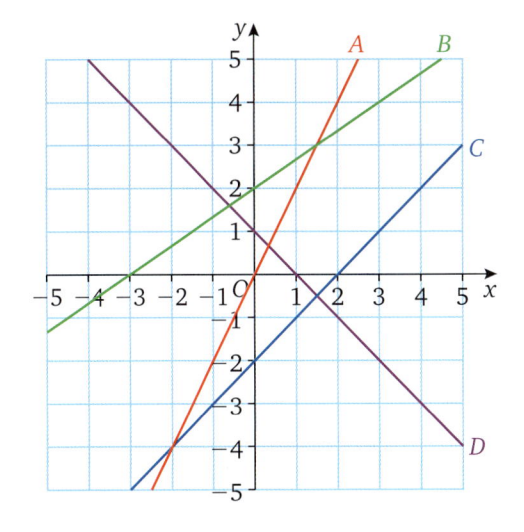

4 Write down the gradient of each graph.

> **Hint**
> Read the vertical scale carefully because it is not the same as the horizontal scale.

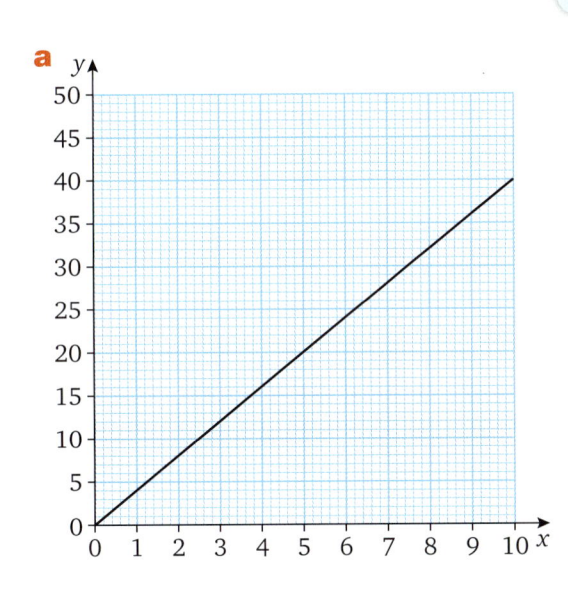

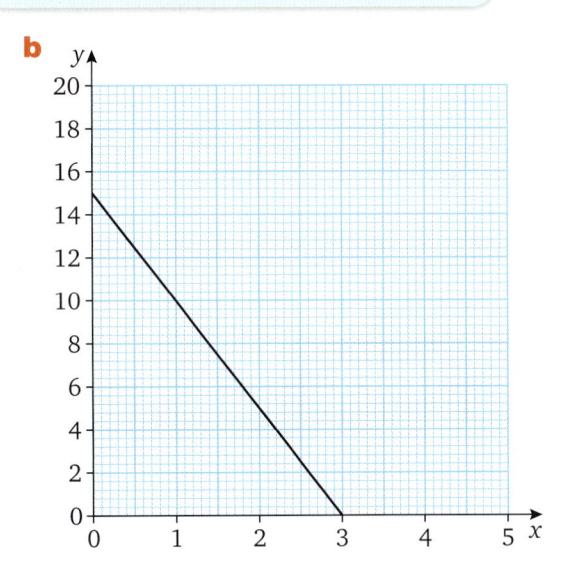

a

b

5 Rearrange each of these equations into the form $y = mx + c$

   a $y - 3x = 6$ **b** $y + 5x = 2$ **c** $2y + x = 6$ **d** $x = 3y - 9$

6 Write down the gradient and intercept of each of these straight lines.

   a $y = 5x + 4$ **c** $y = 3 - 2x$ **e** $2y = 6x - 7$
   b $y = 2 + x$ **d** $y + 5 = 3x$ **f** $4x + y = 9$

7 The diagram shows the line $y = 3x - 5$

   $RQ = 3$ units

   What is the length of PQ?
   Show your working.

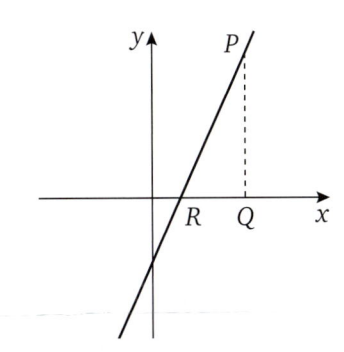

AQA GCSE Mathematics

8 Show that the lines $5x + 2y = 9$ and $4y = 3 - 10x$ have the same gradient.

9 On the same axes, draw the graphs of $y = 2x$, $y = 2x + 4$ and $y = 2x - 5$ for values of x from -4 to 4.

What do you notice?

10 Use your knowledge of gradients and intercepts to match the equations to the sketch graphs.

i $y = 3x$ **ii** $y = -2x$ **iii** $x + y = 4$ **iv** $y = 3x + 8$

a

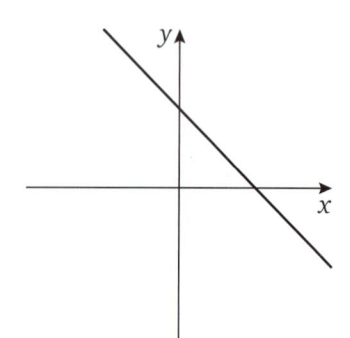

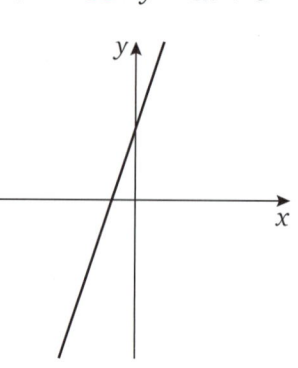

b

c

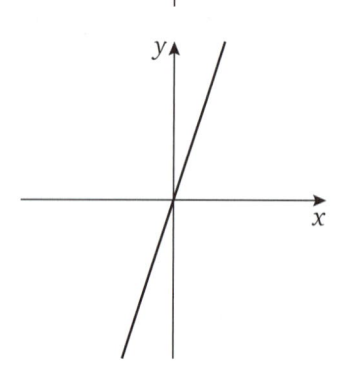

d

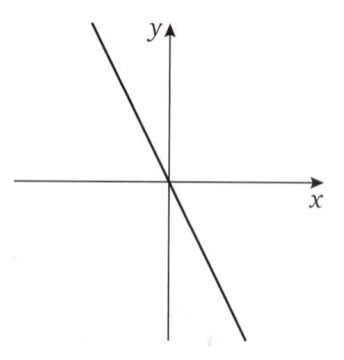

Learn... 5.3 The midpoint of a line segment

A line segment is the part of a line joining two points.
There are two ways to find the midpoint of a line segment.

Method 1:
Measure halfway along the line.

Method 2:
Find the mean of the coordinates of the end points.

Remember, a mean is calculated by adding terms together and then dividing by the number of terms.

Example: A line segment has been drawn from $A(-4, 1)$ to $B(2, 3)$.

Find the midpoint of AB.

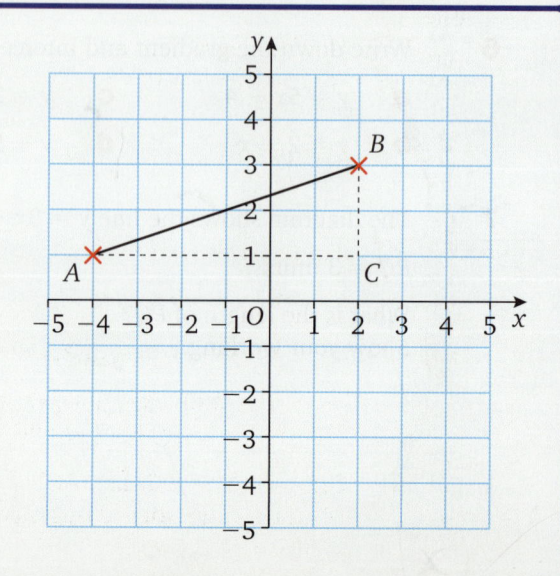

Chapter 5 Graphs of linear functions

Solution: **Method 1**

Measure halfway along the line.

The midpoint of the line is at $(-1, 2)$.

Method 2

Find the mean of the coordinates of the end points.

x-coordinate of the midpoint: $\dfrac{-4 + 2}{2} = -1$ Add the two x-coordinates and divide by 2.

y-coordinate of the midpoint: $\dfrac{1 + 3}{2} = 2$ Add the two y-coordinates and divide by 2.

The midpoint of the line is at $(-1, 2)$.

Practise... **5.3 The midpoint of a line segment**   D C B A A*

1 **a** Work out the coordinates of the midpoint of the line from $(2, 5)$ to $(-4, 1)$.

b Draw a grid with the x-axis and the y-axis labelled from -5 to 5.
Plot the points $(2, 5)$ and $(-4, 1)$.
Use your diagram to check your answer to part **a**.

2 Work out the coordinates of the midpoint of the line from $(0, 4)$ to $(2, 6)$.

3 Joe says that the point $(1, 2\tfrac{1}{2})$ is halfway between $(-4, 3)$ and $(6, -8)$.

Is he correct?

Give a reason for your answer.

4 A is the point $(3, -1)$ and B is the point $(-5, -5)$.

a Work out the coordinates of the midpoint of the line AB.

b Find the gradient of the line AB.

AQA Examiner's tip
It often helps to sketch a diagram and put the points on it. This also gives you a quick check on your calculations.

5 R is the midpoint of the line PQ.
The coordinates of Q are $(3, 2)$.
R is the point $(1, 1)$.

What are the coordinates of P?

6 $A(2, 5)$, $B(5, -2)$ and $C(-2, 2)$ are the vertices of a triangle.

a Find the coordinates of M, the midpoint of AB.

b Find the coordinates of N, the midpoint of BC.

c Draw a grid with the x-axis and y-axis labelled from -3 to 6.
Plot the points A, B, C, M and N.

d Draw the lines MN and AC.
What do you notice about them?

AQA GCSE Mathematics

7 A quadrilateral *PQRS* has these coordinates.

$P(0, 4) \quad Q(6, 2) \quad R(1, -3) \quad S(-5, -1)$

  a Find the gradient of the line *SP*.

  b Find the gradient of the line *RQ*.

  c What do your results tell you about these lines?

  d Find the gradient of the line *PQ*.

  e Find the gradient of the line *SR*.

  f What do your results tell you about the quadrilateral *ABCD*?

8 The quadrilateral *TUVW* is a kite.

Plot $T(1, 3)$, $U(3, 3)$ and $W(-4, -4)$ on a grid.

Find the coordinates of the fourth vertex, *V*.

Learn... 5.4 Lines through two given points and parallel lines

To find the equation of a line that goes through two given points, find the gradient and the intercept.

Example: *P* is the point $(-4, -2)$ and *Q* is the point $(4, 4)$.

Find the equation of the line *PQ*.

Solution:

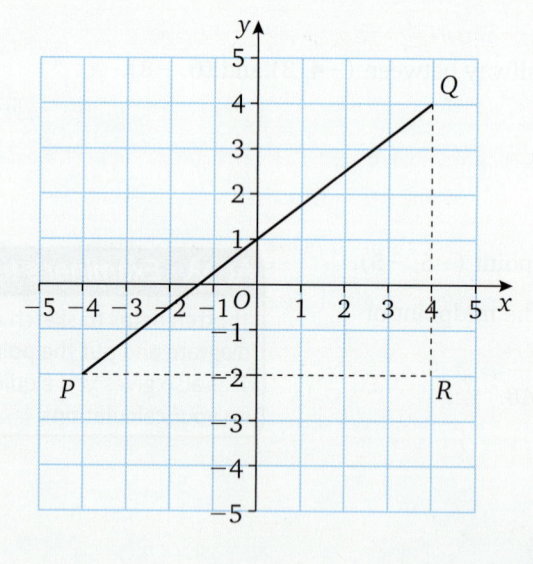

AQA Examiner's tip
Always draw a diagram to help you.

The gradient of the line *PQ* is $\frac{6}{8} \left(= \frac{3}{4}\right)$ — this is *m* — and the intercept is $(0, 1)$ — this is *c*.

The equation of the line is $y = \frac{3}{4}x + 1$

Check by substituting the coordinates of *P* and *Q* into your equation.

At *P*, $x = -4$ and $y = -2$ $-2 = \frac{3 \times -4}{4} + 1$ ✓

At *Q*, $x = 4$ and $y = 4$ $4 = \frac{3 \times 4}{4} + 1$ ✓

If you do not know the intercept, use one pair of coordinates to find *c*.

Example: P is the point (3, 7) and Q is the point (6, 1).

Find the equation of the line PQ.

Solution:

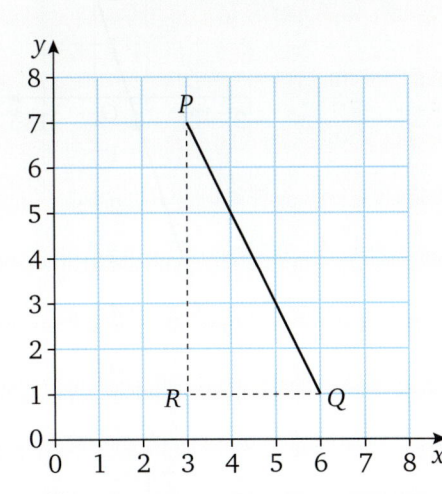

The gradient of the line is $-\frac{6}{3} = -2$

This is m, so the equation of PQ is $y = -2x + c$

The coordinates of P must fit the equation.

Substitute $x = 3$ and $y = 7$ in $y = -2x + c$

$7 = -6 + c$

$c = 13$

The equation of PQ is $y = -2x + 13$

Check by substituting the coordinates of Q in your equation.

At Q, $x = 6$ and $y = 1$ $1 = -2 \times 6 + 13$ ✓

Parallel lines have the same gradient.

Any line parallel to the line $y = 4x + 1$ will have a gradient equal to 4.

The lines $y = 4x$, $y = 4x + 5$, $y = 4x - 2$, $y = 4x - 11$ are all parallel.

In general, the equation of a line parallel to $y = 4x + 1$ will be $y = 4x + c$.

The coordinates of any point on the line will fit this equation.

Example: Find the equation of the line through the point (1, 4) that is parallel to the line $y = 3x - 2$

Solution: The gradient of $y = 3x - 2$ is 3, so the new line is $y = 3x + c$

It goes through (1, 4) so when $x = 1$, $y = 4$ ← substitute these values into the equation $y = 3x + c$

$4 = 3 \times 1 + c$

$c = 1$

The equation of the new line is $y = 3x + 1$

5.4 Lines through two given points and parallel lines

Practise...

1 A is the point (2, 3) and B is the point (3, 7).

Find the equation of the line AB.

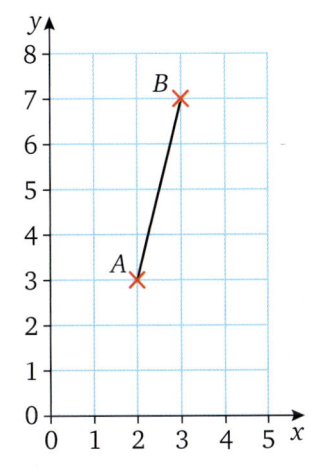

2 C is the point (−2, −4) and D is the point (0, 2).

Find the equation of the line CD.

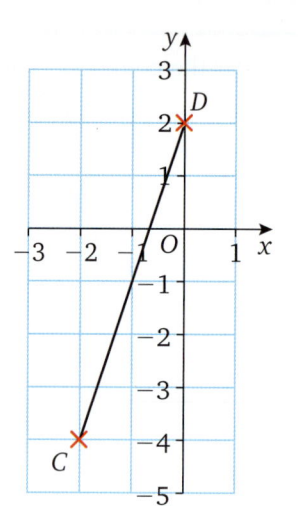

3 E is the point (−1, 6) and F is the point (5, 3).

Find the equation of the line EF.

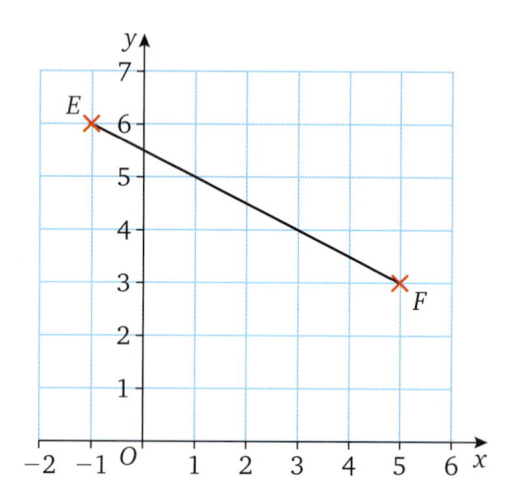

4 Find the equation of the line joining the points (2, 7) and (−2, 6).

5 Anthony says that the line $y = 2x$ is parallel to the line $y = 4 - 2x$

Explain why he is wrong.

6 Find the three pairs of parallel lines in these equations.

$y = 4x$	$y = 1 + 3x$	$x + y = 8$	$x = \dfrac{y}{4} + 2$
$y - 5x = 4$	$2x - y = 7$	$2y - 6x = 5$	$3x + y = 10$
$3y + x = 8$	$4x + y = 2$	$y = 3 - x$	$5y - x = 2$

Hint
Change them to the form $y = mx + c$

7 Find the equation of the line through (0, 2) that is parallel to $y = 3x - 4$

8 Find the equation of the line through (1, 5) that is parallel to $y = 3 - 2x$

9 Find the equation of the line through (−2, −3) that is parallel to $x + y = 4$

10 Find the equation of the line through (4, −1) that is parallel to $3x + 2y = 10$

⚠ 11 The vertices of a triangle are A(3, 6), B(1, 2) and C(7, 4).

M is the midpoint of the side AB.

N is the midpoint of the side AC.

 a Find the equation of the line BC.

 b Find the equation of the line MN.

 c Hence prove that MN is parallel to BC.

Assess

1 a Draw the graph of $y = x - 3$ for values of x from -3 to 4.
 b Write down the coordinates of the point where your graph crosses the y-axis.

2 a Draw the graph of $2x + y = 7$ for values of x from 0 to 5.
 b Write down the coordinates of the point where your graph crosses the line $y = 2$

3 a Which of these points lie on the line $4x - 3y = 4$?
   $(1, 0)$ $(0, 1)$ $(3, 4)$ $(4, 4)$ $(7, 8)$ $(8, 7)$
   Show how you found your answers.
 b Each of these points lies on two of the given lines.
   Match the points to their lines.
   Points: $A(-4, -3)$ $B(-1, 1)$ $C(-3, 6)$ $D(4, 3)$ $E(5, -2)$
   Lines: $y = 6$ $y + x = 3$ $3y = 4x + 7$ $4y - 3x = 0$ $y + 5x = 23$ $y + x = 0$

4 Write down the equation of the line that has:
 a gradient 5 and intercept -6
 b gradient -1 and intercept 4.

5 Rearrange each of these equations into the form $y = mx + c$
 a $y + 6x = 2$
 b $6x - 2y = 5$

6 Show that the lines $y = 9 - x$ and $x + y = 4$ are parallel.

7 The points $A(-3, -3)$ and $B(1, 5)$ are shown on the sketch.

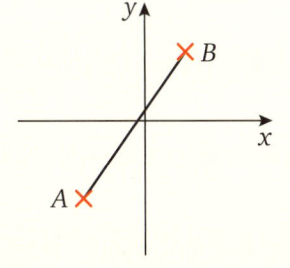

Not drawn accurately

 a Find the gradient of the line segment AB.
 b Work out the coordinates of the midpoint of AB.

8 M is the midpoint of the line PQ.
The coordinates of M are $(-1, 2)$.
The coordinates of P are $(-5, -3)$.

Work out the coordinates of Q.

9 A is the point $(1, 1)$ and B is the point $(4, 9)$.
Find the equation of the line AB.

10 Find the pair of parallel lines in this list.

$3x + 2y = 5$ $2y = 3x - 4$ $2x + 3y = 5$ $3x - 2y = 1$

11 Find the equation of the line through $(2, -3)$ that is parallel to $3y = 5 - 4x$

AQA Examination-style questions

1 The grid shows the graphs of two straight lines A and B.

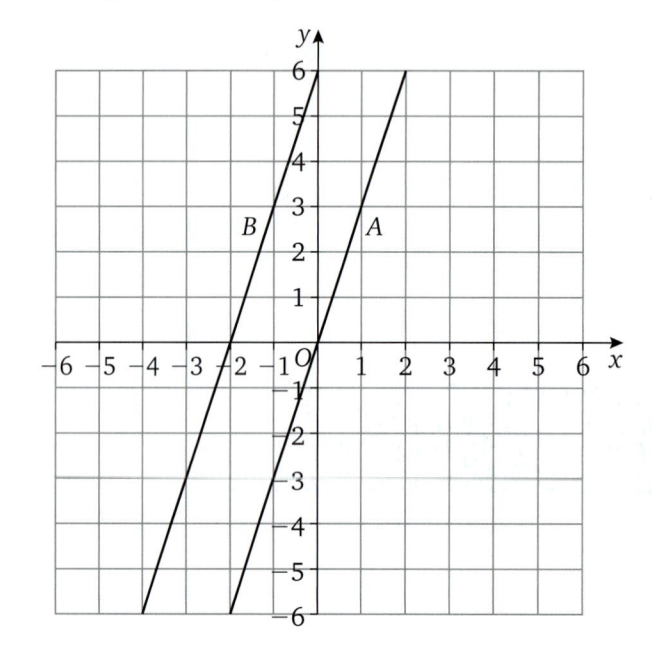

    a Write down the equation of line A. *(2 marks)*
    b Write down the equation of line B. *(1 mark)*
    c Write down a fact about the gradients of lines A and B. *(1 mark)*

AQA 2007

6 Working with symbols

Objectives

Examiners would normally expect students who get these grades to be able to:

D

expand brackets in context such as $x(x + 2)$

factorise an expression such as $x^2 + 4x$

C

expand and simplify an expression such as $x(2x + 1) - x(2x - 3)$

B

expand and simplify two brackets in context such as $(x + 4)(x - 8)$

expand and simplify two brackets in context such as $(3x + 4)(2x - 8)$.

simplify fractions such as $\frac{x}{3} + \frac{x}{5}$ and $\frac{2(x - 1)^2}{x - 1}$

Key terms

expand
expression
simplify
factorise
variable
quadratic expression

Did you know?

Queuing theory

Supermarkets use queuing theory to decide how many people they need to work at the checkout at any time.

There are mathematical formulae used in queuing theory.

This is Little's theorem: $N = \lambda T$

Little's theorem is used in queuing theory.

N stands for the average number of customers.

λ is the average customer arrival rate.

T is the average service time per customer.

Try testing out Little's theorem with real values to see if it makes sense.

You should already know:

✓ number operations and BIDMAS
✓ how to add and subtract negative numbers
✓ how to multiply and divide negative numbers
✓ how to find common factors
✓ how to add and subtract fractions
✓ the meaning of indices
✓ how to collect like terms.

Learn... 6.1 Expanding brackets and collecting like terms

When you **expand** brackets, **all** the terms inside the brackets must be multiplied by the term outside the brackets.

You will be given the instruction **expand** or **multiply out**.

If there is more than one bracket in the **expression**, each is done separately before collecting terms.

If there are terms not included in the bracket they are not included in the expansion.

These terms are collected once the brackets have been expanded.

Once you have the expanded expression, you should **simplify** it by collecting like terms.

Example: Expand $4(2y - 1)$

Solution: Everything inside the bracket is multiplied by the term in front of the bracket.

$$4(2y - 1) = 4 \times 2y - 4 \times 1$$
$$= 8y - 4$$

Example: Multiply out $5a(2a + 1)$

Solution: $5a(2a + 1) = 5a \times 2a + 5a \times 1$ Remember that $a \times a = a^2$
$$= 10a^2 + 5a$$

You may prefer to draw lines on the question to show which terms are multiplied. Using this method saves a line in your working.

$$5a(2a + 1)$$
$$= 10a^2 + 5a$$

Example: Expand and simplify $9x - 2(x - 4)$

Solution: Note that $9x$ is not included in the bracket.

The part of the expression that needs to be expanded is $-2(x - 4)$

$$9x - 2(x - 4) = 9x - 2x + 8$$ Remember that the term in front of
$$= 7x + 8$$ the bracket is -2 and not 2.

Leave $9x$ to be collected once the bracket has been expanded.

Example: Expand and simplify $4(3y + 2) - 5(y - 3)$

Solution: Separate the expression into two brackets to carry out the expansion.

Step 1 First bracket: Expand $4(3y + 2)$
$$4(3y + 2) = 12y + 8$$

Step 2 Second bracket: Expand $-5(y - 3)$
$$-5(y - 3) = -5y + 15$$

Step 3 Put the two answers together and collect like terms.
$$4(3y + 2) - 5(y - 3) = 12y + 8 - 5y + 15$$
$$= 7y + 23$$

Chapter 6 Working with symbols

Example: Write an expression for the area of this rectangle. Expand your answer.

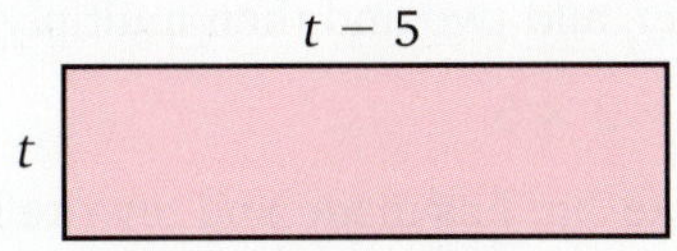

$t - 5$
t

Solution: The area of a rectangle is width × length.

Area = $t(t - 5)$ Put the length in a bracket so both terms are multiplied by t.

Expand the brackets using your own method.

Area = $t^2 - 5t$ There are no terms to simplify because t^2 and t are different types of term.

AQA Examiner's tip
You can use any method to expand brackets as long as it works. Check your answer by substituting values.

Practise... 6.1 Expanding brackets and collecting like terms   D C B A A*

1 Expand:

a $3(x + 4)$
b $5(y - 2)$
c $8(2 - c)$
d $3(2p + 5)$
e $5(5d - 1)$
f $7(2 - 2f)$
g $3(10v + 7)$
h $11(7 + 3m)$
i $3a(a - 2)$
j $2d(3 - 5d)$
k $\frac{t}{2}(t - 4)$
l $6t(\frac{t}{2} - 2)$

2
a Tom expands $4f(2f - 3)$
   Jade expands $6f(f - 2) + 2f^2$
   Show that Tom and Jade get the same answer.

b Micky expands $8f(f - 1)$
   What does Micky have to add to get the same answer as Tom and Jade?

3 Write an expression for the area of each of these rectangles. Expand your answer in each case.

a $5a + 1$ by 3
b $b - 5$ by 2
c $4c + 3$ by 6
d $1.5d$ by $d - 2$
e $2.5e$ by $10 + e$
f $3 - f$ by $5.5f$

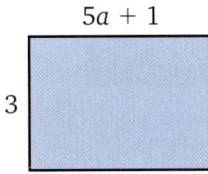

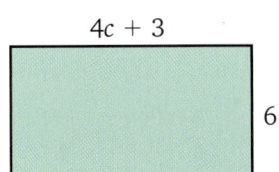

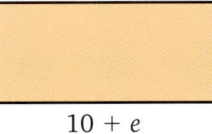

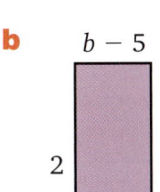

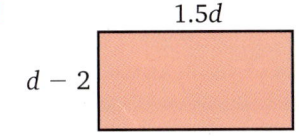

4 Sam and Jim are writing number puzzles using symbols. They use *n* to represent the missing number.

Sam says 'Think of a number, add two and then multiply the answer by 5.'

Jim writes his answer as $n + 2 \times 5$.

a Write down the mistake Jim has made and rewrite his answer correctly.

b Write each of these number puzzles as an expression, using *n* for the missing number.

  i 'Think of a number, subtract 8 and then multiply the answer by 5.'

  ii 'Begin with 10 and subtract the number, multiply the answer by 3 and then add 3 times the number.'

c Travis and his friends wrote these expressions for number puzzles. For each one, expand the brackets and collect like terms.

  i $5(n + 2) - 10$

  ii $3n - 2(n - 1)$

  iii $5(n + 1) + 2(3 - n)$

  iv $7(3 - 2n) + 10n$

  v $3(2 + 3n) - 2(3 + 4n)$

  vi $2(n + 1) + 5(n - 2) - 4n$

Bump up your grade

At Grade C, you may be asked to expand more than one bracket before simplifying.

5 Find an expression for the total area of each coloured shape. Expand and simplify your answer.

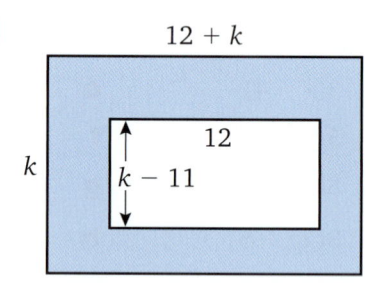

a T-shape: top width $n + m$, top height 6, stem width 5, stem labelled n

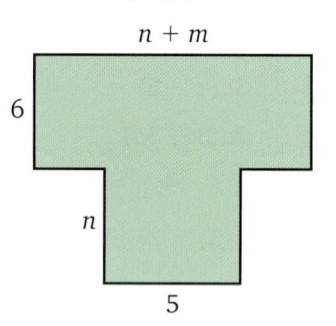

b L-shape: top width $3 - x$, left height 4, vertical side $x - 2$, bottom width 10

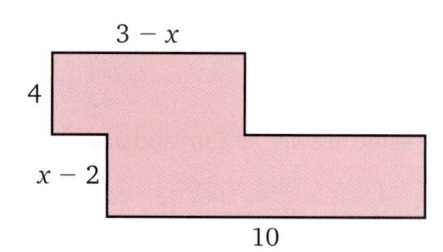

c Square with square hole: outer side $b + c$, inner side b, left side 10, right inner 5

d Rectangle with rectangular hole: outer width $12 + k$, outer height k, inner width 12, inner height $k - 11$

e Rectangle with triangular hole: outer width $3 + t$, left side 3.5, triangle legs 2 and t

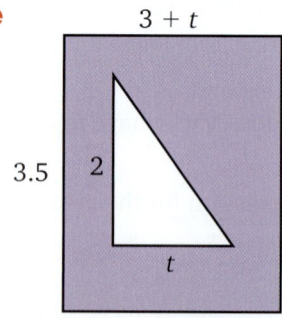

Hint

Remember the area of a triangle $= \frac{1}{2}$ base $\times$ height

f L-shape: left height $3a$, top right height $2a$, bottom right a, bottom width $4a$

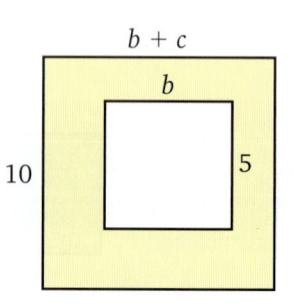

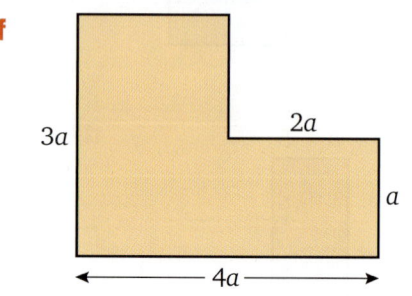

Chapter 6 Working with symbols   85

6 Find the missing numbers to make each pair of expressions equal.
  a $2(a + 4) + 3(a − 1)$ $?(a + 1)$
  b $5(1 − b) − 3(b − 3)$ $?(7 − 4b)$
  c $2(x + 1) − 5(x + ?)$ $−3(x + 6)$
  d $?(2x − 1) + 2(x − 3)$ $10(x − 1)$
  e $5(1 − x) + ?(4x + 5)$ $3(x + 5)$

7 In each diagram the value of the perimeter and the value of the area are the same.
In each question part, which value of x gives the same value for the perimeter and the area?

  a Rectangle with sides $x + 1$ and 3.
     $x = 4$ $x = 5$ $x = 6$

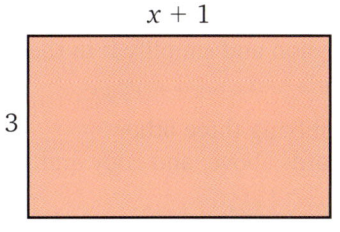

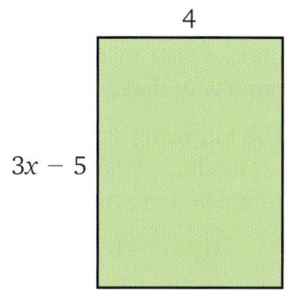

  c Rectangle with sides 4 and $3x − 5$.
     $x = 3.5$ $x = 1.3$ $x = 3.0$

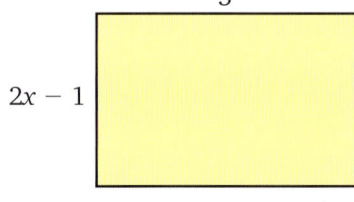

  b Rectangle with sides 3 and $2x − 1$.
     $x = 3.5$ $x = 4.5$ $x = 6.5$

  Hint
  Start by writing an expression for the perimeter and an expression for the area.

8 Here are two rectangles.

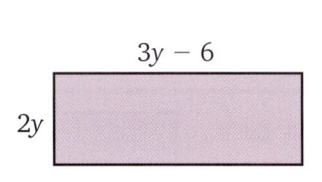

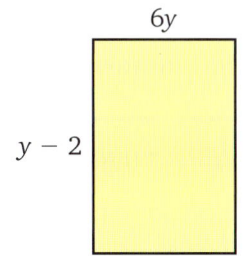

Rectangle 1: sides $3y − 6$ and $2y$.
Rectangle 2: sides $6y$ and $y − 2$.

Show that the areas of the two rectangles are the same.

9 In the diagram below, the expression in the top box is found by multiplying the two adjacent boxes below.

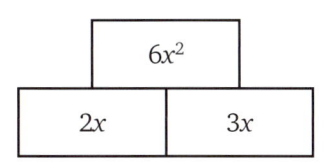

Top: $6x^2$; bottom: $2x$, $3x$.

Fill in the missing boxes in the following diagrams.

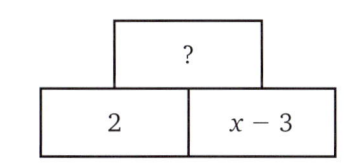

  a Top: $25y^2$; bottom: $5y$, ?

  c Top: $2x^2 + 10x$; bottom: ?, $x + 5$

  b Top: ?; bottom: 2, $x − 3$

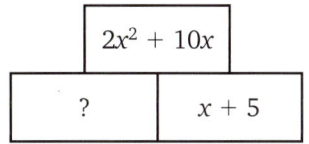

10

| Row A | 3 | 4x | 2 | 3x | 5x | −5 | 2x | −x |

| Row B | 3 − 2x | x − 2 | 2x + 1 | 3 − x | x − 1 | x + 2 | 2 − x | 3x − 1 |

Jess chooses two terms from row A and two terms from row B to make this expression:

$3(3 - x) + 3x(x - 2)$

Jess simplifies the expression in two steps:

$9 - 3x + 3x^2 - 6x$

$3x^2 - 9x + 9$

a Choose your own four terms to make an expression and simplify it in the same way that Jess has.

b The following shows Jess's working when simplifying three other expressions. Find the missing terms from the cards above, and copy and complete her working.

i $?(2x + 1) - 5(x + 2)$
$= 4x^2 + 2x - 5x - 10$
$=$

ii $4x(?) - x(2 - x)$
$= ? - ? - 2x + x^2$
$= 13x^2 - 6x$

iii $5x(x - 1) + ?(?)$
$= 5x^2 - ? + 6 - ?$
$= 5x^2 - 7x + 6$

Learn... 6.2 Factorising expressions

Factorising is the opposite of expanding.

You will usually be given the instruction **factorise**.

Example: An expression for the area of this rectangle is $3xy + 6y$.

Factorise fully the expression to find possible dimensions of the rectangle.

AQA Examiner's tip

If a questions asks you to factorise **fully** then it usually means there is more than one factor to take out. In this case, you can take out 3 and y.

Solution: **Step 1:** Find the common factor of the two terms in the expression.

$3y$ is the common factor because 3 is a factor of 3 and 6

$3xy + 6y$

and y is a factor of xy and y.

Step 2: Divide each term by the common factor.

$3xy \div 3y = x$ $6y \div 3y = 2$

Step 3: Write the common factor outside the bracket and the remaining terms inside the bracket.

$3xy + 6y = 3y(x + 2)$

Chapter 6 Working with symbols • 87

Practise... 6.2 Factorising expressions   D C

1 Factorise each expression.

a $8c + 4$
b $12d - 15$
c $20 - 10p$
d $24 + 18k$
e $20x + x^2$
f $y^2 - 5y$
g $12xy - 9y^2$
h $b^2 + 9ab$
i $4n + 18n^2m$
j $15kl + 27k^2$
k $13f^2 - 65fg$
l $36j^2k - 30jk^2$

AQA Examiner's tip
Multiply out your answers to check you have factorised correctly.

2 In each question, one side of the rectangle and the expression for the area has been given. Find the expression or value for the length of the other side.

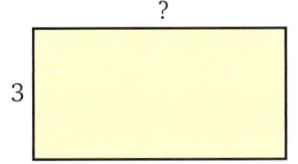

a area = $6x - 21$ 3

b area = $20x^2 - 25x$ 5x

c area = $7p^2 - 5p$ p

AQA Examiner's tip
Always factorise fully. The highest common factor should be taken outside the bracket.

d area = $100t^2 + 125t$ $4t + 5$

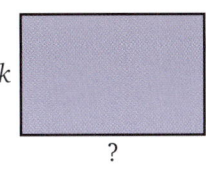

e area = $2kq - 3kr$ k

3 Factorise fully the expressions for the area of these rectangles. Use your answers to give a term for the dimensions of each rectangle.

a area = $5fg + 8fg^2$

b area = $3x^2 + 21xy^2$

c area = $6pq^2 - 2pq^3$

Hint
$q^3 \div q^2 = q$

d area = $10a^2b + 15ab^2$

4 Chris and Sue both factorise the same expression but get different answers.

$12xy^2 - 18x^2y$

Chris's answer is $2x(6y^2 - 9xy)$

Sue's answer is $6xy(2y - 3x)$

Give the reasons why Chris is wrong and Sue is right.

5 These expressions have been factorised fully. Some are wrong and some are right.

For each question part, say whether the answer is wrong or right.

If it is wrong, give the correct answer.

a $3ap - 9p = 3p(a - 3)$

b $12f^2 - 18f = 3f(4f - 6)$

c $36 - 4t^2 + 12t = 4(9 - t^2 + 3t)$

d $15x^2y^2 - 20x^2y = 5xy(3xy - 4x)$

e $55k - 44klm^2 = 11k(5 - 4lm^2)$

6 In this factor puzzle the first expression is factorised. The factors are added. This is repeated until the expression cannot be factorised again.

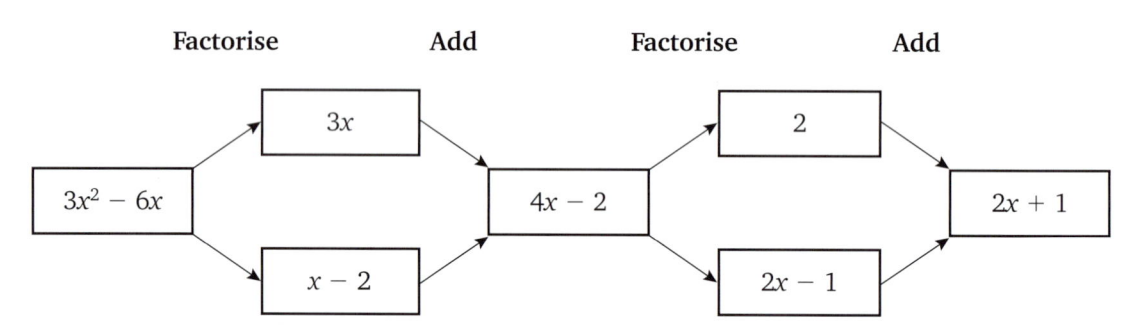

Factorise → $3x^2 - 6x$ → $3x$ and $x - 2$ → Add → $4x - 2$ → Factorise → 2 and $2x - 1$ → Add → $2x + 1$

a Copy and complete this factor puzzle.

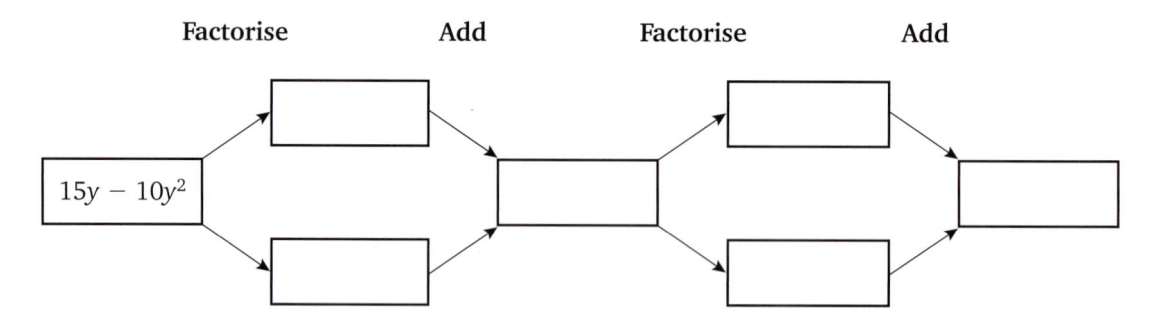

Starting expression: $15y - 10y^2$

b Complete a factor puzzle for each of these starting expressions.

i $7a^2 - 14a$

ii $4p^2 - 12p$

iii $28c - 35c^2$

iv $20q - 25q^2$

Chapter 6 Working with symbols 89

Learn... 6.3 Multiplying two brackets together

When you multiply two brackets together, you have to multiply each term in the second bracket by each term in the first bracket.

$(x + 2)(x + 4) = x(x + 4) + 2(x + 4)$
$= x^2 + 4x + 2x + 8$
$= x^2 + 6x + 8$

$x^2 + 6x + 8$ is a **quadratic expression**, because it contains a term in x^2, but no higher power of x.

The multiplication can be worked out in a table:

×	x	$+2$
x	x^2	$+2x$
$+4$	$+4x$	$+8$

AQA Examiner's tip
Quadratic expressions are usually written with the x^2 term first, then the x term and lastly the number term.

The two like terms, $+2x$ and $+4x$, are combined as $+6x$

$(x + 2)(x + 4) = x^2 + 2x + 4x + 8 = x^2 + 6x + 8$

When there are negative numbers in one or both brackets, using a table helps you to get the signs correct provided your entries are accurate.

Example: Multiply out and simplify $(x - 3)(x - 5)$.

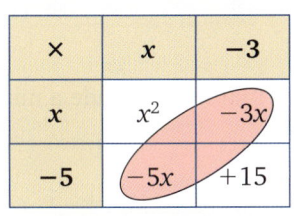

Solution:

×	x	-3
x	x^2	$-3x$
-5	$-5x$	$+15$

AQA Examiner's tip
Make sure you enter each term in the table with its correct sign.

$(x - 3)(x - 5) = x^2 - 3x - 5x + 15 = x^2 - 8x + 15$

Example: Multiply out and simplify $(3x - 1)(2x + 3)$.

Solution:

×	$3x$	-1
$2x$	$6x^2$	$-2x$
$+3$	$+9x$	-3

$(3x - 1)(2x + 3) = 6x^2 - 2x + 9x - 3 = 6x^2 + 7x - 3$

Practise... 6.3 Multiplying two brackets together D C B A A*

1 Multiply out and simplify:

a $(a + 2)(a + 5)$
b $(b + 3)(b + 7)$
c $(c - 1)(c + 4)$
d $(d + 11)(d - 2)$
e $(e - 2)(e - 5)$
f $(4 - f)(9 - f)$
g $(k + 3)(k - 3)$
h $(5 - m)(5 + m)$
i $(p + 1)^2$
j $(q - 5)^2$

AQA Examiner's tip
Write out $(p + 1)^2$ as $(p + 1)(p + 1)$ before you multiply.

2 Multiply out and simplify:
  a $(r + 7)(2r + 1)$ **b** $(t + 4)(3t − 2)$ **c** $(2u − 3)(u − 4)$

3 Multiply out and simplify:
  a $(5v + 2)(2v + 3)$ **c** $(4x − 1)(2x − 5)$
  b $(3w − 1)(2w + 1)$ **d** $(3y + 1)(3y − 1)$

4 Multiply out and simplify:
  a $(5 − 2z)(5 + 2z)$ **b** $(3p + 1)^2$ **c** $(2q − 5)^2$

5 Show that $(4x + 3)(x − 1) − (x − 3)(4x + 1) = 10x$

6 Multiply out and simplify:
  a $(5a + b)(a − 3b)$ **d** $(2x − 3y)^2$
  b $(2c − 7d)(c − 2d)$ **e** $(m + 7n)(m − 7n)$
  c $(4p − q)(4p + q)$ **f** $(3e + 2f)(2e − 3f)$

7 **a** Write down the areas of each of these rectangles.
    i ABED   **ii** BCFE   **iii** DEHG
  b Add your results to find the area of the rectangle ACIG.

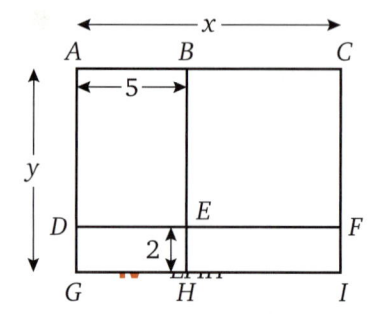

8 Louise says that $(3x + 1)^2 = 9x^2 + 1$
  Why is she wrong?

9 Ed multiplies $(2y − 7)$ by $(3y − 1)$.
  His answer is $6y^2 + 23y + 7$
  How can you tell, **without multiplying the brackets**, that he has made a mistake?

Learn... 6.4 Simplifying algebraic fractions

Algebraic fractions obey the same rules as ordinary fractions.

Multiplying fractions

$\dfrac{3}{4} \times \dfrac{2}{5}$ Multiply numerators together.
Multiply denominators together.

$\dfrac{3}{4} \times \dfrac{2}{5} = \dfrac{\cancel{6}}{\cancel{20}} = \dfrac{3}{10}$ Divide top and bottom by the common factor.

$\dfrac{a}{bc} \times \dfrac{cd}{e}$

$\dfrac{a}{bc} \times \dfrac{cd}{e} = \dfrac{a\cancel{c}d}{b\cancel{c}e} = \dfrac{ad}{be}$ Divide top and bottom by the common factor.

Adding fractions

$\dfrac{1}{3} + \dfrac{2}{5} = \dfrac{5}{15} + \dfrac{6}{15}$ Use the lowest common denominator 15.

$= \dfrac{11}{15}$ Add the numerators.

$\dfrac{x}{3} = \dfrac{5x}{15}$ $\dfrac{2x}{3} = \dfrac{6x}{15}$ $\dfrac{x}{3} + \dfrac{2x}{5} = \dfrac{5x}{15} + \dfrac{6x}{15}$

× 5   × 3

× 5   × 3

$= \dfrac{11x}{15}$

To simplify algebraic fractions, you should factorise the numerator and/or the denominator.
Then divide the numerator and denominator by common factors.

Chapter 6 Working with symbols

Example: Simplify $\dfrac{4x+6}{6x-18}$

Solution: Factorise the numerator $4x + 6 = 2(2x + 3)$

Factorise the denominator $6x - 18 = 6(x - 3)$

Rewrite the fraction as $\dfrac{2(2x+3)}{6(x-3)}$

Divide top and bottom by the common factor which is 2 $\dfrac{{}^{1}\!\cancel{2}(2x+3)}{{}^{3}\!\cancel{6}(x-3)} = \dfrac{2x+3}{3(x-3)}$

AQA Examiner's tip
If there is no common factor in a question like this you are likely to have made an error.

Practise... 6.4 Simplifying algebraic fractions   D C B A A*

1 Simplify:

a $\dfrac{ab}{4a}$

b $\dfrac{6cd}{8d^2}$

c $\dfrac{12e}{3f}$

d $\dfrac{3(x+1)}{6x}$

e $\dfrac{5yz}{y(t-4)}$

f $\dfrac{pqrs}{q^2 r}$

g $\dfrac{a-5}{3a-15}$

h $\dfrac{10+5b}{b+2}$

2 Simplify:

a $\dfrac{a}{2} + \dfrac{3a}{8}$

b $\dfrac{2b}{3} + \dfrac{b}{6}$

c $\dfrac{3c}{8} + \dfrac{3c}{16}$

d $\dfrac{3d}{5} - \dfrac{d}{2}$

e $\dfrac{e}{3} - \dfrac{e}{9}$

f $\dfrac{5f}{8} - \dfrac{f}{4}$

g $\dfrac{11x}{12} - \dfrac{5x}{6}$

h $\dfrac{2y}{5} + \dfrac{y}{6}$

i $\dfrac{4z}{9} + \dfrac{5z}{6}$

3 Simplify:

a $\dfrac{3p}{5} + \dfrac{p}{4} - \dfrac{7p}{10}$

b $\dfrac{7t}{8} - \dfrac{5t}{6} + \dfrac{t}{12}$

c $\dfrac{4m}{15} + \dfrac{m}{6} - \dfrac{2m}{5}$

Simplify:

⚠ **4** $\dfrac{3}{8x} + \dfrac{1}{2x}$

⚠ **5** $\dfrac{3}{4y} - \dfrac{5}{16y}$

⚠ **6** $\dfrac{3}{5t} + \dfrac{2}{3t} - \dfrac{9}{10t}$

⚠ **7** $\dfrac{1}{x} + \dfrac{4}{2-x}$

6 Assess

1 Multiply out:

a $7(a-2)$

b $3(2b-1)$

c $4(c+d)$

d $5(e-3f)$

e $2m(n+2p)$

f $3t(2u-3v)$

g $x(x+2)$

h $y(3-y)$

i $5z(z-1)$

2 Factorise:

a $3a - 12$

b $2b + 10$

c $9 - 6c$

d $14 - 7d$

e $4p - 2q + 8r$

f $12x + 6y - 4z$

g $x^2 - 4x$

h $yz + z^2$

i $w^2 + vw - 3w$

3 Expand and simplify:

a $3(a + 2) + 2(a - 1)$
b $3(b - 2) + 3(b + 5)$
c $2(3c + 4) - 3(c - 4)$
d $5(x + 1) + 6(x + 7)$
e $6(2y - 3) - 4(3y - 2)$
f $8(w - 1) + 2(4 + 2w)$
g $2(x + y) + 5(2x + y)$
h $3(4p - q) + 2(p - 3q)$
i $5(2a + 3b) - 2(3a + 4b)$
j $4(m - 3n) - (3m - 5n)$

4 Show that $5(x + 1) + 2(5 - x) = 3(x + 5)$

5 Multiply out and simplify:

a $(a + 1)(a + 3)$
b $(b - 2)(b + 8)$
c $(c - 6)(c + 6)$
d $(d - 7)(d - 4)$
e $(e - 4)^2$
f $(f + 2)(f - 1)$
g $(h - 9)(h - 2)$
h $(m + 2)(m - 2)$
i $(2x + 1)(x + 4)$
j $(3y + 4)(y - 2)$
k $(5z - 3)(z + 1)$
l $(2t + 3)(3t - 2)$
m $(2w + 3)^2$

6 Simplify:

a $\dfrac{3xy}{6x}$
b $\dfrac{pqr}{qr^2}$
c $\dfrac{6t}{2t - 4}$
d $\dfrac{v + 5}{2v + 10}$
e $\dfrac{y^2 - 3y}{5y}$
f $\dfrac{3c - 9}{2c - 6}$
g $\dfrac{(z + 5)(z - 7)}{(z - 1)(z + 5)}$

7 Simplify:

a $\dfrac{x}{8} + \dfrac{3x}{4}$
b $\dfrac{5y}{8} - \dfrac{y}{4}$
c $\dfrac{2z}{9} + \dfrac{z}{6}$
d $\dfrac{t}{2} - \dfrac{3t}{16}$
e $\dfrac{9a}{10} - \dfrac{8a}{15}$
f $\dfrac{7c}{12} + \dfrac{4c}{9}$

8 Write an expression for the area of each polygon. Expand and simplify your answer.

a Rectangle with sides $h + 1$ and $h - 3$

b Trapezium with parallel sides 8 and $3d$, height $d - 1$

9 a Expand and simplify:

i $(x + 1)(x + 3) + (x + 4)(x - 1)$
ii $(t + 4)(t - 3) - (t + 3)(t - 4)$

b Show that $(n + 1)^2 - n(n + 2) = 1$

10 Any even number can be written as $2n$ and any odd number can be written as $2n + 1$.

Show that the product of an odd and even number is always even.

AQA Examination-style questions

1 a Simplify $y + 2 \times y \times y$ *(1 mark)*
b Factorise $15y + 25$ *(1 mark)*
c Factorise $z^2 + 8z$ *(1 mark)*
d Expand and simplify $(2n - 1)(n + 1)$ *(1 mark)*

AQA 2008

7 Percentages

Objectives

Examiners would normally expect students who get these grades to be able to:

D
compare harder percentages, fractions and decimals

work out more difficult percentages of a given quantity

increase or decrease by a given percentage

express one quantity as a percentage of another

C
work out a percentage increase or decrease

B
understand how to use successive percentages

work out reverse percentage problems

work out compound interest

understand how to use successive percentages

use a multiplier raised to a power to solve problems involving repeated percentage changes

work out reverse percentage problems.

Did you know?

I gave 110%!

Some sports personalities have claimed 'I gave 110%'

Is this possible?

When is it possible to have more than 100%?

What about these?

'I got more than 100% in the maths test!'

'The price went up by more than 100%'

'The company made a loss of more than 100%'

'I'm more than 100% certain that it happened.'

Key terms

percentage
VAT (Value Added Tax)
rate
amount
discount
deposit
credit
balance
interest
depreciation
compound interest

You should already know:

✔ about place values in decimals and how to put decimals in order of size

✔ how to simplify fractions

✔ how to change fractions to decimals and vice versa

✔ how to add, subtract, multiply and divide whole numbers, fractions and decimals.

Learn... 7.1 Percentages, fractions and decimals

1% (1 per cent) means '1 part out of 100' or 'one hundredth'.
It is equivalent to the fraction $\frac{1}{100}$ and the decimal 0.01
In money it is equivalent to '1p in the £1'.

To write other percentages as fractions or decimals, divide by 100.

For example, $35\% = \frac{35}{100} = \frac{7}{20}$ (35 hundredths, simplifying by dividing by 5) and $35\% = 35 \div 100 = 0.35$ (The figures move two places to the right.)

On the calculator paper, use your fraction key to simplify fractions.

To write a decimal or fraction as a percentage, you multiply by 100% (the inverse operation).

For example, $0.3 = 0.3 \times 100\% = 30\%$ and $\frac{2}{5} = \frac{2}{\cancel{5}_1} \times \frac{\cancel{100}^{20}}{1}\% = \frac{40}{1}\% = 40\%$

In some cases, like this one, you can also use equivalent fractions: $\frac{2}{5} = \frac{20}{50} = \frac{40}{100} = 40\%$ (×10, ×2)

This is usually the easiest way to change a fraction to a percentage.

Example:

a Which of these fractions is nearest in size to 30%?

$\frac{2}{5} \quad \frac{1}{3} \quad \frac{2}{7}$

b Write down a fraction, in its simplest form, which is exactly equal to 30%.

Solution:

a Comparing decimals, fractions and percentages is easiest if they are all written as percentages.

$\frac{2}{5} = 40\%$ (see working above)

To change the other fractions to decimals, multiply them by 100:

$\frac{1}{3} \times \frac{100}{1}\% = \frac{100}{3}\% = 33\frac{1}{3}\%$ $\frac{2}{7} \times \frac{100}{1}\% = \frac{200}{7}\% = 28\frac{4}{7}\%$

Compare 40%, $33\frac{1}{3}\%$ and $28\frac{4}{7}\%$ with 30%

$28\frac{4}{7}\%$ is nearest, so $\frac{2}{7}$ is the fraction that is nearest to 30%

> **AQA Examiner's tip**
> Give the fraction from the question as your answer, not the percentage that you have worked out.

b To change 30% to a fraction, divide it by 100:

$30\% = \frac{30}{100} = \frac{3}{10}$ (÷10)

Divide the top and bottom of the fraction until you get the smallest whole numbers you can. This is the simplest form.

Chapter 7 Percentages

There are many ways to find the percentage of a quantity.

Here are two ways to find 45% of £600:

$$45\% \text{ of } £600 = \frac{45}{\cancel{100}_{1}} \times \frac{\cancel{600}^{6}}{1} = \frac{270}{1} \quad \text{or} \quad 0.45 \times 600 = 45 \times 6 = 270 \quad \text{Using a 'decimal multiplier'.}$$

45 hundredths of 600

Without a calculator, the best method is often to start by finding 1% or 10%

$1\% = \frac{1}{100}$ To find 1% of a quantity, divide it by 100.
In the example above, 1% of £600 = £6, so 45% is 45 × £6 = £270

$10\% = \frac{10}{100} = \frac{1}{10}$ To find 10% of a quantity, divide it by 10.

Example: Find:

     a   35% of £4.20   **b**   97% of £240

Solution: **a**   10% of £4.20 = $\frac{£4.20}{10}$ = £0.42

     30% of £4.20 = 3 × £0.42 = £1.26   30% is 3 × 10%

     5% of £4.20 = $\frac{£0.42}{2}$ = £0.21+   5% is half of 10%

     35% of £4.20 = 30% + 5% = **£1.47**

b   1% of £240 = $\frac{£240}{100}$ = £2.40

     Here is one way to check this:

     3% of £240 = 3 × £2.40 = £7.20   3% is the same as 3p in every £.

     97% of £240 = £240 − £7.20 = **£232.80**   So 3% of £240 = 240 × 3p = 720p

> **AQA Examiner's tip**
> Always check whether the answer looks reasonable.
> For example, 97% of £240 is nearly all of it, so £232.80 is reasonable.

Occasionally other ways may be quicker and easier.

For percentages with a simple, equivalent fraction, using these is quicker and easier.

For example:

$50\% = \frac{1}{2}$ To find 50% of a quantity, divide it by 2.

$25\% = \frac{1}{4}$ To find 25% of a quantity, divide it by 4 (or halve it, then halve again).

75% = 50% + 25%   To find 75% of a quantity, find 50% and 25%, then add.
     Halving, then halving again is the quickest way to do this.

Practise... 7.1 Percentages, fractions and decimals   k!   D C B A A*

1 Write these in order of size, smallest first.

     a $\frac{1}{4}$ 0.4   4% $\frac{4}{9}$

     b $\frac{16}{25}$ 0.67 $\frac{2}{3}$ 66% $\frac{13}{20}$ $62\frac{1}{2}\%$

2   **a**   Which of these is nearest in size to 0.4?   38% $\frac{3}{8}$ 43% $\frac{3}{7}$

     b   Which of these is nearest in size to $\frac{3}{4}$?   0.7   72% $\frac{7}{9}$ 0.79

3 Use three different ways to work out 25% of half a million pounds.

4 a Find:
  i 10% of 840 kg
  ii 20% of 150 m
  iii 80% of 45 000
  iv 90% of 6 million
  v 1% of 180 litres
  vi 4% of 750 km
  vii 6% of £3500
  viii 120% of £50
  ix 150% of £3000

  b Check each answer in part **a** using a different method.
  For example, if you found 10% of 840 g in part **a i** by dividing by 10 you could check using fractions: 10% of 840 = $\frac{10}{100} \times \frac{840}{1}$
  or using a multiplier: 10% of 840 = 0.1 × 840

5 In a school, there are 630 boys and 660 girls.
90% of the boys and 95% of the girls have a mobile phone.
How many students altogether have mobile phones?

6 Paula earns £840 per week.
She spends 25% of this on rent and 40% on shopping.
How much does she have left?

7 Carl explains how he finds $12\frac{1}{2}$%

  a Use Carl's method to find $12\frac{1}{2}$% of £560.
  b Use a different way to find $12\frac{1}{2}$% of £560.

> I divide by 10 to find 10%. Then I divide by 2 to find 5%. Then I divide again by 2 to find 2½%. Adding the 10% and the 2½% gives the answer

8 Gas and electricity companies charge 5% VAT on their bills
Find the VAT on each of these bills.

  a Cost of electricity used
  (without VAT) = £96.40

  Note: **VAT** is **Value Added Tax**.

  b Gas you've used
  (without VAT) = £135.80

9 A shop adds 17.5% VAT to all the goods it sells.
Find the VAT on each of these.

Hint 17.5% = 10% + 5% + 2.5%

  a £160 plus VAT
  b £24 plus VAT
  c £16.80 plus VAT

10 There are 32 000 football supporters at a match.
65% of these are men, 25% are women and the rest are children.

  a How many more men than women are at the match?
  b What fraction of the football supporters at the match are children?

11 Karen says you can find 8% of £5200 by dividing 5200 by 8.
Sanjay says that you can find 8% of £5200 by multiplying 5200 by 0.8.
Are either of these methods correct? Explain your answer.

12 Which is greater? $\frac{4}{5}$ of £2 million or 45% of £4 million

13 A science examination consists of a practical and a theory test.
70% of the candidates pass the practical. 45% pass the theory test.
These percentages include 25% of the candidates who pass both parts.
What fraction of the candidates fail both parts?

14 In 2009 a laptop cost £400 **excluding** VAT.
During 2009 the **rate** of VAT was reduced from 17.5% to 15%
How much less was the cost of the laptop **including** VAT after the VAT rate was reduced?

15 The table shows the tax rates in the country where Yusef lives.

Taxable income	Taxed at
Up to £40 000	20%
Amount over £40 000	40%

Yusef's taxable income is £45 000.

a How much tax does Yusef pay?

b How much extra tax will Yusef pay if he gets a 2% pay rise?

16 Rowan, Sue and Terry share a £60 000 inheritance.
Rowan gets 30% of what Sue gets and Terry gets 20% of what Sue gets.

a Work out what each person gets.

b Show how to check your answers to part **a**.

7.2 Increasing or decreasing an amount by a percentage

Learn...

Without a calculator, it is usually best to find the percentage increase or decrease first (using any of the methods in Learn 8.1). Then add the increase to the original **amount** or subtract the decrease from the original amount.

Sometimes there are more direct ways.

For example, suppose you want to reduce £150 by 60%

The final amount = 100% − 60% = 40% of £150

To reduce something by 60% you could:
find 60% of it then subtract
or just find 40% of it.
This way is quicker.

Here are three ways to find 40% of £150:

10% of £150 = £15   or $\frac{\cancel{40}^{\,20}}{\cancel{100}_{\,2}} \times \frac{\cancel{150}^{\,3}}{1} = \frac{60}{1}$ or   0.4 × 150 = 60

40% of £150 = £15 × 4 = £60

40 hundredths of £150   Using a multiplier 0.40 is the same as 0.4

Any method is acceptable. You could use a second method to check your answer.

Example: a Increase 800 by 15% b Decrease 500 by 7%

Solution:
a 10% of 800 = 800 ÷ 10 = 80
5% of 800 = 80 ÷ 2 = 40   5% is half of 10%
15% of 800 = 10% + 5% = 120
Increased amount = 800 + 120 = **920**

b 1% of 500 = 500 ÷ 100 = 5
7% of 500 = 7 × 5 = 35
Decreased amount = 500 − 35 = **465**

7.2 Increasing or decreasing an amount by a percentage

Practise… D C B A A*

1
a Increase £500 by 20%   e Increase 80 000 by 5%
b Increase 750 kg by 40%   f Increase £12.80 by 15%
c Decrease £650 by 30%   g Decrease 7000 by 45%
d Decrease 360 km by 75% h Decrease 480 by 95%

2 The normal price for an album is £15.
The shop reduces this by 20% in a sale.
What is the sale price?

3 A late offer gives 25% **discount** on a holiday that usually costs £720.
a What does the holiday cost after the discount?
b Check your answer using a different method.

4 The cost of a coach trip is £36.
What is the new price after a 5% increase?

5
a Copy and complete these tables.

To increase by	10%	20%	90%
Multiply by			

To decrease by	10%	20%	90%
Multiply by			

b Use the multipliers from your table to work out:
  i   £400 increased by 10%   iv £400 decreased by 10%
  ii 5000 increased by 20%   v   5000 decreased by 20%
  iii 200 g increased by 90%   vi 200 g decreased by 90%

c Check your answers using a different method.

6 An evening cinema ticket costs £8. It costs $12\frac{1}{2}$% less in the afternoon.
What is the price in the afternoon?

Chapter 7 Percentages

7 Find the total cost of each of these.

  a £56 + 17.5% VAT

  b Cost of gas £328 + 5% VAT

  c £26.80 + 17½% VAT

8 Lee wants to buy a digital camera priced at £490.
He pays a **deposit** of £90.
There is a 3% charge for **credit** on the **balance**.
How much extra does Lee pay for credit?

9 Kate invests £6000 in a savings account with an **interest** rate of 5%.
What is the amount in the account at the end of 2 years?

10 Toby's salary is £19 500 per year. He is paid the same every month.
He gets a 4% pay rise.
What is his new monthly salary?

11 Carol is paying for a dress priced at £35.
She gets a discount of 2% for paying by cash.
To find the new price Carol writes down 0.8 × 35.

  a What mistake has she made?   **b** Work out the new price correctly.

12 A new car costs £20 000. Its value **depreciates** by 10% each year.
How much will it be worth when it is 3 years old?

13 An internet website advertises watches at 20% off, but adds £4 for postage and packing. The final cost of buying a watch from this website is £32.
Using £x to represent the original price of the watch:

  a write down an equation for x

  b solve the equation to find the original price of the watch.

14 A games console is advertised for sale in two shops.

  Arkos — £79.95 including VAT

  Playshop — £68 plus VAT

  VAT is $17\frac{1}{2}$%

  Which shop is cheaper and by how much?

15 A clothes shop aims to make at least 30% profit on everything it sells.
First the manager adds 30% to the cost price of an item.
Then he increases the result to a penny less than the next pound.
So, for example, if the 30% markup on an item gives £27.30, the manager prices it at £27.99.

Find the manager's price for each item in the table.

Item	Cost price
Shirt	£12
Skirt	£25
Shorts	£7
Trousers	£36
Jacket	£47

16 A shop sells 200 g packets of peanuts. A poor peanut harvest means that the shop now has to pay more for its supplies. The manager considers two options:

  Option 1 Increase the price of a bag of peanuts by 20%
  Option 2 Keep the price the same, but reduce the quantity by 20%

Which of these would you advise the manager to choose?
Give reasons for your choice and include calculations to support it.

Learn... 7.3 Successive percentages

Multipliers give a quick way to work out the effect of more than one percentage.

For example, suppose you know that 56% of the 1250 people at a festival are male.
The multiplier for 56% is 0.56, so the number of males at the festival = 1250 × 0.56 = 700

If you also know that 35% of these males are under 20 years old.
Then the number of males under 20 years old at the festival = 700 × 0.35 = 245 ← Multiplier for 35%

You can do all of this in one calculation:
The number of males under 20 years old at the festival = 1250 × 0.56 × 0.35 = 245

If you just want to know what percentage of the festival-goers are males under 20 years old, you just need to multiply the multipliers:

0.56 × 0.35 = 0.196 so 19.6% of the festival-goers are males under 20

You can combine percentage changes in the same way.

Example: Jan buys a car for £12 800.
It depreciates by 25% in the first year and 20% in the second year.
What is the car worth after 2 years?

AQA Examiner's tip
Use multipliers to save time.

Solution: The original price is 100%. In the 1st year the car depreciates by 25%
This means its value goes down from 100% to 75% of the original value.

The multiplier is 0.75

At the end of the 1st year the car is worth £12 800 × 0.75 = £9600

At the start of the 2nd year, the car is worth £9600 ← Count this as 100% at start of 2nd year.

After the 2nd year it is worth (100 − 20)% = 80% of this. The multiplier is 0.80

After 2 years the car is worth £9600 × 0.80 = £7680

Check this on your calculator using a single calculation:

Value of car after 2 years = £12 800 × 0.75 × 0.80 = £7680

Multiplier for the 1st year   Multiplier for the 2nd year

0.75 × 0.80 = 0.6 = 0.60 so the car is now worth 60% of its original value.
It has lost 40% of its value.

Practise... 7.3 Successive percentages   D C B A A*

1 A school has 1480 students. 20% of the students take part in a survey and 75% of these students say they have the internet at home.

    a How many students took part in the survey?

    b How many of those surveyed have the internet at home?

    c Show how you could work out the answer to part **b** in one line using multipliers.

    d Estimate the number of students at the school who have the internet at home.

Chapter 7 Percentages

2 There are 39 375 people at a football match.
24% of these are teenagers. 32% of these teenagers are under 16 years old.
How many teenagers under 16 years old are at the match?

3 Rowan earns £120 for delivering papers.
He spends 5% of his earnings at the newsagents.
45% of his spending at the newsagents is on magazines.
How much does Rowan spend on magazines?

4 A questionnaire about a new speed limit is sent to 2500 villagers.
72% of the questionnaires are returned.
65% of these are in favour of the new speed limit.

How many of the returned questionnaires are in favour of the new speed limit?

5 A new house costs £95 000 to build and is sold for 26% more.
A year later an estate agent tells the owner that house prices have gone down by 8%

What is the house worth after the price fall?

6 Val buys shares for £25 000. In the first month they lose 4.8% of their value.
In the following month, the value of the shares increases by 8.5%
What are Val's shares worth at the end of the second month?

7 Ed earns £9.60 per hour. On promotion he gets a pay rise of 5%

After a year in his new job, Ed gets another pay rise of $2\frac{1}{2}$%
How much is Ed paid per hour after the $2\frac{1}{2}$% increase?

8 An insurance company gives Don a 50% discount on the price of his insurance for making no claims in the past. He gets a further 15% reduction on the discounted price for agreeing to pay the first £200 on any claim he makes.
What percentage of the original price of the insurance does Don pay?

9 Mr Marks asks, 'Which of these is bigger? An 18% increase followed by a 12% increase or a 12% increase followed by an 18% increase.'

Katie says that they both give an increase of 30%

   a What mistake has Katie made?

   b What is the correct answer to Mr Marks' question?

10 52% of the adults in a town are women. 86% of these women have jobs and 28% of the women who have jobs work full-time.

What percentage of the town's adult population are:

   a women who work full-time

   b women who work part-time?

11 A bookshop is closing down.
In its final week, books are reduced by 5% more each day as shown in the table.

Monday	Reduced by 10% of usual price
Tuesday	Reduced by 15% of Monday's price
Wednesday	Reduced by 20% of Tuesday's price

   a Pete buys a book at the shop on Wednesday. What percentage of the usual price does he pay?

   b Assume the shop continues to reduce prices in this way until it closes on Saturday. On which day would the price of a book be reduced to less than a quarter of its usual price?

   c Should Pete have delayed his purchase until Saturday? Explain your answer.

12 A shop buys clothes and usually sells them at a profit of 30%
In a sale it reduces its usual prices by 25%
Does the shop still make a profit? Explain your answer.

13 A shop usually sells trainers at prices that include a markup of 50% for profit.
The manager decides to have a sale, but still wants to make 20% profit on the trainers sold.

By what percentage of the usual selling price should the manager reduce the prices of the trainers for the sale?

Learn... 7.4 Compound interest

When money is put into a savings account at a bank or building society, interest is paid each year.

Usually the interest is added on to the **amount** already in the account (this is called 'compounding' or paying **compound interest**). For the next year, the amount of money in the account is greater so more interest is paid. This is an example of **repeated proportional change**.

For example, suppose you invest £500 in an account at a fixed **rate** of interest of 4% per year.

At the end of the first year you will have £500 plus 4% of £500, which is 104% of £500.

The multiplier is 1.04

Repeated use of this multiplier gives the amount in the bank after 1 year, 2 years, 3 years and so on. Each calculation can be done in one step on your calculator.

After 1 year, the amount is £500 × 1.04

After 2 years, the amount is £500 × 1.04 × 1.04 = £500 × 1.04^2

After 3 years, the amount is £500 × 1.04 × 1.04 × 1.04 = £500 × 1.04^3

If left in the account for 10 years, the amount would grow to £500 × 1.04^{10}

You can work this out on your calculator one year at a time or all at once.

For one year at a time:

Press 5 0 0 = × 1 . 0 4 = then = = = ... (count to 10)   *Using the power key is more efficient.*

To do it all at once, work out 500 × 1.04^{10} using the power key.

The amount after 10 years is £740.12, so the interest earned is £740.12 − £500 = £240.12

You can write a formula for the amount in the account after t years.

After every year, the amount in the account is multiplied by 1.04
So after t years, the amount has been multiplied by 1.04^t

An increase of 4% a year for 10 years leads to an overall increase of about 48%

So the amount in the account after t years is £500 × 1.04^t

Example: A ball falls to the ground from a height of 5 metres.

The height it reaches after each bounce is reduced by 20%

a Find the height it reaches after the fourth bounce.

b Show that it will take 8 bounces for the height reached in a bounce to reduce to less than 1 metre.

Chapter 7 Percentages 103

Solution:

a The multiplier is 0.8 (because the height reached is reduced by 20% to 80% after each bounce).

Height after 4 bounces = $5 \times 0.8 \times 0.8 \times 0.8 \times 0.8 = 5 \times 0.8^4$
= 2.048 = 2.05 metres (to 3 s.f.)

b Height after 7 bounces = 5×0.8^7
= 1.048576

Height after 8 bounces = 1.048576 × 0.8
= 0.8388608

It takes 8 bounces for the height to reduce to less than 1 metre.

AQA Examiner's tip
Use this way to save time and avoid errors when you copy amounts.

Practise... 7.4 Compound interest   D C B A A*

1 Will invests £600 for two years at 5% compound interest.
Find the amount in the account at the end of two years.

Hint The initial amount invested is sometimes called the **principal**.

2 £4500 is invested at 4.3% compound interest.
Work out the amount in the account at the end of 3 years.

3 £2000 is invested at 6% compound interest.
  a Write down the amounts in the bank after:
    i 5 years
    ii 10 years.
  b How much interest was earned in:
    i the first 5 years
    ii the second 5 years?
    iii Why is your answer to part **bii** larger than your answer to part **bi**?

4 Work out the compound interest on £16 000 invested for 4 years at $5\frac{3}{4}$%

5 Carmen puts £2500 into a savings account that pays 4% per year.
She says that after 5 years she will have 20% more.
Is Carmen correct? Explain your answer.

6 Roy wants to invest £5000 for 3 years. He considers two accounts.

Account	Interest Rate	Conditions
Simple Saver	4.6%	Take out the interest at the end of each year
Compound Saver	4.6%	Add the interest to the account each year

Work out how much more interest Roy will get if he uses the Compound Saver.

7 Paul buys a car for £7900. Its value depreciates by 20% each year.

    a Complete a table to show how the car's value reduces over the next 8 years.

    b Sketch a graph of the car's value against time.

8 A young manager has a job with a starting salary of £19 000 increasing by 2.4% per year.

    a What is her salary after one year?

    b What is her salary after five years?

    c Why may your answer to part **b** not be very realistic?

9 £8000 is invested at $5\frac{1}{2}$% compound interest.

The interest is added at the end of each year. Show that it takes 5 years for the amount to grow to more than £10 000.

10 A report says that the cost of mobile phone calls is falling by 4% per year and that the average cost now is 12 pence per minute. Use this information to estimate how many years it will take for the average cost to fall to:

    a less than 10 pence per minute

    b less than 7.5 pence per minute.

11 Rita has earned £16 000 this year. Each year she gets a pay rise of 2%
Rita wonders how long it will be until her yearly earnings reach £20 000.

    a Show that after 10 pay rises, her yearly earnings will still be less than £20 000.

    b After how many pay rises will Rita's yearly earnings be more than £20 000?

12 Mike is going to a slimming club. He weighs 112 kg. His target weight is 80 kg.

He aims to lose 3.5% of his body weight per month.
Show that it takes him 10 months to reach his target weight.

13 The table gives details of a bank's different savings accounts.
All interest is paid into the accounts after the periods shown.

Account	Interest Rate
Emerald	3.90% paid annually
Ruby	1.94% paid every 6 months
Sapphire	0.96% paid every 3 months

Work out which account gives the best return on £15 000 saved for a year.

14 It is thought that about 22 000 polar bears are living in the wild today, but that this number is decreasing by 8% per decade.

Write a short report to illustrate how the number of polar bears is likely to decrease over the next century.

Include calculations and state any assumptions you make.

Investigate the situation for other endangered animals such as the giant panda or black rhino.

15 £2000 is invested at x% interest over three years.
At the end of three years the money has grown to £2963.
To the nearest percentage find the rate of interest.

Learn... 7.5 Writing one quantity as a percentage of another

To write one quantity as a percentage of another
- Make sure they are in the same units.
- Divide the first quantity by the second. This gives you a decimal (or write the first quantity as a fraction of the second).
- Then multiply by 100. This changes the decimal or fraction to a percentage.

Example: The table shows the marks students get in a test.

a What percentage of students get less than 10?

b Students must get 20 or more to pass.

   i What percentage of students pass?

   ii What percentage of students fail?

Marks	Frequency
0–9	4
10–19	7
20–29	9
30–39	8
40–49	4

Solution:

a The total number of students = 4 + 7 + 9 + 8 + 4 = 32

4 out of 32 students get less than 10 — divide by the total

Percentage of students who get less than 10 = 4 ÷ 32 × 100% = 12.5%

or $\frac{4}{32} \times 100 = 12\frac{1}{2}\%$

b The number of students who get 20 or more = 9 + 8 + 4 = 21

i Percentage of students who pass = 21 ÷ 32 × 100 = 65.6% (to 3 s.f.)

ii Percentage of students who fail = 100% − 65.6% = 34.4% (to 3 s.f.)

The number who fail = 4 + 7 = 11

Percentage of students who fail = $\frac{11}{32} \times 100\%$ = 11 ÷ 32 = 100% = 34.4% (to 3 s.f.)

Note: Check that 65.6% + 34.4% = 100%

Practise... 7.5 Writing one quantity as a percentage of another D C B A A*

AQA Examiner's tip

When answers are not exact, the accuracy you use should reflect the accuracy of the values given. They should be appropriate for the real-life context. Usually three significant figures are sufficiently accurate for most purposes.

1 Out of 52 people who take a driving test, 34 pass. What percentage of the people:

a pass

b fail?

2 It snowed on 4 days in January. What percentage of the days is this?

3 Write:

a 65p as a percentage of £5.20

b 5 cm as a percentage of 2 m

c 250 g as a percentage of 5 kg

d 850 mm as a percentage of 5 m

e 280 ml as a percentage of 2 litres

f £18 500 as a percentage of £25 000

g 63 000 as a percentage of 4 million

h $1\frac{3}{4}$ of an hour as a percentage of 1 day.

Hint

1 m = 100 cm = 1000 mm   1 kg = 1000 g   1 litre = 1000 ml

4 A school has 6 part-time teachers and 29 full-time teachers.

What percentage of the teachers are:

a part-time

b full-time?

5 Ten out of fifteen boys and eight out of seventeen girls in a class have school dinners.

What percentage of the whole class:

a have school dinners

b do not have school dinners?

6 This is Ian's tally chart. It shows the hair colour of the students in his class.

Colour	Tally	Frequency
Blonde	|||| ||||	10
Brown	|||| |||| |||	13
Black	||||	5
Red	||	2

a Ian says 10% of the class has blonde hair. Do you agree? Explain your answer

b Find the percentage of the class that has each hair colour.

c Show how you can check your answer to part **b**.

7 The surface area of the Earth is 510 million km². 149 million km² is land and the rest is water.

What percentage of the Earth's surface is water?

8 A class is asked to vote on whether or not they want to take part in a sponsored swim.

The table shows the results.

a What percentage of boys want to take part?

b What percentage of girls want to take part?

c What percentage of the whole class want to take part?

d What percentage of those who want to take part are boys?

	Vote Yes	Vote No
Girls	8	6
Boys	10	4

9 The table gives the ages of the people who go on an activity holiday.

a What percentage of the people are under 20 years old?

People who are 40 or over must pay extra insurance.

b What percentage of people are 40 or over?

Age	Frequency
0–9	1
10–19	36
20–39	33
40–59	8
60 and over	2

10 The table gives the number of people who take part in a survey.

a What percentage of the people are:

i men **ii** women?

b What percentage of the people are:

i under 20 **ii** 40 or over?

c What percentage of the men are under 20?

d What percentage of those under 20 are men?

Age x	Number of Men	Number of Women
$x < 20$	24	25
$20 \leq x < 40$	26	28
$40 \leq x < 60$	18	23
$60 \leq x$	12	14

11 A national travel survey asked people how often they cycled last year.
Use the data to compare the results given in the table below.

Cycled (during last year)	Number of people aged 5–15 years	Number of people aged 16 years and over
Once or more per week	1371	1576
At least once, but less than once per week	792	2627
Never	883	13 310

Learn... 7.6 Finding a percentage increase or decrease

To write an increase or decrease as a percentage
- Subtract to find the increase or decrease.
- Divide the increase (or decrease) by the **original** amount or write the increase (or decrease) as a fraction of the original amount.
- Then multiply by 100 to change the decimal or fraction to a percentage.

$$\% \text{ increase} = \frac{\text{increase}}{\text{original amount}} \times 100\%$$

Example: A worker takes $1\frac{1}{4}$ minutes to pack a box.
After training he can do it in 50 seconds.
What is the percentage decrease in time?

Solution: Before training, he takes 75 seconds. ← $1\frac{1}{4} \times 60 = 75$

Decrease in time = 75 − 50 = 25 seconds

Percentage decrease = 25 ÷ 75 × 100 = 33.3% (to 1 d.p.)

or $\frac{25}{75} \times 100 = 33\frac{1}{3}\%$

Example: The table shows how the food consumed has changed in the last 4 years.

Food	Average consumption per person per week	
	4 years ago	Now
Meat	462 g	448 g
Fish	98 g	84 g
Vegetables	1.11 kg	1.14 kg
Fruit	1.17 kg	1.28 kg

AQA Examiner's tip
You must use the **same units**.

Compare these results.

Solution: The amounts are very different, so use percentages to compare the changes.

Work in grams for the meat and fish, and kilograms for the vegetables and fruit.

Meat Decrease = 462 − 448 = 14   % decrease = 14 ÷ 462 × 100 = **3.0%**
Fish   Decrease = 98 − 84 = 14   % decrease = 14 ÷ 98 × 100 = **14.3%**
Veg   Increase = 1.14 − 1.11 = 0.03   % increase = 0.03 ÷ 1.11 × 100 = **2.7%**
Fruit Increase = 1.28 − 1.17 = 0.11   % increase = 0.11 ÷ 1.17 × 100 = **9.4%**

These percentages have been rounded to one decimal place.

AQA Examiner's tip
Remember to divide by the **original** amount.

The greatest change was in the amount of fish we eat, down by 14.3%
The amount of meat also went down but by a smaller percentage.

The amount of vegetables and fruit both increased. The biggest percentage increase was in fruit.

Practise... 7.6 Finding a percentage increase or decrease

D C B A A*

AQA Examiner's tip
When answers are not exact, round them to an appropriate degree of accuracy.

1 This year a school has 984 students.
Last year it had 1023 students.
What is the percentage decrease?

Bump up your grade
For Grade C you must be able to write an increase or decrease as a percentage.

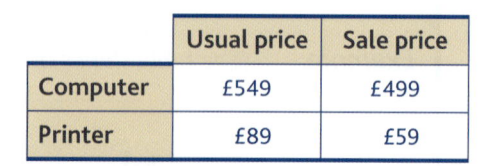

2 The price of a bus ride goes up from 95 pence to £1.05
What is the percentage increase?

3 A company employs fewer employees than 10 years ago.
The number of male workers decreased from 8530 to 5380.
The number of female workers decreased from 3150 to 1420.

   a Compare the percentage decrease in the number of male and female workers.

   b Work out the percentage decrease for all workers.

4 The table gives the usual price and sale price of a computer and printer.

Find the percentage reduction in the price of:

	Usual price	Sale price
Computer	£549	£499
Printer	£89	£59

   a the computer

   b the printer

   c the total price.

5 The rent of Sophie's flat has gone up from £120 to £150 per week.
Sophie works out 30 ÷ 150 × 100.
She says the rent has increased by 20%

Bump up your grade
For Grade C you must be able to explain why something is wrong.

   a What mistake has she made?

   b What is the actual percentage increase in Sophie's rent?

6 A sports club advertises on local TV. The table shows the number of male and female members before and after the advert.

	Before	After
Male	46	51
Female	39	44

Compare the percentage increase in the number of male and female members.
Was the advert more successful with males or females?

Chapter 7 Percentages   109

7 A shopkeeper buys a box of 25 pens for £3. He sells them for 20 pence each.

Find the percentage profit.

25 pens for £3

20p each

8 It costs a company £0.75 million to make 50 thousand teapots.
The teapots do not sell well. The company sells them off at £12 each.

Find the percentage loss.

9 What is the percentage increase if the value of a painting

  a   increases by a half of its previous value

  b   doubles

  c   goes up to five times its previous value?

10 Tanya says that you can make more than 100% profit, but you can't make more than 100% loss.

Is she correct? Explain your answer.

11 The table shows differences in what we drink now and 4 years ago.

Drink	Average consumption per person, per week	
	4 years ago	Now
Fruit juice	280 ml	340 ml
Low calorie soft drinks	442 ml	508 ml
Other soft drinks	1.39 litres	1.18 litres
Beverages (e.g. tea, coffee)	5.6 litres	5.6 litres
Alcoholic drinks	763 ml	772 ml

Compare these results.

12 The table gives the UK population in millions.

Year	1971	1976	1981	1986	1991	1996	2001	2006
Population	55.9	56.2	56.4	56.7	57.4	58.2	59.1	60.6

  a   In which 5 year interval was the percentage increase the greatest?

  b   Use the data to estimate what the population will be in:

     i 2011   **ii** 2016   **iii** 2021   **iv** 2026   **v** 2031

     Explain your method and any assumptions you make.

110 AQA GCSE Mathematics

Learn… 7.7 Reverse percentages

In a reverse percentage problem you start with the final amount and work back to the original amount.

One way of working this out is by using the **unitary** method.
It is based on finding the amount or cost of **one** unit (hence the name 'unitary').
Here the problem is solved by finding **1%**

For example, a digital camera is priced at £156.72 in a sale. It has been reduced by 20%.
What was the original price and how much is saved?

£156.72 is 80% of the original price (since 100% − 20 % = 80%)

So, 1% of the original price = £156.72 ÷ 80 = £1.959

and 100% of the original price = £1.959 × 100 = £195.90

The original price was £195.90.
The saving is £195.90 − £156.72 = £39.18   (or work out 20% of £195.90)

An alternative method is by using the decimal multiplier.

In Learn 4.2 you started with an original amount and found the final amount by multiplying by the multiplier. To reverse the process, you just need to **divide** by the multiplier.

In this case the sale price is 80% of the original price, so the multiplier is 0.80 or 0.8

sale price = 0.8 × original price so original price = sale price ÷ 0.8
                                                   = £156.72 ÷ 0.8 = £195.90 (as before)

Both the unitary and multiplier methods also work when amounts have been increased.

Example: A plumber charges £493.50 for a job.

This includes VAT at $17\frac{1}{2}$%

What was the cost before VAT?

AQA Examiner's tip
Look out for examples like this when you need to work out the *original* amount, rather than the final amount.

Solution: The final price = 100% + 17.5% = 117.5% of the original price.

Unitary method

117.5% of the original price = £493.50
1% of the original price   = £493.50 ÷ 117.5
                             = £4.2
100% of the original price   = £4.2 × 100
Original price   = £420

Multiplier method

1.175 × original price = £493.50
Original price   = £493.50 ÷ 1.175
Original price   = £420

AQA Examiner's tip
Check that your answer is the correct original price. Do this by increasing it by 17.5%. You should get back to £493.50.

As you can see from the example, the multiplier method is a more efficient and powerful method if you can use it successfully.

Practise… 7.7 Reverse percentages   D C B A A*

1 **a** A film on DVD is reduced by 20% in a sale. The sale price is £7.16.
             Work out the price of the DVD before the sale.

   b The cost of insurance for Doug's mountain bike has gone up by 12% this year.
          It now costs £39.20.
          What was the price of his insurance last year?

   c The population of an island has risen 8% since last year. The population is now 280 000.
          What was it a year ago? Give your answer to a suitable degree of accuracy.

B

Chapter 7 Percentages

2 A department store reduces its prices by 30% in a sale.
The reduced price of a television is £875

  a What was the price before the sale?

  b How much do you save by buying the television in the sale?

SALE 30% OFF Now only £875

3 The number of students from a school who are going to university this year has gone up by 16% to 145. How many went to university last year?

4 A website says that the price of a download is 40% less than the price of a CD.
It charges £3.99 to download an album.
How much does the website say you save by downloading the album instead of buying a CD?

5 Sumira wants to buy a computer.

Compsave Price
£564
including 17.5% VAT

PC Perfect Price
£498
+ 17.5% VAT

In which store would Sumira pay less?

6 Kev buys a car for £3150. The price was reduced by 10% for paying by cash.
Kev says 'I saved £315 by paying by cash.'

  a Explain why Kev is wrong.   **b** Work out how much Kev saved.

7 A finance company charges 12% interest per annum. Helen borrows a sum of money and 2 years later gives the company £6272 to pay off the loan.

How much did Helen borrow?

8 A charity can reclaim VAT on goods and services that it buys.
The table shows the prices it paid for an extension.

Item	Price including VAT (17.5%)
Building materials	£1739.00
Builder's labour charge	£6345.00
Plumber's bill	£493.50
Electrician's bill	£465.30
Decorating bill	£181.89

Work out the total amount of VAT that the charity can reclaim.

9 Stacey has inherited some money. She wants to invest some of it to help with the cost of going to university. She decides to use a building society account that gives a fixed rate of interest of 6% per annum.

How much does Stacey need to put into the account if she wants it to grow to at least £12 000 at the end of four years?

Give your answer to the nearest £.

Assess

1 The table shows Carl's marks in two tests.

In which test did Carl do better?
You **must** show your working.

Test	Mark
A	52 out of 80
B	60 out of 100

2 Meera asks 250 of the 1246 students in her school what they like to read.

a What percentage of the school population does she ask?

b The table gives her results.

	Number of students
Books	102
Comics	146
Magazines	215
Newspapers	76
Other	85

i Why is the total more than 250?

ii What percentage of the students in the survey like to read magazines?

iii What percentage of the students in the survey like to read newspapers?

3 The table shows the results of a cycling test.

	Boys	Girls
Pass	34	28
Fail	16	12

Compare the percentage of boys who passed with the percentage of girls who passed.

4 The price of an mp3 player is reduced from £69.95 to £55.96 in a sale.
Find the percentage reduction.

5 William invests £1500 in a building society for 2 years.
The compound interest rate is 4% per annum.

How much will William have in the building society at the end of the second year?

6 Foollah got 32 out of 60 for her first maths paper. She sits the second paper next week. It is out of 75. Foollah needs to get an overall 60% to pass maths.

	Mark	Total
Paper 1	32	60
Paper 2	?	75

What mark does she need to get on the second paper?

Chapter 7 Percentages

7 In a survey, 300 students are asked how they travel to school. 70% say they use public transport. Of these, 90% say they travel by bus.

How many students in the survey travel by bus to school?

8 A dish contains 5000 bacteria. The number of bacteria increases by 18% per hour.

   a How many bacteria will be in the dish after 6 hours?

   b Show that it will take over 13 hours for the number of bacteria to exceed fifty thousand.

9 Jensen's speedometer overestimates his speed by 10%

At what speed is he travelling when his speedometer says 66 mph?

10 The price of a games console is £236 after a reduction of 20%

What was the price before the reduction?

11 The table shows Debbie's English and maths test scores in Years 8 and 9.

	Year 8	Year 9
English	53%	75%
Maths	41%	63%

In which subject has Debbie's test score improved the most?

You **must** show your working.

AQA Examination-style questions

1 John has £2000 to invest.
He sees this advert.

> **SureFire Investments**
>
> *Don't see your money go up in smoke!*
>
> **Double your money in 10 years.**
>
> The average annual growth of our investment account is **7.2%**

Will John double his money in ten years with SureFire Investments?
You **must** show your working.   *(4 marks)*

AQA 2006

2 a In a sale the price of a television decreases from £750 to £660.
Work out the percentage decrease in price.   *(3 marks)*

   b In a sale the price of a camcorder decreases by 60%.
The sale price is £372.
Work out the price before the sale.   *(3 marks)*

3 The value of a vintage car rises from £36 000 to £63 000.
Work out the percentage increase in the price of the car.   *(3 marks)*

AQA 2008

8 Statistical measures

Objectives

Examiners would normally expect students who get these grades to be able to:

D
calculate the mean for a frequency distribution

find the modal class for grouped data

C
find the mean for grouped data

find the median class for grouped data

B
find the upper and lower quartiles and calculate the inter-quartile range for a frequency distribution.

Key terms

frequency distribution
discrete data
average
mean
mode
median
range
inter-quartile range
grouped data
continuous data
modal class or modal group
class interval

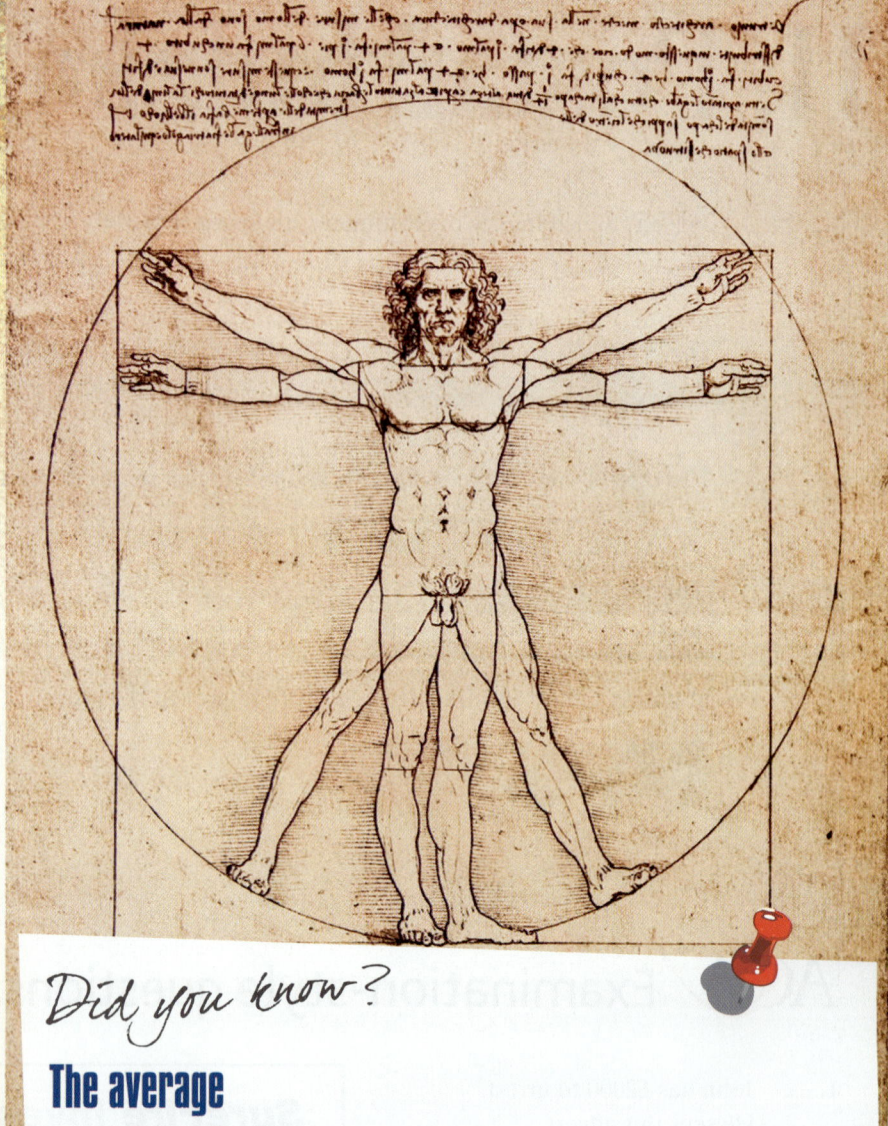

Did you know?

The average

The **Vitruvian Man** is a famous drawing created by Leonardo da Vinci around 1487. His notes offer an explanation of the average man including:

- the length of a man's outspread arms is equal to his height
- the length of a man's foot is one-sixth of a man's height
- the length of the hand is one-tenth of a man's height
- the distance from the elbow to the armpit is one-eighth of a man's height.

Do these measurement still apply to the average man? What about the average woman?

You should already know:

✓ how to use a calculator to work with the four rules of arithmetic

✓ how to calculate the mean, mode, median and range

✓ what discrete and continuous data are.

Chapter 8 Statistical measures   115

Learn... 8.1 Frequency distributions

A **frequency distribution** shows how often individual values occur (the frequency).

The information is usually shown in a frequency table.

A frequency table shows the values and their frequency.

Frequency distributions are usually used with **discrete data**.

Discrete data are data that can only take individual values.

For example, the number of cars is discrete data. You cannot have 2.3 cars!

This frequency table shows the number of pets for students at a school.

There are 5 students with no pets, 11 students with 1 pet, 8 students with 2 pets, ... and so on.

You can use the frequency table to calculate measures of average and measures of spread.

Number of pets (x)	Frequency (f)
0	5
1	11
2	8
3	5
4	2

Example: For the frequency distribution above, find:

a the average

b the spread.

AQA Examiner's tip

The average and the spread are useful measures to compare sets of data. You should appreciate the difference between measures of average and measures of spread.

Solution: a The most common measures of **average** are the **mean**, the **mode** and the **median**.

Mean

The mean is the total of all the values divided by the number of values.

The mean here is the total number of pets divided by the total number of students.

$$\text{Mean} = \frac{\text{the total of (frequencies} \times \text{values)}}{\text{the total of frequencies}} = \frac{\Sigma fx}{\Sigma f}$$

where Σ means 'the sum of'.

Number of pets (x)	Frequency (f)	Frequency × number of pets (fx)
0	5	0 × 5 = 0
1	11	1 × 11 = 11
2	8	2 × 8 = 16
3	5	3 × 5 = 15
4	2	4 × 2 = 8
	$\Sigma f = 5 + 11 + 8 + 5 + 2 = 31$	$\Sigma fx = 0 + 11 + 16 + 15 + 8 = 50$

$$\text{Mean} = \frac{\text{the total of (frequencies} \times \text{values)}}{\text{the total of frequencies}} = \frac{\Sigma fx}{\Sigma f}$$
$$= \frac{50}{31}$$
$$= 1.6129...$$

Mean = 1.6 (to 1 d.p.)

The mean is a useful measure of average.

AQA Examiner's tip

Always check that your answers are reasonable. Candidates often mistakenly divide by the number of rows instead of the total frequency. This will usually give a silly answer.

Mode

The mode is the value which has the highest frequency next to it (i.e. the value occurring most often).

'Number of pets is 1' has a frequency of 11 and all the other frequencies are less than this.

Mode = 1

The mode is the number that occurs most frequently.

AQA Examiner's tip
Candidates often write down the frequency of the value rather than the value when asked for the mode. Make sure your answer is sensible.

Median

The median is the middle value when the data are listed in order.

It does not matter whether you go from smallest to highest or the other way round.

The data have 31 values so the median is the $\left(\frac{31+1}{2}\right)$th value = 16th value. The data are already ordered in the table.

The first 5 values are 0, the next 11 are 1, so the 16th value is 1.

0 0 0 0 0 1 1 1 1 1 1 1 1 1 1 1 2 2 2 ...

                              16th

Median = 1

The median is the middle value when the data are arranged in order.

The median can also be found using the 'running totals' of the frequencies as follows:

Number of pets (x)	Frequency (f)	Running total
0	5	5
1	11	5 + 11 = 16
2	8	5 + 11 + 8 = 24
3	5	5 + 11 + 8 + 5 = 29
4	2	5 + 11 + 8 + 5 + 2 = 31

The 16th value will lie in this interval so the median is 1.

b The most common measures of spread are the **range** and the **inter-quartile range**.

Range

The range is the difference between the highest value and the lowest value.

The range = 4 − 0 = 4

Range = 4

The range is a measure of how spread out the data are.

AQA Examiner's tip
Remember that the range should always be presented as a single answer (not a range!). The range is the difference between the highest value and the lowest value.

Inter-quartile range

The inter-quartile range is the difference between the upper quartile and the lower quartile.

The lower quartile is the $\frac{1}{4}(n+1)$th value = $\frac{1}{4}(31+1)$th value = 8th value

The upper quartile is the $\frac{3}{4}(n+1)$th value = $\frac{3}{4}(31+1)$th value = 24th value

The quartiles can be found using the same method as the median or else you can consider the 'running totals' of the frequencies as follows.

Number of pets (x)	Frequency (f)	Running total
0	5	5
1	11	5 + 11 = 16
2	8	5 + 11 + 8 = 24
3	5	5 + 11 + 8 + 5 = 29
4	2	5 + 11 + 8 + 5 + 2 = 31

The 8th value will lie in this interval so the lower quartile is 1.

The 24th value will lie in this interval so the upper quartile is 2.

The inter-quartile range = 2 − 1 = 1

Inter-quartile range = 1

The inter-quartile range is a measure of how spread out the data are.

It focuses on the middle 50 per cent of the distribution and is not affected by extreme values.

Practise... 8.1 Frequency distributions   D C B A A*

1 Andy keeps a record of the points he scores in tennis games.

The table shows results for 40 games he lost.

For the data work out:

Score	Frequency
0	5
15	11
30	20
40	7

a the mean
b the median
c the mode
d the range
e the inter-quartile range
f the percentage of these games where Andy scored 30 points.

2 The frequency table shows the speed limit of all the roads in one county.

Speed limit (miles per hour)	20	30	40	50	60	70
Number of roads	8	88	52	23	150	3

a Work out the number of roads that have a speed limit of:
   i less than 40 miles per hour
   ii 50 miles per hour or more.
b What percentage of roads have a speed limit of 30 miles per hour? Give your answer to two decimal places.
c What is the range of speed limits in this county?
d Work out the modal speed limit for the county.
e Work out the median speed limit for the county.
f Work out the mean speed limit for the county.

3 Ryan throws a dice 100 times. The frequency distribution shows his scores.

Score (x)	Frequency (f)	Frequency × score (fx)
1	18	
2	19	
3	16	
4	12	
5	15	
6	20	

AQA Examiner's tip
It is possible to use a calculator's statistical functions to find the mean of a frequency distribution. Make sure you are in statistical mode and enter the data value or midpoint followed by its frequency each time.

a Find his mean score.
b Find the median score.
c What is the modal score?
d Work out the range of scores from these 100 dice throws.
e What fraction of the throws resulted in a 6?
Give your answer in its simplest form.

4 The number of people in a sample of 100 cars is given in the frequency table.

Number of people	1	2	3	4
Frequency	60	32	6	2

a Write down the median number of people in these cars.
b Work out the mean number of people in these cars.
c Which is more useful in predicting the number of people in the next car to come along? Explain your answer.

5 This table shows some information about storms in the USA.

	Number of rumbles of thunder
Mean	3.1
Median	3
Mode	3

This table shows the number of rumbles of thunder heard in one minute time periods during a storm in another country.

Number of rumbles of thunder	Frequency
0	11
1	24
2	14
3	3
4	1
5	2

Hint
To compare this storm with storms in the USA you need to work out the average values even though you have **not** been asked to.

Compare this storm with storms in the USA.

⚠ 6 Fill in the frequencies so that the median is 10 and the mode is 9.

x	f
8	
9	
10	
11	

7 Make four copies of this frequency table.

x	f
2	35
4	65
6	19
8	

a Complete one copy of the table so that x has a mode of 8.
b Complete one copy of the table so that x has a median of 4.
c Complete one copy of the table so that x has a median of 5.
d Complete one copy of the table so that x has a mean of 4.

8 The table shows the number of bedrooms in a sample of houses from a town centre and a village.

Number of bedrooms	Number of houses	
	Town centre	Village
1	8	3
2	19	9
3	6	10
4	2	8
5	0	5

Compare the number of bedrooms in these two samples.

Hint
As well as using measures of average and spread to make the comparisons you could also use percentages.

9 Two bus companies, Super Express and Big Bus, run a bus service between the same two towns along the same route.

George is investigating the punctuality of their buses on this route.

He records the number of minutes late, rounded to the nearest 5 minutes, for a sample of buses from each company over a one week period.

Here are the data George collects for Big Bus.

0	0	0	0	0	0	0	0	0	0
0	0	0	0	0	0	0	0	5	5
5	5	5	5	5	5	10	10	10	10
10	10	10	10	10	10	15	15	25	35

Here are the data George collects for Super Express.

0	0	0	0	5	5	5	5	5	5
5	5	5	5	5	5	5	5	5	5
5	5	5	10	10	15	15	15	15	15
15	15	15	15	15	15	15	15	15	15
15	20	20	20	20	20	20	20	20	20

Hint
When you are given sets of raw data, the first thing to do is sort out the data in a frequency table.

a Compare the punctuality of the two bus companies.
b Give a reason why you might be more interested in the range of the times late rather than the average.

10 A frequency distribution for the variable x has the following features.

The total number of pieces of data is 100.

The mean of x is 5.   The mode of x is 3.
The median of x is 4.   The range of x is 7.

Copy and complete this frequency table to show a possible distribution for x.

x	0	1	2	3	4	5	6	7	8	9	10
Frequency											

Learn... 8.2 Grouped frequency distributions

A grouped frequency distribution shows how often **grouped data** values occur (the frequency).
The information is usually shown in a grouped frequency table.
A grouped frequency table shows the values and their frequency.
Grouped frequency distributions are usually used with **continuous data**.
Continuous data are data which can take any numerical value. Length and weight are common examples of continuous data.
Discrete data can only take individual values. Shoe sizes are an example.
You can use the grouped frequency table to calculate measures of average and measures of spread as before.

Mean

The mean is the total of all the values divided by the number of values.

$$\text{Mean} = \frac{\text{the total of (frequencies} \times \text{values)}}{\text{the total of frequencies}} = \frac{\Sigma fx}{\Sigma f}$$

where Σ means 'the sum of'.

As the data are grouped, you will need to use the midpoint of each group to represent the value.

Discrete data	Continuous data
To find the midpoint, add together the largest and smallest values of each group and divide the answer by two.	To find the midpoint, add together the smallest possible value (lower bound) and the largest possible value (upper bound) for each group and divide the answer by two.

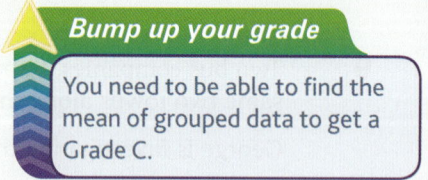

Bump up your grade

You need to be able to find the mean of grouped data to get a Grade C.

Mode

The mode is the value which has the highest frequency next to it (i.e. the value occurring most often).
For grouped data it is more usual to find the **modal class**.
The modal class is the class with the highest frequency.

Median

The median is the middle value when the data are listed in order.
For grouped data it is more usual to find the group containing the median.
Graphical work (see Chapter 7) is often used to estimate the median.

Range

The range is the highest value take away lowest value.
For grouped data it is not always possible to identify the highest value and the lowest value. However, it can be estimated as: Highest value in highest group − lowest value in lowest group.

Inter-quartile range

The inter-quartile range is the difference between the upper quartile and the lower quartile.
For grouped data it is not always possible to identify the upper quartile and the lower quartile.
Graphical work (see Chapter 7) is often used to estimate the quartiles.

Example: The table shows the time taken for students to solve a simple puzzle.

$20 \leq t < 30$ covers all the values between 20 and 30 seconds. The 20 is included in the group whereas the 30 will be in the $30 \leq t < 40$ group. The range of values is called a **class interval**.

Time, t (seconds)	Frequency
$10 \leq t < 20$	30
$20 \leq t < 30$	35
$30 \leq t < 40$	20
$40 \leq t < 50$	10
$50 \leq t < 60$	5

Use the information in the grouped frequency table to:

a write down the modal class

b work out the class which contains the median

c calculate an estimate of the mean time taken to solve the puzzle.

Solution:

a The modal class is the class with the highest frequency.

This is the class $20 \leq t < 30$ (as there are 35 students in this class).

b The median is the middle value when the data are listed in order.

In this case the middle value is the 50th value.

> **Hint**
> The median is the $\frac{1}{2}(n + 1)$th value but for large numbers the $\frac{n}{2}$th value is sufficient.

The median can also be found using the 'running totals' of the frequencies as follows.

The 50th value will lie in this interval so the median lies in the $20 \leq t < 30$ class.

Time, t (seconds)	Frequency	Running total
$10 \leq t < 20$	30	30
$20 \leq t < 30$	35	30 + 35 = 65
$30 \leq t < 40$	20	30 + 35 + 20 = 85
$40 \leq t < 50$	10	30 + 35 + 20 + 10 = 95
$50 \leq t < 60$	5	30 + 35 + 20 + 10 + 5 = 100

The $20 \leq t < 30$ class contains the median.

c The mean is the total of all the values divided by the number of values.

$$\text{Mean} = \frac{\text{the total of (frequencies} \times \text{values)}}{\text{the total of frequencies}} = \frac{\Sigma ft}{\Sigma f}$$

where Σ means 'the sum of'.

As the data are grouped, you will need to use the midpoint of each group.

An additional column should be added to the table for the midpoints.

Time, t (seconds)	Frequency (f)	Midpoint (t)	Frequency × midpoint (ft)
$10 \leq t < 20$	30	15	30 × 15 = 450
$20 \leq t < 30$	35	25	35 × 25 = 875
$30 \leq t < 40$	20	35	20 × 35 = 700
$40 \leq t < 50$	10	45	10 × 45 = 450
$50 \leq t < 60$	5	55	5 × 55 = 275
	$\Sigma f = 100$		$\Sigma ft = 2750$

$$\text{Mean} = \frac{\text{the total of (frequencies} \times \text{values)}}{\text{the total of frequencies}} = \frac{\Sigma ft}{\Sigma f}$$
$$= \frac{2750}{100}$$
$$= 27.5$$

Mean = 27.5 seconds

> **Hint**
> Remember that this is only an estimate of the mean as we do not know how the numbers are distributed within each group. Using the midpoint gives an approximation only.

> **AQA Examiner's tip**
> Remember to check that the answer you have obtained is sensible for the data. Your answer must lie within the range of the data. If it doesn't you have made a mistake.

Practise... 8.2 Grouped frequency distributions   D C B A A*

1 The table shows the time in minutes people have to wait to be served in a shop.

Time, t (minutes)	Frequency
$0 \leq t < 2$	8
$2 \leq t < 4$	14
$4 \leq t < 6$	6
$6 \leq t < 8$	4
$8 \leq t < 10$	2

a Write down the modal class.

b In which group does the median lie?

c What percentage of people waited more than 8 minutes?
Give your answer to one significant figure.

d Calculate an estimate of the mean waiting time.
Explain why your answer is an estimate.

e Estimate the range of the waiting times.

2 In a survey of reading ability the scores obtained are given in this table.

Reading score	0–4	5–9	10–14	15–19	20–24	25–29	30–34
Frequency	15	60	125	260	250	200	90

What is the modal class?

Calculate an estimate of the mean reading score.

3 The table shows the weights of 10 letters.

Weight, x (grams)	$0 \leq x < 20$	$20 \leq x < 40$	$40 \leq x < 60$	$60 \leq x < 80$	$80 \leq x < 100$
Number of letters	2	3	2	2	1

Calculate an estimate of the mean weight of a letter.

4 The table shows the weekly wages of 40 staff in a small company.

Wage, x (£)	$50 \leq x < 100$	$100 \leq x < 150$	$150 \leq x < 200$	$200 \leq x < 250$	$250 \leq x < 300$	$300 \leq x < 350$
Frequency	5	13	11	9	0	2

a Work out:

  i the modal class

  ii the class that contains the median

  iii an estimate of the mean.

b Which average should you use to compare the wages with another company?
Give a reason for your answer.

5 A company produces three million packets of crisps each day.
It states on each packet that the bag contains 25 g of crisps.
To test this, the crisps in a sample of 1000 bags are weighed.
The results are shown in the table.

Weight, w (grams)	Frequency
$23.5 \leqslant w < 24.5$	20
$24.5 \leqslant w < 25.5$	733
$25.5 \leqslant w < 26.5$	194
$26.5 \leqslant w < 27.5$	53

a Calculate an estimate of the mean weight of a packet of crisps.

b Is the company justified in stating that each bag contains 25 g of crisps?

c What percentage of the packets of crisps weigh under 25 g?

d Estimate the number of bags weighing under 25 g produced in one day.

6 Two machines are each designed to produce paper 0.3 mm thick.

The frequency distributions below show the actual output of a sample for each machine.

	Machine A	Machine B
Thickness, t (mm)	Frequency	Frequency
$0.27 \leqslant t < 0.28$	2	1
$0.28 \leqslant t < 0.29$	7	50
$0.29 \leqslant t < 0.30$	32	42
$0.30 \leqslant t < 0.31$	50	5
$0.31 \leqslant t < 0.32$	9	2

Compare the outputs of the two machines using suitable calculations.

Which machine is producing paper closer to the required thickness?

7 The table shows the weights of 100 vehicles travelling on a road.

Weight, w (tonnes)	$0 < w \leqslant 1$	$1 < w \leqslant 2$	$2 < w \leqslant 3$	$3 < w \leqslant 4$
Frequency	53	43	5	2

a Estimate the mean weight of the vehicles on the road.

b Explain why this value is only an estimate.

8 The frequency distribution shows the time taken by 50 people to complete a supermarket shop.

Time, t (minutes)	$10 \leqslant t < 20$	$20 \leqslant t < 30$	$30 \leqslant t < 40$	$40 \leqslant t < 50$	50 or over
Frequency	13	21	8	5	3

a Find the class which contains the median length of time.

b Explain why the class '50 or over' makes estimating the mean time difficult.

c Yasmin uses the table to estimate the mean length of time spent shopping for these 50 people.

She correctly obtains a value of 28.4

Work out the class interval she used instead of '50 or over'.

8 Assess

1 a Look at this set of numbers.

1 2 2 3 4 4 4 4 7 7 33 37

How can you tell at a glance that the mean is **larger** than the median?

b Look at this set of numbers.

1 1 22 23 25 25 25 25 26 26 26 27

How can you tell at a glance that the mean is **smaller** than the median?

c Remember that an average is one number that best represents a set of numbers.

In parts **a** and **b** which average, the mean or the median, best represents each set of values?

Give a reason for your answer.

2 a Write down two **different** sets of five numbers that have the **same** median and mode but a different mean.
Work out the range of each set.

b Write down two **different** sets of five numbers that have the same mean and range but a different mode.
Work out the median of each set.

3 Leela rolls an eight-sided dice 200 times. Her results are shown in the frequency table below.

Score	1	2	3	4	5	6	7	8
Frequency	19	26	24	25	22	33	21	30

a Write down the modal score.

b Work out the median score.

c Work out the mean score.

4 Debbie asks students in her class how many brothers and sisters they have.
She puts the information in a table.

```
              5 | 1
              4 | 0  2
Number        3 | 2  2  1
of            2 | 4  3  3  1
brothers      1 | 5  3  2  1  1
              0 | 5  6  2  1     1
                  0  1  2  3  4  5
                    Number of sisters
```

a How many people have no sisters?

b How many people have only one brother?

c How many people have equal numbers of brothers and sisters?

d How many people did Debbie survey altogether?

e What is the modal number of sisters?

f Calculate the mean number of brothers.

Chapter 8 Statistical measures 125

5 The table shows the number of letters in the words in a game of scrabble.

Numbers of letters in word	2	3	4	5	6	7
Frequency	10	7	5	5	6	3

a Write down the modal word length.

b Work out the median word length.

c Work out the mean word length.

d Which of these averages do you feel is most suitable for these data? Give a reason for your answer.

6 In a survey of the number of people in a household the following information was collected from 50 houses.

Number of people in a household	Number of households
1	9
2	19
3	9
4	8
5	4
6	1
Total	50

a Find the mean, median, mode and range of household sizes.

b Which average is the best one to use to represent the data? Give a reason for your answer.

7 This table gives the number of years' service by 50 teachers at the Clare School.

Number of years' service	0–4	5–9	10–14	15–19	20–24	25–29
Number of teachers	11	15	4	10	6	4

a Find the modal class.

b Calculate an estimate of the mean.

8 The heights achieved by Year 10 high jumpers in a trial are summarised below.

Height, h (cm)	$149.5 \leq h < 154.5$	$154.5 \leq h < 159.5$	$159.5 \leq h < 164.5$	$164.5 \leq h < 169.5$
Frequency	4	21	18	7

a Estimate the mean height jumped in the trial.

b John says 'I won the trial, I jumped 1 metre 65 cm.' Comment on John's statement.

9 The length of 40 political speeches in 1900 in the House of Commons is given in the table.

Length, x (minutes)	$10 \leq x < 20$	$20 \leq x < 30$	$30 \leq x < 40$	$40 \leq x < 50$	$50 \leq x < 60$
Frequency	7	8	16	6	2

By 2008 the mean speech length was 45% longer than 1900.

Estimate the mean speech length for 2008.

10 In a science lesson 30 runner bean plants were measured.
Here are the results correct to the nearest centimetre.

6.2	5.4	8.9	12.1	6.5	9.3	7.2	12.7	10.2	5.4
7.7	9.5	11.1	8.6	7.0	13.5	12.7	5.6	15.4	12.3
13.4	9.5	6.7	8.6	9.1	11.5	14.2	13.5	8.8	9.7

The teacher suggested that the data were put into groups.

Length, l (cm)	Tally	Frequency
$5 \leq l < 7$		
$7 \leq l < 9$		
$9 \leq l < 11$		
$11 \leq l < 13$		
$13 \leq l < 15$		
$15 \leq l < 17$		

a Copy and complete the table.

b Use the information to work out an estimate of the mean height of the plants.

c Calculate the mean from the original data.

d Why is your answer to part **b** only an estimate of the mean?

11 The table shows the distribution of three sets of discrete data A, B and C.

	Frequency		
x	Set A	Set B	Set C
0	1	1	0
1	1	2	6
2	7	7	2
3	6	6	10
4	0	4	1

Find as many reasons as you can for each data set to be the odd one out.

Show working to justify your answers.

12 Tom and Sara are investigating this hypothesis about the game of Snakes and Ladders.

'The higher the average score you get when you roll the dice the more likely you are to win.'

Here are the scores in games that Tom won.

Score	Frequency	
	Tom	Sara
1	9	7
2	11	10
3	8	12
4	8	11
5	14	8
6	12	9

Hint

Snakes and Ladders

In a game of Snakes and Ladders you can land on squares that tell you to miss a turn or throw again.

So Tom and Sara are likely to throw the dice a different number of times in a game.

Here are the scores in games that Sara won.

Score	Frequency	
	Tom	Sara
1	11	8
2	8	7
3	11	9
4	7	10
5	8	8
6	10	14

Investigate the hypothesis.

Hint

When you are given sets of data and are asked to investigate a hypothesis you often have to **compare** measures of average and spread.

In this question there are four different sets of data. You have to work out the average score for all four sets. Then you have to decide what comparisons to make that will help you decide whether the hypothesis is true or not.

In this question, you don't have to work out the range. Why?

The best average to use is the mean. Why?

Don't forget to write a conclusion.

AQA Examination-style questions

1   The table shows the heights of 30 students in a class.

Height, h (cm)	Number of students
$140 < h \leq 144$	4
$144 < h \leq 148$	5
$148 < h \leq 152$	8
$152 < h \leq 156$	7
$156 < h \leq 160$	5
$160 < h \leq 164$	1

By using the midpoints of each group, calculate an estimate for the mean height of the students.

(3 marks)

AQA 2007

9 Sequences

Objectives

Examiners would normally expect students who get these grades to be able to:

D
write the terms of a sequence or a series of diagrams given the nth term

C
write the nth term of a linear sequence or a series of diagrams.

Did you know?

Sequences in nature

Have you ever wondered why four-leaf clovers are so rare? It's because four isn't a number in the Fibonacci sequence.

The Fibonacci sequence 0, 1, 1, 2, 3, 5, 8, 13, … is well known in nature and can be applied to seashell shapes, branching plants, flower petals, pine cones and pineapples.

If you count the number of petals on a daisy, you are most likely to find 13, 21, 34, 55 or 89 petals… all numbers in the Fibonacci sequence.

Key terms
sequence
term-to-term
nth term
linear sequence

You should already know:

✓ how to continue a sequence of numbers or diagrams
✓ how to write terms in a sequence of numbers or diagrams
✓ how to write the term-to-term rule in a sequence of numbers or diagrams.

Chapter 9 Sequences 129

Learn... 9.1 The *n*th term of a sequence

A **sequence** is a set of patterns or numbers with a given rule.

☐ ☐☐ ☐☐☐ ... is a sequence of patterns.

2, 4, 6, 8, 10, ... is a sequence of numbers.

A linear sequence is one where the differences between the terms are all the same.

5, 10, 15, 20, ...

5, 10, 15, 20, ...
 +5 +5 +5   The **term-to-term** rule is +5.

To find the **nth term** of a **linear sequence**, you can use the formula:

nth term = difference × n + (first term − difference)
           = $dn + (a - d)$

For 7, 10, 13, 16, ... d is the difference = +3
                          a is the first term = 7

nth term = difference × n + (first term − difference)
           = $dn + (a - d)$
           = $3n + (7 - 3)$
           = $3n + 4$

You can check this as follows.
1st term = 3 × 1 + 4 = 7
2nd term = 3 × 2 + 4 = 10
3rd term = 3 × 3 + 4 = 13

Example: The first four terms of a sequence are 3, 7, 11, 15.

Find the nth term.

Solution:

1st term	2nd term	3rd term	4th term
3,	7,	11,	15,
	+4	+4	+4

The sequence goes up in 4's, just like the 4 times table, so the rule begins 4 × n (4n, for short).

The term-to-term rule is +4.

AQA Examiner's tip
The nth term is sometimes called the general term.

This tells you that the rule is of the form 4n + ...
1st term = 4 × 1 + ... = 3
2nd term = 4 × 2 + ... = 7
3rd term = 4 × 3 + ... = 11
4th term = 4 × 4 + ... = 15

This method only works for linear sequences.

From the above you can see that the nth term is 4n − 1.

Bump up your grade
You need to be confident in finding the nth term for a Grade C.

Practise... 9.1 The nth term of a sequence

1 Write down the term-to-term rule for the following sequences.

a 0, 3, 6, 9, ...
b 3, 7, 11, 15, ...
c 1, 2, 4, 8, 16, ...
d 3, 4.5, 6, 7.5, ...
e 25, 20, 15, 10, ...
f 2, 3, 4.5, 6.25, ...
g 54, 18, 6, 2, ...
h 0.01, 0.1, 1, 10, ...

2 The term-to-term rule is +6.

Write down five different sequences which fit this rule.

AQA Examiner's tip
Always check your nth term to see that it works for the sequence.

3 Write down the first five terms of the sequence whose nth term is:

a $n + 3$
b $n + \frac{1}{2}$
c $5n - 3$
d $n^2 + 3$
e $n^2 - 5$
f $4n^2$
g $\frac{n}{n + 11}$

4 Aisha writes down the sequence 2, 6, 10, 14, ...

She says that the nth term is $n + 4$.

Is she correct? Give a reason for your answer.

5 The nth term of a sequence is $3n - 1$.

a Colin says that 31 is a number in this sequence.
   Is Colin correct? Give a reason for your answer.

b Diane says the 20th term is double the 10th term.
   Is Diane correct? Give a reason for your answer.

6 Copy and complete the following table.

Pattern (n)	Diagram	Number of matchsticks (m)
1		3
2		5
3		7
4		
5		

a What do you notice about the pattern of matchsticks?

b Write down the formula for the number of matchsticks m in the nth pattern.

c How many matchsticks will there be in the 10th pattern? Check your answer by drawing the 10th pattern and counting the number of matchsticks.

d There are 41 matchsticks in the 20th pattern. How many matchsticks are there in the 21st pattern? Give a reason for your answer.

Chapter 9 Sequences

7 Write down the nth term in the following sequences.

- a   3, 6, 9, 12, ...
- b   0, 5, 10, 15, ...
- c   8, 14, 20, 26, ...
- d $\frac{1}{5}, \frac{2}{7}, \frac{3}{9}, \frac{4}{11},$ ...
- e   23, 21, 19, 17, ...
- f   105, 100, 95, 90, ...
- g   −5, −1, 3, 7, ...
- h   4, 6.5, 9, 11.5, ...
- i   −5, 3, 11, 19, ...
- j $\frac{2}{7}, \frac{4}{13}, \frac{6}{19}, \frac{8}{25},$ ...

8 Write down the formula for the number of squares in the nth pattern.

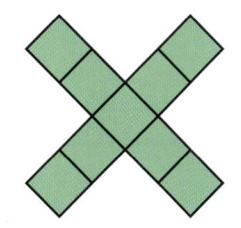

9 Stuart says that the number of cubes in the 100th pattern is 300.

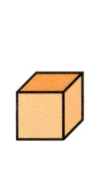

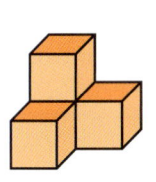

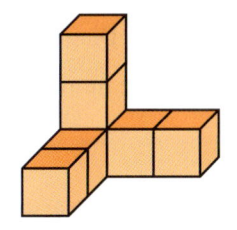

How can you tell that Stuart is wrong? Give a reason for your answer.

10 Jacob is exploring number patterns.

He writes down the following products in a table.

1 × 1	1
11 × 11	121
111 × 111	12 321
1111 × 1111	1 234 321
11 111 × 11 111	
111 111 × 111 111	

Copy and complete the next two rows for the table.

Jacob says he can use the table to work out 1 111 111 111 × 1 111 111 111

Is he correct? Give a reason for your answer.

11 Write down the nth term in the following non-linear sequences.

- a   1, 4, 9, 16, ...
- b   2, 5, 10, 17, ...
- c   2, 8, 18, 32, ...
- d   1, 8, 27, 64, 125, ...
- e   0, 7, 26, 63, 124, ...
- f   10, 100, 1000, ...

Hint Use your answer to part **a** to help you with parts **b** and **c**.

12 Write down the nth term in the following sequences.

- a   1 × 2, 2 × 3, 3 × 4, ...
- b $\frac{2}{3}, \frac{3}{4}, \frac{4}{5}, \frac{5}{6}$ ...
- c   1 × 2 × 5, 2 × 3 × 6, 3 × 4 × 7, 4 × 5 × 8, ...
- d   0.1, 0.2, 0.3, 0.4, ...
- e   0.11, 0.22, 0.33, 0.44, ...

13

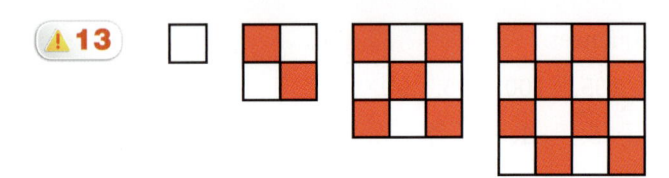

a Write down the formula for the number of white tiles in the nth pattern.

b Write down the formula for the number of red tiles in the nth pattern.

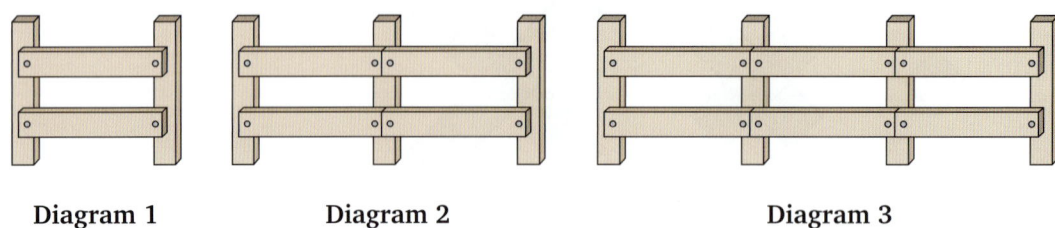

14 Jenny builds fencing from pieces of wood as shown below.

Diagram 1
4 pieces of wood

Diagram 2
7 pieces of wood

Diagram 3
10 pieces of wood

a How many pieces of wood will there be in Diagram n?

b Use your answer to part **a** to work out the number of pieces of wood needed for Diagram 10.

15 The diagram shows the stopping distances for cars travelling at different speeds.

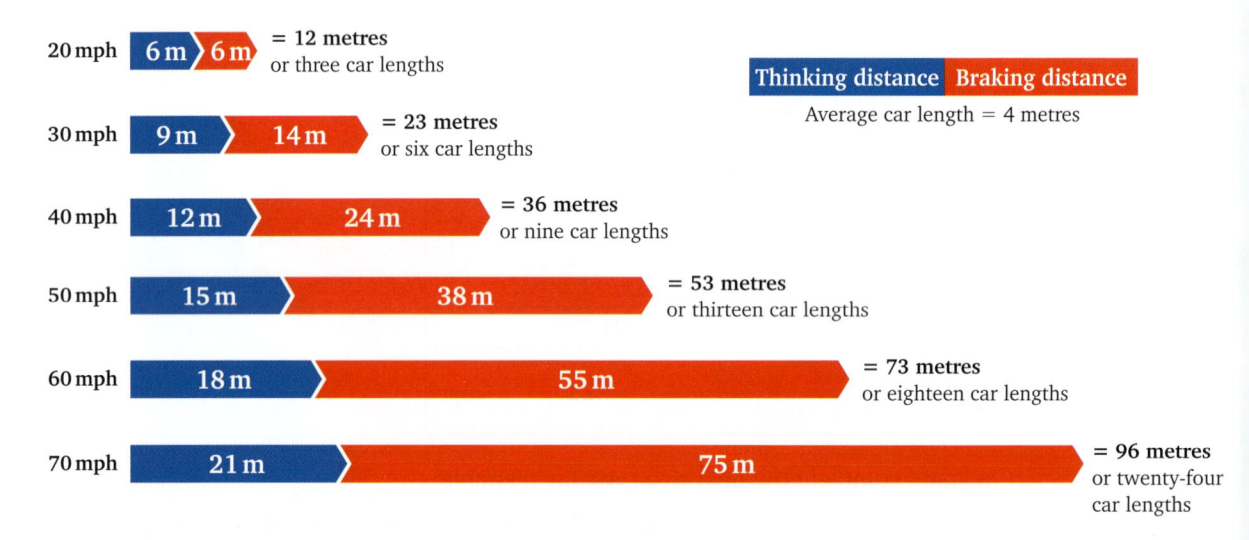

20 mph 6 m 6 m = 12 metres or three car lengths

30 mph 9 m 14 m = 23 metres or six car lengths

40 mph 12 m 24 m = 36 metres or nine car lengths

50 mph 15 m 38 m = 53 metres or thirteen car lengths

60 mph 18 m 55 m = 73 metres or eighteen car lengths

70 mph 21 m 75 m = 96 metres or twenty-four car lengths

Thinking distance | Braking distance
Average car length = 4 metres

a Work out a formula for the thinking distance.

b Work out the thinking distance for these speeds.

  i 80 mph   ii 35 mph

16 Here are the first four terms of a sequence.

45, 31, 14, 15

Here is the rule for the sequence.

> To get the next number, multiply the digits of the previous number and add 11 to the result.

Work out the 100th number of the sequence.

9 Assess

1 Write down the first three terms, then the 5th, 25th and 50th terms of the sequences that have the nth term:

   a $2n + 1$ **b** $5n - 2$ **c** $n^2 + 1$

2 The nth term of a sequence is $3n + 15$.

   a   Work out the 5th term.

   b   Show that every term of the sequence is a multiple of 3.

3 The nth term of a sequence is $36 - 2n$.

   a   Work out the first four terms.

   b   Explain why one of the terms of the sequence will be zero.

4 Information about some squares is shown.

Side of square (cm)	1	2	3	4	n
Area of square (cm²)	1	4	9	16	

Copy and complete the table.

5 The sequence 3, 7, 11, 15, ... has nth term $4n - 1$

   a   What is the nth term of this sequence?

         $\frac{1}{3}, \frac{2}{7}, \frac{3}{11}, \frac{4}{15}, \ldots$

   b   Here is another sequence.
         $2 \times 3, \ 4 \times 7, \ 6 \times 11, \ 8 \times 15, \ldots$

        Explain why the nth term is $8n^2 - 2n$.

6 The diagrams show a quadrilateral, a pentagon and a hexagon with all possible diagonals drawn in.

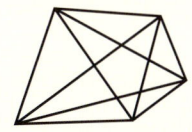

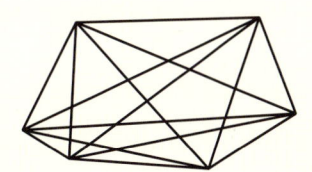

   a   Draw figures with seven and eight sides and fill in all the possible diagonals.

   b   Copy and complete the table.

Number of sides	4	5	6	7	8
Number of diagonals	2				

   c   Use your table to predict the number of diagonals in polygons having:

        i   9 sides   **ii**   10 sides   **iii**   11 sides   **iv**   12 sides.

   d   Use your answers to find the formula which gives the number of diagonals for a polygon with n sides.

   e   Use your formula to predict the number of diagonals in polygons with:

        i   15 sides   **ii**   20 sides   **iii**   50 sides   **iv**   100 sides.

7 The nth term of a sequence is $4n - 5$.

The nth term of a different sequence is $8 + 2n$.

Jo says that there are no numbers that are in both sequences.

Show that Jo is correct.

8 Write down a linear sequence where the 4th term is twice the 2nd term.

Scotty says that this is always true if the first term is equal to the difference.

Is Scotty correct?

Give a reason for your answer.

9 Here is a sequence.

1000, 100, 10, 1, …

a Write the terms of the sequence as powers of 10.

b Write the next term of the sequence.
Give your answer as a fraction.

10 Four numbers add up to 80.

The numbers form part of a sequence.

Each number in the sequence is three times the number before it.

Work out the largest number in the sequence.

AQA Examination-style questions

1 In a sequence, the next term is made by taking the last term, subtracting 1 and then squaring the result.

Here are two adjacent terms in the sequence.

p, $(p - 1)^2$

a Show that the next term in the sequence can be simplified to:

$[p(p - 2)]^2$ *(3 marks)*

b Find an expression for the term that precedes p in the sequence. *(2 marks)*

AQA 2009

10 Ratio and proportion

Objectives

Examiners would normally expect students who get these grades to be able to:

D

use ratio notation, including reduction to its simplest form and its links to fraction notation

divide a quantity in a given ratio

solve simple ratio and proportion problems, such as finding the ratio of teachers to students in a school

C

solve more complex ratio and proportion problems such as sharing money in the ratio of people's ages

solve ratio and proportion problems using the unitary method.

Did you know?

A fair world?

Many African countries do not have good healthcare. In Tanzania, the ratio of doctors to people is 0.02 to 1000. This means one doctor for every fifty thousand people!

People in other countries of the world have better access to a doctor. In Cuba, the ratio is 5.9 to 1000.

In the UK, it is 2.2 to 1000. Think about this next time you are in a surgery waiting room.

Key terms

ratio
unitary ratio
proportion
unitary method

You should already know:

✓ how to add, subtract, multiply and divide simple numbers by hand and all numbers with a calculator

✓ how to simplify fractions by hand and by calculator.

Learn... 10.1 Finding and simplifying ratios

Ratios are a good way of comparing quantities such as the number of teachers in a school and the number of students.

The colon symbol is used to express ratio.

In a school with 50 teachers and 800 students, the teacher : student ratio is 50 : 800

You read 50 : 800 as '50 to 800'.

Ratios can be simplified like fractions.

Each number has been divided by 10.

Ratio = 50 : 800 = 5 : 80 = 1 : 16

Each number has been divided by 5.

This is just like simplifying fractions $\frac{50}{800} = \frac{5}{80} = \frac{1}{16}$

Ratios with 1 on one side are called **unitary ratios**.

Remember that you can use your calculator to simplify fractions by pressing the = button.

The simplest form of the ratio 50 : 800 is 1 : 16

This means there is one teacher for every 16 students, and $\frac{1}{16}$ of a teacher for every student.

The **proportion** of teachers in the school is $\frac{1}{17}$ and the proportion of students is $\frac{16}{17}$

Example: A photo is 15 cm high and 25 cm wide.
What is the ratio of height to width in its simplest form?

Solution: The ratio of height to width is 15 cm : 25 cm = 15 : 25 = 3 : 5 (Dividing both numbers by 5).

Why is it important to keep the ratio of height to width the same when changing the size of photos?

Example: The total charge for a meal is £6.16 including 66p service charge.

a What is the ratio of the original meal price to the service charge?

b The ratio of the original meal price to service charge is the same for all meals. Another meal costs £7.50. What is the service charge on this meal?

Solution: **a** The original price is £6.16 − £0.66 = £5.50.

So the ratio of original price to service charge is

£5.50 : 66p = 550p : 66p = 550 : 66

> **AQA Examiner's tip**
> The units must be the same in a ratio. In this example, £5.50 was changed to pence to match the 66p.

(Both amounts are changed to pence so that the numbers both represent the same thing. You could change them both to pounds but it is probably easier to work with integers rather than decimal numbers.)

550 : 66 = 50 : 6 (dividing both numbers by 11)
and   50 : 6 = 25 : 3 (dividing both numbers by 2)

The ratio of the original price to the service charge in its simplest form is 25 : 3

So for every 28 pence paid, 25p is for food and 3p is for service.

$\frac{25}{28}$ is the proportion that is for food

so $\frac{3}{28}$ is the proportion of the total charge that is for service.

Chapter 10 Ratio and proportion

b The ratio of the original price to the service charge in its simplest form is 25 : 3

To find the service charge on a meal costing £7.50, multiply both sides of this ratio by 30.
25 : 3 = 750 : 90, so when the meal costs £7.50, the service charge is 0.90 or 90p.

This works well because 750 is a multiple of 25. But what if the meal had cost £7.85 instead of £7.50?

When the numbers are difficult, use a calculator to find a unitary ratio.

This means writing the ratio in the form 1 : n or n : 1.
The working (in pence) is shown below.

original price : service charge

This is the 1 : n form of the ratio.

÷ 25 (25 : 3) ÷ 25
1 : 0.12
× 785 (785 : 94.2) × 785

Starting from the 1 : 0.12 ratio, you can find the service charge on any meal just by multiplying by the price of the meal in pence.

The service charge on the £7.85 meal is 94p to the nearest penny.

AQA Examiner's tip
Remember that working with ratios is all about multiplying and dividing not about adding and subtracting.

Practise... 10.1 Finding and simplifying ratios   D C B A A*

1 Write each of these ratios as simply as possible.

a	2 : 4	**e**	2 : 12	**i**	36 : 24	**m**	1.5 : 2.5
b	2 : 6	**f**	2 : 14	**j**	25 : 100	**n**	$\frac{2}{3} : \frac{4}{9}$
c	2 : 8	**g**	36 : 12	**k**	25 : 200	**o**	$2\frac{1}{2} : 7\frac{1}{2}$
d	2 : 10	**h**	24 : 18	**l**	0.3 : 0.8	**p**	20% : 80%

2 Simplify each ratio:

a 50 cm : 1 m
b 20 min : 1 hour
c 1 kg : 500 g
d 2 litres : 250 ml
e 100 m : 2 km
f 330 ml : 1½ litres
g 750 mm : 5 m
h 1.6 kg : 300 g

Hint
Remember, 1 m = 100 cm = 1000 mm
1 kg = 1000 g and 1 litre = 1000 ml.

3 **a** Write down three different pairs of numbers that are in the ratio 1 : 2

b Explain how you can tell that two numbers are in the ratio 1 : 2

4 The simplest version of all these ratios is 1 : 3. Fill in the gaps.

a 2 : __   **b** 5 : __   **c** __ : 21   **d** __ : 3600   **e** a : __

5 Four of these ratios are the same. Which four?

1 : 2.5 $2\frac{1}{2} : 5\frac{1}{2}$ 3 : 6   0.2 : 0.5   25 : 55   2 : 5   3 : 7.5

6 Pippa writes the three pairs of numbers 6 and 9, 9 and 12, and 12 and 15.

She says these pairs of numbers are all in the same ratio.

Is Pippa right? How do you know?

7 On a music download site, a song costs 65p and an album costs £6.50.

Find the ratio of the cost of a song to the cost of an album in its simplest form.

8 A book group has men and women in the ratio 2 : 7

a There are 21 women in the group.
How many men are there?

b Two more men join the group.
How many more women are needed to keep the ratio the same?

9 The numbers a and b are in the ratio 2 : 3

a If a is 4, what is b?

b If b is 12, what is a?

c If a is 1, what is b?

d If b is 1, what is a?

e If a and b add up to 10, what are a and b?

10 Invent your own question like the one above and find the answers.

11 **a** A photo is 20 cm high and 30 cm wide.
What is the ratio of width to height in its simplest form?

b Another photo measures 25 cm high and 35 cm wide.
Is the ratio of its width to its height the same as the photo in part **a**?

12 A recipe for pastry needs 50 grams of butter and 100 grams of flour.

a What is the ratio of butter to flour? What is the ratio of flour to butter?

b How much butter is needed for 200 grams of flour?

c How much flour is needed for 30 grams of butter?

d What fraction is the butter's weight of the flour's weight?

13 **a** Find, in their simplest forms, the teacher : student ratios for these schools.

School	Number of teachers	Number of students
School 1	75	1500
School 2	15	240
School 3	22	374
School 4	120	1800
School 5	65	1365

b **i** A school with 50 teachers has the same teacher : student ratio as School 1. How many students does it have?

ii A school with 2000 students has the same teacher : student ratio as School 1. How many teachers does it have?

c Which school has the smallest number of students for each teacher?

Chapter 10 Ratio and proportion 139

14 Map scales are often expressed in ratio form, such as 1 : 100 000

Look at some maps (perhaps you can use examples from geography).

a How are the scales of the maps shown?
Write down some examples.

b A scale is written as '2 cm to 1 km'.
Write this scale as a unitary ratio.

c The scale 1 : 100 000 can be written as '1 cm to n km'.
Work out the value of n.

d What distance in real life does 3 cm represent on a 1 : 100 000 map?

> **Hint**
> You will need to use these conversions.
> 100 cm = 1 m
> 1000 m = 1 km

15 Copy and complete the table to show the ingredients needed for 18 choux puffs.

	12 choux puffs	18 choux puffs
Flour	3 ounces	
Water	5 ounces	
Eggs	2	

16 Here is a pattern sequence.

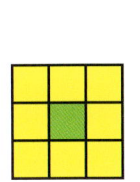

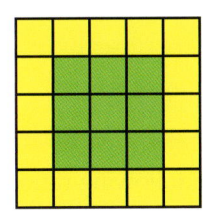

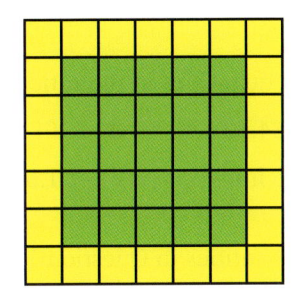

a Does the ratio 'number of green squares : number of yellow squares' increase, decrease or stay the same as the shapes get bigger?
Show how you worked out your answer.

b Draw your own sequence where the ratio of the number of green squares to the number of yellow squares stays the same as the shapes get bigger.

Learn... 10.2 Using ratios to find quantities

You can use ratios to find numbers and quantities.

You can find:
- the number of boys and the number of girls in a school

if you know
- the ratio of boys to girls

and
- the total number of students.

For example, in a school of 1000 students, the ratio of boys to girls is 9 : 11

This means that for every 9 boys there are 11 girls, whatever the size of the school.

9 + 11 = 20, so

9 out of every 20 students are boys so $\frac{9}{20}$ of the students are boys. 11 out of every 20 students are girls so $\frac{11}{20}$ of the students are girls.

The school has 1000 students, so to find the number of boys, work out $\frac{9}{20}$ of 1000.

To find the number of girls work out $\frac{11}{20}$ of 1000.

$\frac{1}{20}$ of 1000 = 1000 ÷ 20 = 50

Number of boys = 50 × 9 = 450

Number of girls = 50 × 11 = 550

> **AQA Examiner's tip**
> Check that the number of boys and the number of girls add up to the total number of students in the school.

Example: Jane is 6 years old and Karl is 10 years old.

Their grandmother gives them £24 to share between them in the ratio of their ages.

How much does each child receive?

Solution: The ratio of the Jane's age to Karl's age is $6:10 = 3:5$

The total number of parts is $3 + 5 = 8$, so Jane gets $\frac{3}{8}$ of £24 and Karl gets $\frac{5}{8}$ of £24.

$\frac{1}{8}$ of £24 is £24 ÷ 8 = £3

So Jane gets $3 \times \frac{1}{8} = 3 \times £3 = £9$ and Karl gets $5 \times \frac{1}{8} = 5 \times £3 = £15$

AQA Examiner's tip
Remember to add the numbers in the ratio to find the total number of parts. This is what you have to divide by to find the size of each part.

Practise... 10.2 Using ratios to find quantities

1 Divide these numbers and quantities in the ratio 1 : 2

a 150
b 300
c £4.50
d 6 litres
e £1.50
f 1.5 litres

2 Divide the numbers and quantities in Question 1 in the following ratios.

a 1 : 4
b 2 : 3
c 3 : 7
d 1 : 2 : 7

3 In a savings account, the ratio of the amount invested to the interest paid is 50 : 1

Approximately how much is the interest paid on a savings account that has a total of £10 525 in it?

4 The angles of any pentagon add up to 540 degrees.
The angles of one pentagon are in the ratio 2 : 3 : 4 : 5 : 6
What is the size of the largest angle?

5 This table shows the ratio of carbohydrate to fat to protein in some foods.

Food	Carbohydrate : fat : protein
Chicken sandwich	1 : 1 : 1
Grilled salmon	0 : 1 : 1
Yoghurt (whole milk)	1 : 2 : 1
Taco chips	10 : 4 : 1
Bread	7 : 2 : 1
Milk	2 : 3 : 2

a Work out the amount of fat in 150 g of each of the foods.
Use a calculator for the milk ratios as they do not work out easily.
Round your answers to the nearest 5 grams.

b Which of these foods would you avoid if you were on a low-fat diet?

c How many grams of yoghurt would you need to eat to have 100 g of protein?

d Which of these foods would you avoid if you were on a low-carbohydrate diet?

Chapter 10 Ratio and proportion

6 Bronze for coins can be made of copper, tin and zinc in the ratio 95 : 4 : 1

  a How much of each metal is needed to make 1 kilogram of bronze?

  b How much of each metal is needed to make 10 kilograms of bronze?

  c How much of each metal is needed to make half a kilogram of bronze?

  d How much zinc would there be in a coin weighing 6 grams?

7 Leena invested £10 000 in a business and Kate invested £3500.

At the end of the year, Leena and Kate share the profits of £70 000 in the ratio of their investments.

How much does each receive?

8 The table shows the number of pupils in five schools together with the ratio of the numbers of boys to the number of girls.

  a Which school has the greatest number of boys? Show working to justify your answer.

  c Which school has the greatest proportion of boys? Show working to justify your answer.

School	Total number of students	Boy : girl ratio
School A	750	1 : 1
School B	900	4 : 5
School C	1800	4 : 5
School D	1326	6 : 7
School E	1184	301 : 291

Learn... 10.3 The unitary method

You can use the **unitary method** to do all types of percentages as well as ratio and proportion. The method is based on finding the amount or cost of **one** unit (hence the name 'unitary').

So if you know how much 20 litres of petrol cost, you can find the cost of one litre and then the cost of any number of litres.

Example: A teacher pays £27.60 for 6 calculators.

How much does he pay for 15 calculators at the same price each?

Solution: 6 calculators cost £27.60

So 1 calculator costs $\frac{£27.60}{6}$ = £4.60 (divide the cost of 6 calculators by 6)

So 15 calculators cost 15 × £4.60 = £69 (multiply the cost of 1 calculator by 15)

All the calculating can be left to the end if you prefer:

6 calculators cost £27.60

1 calculator costs $\frac{£27.60}{6}$

15 calculators cost $15 \times \frac{£27.60}{6}$ = £69

Dividing by 6 and multiplying by 15 can be done in one step using the multiplier $\frac{15}{6}$, which is $2\frac{1}{2}$

Cost of 15 calculators = £27.60 × $2\frac{1}{2}$ = £69

This is the same as $\frac{£27.60}{6} \times 15$ or £27.60 × $\frac{15}{6}$

If you feel confident with problems like this, you can do them in one step by combining the multiplication and division, but be careful and check that your answer is sensible.

AQA Examiner's tip

Check that your answer is reasonable.

Bump up your grade

To get a Grade C, you should be able to use the unitary method to work out, for example, the cost of 27 items when you know the cost of 5.

Practise... 10.3 The unitary method

1. To make chilli con carne for 4 people you need 500 g of beef mince. How much do you need for 9 people?

2. Katy can type 8 pages in a hour. How long does she take to type 12 pages?

3. Six identical textbooks weigh 1.8 kg. How much do ten of these textbooks weigh?

4. Tom earns £91.80 for 12 hours work. How much does he earn for 15 hours work at the same rate of pay?

5. A recipe for 12 cheese scones needs 240 g of flour, 60 g of butter and 75 g of cheese. How much of each ingredient do you need to make 20 cheese scones?

6. Six musicians play a piece of music in 15 minutes. How long do nine musicians take to play the piece?

7. Abby travelled for three hours on the motorway and covered 190 miles.
   a How far would Abby travel in five hours at the same average speed?
   b How far would she travel in half an hour?
   c How long would it take her to travel 250 miles?

8. Dave drove 246 miles and used 25.4 litres of diesel.
   a How many litres of diesel does Dave need for a 400 mile journey?
   b How far can he go on 10 litres of diesel?
   c What assumption do you have to make to answer these questions?

9. Here are prices for Minty toothpaste.

Size	Amount of toothpaste	Price
Small	50 ml	£0.99
Standard	75 ml	£1.10
Large	100 ml	£1.28

   Which size gives the best value for money?
   You must show your working.

10. These are prices for different packs of bird seed.

Pack size	Price
5.50 kg	£15.65
12.75 kg	£28.00
25.50 kg	£53.00

    a Find the cost of 1 kg of bird seed for each of the different pack sizes.
    b Which pack offers best value for money?
    c Find the cost of a 25.50 kg pack if the price per kg was the same as for the 5.50 kg pack.
    d Give one advantage and one disadvantage of buying a 25.50 kg pack.

Chapter 10 Ratio and proportion 143

11 The weights of objects on other planets are proportional to their weights on Earth. A person weighing 540 newtons on Earth would weigh 90 newtons on the Moon and 1350 newtons on Jupiter.

    a What would a teenager weighing 360 newtons on Earth weigh on Jupiter?

    b What would a rock weighing 10 newtons on the Moon weigh on Earth?

    c What would an astronaut weighing 130 newtons on the Moon weigh on Jupiter?

    d Express the ratio 'weight of object on Earth : weight of object on Moon : weight of object on Jupiter' in its simplest form.

12 Sajid worked for 8 hours and was paid £30.

    a How much will he be paid for working 10 hours at the same rate of pay?

    b Complete a copy of this table. Plot the values in the table as points on a graph, using the numbers of hours worked as the x-coordinates and the money earned as the corresponding y-coordinates.

Number of hours worked	0	2	4	6	8	10
Money earned (£)						

    c Explain why the points should lie in a straight line through (0, 0).

    d Show how to use the graph to find out how much Sajid earns in 5 hours.

13 You may already know about Fibonacci sequences.

Each term is found by adding together the previous two terms.

Starting with 1, 1, the series continues:

1, 1, 2 (as 1 + 1 = 2)
1, 1, 2, 3 (as 1 + 2 = 3)
1, 1, 2, 3, 5, 8, ...

Carry on the sequence until you have at least 20 terms (you could use a spreadsheet).

Work out, in the form $1 : n$, the ratio of:

    term 1 to term 2
    term 2 to term 3
    term 3 to term 4
    and so on.

What do you notice about the ratios as you go through the series?

10 Assess

1 A school has 45 teachers and 810 students.
  a Express the ratio of teachers to students in its simplest form.
  b How many teachers would a school of 1200 students need to have the same teacher : student ratio?

2 In a dance class, 30% of the dancers are male.
What is the ratio of male dancers to female dancers?
Give your answer in its simplest form.

3 **a** Write each of the following ratios in its simplest form.
  i $6:8$ **iii** $1000:10$ **v** $2\frac{1}{2}:3\frac{1}{2}$
  ii $27:81$ **iv** $\frac{1}{4}:2$

  b In a choir there are 12 boys and 18 girls.
  i Express this as a ratio in its simplest form.

  Two more boys and two more girls join the choir.
  ii Express the new ratio in its simplest form.

4 To make sugar syrup, 100 grams of sugar is mixed with 250 ml of water.
  a How many grams of sugar are mixed with 1000 ml (one litre) of water?
  b How much water is mixed with 150 grams of sugar?

5 Darren gets 16 out of 20 in Test A and 20 out of 25 in Test B.
  a In which test did he do better?
  b The next test is marked out of 30. How many marks will Darren need to do as well as he did on Test A?

6 Divide £12 in the ratio:
  a $1:2$ **b** $1:5$ **c** $1:6$

Explain why part **c** is more difficult than part **a** and part **b**.

7 Jamie is cooking omelettes.

To make omelettes for 4 people he uses 6 eggs.

How many eggs does Jamie need to make omelettes for 10 people?

8 Gary, Helen and Izzy start a business.
Gary invests £2000, Helen invests £1500 and Izzy invests £2500.
They agree to share any profits in the ratio of their investments.

In one year the business makes £8100 profit.
How much more does Izzy receive than Helen?

9 The supermarkets 'Lessprice' and 'Lowerpay' both sell packs of pens.

'Lessprice' sells a pack of 5 pens for £1.25.

'Lowerpay' sells a pack of 6 pens for £1.44.

Which supermarket gives the greater value?

10 It takes Kelly 25 seconds to run 200 m. At the same pace, how long will it take her to run:

   a 56 m

   b 128 m?

11 The table shows the approximate population and the number of doctors in some countries of the world.

Country	Population (millions)	Number of doctors
Cuba	10.9	64 300
Israel	5.4	20 600
Italy	57.2	240 000
Nigeria	108.4	30 400
Tanzania	29.7	594
Thailand	58.4	21 600
UK	58.3	128 000
USA	263.6	606 000

   a In which country is the ratio of doctors : population the greatest?

   b Work out the number of doctors in each country if the doctors are shared out equally among the total population.

12 A litre of paint covers 15 m^2 of woodwork.

   a How much paint is needed for 50 m^2 of woodwork?

   b You can buy the paint in the different sizes of tin shown.
          What would you buy to paint 50 m^2 of woodwork?
          Explain your answer.

   750 ml £8.98   1 litre = 1000 ml

   2.5 litres £13.98   1 litre = 1000 ml

AQA Examination-style questions

1 Year 10 and Year 11 students are in an assembly.
Here are some facts about the students in the assembly.

Year	boys : girls	Student data
10	4 : 5	84 boys
11	2 : 3	150 students

Work out the total number of girls in the assembly.
You **must** show your working.

(5 marks)

AQA 2008

11 Area and volume 1

Objectives

Examiners would normally expect students who get these grades to be able to:

D
convert between square units such as changing 2.6 m² to cm²

C
convert between cube units such as changing 3.7 m³ to cm³

find the volume of prisms including cylinders

find the surface area of simple prisms.

Did you know?

Optical prisms

In the study of light, a **prism** is a transparent optical element with flat, polished surfaces that can be used to refract light (break light up) into different colours.

In Isaac Newton's time, it was believed that white light was colourless, and that the prism itself produced the colour. Newton's experiments convinced him that all the colours already existed in the light, and that particles of light were fanned out because particles with different colours travelled with different speeds through the prism. This causes light of different colours to leave the prism at different angles, creating an effect similar to a rainbow. So a prism can be used to separate a beam of white light into its spectrum of colours.

The traditional geometrical shape is that of a triangular prism with a triangular base and rectangular sides, but there are other shapes that are also known as prisms.

Key terms

dimension
solid
cross-section
prism
volume
surface area
face
net

You should already know:

✔ how to find the area of rectangles, triangles, parallelograms and circles

✔ how to convert between metric units, such as centimetres to metres

✔ how to find the volume of a solid by counting cubes

✔ that area is measured in square units and volume in cube units

✔ how to draw simple nets.

Chapter 11 Area and volume 1

Learn... 11.1 Volume of a prism

Shapes such as rectangles have two **dimensions**: length and width.

Shapes that have a third dimension such as thickness or height are called **solids**.

Solids that have the same **cross-section** all the way through the shape are called **prisms**.

Here are some prisms with their cross-sections shaded.

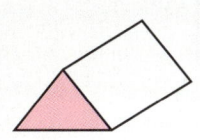

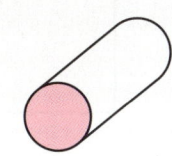

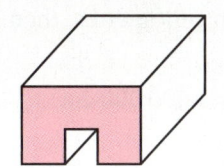

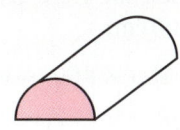

The formula for calculating the **volume** of a prism is:

volume = area of cross-section × length

Remember that the units should always be stated.

AQA Examiner's tip
This formula will be given on the exam paper.

Example: Work out the volume of each of these prisms.

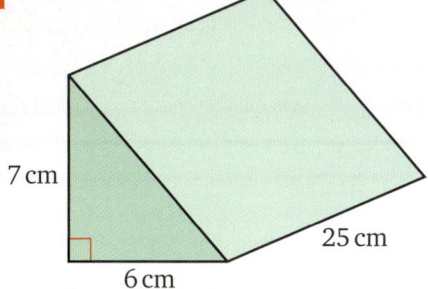

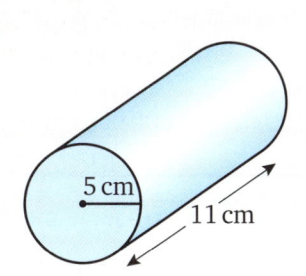

Not drawn accurately

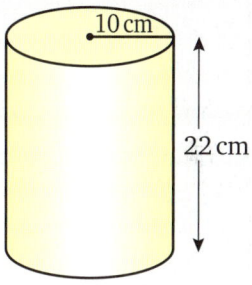

a 7 cm, 6 cm, 25 cm

b 5 cm, 11 cm

c 10 cm, 22 cm

Solution:

a The cross-section of this prism is a right-angled triangle with base 6 cm and perpendicular height 7 cm.

Area of cross-section = $\frac{1}{2}$ × base × height = $\frac{1}{2}$ × 6 × 7 = 21 cm^2

Volume = area of cross-section × length
= 21 × 25 = 525 cm^3

AQA Examiner's tip
Remember:
- area is measured in square units (such as cm^2)
- volume is measured in cube units (such as cm^3).

b The cross-section of this prism is a circle of radius 5 cm.

Area of a circle = πr^2 so area of cross-section = $\pi × 5^2 = 25\pi$ cm^2

Volume = area of cross-section × height
= 25 × π × 11 = 863.9 cm^3 (to 1 d.p.)

c The cross-section of this prism is a circle of radius 10 cm.

Area of a circle = πr^2 so area of cross-section = $\pi × 10^2$ cm^2 = 100π cm^2

Volume = area of cross-section × height
= 100 × π × 22
= 2200π cm^3
= 6911.5 cm^3 (to 1 d.p.)

Notice that all the lengths in the prism (cylinder) in **c** are two times the corresponding lengths in the prism in **b**. The volume of the prism in **c**, however, is eight times the volume of the prism in **b**.)

Volume is always measured in cube units such as mm³, cm³, m³.

Sometimes it is necessary to convert between these units.

You should know that there are 100 centimetres in 1 metre but how many cubic centimetres (cm³) are there in 1 cubic metre (m³)?

This cube has sides of 1 metre. Its volume is $1 \times 1 \times 1 = 1\,m^3$

If the dimensions of the cube were given in centimetres, then each side would measure 100 cm.

The volume would be $100 \times 100 \times 100 = 1\,000\,000\,cm^3$

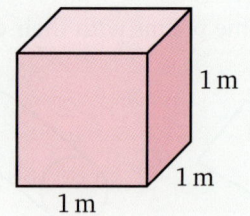

So $1\,m^3 = 1\,000\,000\,cm^3$

In the same way, the area of the base can be found in square metres or square centimetres.

The area of the base of this cube is $1 \times 1 = 1\,m^2$

In centimetres the area of the base is $100 \times 100 = 10\,000\,cm^2$

So $1\,m^2 = 10\,000\,cm^2$

So:
$1\,m = 100\,cm$
$1\,m^2 = 100\,cm \times 100\,cm = 10\,000\,cm^2$
$1\,m^3 = 100\,cm \times 100\,cm \times 100\,cm = 1\,000\,000\,cm^3$

Example: a Convert $24\,500\,cm^2$ to square metres.
  b Convert $5\,m^2$ to square centimetres.
  c Convert $7\,250\,000\,cm^3$ to cubic metres.

Solution: a To convert cm² to m² divide by 10 000.
    $24\,500 \div 10\,000 = 2.45\,m^2$
  b To convert m² to cm² multiply by 10 000.
    $5 \times 10\,000 = 50\,000\,cm^2$
  c To convert cm³ to m³ divide by 1 000 000.
    $7\,250\,000 \div 1\,000\,000 = 7.25\,m^3$

Practise... 11.1 Volume of a prism D C B A A*

1 Find the volume of these solids.

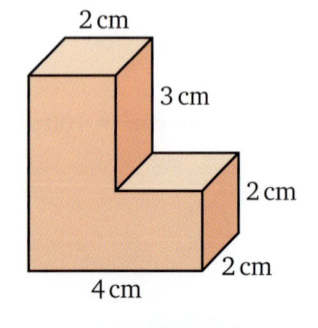

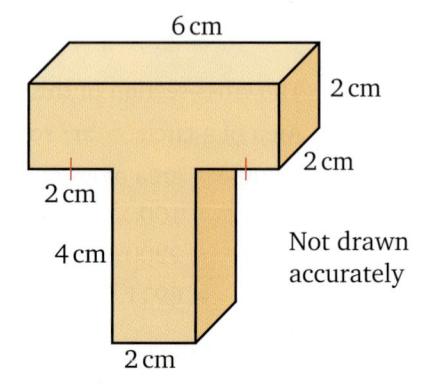

a 2 cm, 3 cm, 2 cm, 4 cm, 2 cm

b 6 cm, 2 cm, 2 cm, 2 cm, 4 cm, 2 cm

Not drawn accurately

Hint
Divide each solid into cuboids.

2 **a** Convert the following areas to square centimetres.
  - **i** 4.6 m²
  - **ii** 23 m²
  - **iii** 9 m²
  - **iv** 0.5 m²
  - **v** 270 mm²
  - **vi** 8000 mm²

b Convert the following areas to square metres.
  - **i** 300 000 cm²
  - **ii** 75 000 cm²
  - **iii** 57 600 cm²
  - **iv** 8500 cm²

3 This cuboid has a volume of 432 m³.

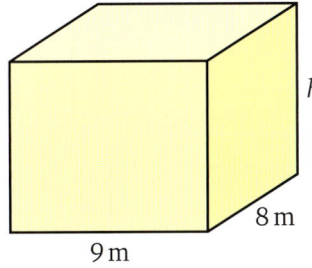

8 m, 9 m, h — Not drawn accurately

Work out the height, h, of the cuboid.

4 The area of cross-section of each prism is given in these diagrams.

Work out the volume of each prism.
Remember to state the units of each answer.

a 22 cm², 8 cm

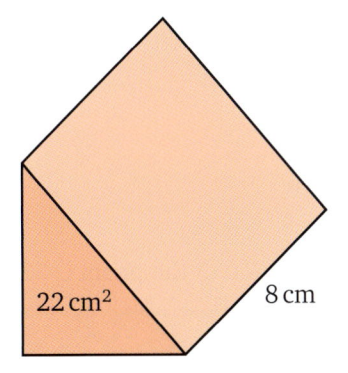

c 36 cm², 15 cm

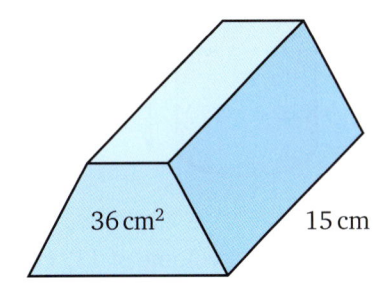

Not drawn accurately

b 14.5 cm², 10 cm

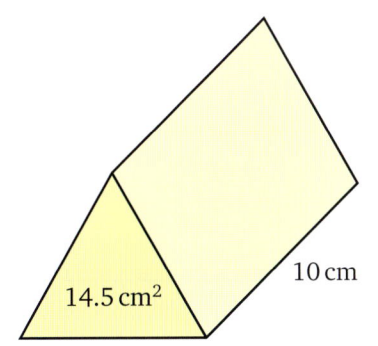

d 9.2 m², 12 m

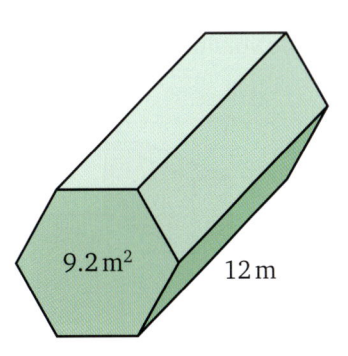

5 **a** Convert the following volumes to cubic centimetres.
  - **i** 8 m³
  - **ii** 3.2 m³
  - **iii** 0.765 m³
  - **iv** 0.0568 m³
  - **v** 15 600 mm³
  - **vi** 950 mm³

b Convert the following volumes to cubic metres.
  - **i** 2 360 000 cm³
  - **ii** 56 000 000 cm³
  - **iii** 473 100 cm³

6 Work out the volume of each of these triangular prisms.

a 9 mm, 8 mm, 15 mm

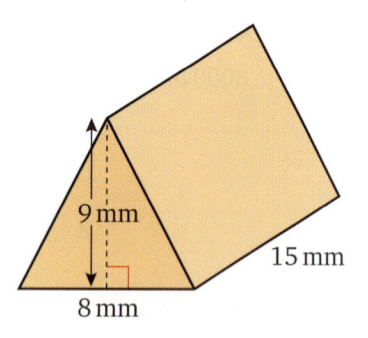

b 7.4 cm, 11.2 cm, 4 cm

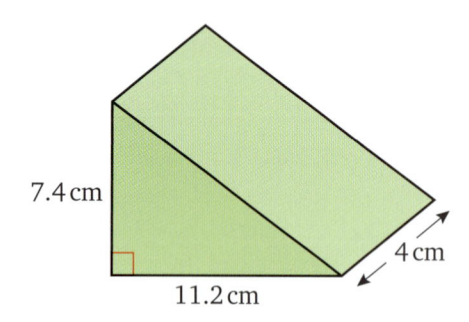

c 4 m, 6 m, 8 m

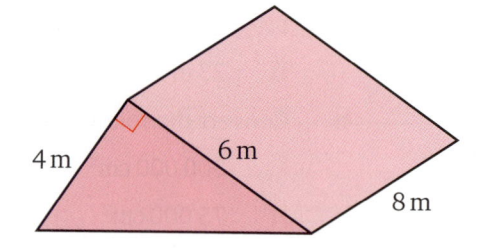

Not drawn accurately

7 Work out the volume of each cylinder.

a 6 cm, 14 cm

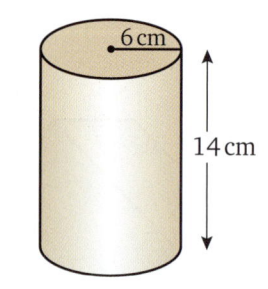

b 8.4 m, 32 m

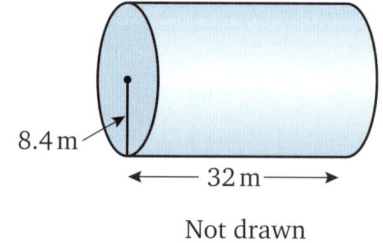

Not drawn accurately

c 17.5 mm, 10 mm

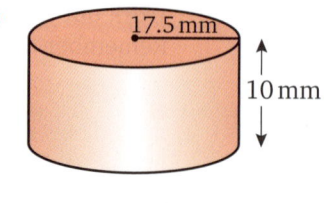

8 A prism has a volume of 132 cm³. The area of the cross-section of the prism is 33 cm². Work out the height of the prism.

9 For each prism shown below, work out:

i   the area of the cross-section
ii the volume.

Hint
Draw a sketch of the cross-section to help you.

a 1 cm, 10 cm, 8 cm, 6 cm, 7 cm

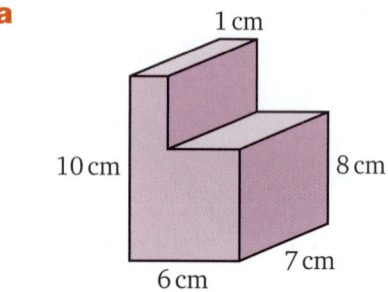

c 3 cm, 4 cm, 17.5 cm, 8 cm

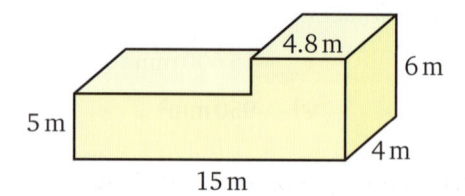

b 4.8 m, 6 m, 5 m, 15 m, 4 m

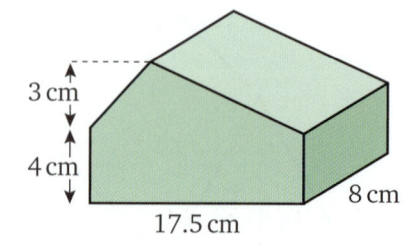

Not drawn accurately

Chapter 11   Area and volume 1   151

10   A cylinder of height 3.2 m has a volume of 15.68 m³.

Work out the area of the base of the cylinder.

> **Bump up your grade**
>
> To get a Grade C you need to know how to work out the volume of a solid from its dimensions. You also need to know how to do reverse calculations where you are given the volume and a dimension, and then work out the area of cross-section.

11   A 25 mm square hole is cut right through the centre of a cuboid as shown.

Find the volume of the remaining cuboid.

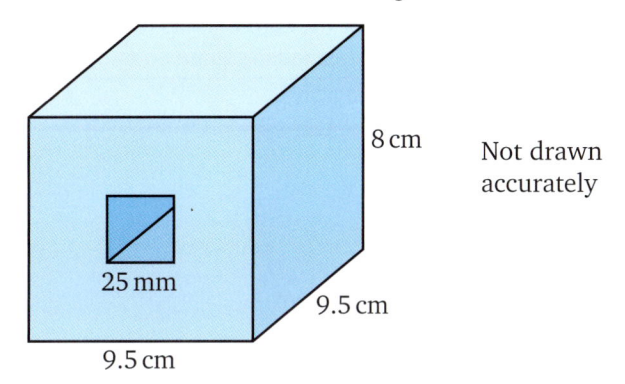

8 cm

25 mm

9.5 cm

9.5 cm

Not drawn accurately

12   The diagram shows a plastic pipe of internal radius 4 cm and length 60 cm.
The plastic has a thickness of 1 cm.

Calculate the volume of plastic in the pipe.

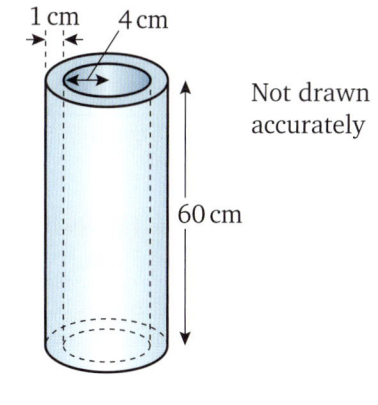

1 cm   4 cm

60 cm

Not drawn accurately

13   The diagram shows a swimming pool.
The pool is filled with water at a rate of 350 litres per minute.

How long will it take to fill the pool?
Give your answer in hours and minutes. (1 m³ = 1000 litres)

25 m

1 m

1.8 m

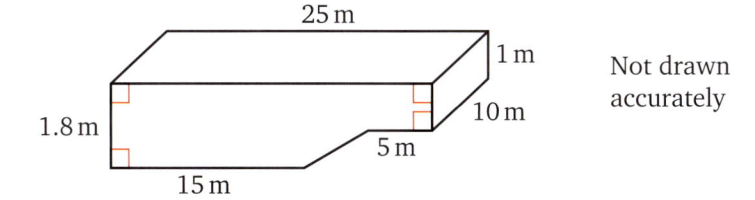

10 m

5 m

15 m

Not drawn accurately

14   At a pre-school playgroup, each of the 36 children are given a beaker of milk.
The beakers are cylinders of radius 3 cm and height 8 cm and are three quarters full.
Each milk carton contains 2.2 litres of milk.
Susie says that three cartons will be enough for all the children.

Is she correct?
Show your working.

> **Hint**
>
> 1000 cm³ = 1 litre

15   The volume of a prism is 90 cm³.

Find three different types of prism with this volume, giving the dimensions of each one.

Learn... 11.2 Surface area of a prism

The total **surface area** of a three-dimensional shape is the sum of the area of all the **faces** (sides) of the shape.

For example, a cube of side 3 cm is made up of six square faces, each measuring 3 cm by 3 cm.

The area of each face is $3 \times 3 = 9 \text{ cm}^2$

The total surface area of all six faces is $6 \times 9 = 54 \text{ cm}^2$

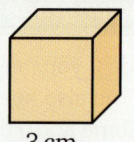

It is often useful to draw the **net** of a solid to help you to see the individual areas.

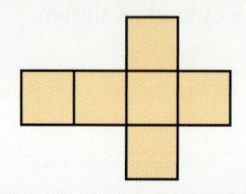

AQA Examiner's tip
Remember to give the correct units for your answer. Area is always measured in square units.

Example: Work out the surface area of this triangular prism.

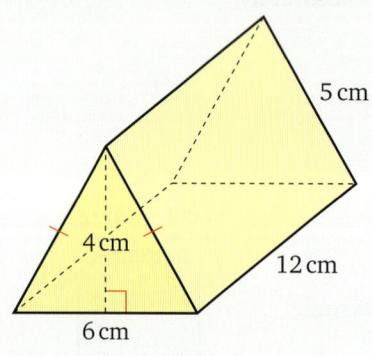

Not drawn accurately

Solution: Draw the net.

The middle rectangle, which is the base, has area $6 \times 12 = 72 \text{ cm}^2$

The two outer rectangles, which are the sloping faces, each have area $5 \times 12 = 60 \text{ cm}^2$

The triangles each have area $\frac{1}{2} \times 6 \times 4 = 12 \text{ cm}^2$

Total surface area $= 72 + (2 \times 60) + (2 \times 12)$
$= 216 \text{ cm}^2$

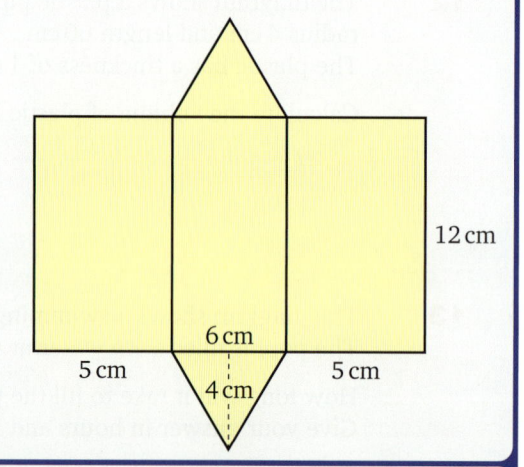

Example: Work out the surface area of this hollow cylinder.

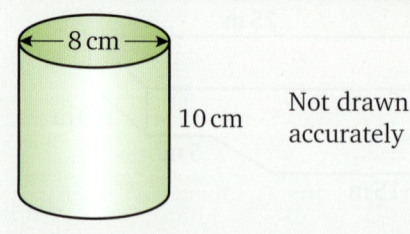

Not drawn accurately

Solution: A hollow cylinder has no base or top and is also called an open cylinder.

The curved surface of the cylinder forms a rectangle when the net is drawn.

The length of the rectangle is equal to the circumference of the circular end of the cylinder.

Circumference $= 2\pi r$ so the curved surface area $= 2\pi r \times h$

In the cylinder shown, the radius is 4 cm (half the diameter).

Area of the curved surface $= 2 \times \pi \times 4 \times 10 = 80\pi$ or 251.3 cm^2 (to 1 d.p.)

If a cylinder has a top or a base then the area of the circular top and/or base must be added to find the total surface area.

Chapter 11 Area and volume 1 153

Practise... 11.2 Surface area of a prism | D C B A A*

The shapes in these exercises are not drawn accurately.

1 Here is a net of a cuboid.

Work out the surface area of the cuboid.

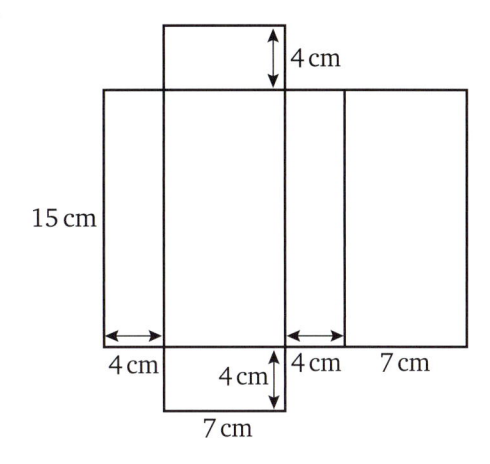

15 cm, 4 cm, 4 cm, 4 cm, 7 cm, 7 cm, 4 cm

2 Here is a net of a triangular prism.

Work out the surface area.
Give your answer in:

a m²   **b** cm²

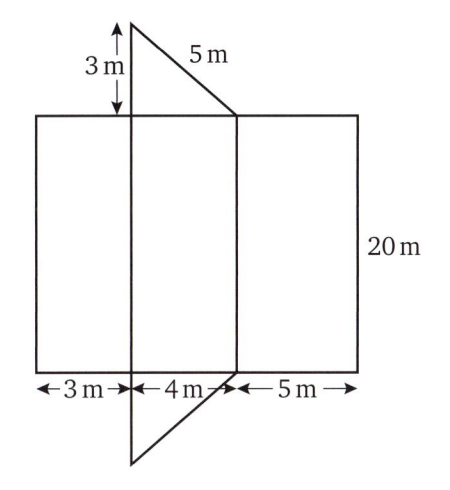

3 m, 5 m, 20 m, 3 m, 4 m, 5 m

3 Calculate the total surface area of cubes with these side lengths.

a 7 cm   **b** 10 cm   **c** 5.4 cm

4 Calculate the total surface area of these cuboids.

a 3 cm, 8 cm, 4 cm

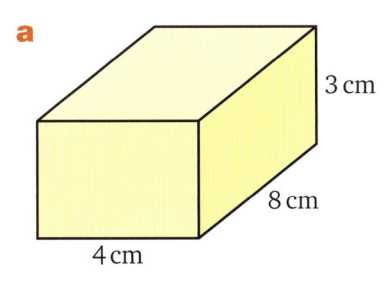

b 22 mm, 18 mm, 5.5 mm

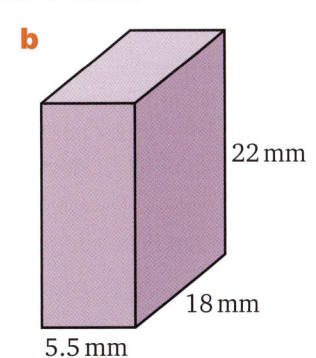

c 3.2 m, 4 m, 7.5 m

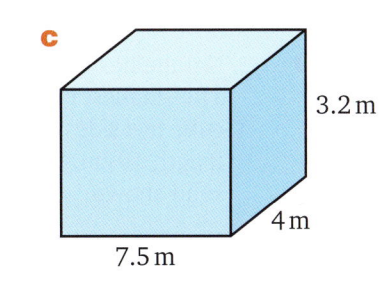

5 Work out the surface area of each triangular prism.

AQA Examiner's tip
Sketch a net to help you.

a 9.85 mm, 9 mm, 15 mm, 8 mm

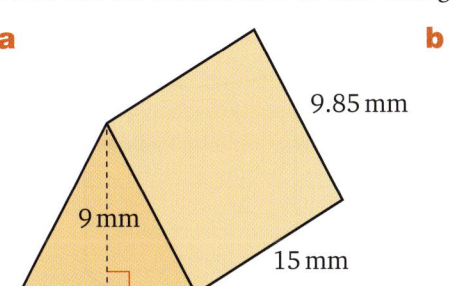

b 7.4 cm, 13.4 cm, 11.2 cm, 4 cm

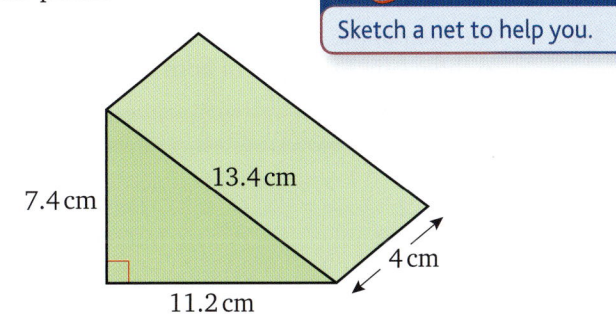

6 Calculate the curved surface area of each of these cylinders.

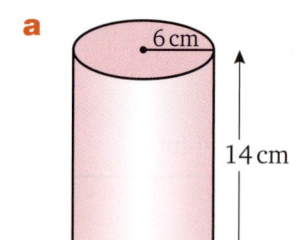

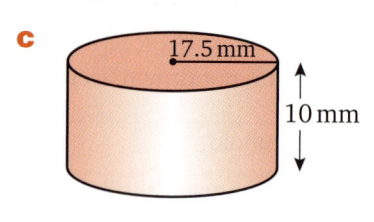

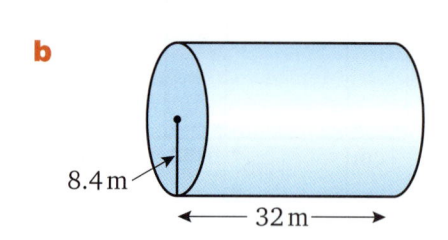

a 6 cm, 14 cm

b 8.4 m, 32 m

c 17.5 mm, 10 mm

7 Here are two closed cylinders. (They have a top and a base.)
Work out the surface area of each cylinder.

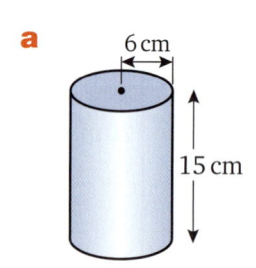

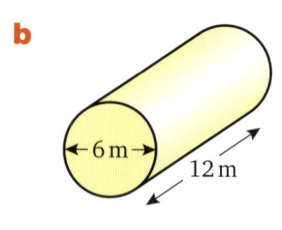

a 6 cm, 15 cm

b 6 m, 12 m

8 Andrew makes wooden jewellery boxes in the shape of cuboids of length 20 cm, width 15 cm and depth 10 cm. Each box has a lid.
The wood costs £18.75 for 1 square metre and on average he wastes 10% of each square metre.
He varnishes the outside of each box when he has made them.
A tin of varnish will cover an area of 1.5 m² and costs £7.99.

What is the cost of making each jewellery box?

9 Natalie has three wooden cubes that she is using in DT.
The smallest cube has sides of length 3 cm. The medium-sized cube has sides of length 6 cm. The largest cube has sides of length 10 cm. She sticks them together to make the solid shown.

Natalie wants to paint the solid red. The tin of red paint she uses will cover an area of 0.5 m².

Will she have enough paint? Show your working.

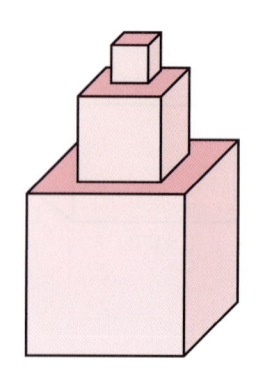

Not drawn accurately

10 The area of the curved surface of this cylinder is equal to three times the area of both ends added together.
Express h in terms of r.

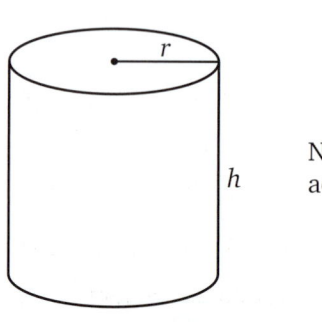

Not drawn accurately

Chapter 11 Area and volume 1   155

11 Assess k!

1 A prism has a total surface area of 0.75 m².

Write this area in cm².

2 The table shows the measurements of some cuboids.

Calculate the total surface area of each cuboid. Remember to state the units of each answer.

Cuboid	Length	Width	Height
a	14 cm	6 cm	3 cm
b	45 mm	22 mm	10 mm
c	3.2 m	6 m	4 m
d	12.4 cm	15.5 cm	11 cm

3 Calculate the volume of this cuboid.

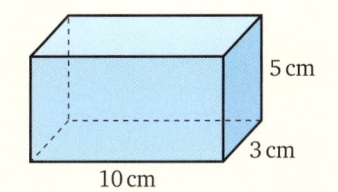

Not drawn accurately
5 cm
3 cm
10 cm

Give your answer in: **a** cm³   **b** mm³

4 Calculate the volume of each of these prisms.

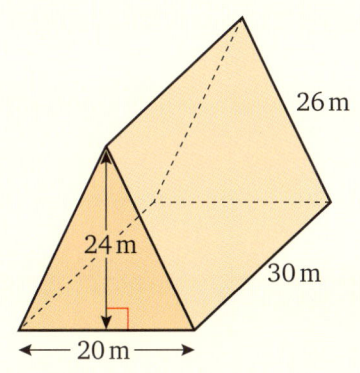

a
26 m
24 m
30 m
20 m

b
4 m
5 m
4 m
15 m
10 m

5 a Work out the total surface area of this triangular prism.

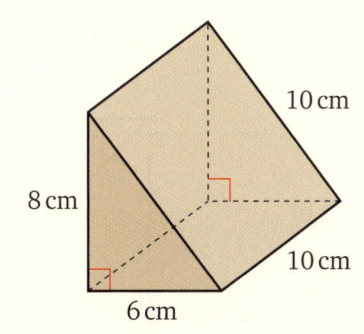

Not drawn accurately
10 cm
8 cm
10 cm
6 cm

b Another triangular prism has measurements double those of the triangular prism above.

What is its total surface area?

Copy and complete the statement 'The new surface area is _____ times the original surface area.'

6 A metal pole is in the shape of a cylinder. It has a radius of 1.5 m and a length of 17 m.

Work out the volume of metal used for the pole.

AQA Examination-style questions

1 The diagram shows a block of wood with uniform cross-section.
The cross-section is made of rectangles.
The block is 65 cm long.

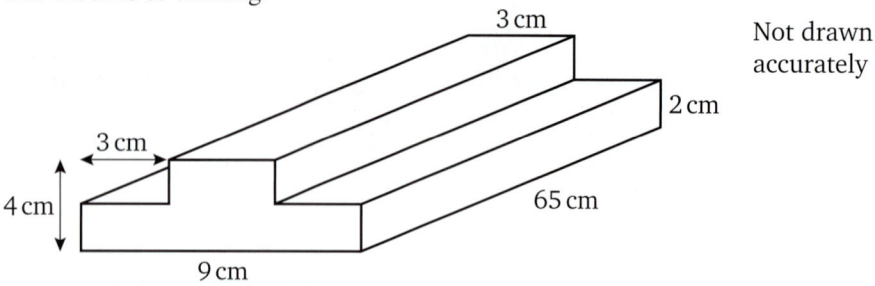

Not drawn accurately

Calculate the volume of the block.
State the units of your answer. *(5 marks)*

AQA 2008

2 The diameter of a solid cylinder is 9.2 cm.
The cylinder is 25 cm long.

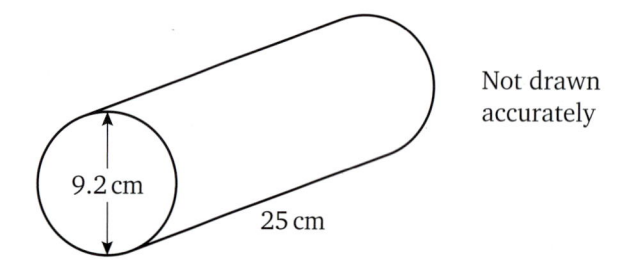

Not drawn accurately

a Calculate the area of one end of the cylinder. *(2 marks)*
b Calculate the **total** surface area of the cylinder.
You **must** show your working. *(3 marks)*

AQA 2007

3 A cuboid is made from centimetre cubes.
The area of the base of the cuboid is 5 cm^2.
The volume of the cuboid is 10 cm^3.
Work out the surface area of the cuboid.
State the units of your answer. *(5 marks)*

AQA 2005

4 The diagram shows a cube.
The volume of the cube is 1000 cm^3.

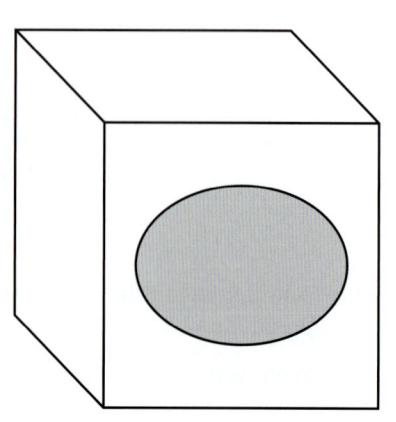

a A label covers half the area of the front of the cube.
Calculate the area of the label.
Show your working. *(3 marks)*

b The cube contains 200 cm^3 of water.
How much more water is needed for the cube to be three-quarters full?
Give your answers in litres. *(3 marks)*

AQA 2007

12 Real-life graphs

Objectives

Examiners would normally expect students who get these grades to be able to:

D

interpret real-life graphs

find simple average speed from distance–time graphs

recognise from a distance–time graph when the fastest average speed takes place

C

find the average speed in km/h from a distance–time graph with time in minutes

B

discuss and interpret graphs modelling real situations.

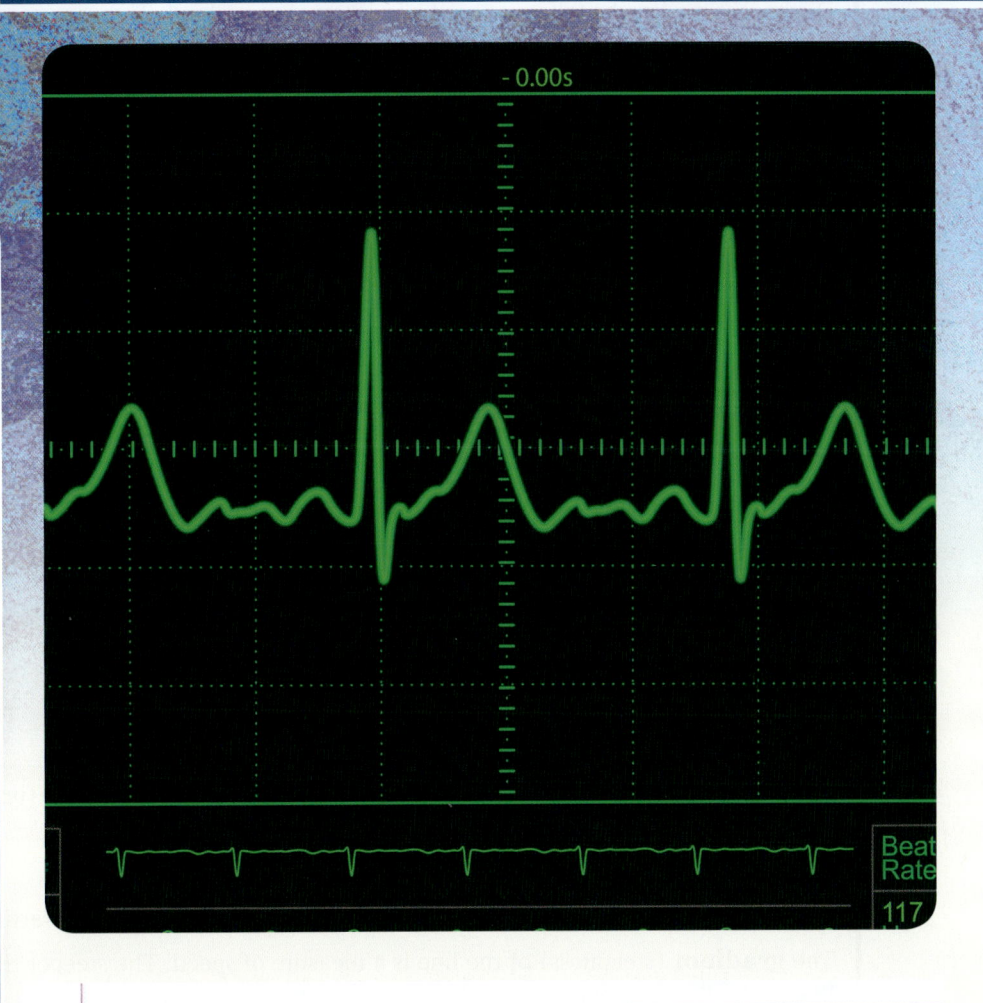

Key terms

speed
gradient

Did you know?

...how important graphs can be?

Graphs that record information such as heart rate, heart beats and blood pressure are very important. Real-life graphs such as these are used in hospitals and can save lives.

You should already know:

✔ how to plot points
✔ how to draw, scale and label axes
✔ how to plot and interpret a line graph
✔ how to plot and use conversion graphs
✔ how to solve simple problems involving proportion
✔ common units for measuring distance, speed and time
✔ how to interpret horizontal lines on a distance–time graph
✔ how to find distances from distance–time graphs.

Learn... 12.1 Distance–time graphs

Distance–time graphs tell you about a journey of some kind. They are used to compare **speeds**.
The diagrams show how far Sam and Richard have cycled over a race of 30 metres.

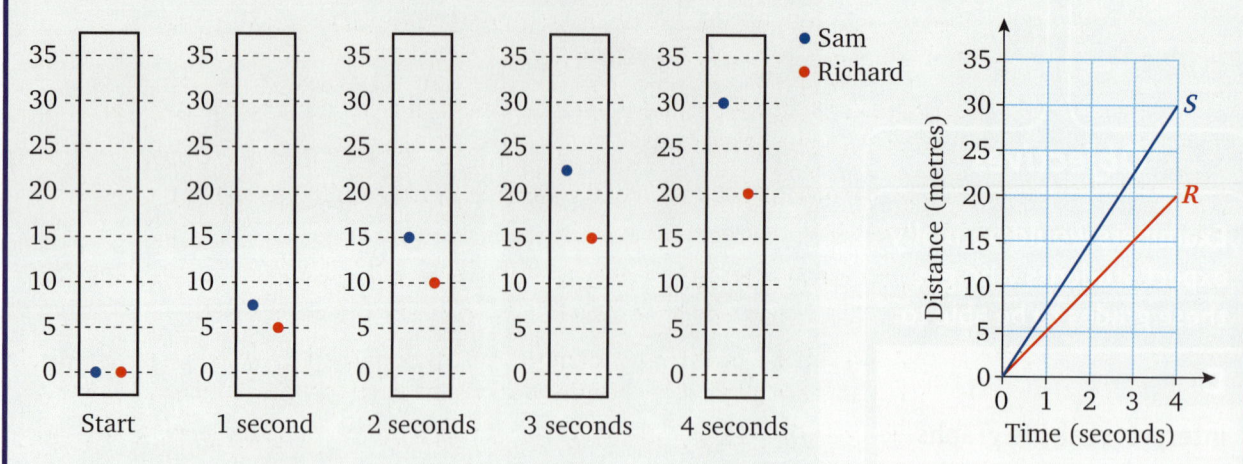

It is easy to compare the speed of the two cyclists.

The vertical axis is always distance.
The horizontal axis is always time.

The distance is always from a particular point, usually the starting point.
The higher up the graph, the further the distance from the starting point.

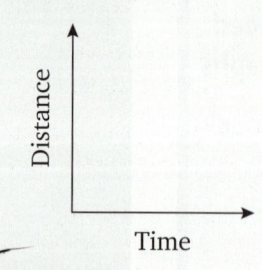

Time may be the actual time using am and pm or the 24 hour clock.
Time could be the number of minutes or hours from your starting point.

If the graph goes back to the horizontal axis, it shows a return to the starting point.

The **gradient** (steepness) of the line is a measure of speed. The steeper the line the faster the speed. A horizontal line represents a speed of zero (i.e. stopped).

In Chapter 6 you learnt how to find the gradient of a straight line. The same method is used to find speeds from a distance–time graph, i.e. use

$$\text{Speed} = \frac{\text{distance travelled}}{\text{time taken}}$$

For the speed to be worked out in miles per hour the distance must be in miles and the time in hours.

To find the average speed for a whole journey, use

$$\text{Average speed} = \frac{\text{total distance travelled}}{\text{total time taken}}$$

Example: The distance–time graph shows Michael's journey to and from the beach.

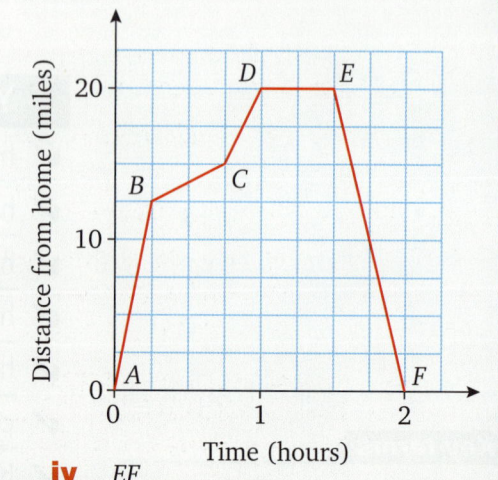

a Describe the journey giving reasons for the shape of the graph.

b How far is it to the beach?

c During which part of the journey is Michael travelling the fastest?

d During which part of the journey was Michael most likely to have been held up by road works?

d Calculate Michael's speed in miles per hour for the following sections of the graph
   i   AB   ii   BC   iii   CD   iv   EF

e What was Michael's average speed for the journey to the beach?

f What was Michael's average speed over the two hours?

Solution:

a Michael left home at *A* and travelled at a constant speed for $\frac{1}{4}$ hour to *B*.

He then travelled at a slower constant speed for $\frac{1}{2}$ hour from *B* to *C*.

He then travelled at a faster constant speed for $\frac{1}{4}$ hour from *C* to *D*.

He then stopped for $\frac{1}{2}$ hour.

Then it took $\frac{1}{2}$ hour to return home from *E* to *F*. The graph returns to the horizontal axis. This shows the return journey home.

b The furthest distance Michael goes from *A* is 20 miles. This is the distance from *A* (home) to *D* (the beach).

c Michael is travelling fastest between *AB* as the gradient (steepness) of the line is greatest then.

d Michael is likely to have been held up by road works between *BC* as he is travelling much slower. The gradient (steepness) of the line is least then.

e **i** *AB*: In $\frac{1}{4}$ hour, he travels 12.5 miles. In 1 hour he would travel $4 \times 12.5 = 50$ miles. His speed is 50 miles per hour (mph) (as he would travel 50 miles in 1 hour).

ii *BC*: In $\frac{1}{2}$ hour, he travels 2.5 miles. In 1 hour he would travel $2 \times 2.5 = 5$ miles. His speed is 5 miles per hour (mph).

iii *CD*: In $\frac{1}{4}$ hour, he travels 5 miles. So in 1 hour he would travel $4 \times 5 = 20$ miles. His speed is 20 miles per hour (mph).

iv *EF*: In $\frac{1}{2}$ hour, he travels 20 miles. So in 1 hour he would travel $2 \times 20 = 40$ miles. His speed is 40 miles per hour (mph).

e In 1 hour, he travels 20 miles. His average speed is 20 miles per hour (mph)

f For the whole journey the distance travelled is 40 miles (there **and** back). The time taken is 2 hours.

Average speed = total distance ÷ total time = 40 ÷ 2 = 20 mph.

> **AQA Examiner's tip**
>
> Remember to divide by the time **in hours** when you want to find the average speed in miles per hour, or km per hour.

Practise... 12.1 Distance–time graphs   D C B A A*

1 Sam walks to town to buy a CD and then walks home. The distance–time graph shows his journey.

a How far does Sam walk altogether?

b Sam stops to talk to a friend on his way into town. How long does he stop for?

c When is Sam walking at his fastest? What is his average speed for this part of the journey?

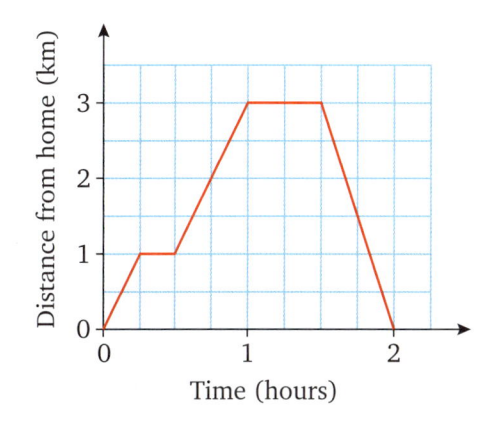

> **AQA Examiner's tip**
>
> The horizontal axis has 4 squares for each hour. This tells you each square is $\frac{1}{4}$ hour. Remember $\frac{1}{4}$ hour = 0.25 hours.

2 Helen completed a short mountain-bike trail. The distance–time graph shows her ride.

  a What was the total distance Helen travelled?

  b Helen enjoyed the ride as there was a really fast section.
   i Between which letters on the graph is this indicated?
   ii How long was this section? Give your answer in km.
   iii How long did it take Helen to ride this section?

  c There was one very steep uphill section.
   i Between which two letters on the graph is this indicated?
   ii How long was this section?
   iii How long did it take Helen to get up the hill?

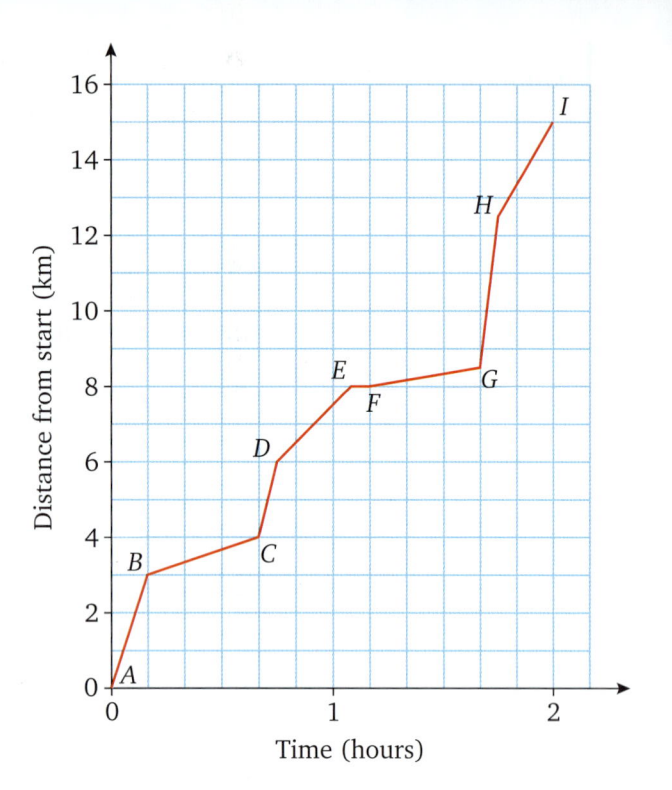

  d Calculate the average speed in km/h for each of the eight sections of the ride.

  e Calculate Helen's average speed for the whole ride.

3 A coach travels from Kendal to Birmingham. The journey is shown in the distance–time graph.

  a The coach stops at some services.
   i What time does it stop at the services?
   ii How long does the coach stop for?
   iii How far are the services from Kendal?

  b At what stage on the graph does the coach join the motorway?

  c How far is the coach from Birmingham when it leaves the motorway?

  d Work out the average speed in mph for each of the five stages in the journey.

  e Find the average speed of the coach between Kendal and Birmingham.

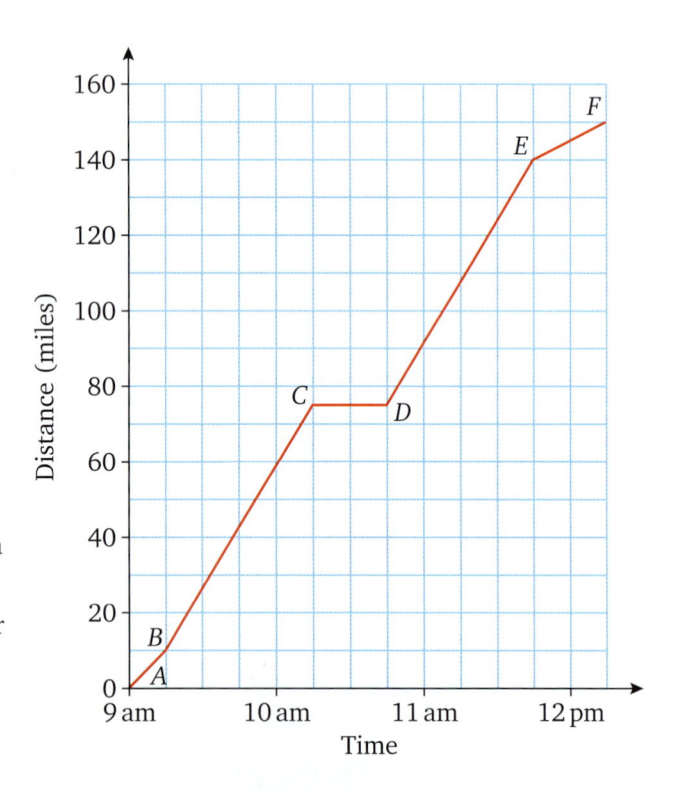

4 Giovanni goes for a ride on his bike in the country.

He starts from the car park and rides for 30 minutes at a steady 12 mph.

He then goes up a hill at 8 mph for 15 minutes.

At the top he stops to admire the view for 15 minutes.

He then rides down back to the car park, which takes him 30 minutes.

Work out Giovanni's average speed in mph for the whole journey.

Hint
You may use a distance–time graph to help answer Question 4.

AQA Examiner's tip
When asked to find the average speed in km/h when time is given in minutes remember to divide by the time taken in **hours**.

Chapter 12 Real-life graphs 161

5 The graph shows the journeys of four students to school in the morning.

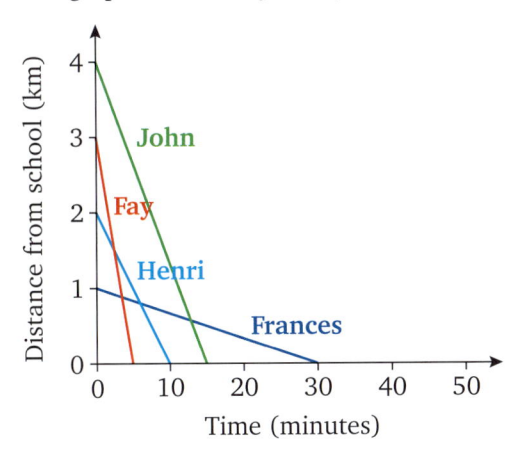

The four students used different ways to get to school.
One student walked, one cycled, one caught the bus and one used the train.

  a How did each student travel to school?
  Give reasons for your answers.

  b Calculate the speed of each student in km/h.

6 Hamish goes for a ride on his bike. His journey is shown in the distance–time graph.

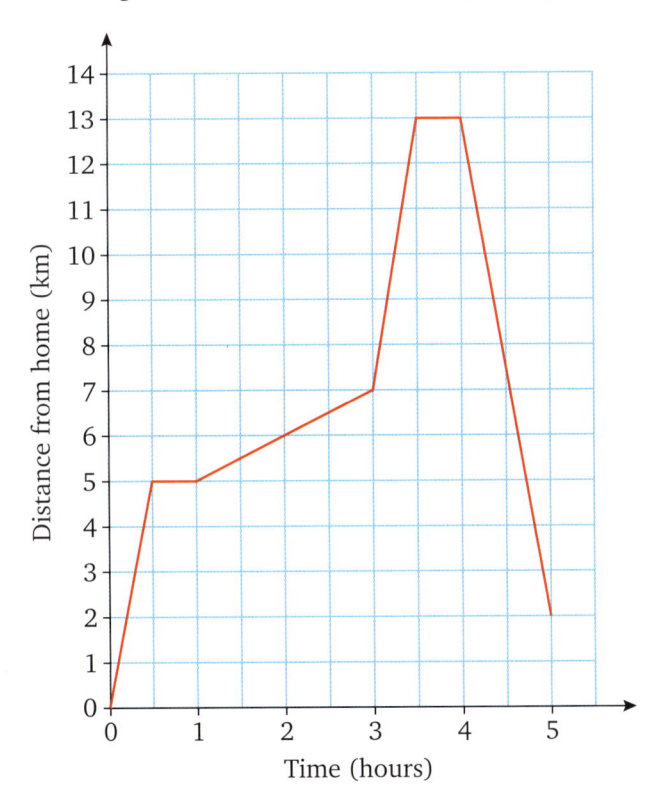

  a When did Hamish fall off his bike?
  b When was Hamish going fastest?
  c Describe his journey in words.
  d What was his average speed for the whole journey?
  e What could be changed in the graph for his average speed to have been 5 km/h?
  f How would the graph be different if Hamish had been unable to cycle after he fell off?

Learn... 12.2 Other real-life graphs

Graphs are useful for tracking changes in a variable such as value, population size, height of a ball or temperature over time.

Examples of graphs

A. Graph showing temperature of a cup of coffee from the time it is made.

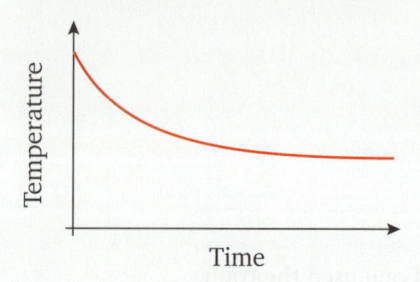

B. Graph showing height of a ball from the time it is thrown.

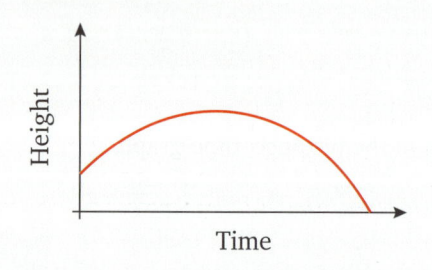

C. Graph showing population growth for a population.

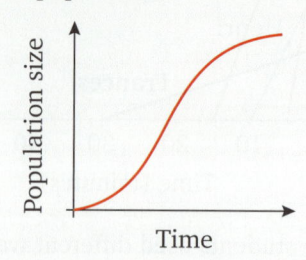

Example: The graph shows how the value of a car has changed over the last eight years.

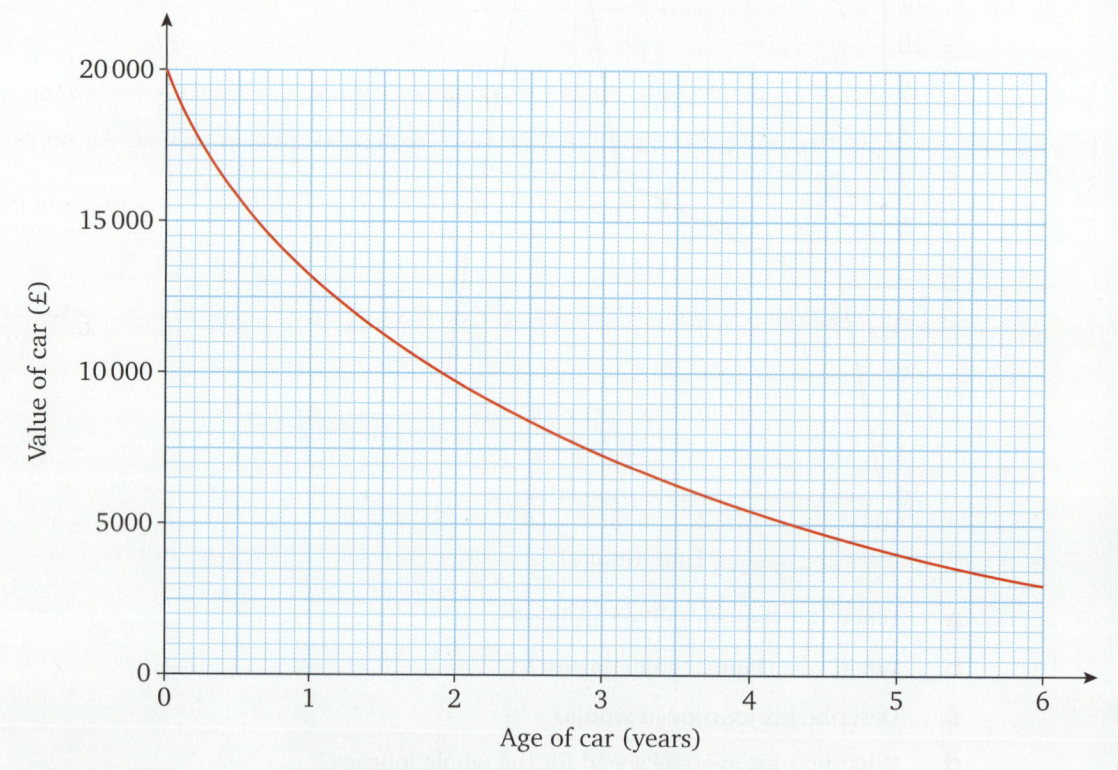

a Describe how the value of the car changes as it gets older.

b How much was the car when it was new?

c How old is the car when it is worth 50% of its initial value?

d Is it appropriate to use the graph to find the value of the car when it is 10 years old? Explain your answer.

Solution:

a The car starts decreasing in value very quickly at the start. As it gets older its value continues to decrease, but it loses value less quickly.

b The car was worth £20 000 when new. This is the value at the 'start' of the graph, when the age was 0 years.

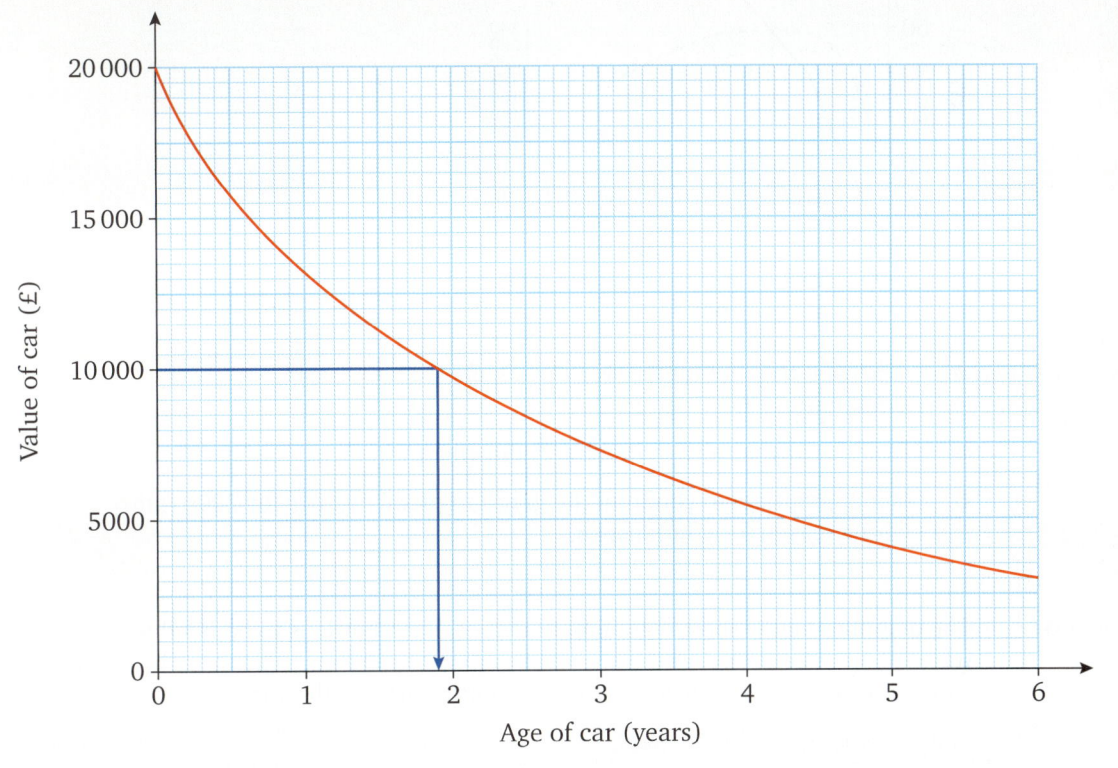

c 50% of £20 000 is £10 000. Read across from £10 000 and down to the 'Age' axis. The car is almost two years old when it is worth 50% of its initial value. The blue arrow shows this on the graph.

d No.
It is difficult to use a curve to make predictions, even if the same pattern continues.

There is no information as to what happens to the car's value after it is six years old so the same pattern may not continue.

Practise... 12.2 Other real-life graphs   D C B A A*

1 The graph shows the temperature of a cup of tea as it cools.

  a What temperature is the tea when it is made?

  b How long does it take the tea to cool to half of its original temperature?

  c Joe looked at the graph and said 'If it carries on cooling like this it will freeze in another half hour'.
  Do you think Joe is correct? Explain your answer.

  d Max said 'If the graph carries on curving like that it will soon start warming up again'.
  Do you think Max is correct? Explain your answer.

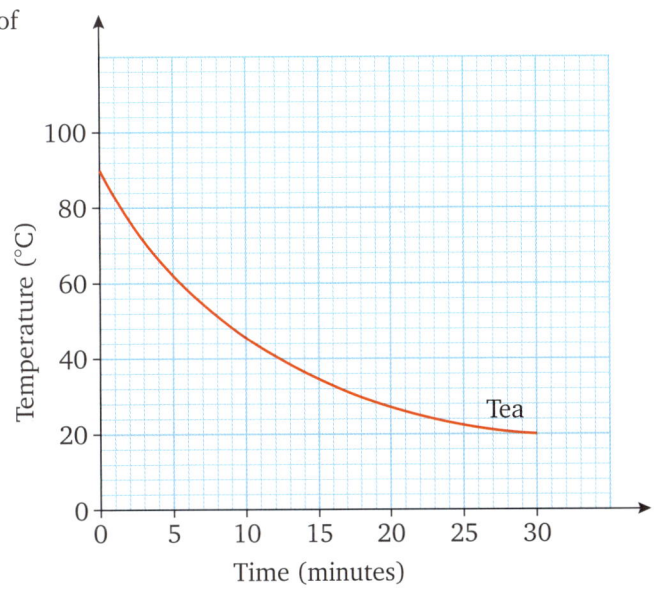

2 The following graph shows how power (kW) and torque (Nm) vary with the speed of the engine (rpm) for a particular car engine.

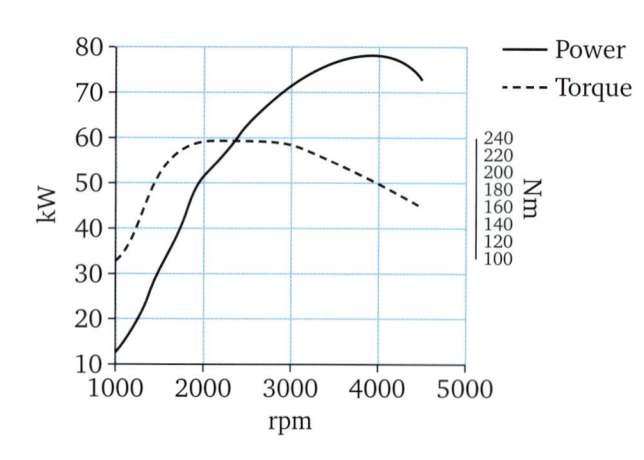

a John said that the torque was at its highest at 4000 rpm.
What mistake has John made?

b Describe any pattern in the graph showing torque.

c Is it appropriate to continue the graph to predict values for 7000 rpm?
Give a reason for your answer.

3 The diagrams below show eight empty bottles. Each bottle is to be filled with water at a constant rate. There are eight graphs, one for each picture. The graph shows how the depth of water, d, in each bottle varies with time, t.

Match each bottle with its graph.

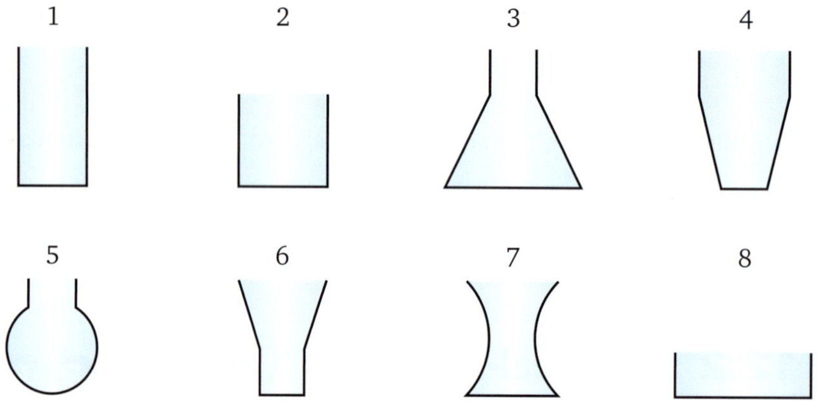

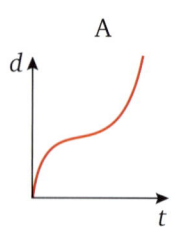

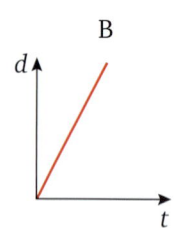

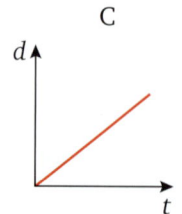

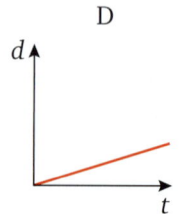

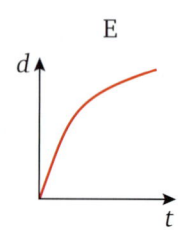

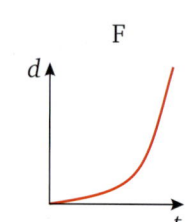

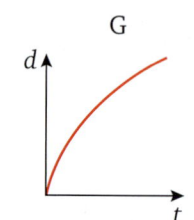

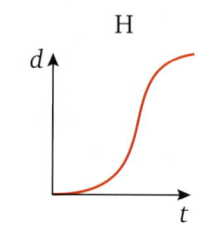

Chapter 12 Real-life graphs   165

4 The following graph shows the depth of water at the end of a pier over a weekend.

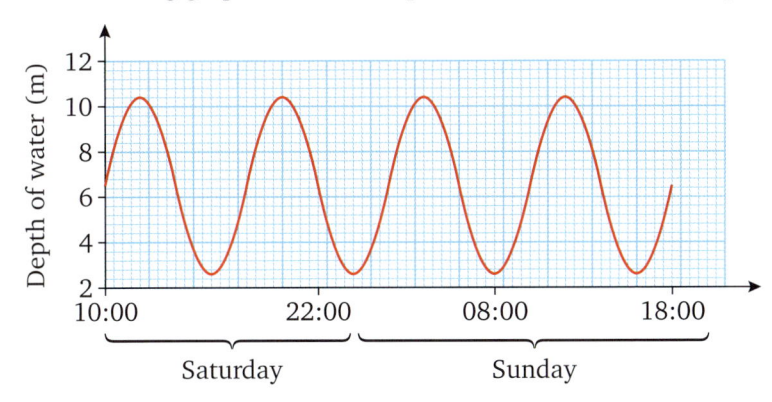

[Graph: Depth of water (m) vs time, showing wave pattern from 10:00 Saturday through 18:00 Sunday, oscillating between approximately 2m and 10m]

- **a** At what time are the high tides on Saturday?
- **b** What is the maximum depth of water at the end of the pier?
- **c** What is the minimum depth of water at the end of the pier?
- **d** What is the length of time between consecutive high tides?
- **e** Cara is on holiday and wants to fish from the end of the pier. She thinks the best time to fish is when the tide has been fully out and is on its way in.
  She has to leave at 17:00 on Saturday to go for tea. She has to leave at 12:00 on Sunday for lunch.
  How much time will she be able to spend fishing on:
  - **i** Saturday
  - **ii** Sunday morning?
- **f** Wendy sails her boat from the end of the pier.
  She needs at least 5 metres of water to launch and land her boat safely.
  She launches her boat at 11 o'clock on Saturday morning.
  - **i** How long does she have before she will not be able to land her boat?
  - **ii** If she is late arriving, what is the next earliest time that she will be able to land her boat?

5 The following graph shows the daylight hours throughout the year at Longtown in hours.

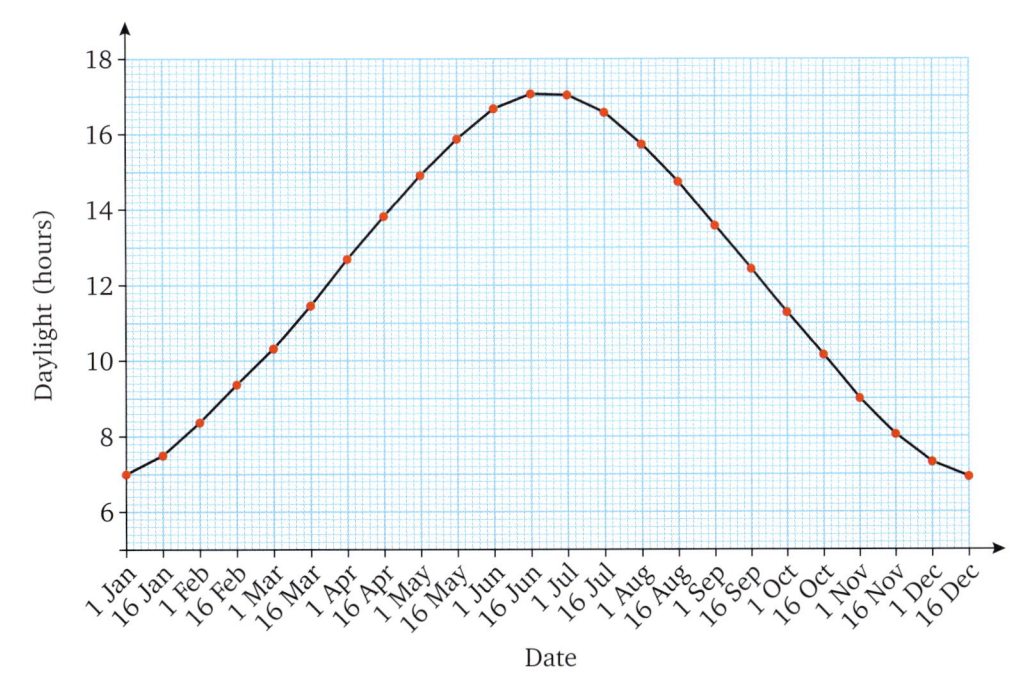

[Graph: Daylight (hours) vs Date, from 1 Jan to 16 Dec, showing curve peaking around late June at about 17 hours and minimum around December/January at about 7 hours]

Use the graph to find:
- **a** the daylight hours for the longest day
- **b** the daylight hours for the shortest day
- **c** the number of hours daylight on George's birthday, 16 April.

6 The following graph shows the thinking distances (blue) and stopping distances (red) for different speeds. (Source: Highway Code.)

The thinking distance is the distance travelled by a car between the driver deciding to brake and actually starting to brake.

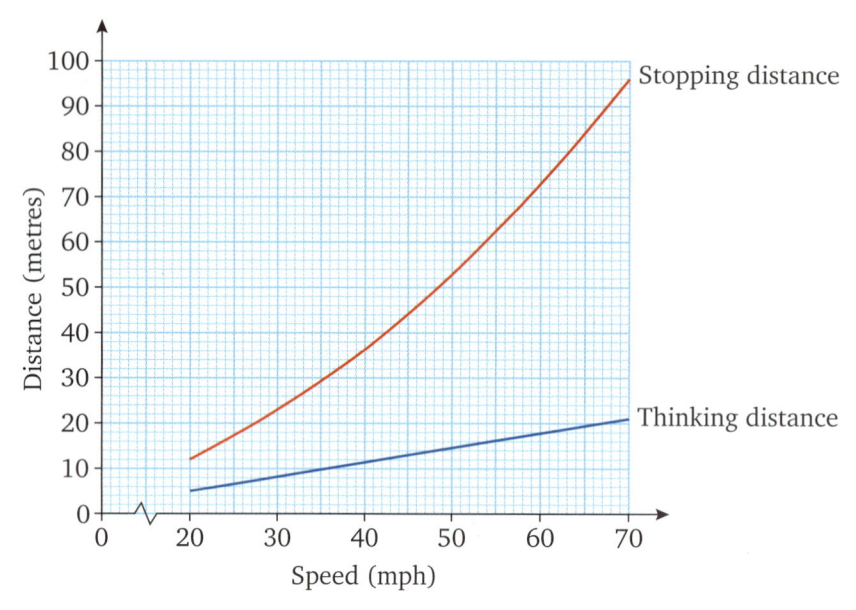

a Describe the patterns in:

  i the thinking distance

  ii the stopping distances.

b Use the graph to find:

  i the thinking distance for a car travelling at 40 mph

  ii the thinking distance for a car travelling at 55 mph

  iii the **stopping** distance for a car travelling at 30 mph

  iv the **stopping** distance for a car travelling at 40 mph.

c The braking distance is the difference between the thinking distance and the stopping distance.

Fred said 'the braking distance for travelling at 60 mph is two times the braking distance for travelling at 30 mph'. Is Fred correct? Explain your answer.

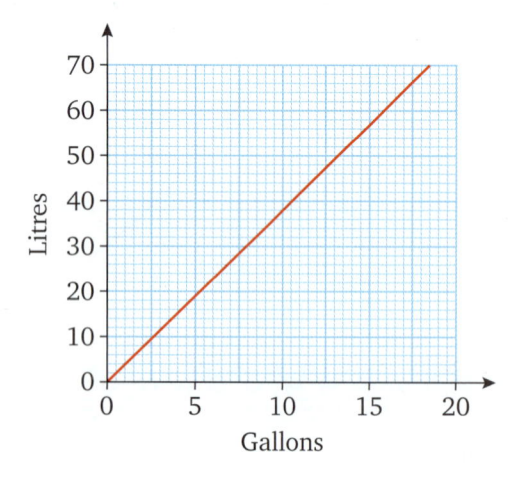

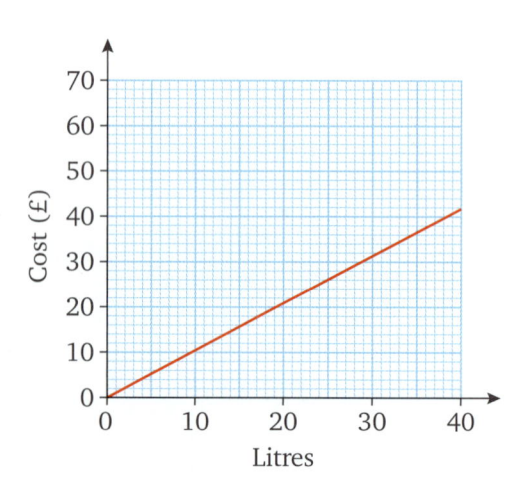

7

Andrew is filling his car with fuel.
The tank will hold 15.5 gallons when full.
The car's trip computer said the car had 3 litres left in the tank when he stopped at the filling station.

How much will it cost Andrew to fill his car's fuel tank?

Chapter 12 Real-life graphs

12 Assess

1 Colin takes his dog Ben for a walk over Cartmel Fell.
The distance–time graph shows his distance from home.

  a What time did Colin and Ben set off?

  b Colin had his lunch the first time they stopped.

    i What time was this?

    ii How long did they stop for lunch?

  c What was their average speed in km per hour before lunch?

  d On the way back they stopped several times for Colin to admire the view.
At what times did Colin make these stops?

  e How far did they walk?

  f What was their average speed in km/h for the whole walk?

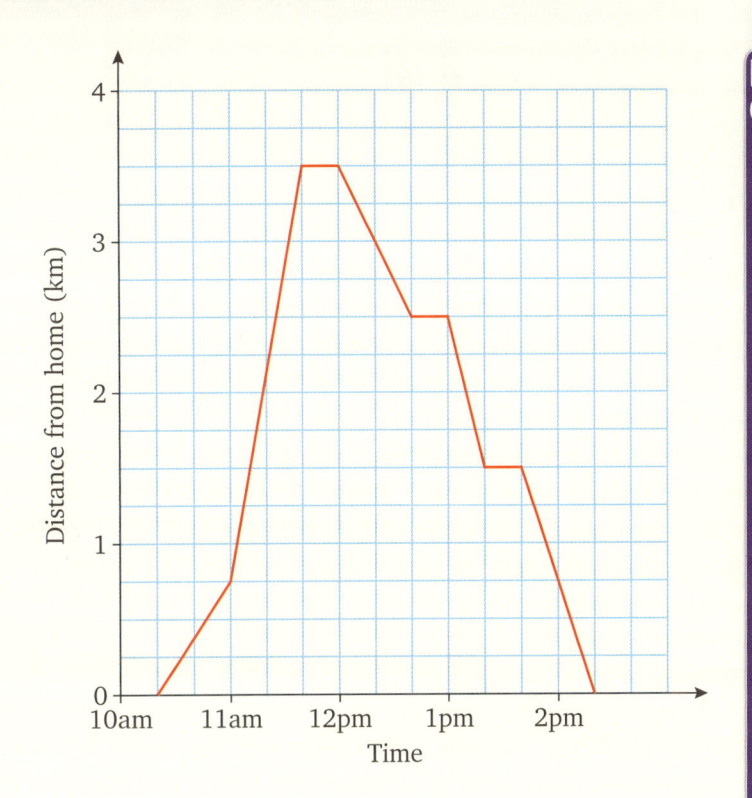

2 Sophie and Beckie are running to keep fit.

  a Beckie and Sophie go for a training run one night. Describe their runs.

  b What does the graph show about Sophie between A and B?
Give a possible reason for this.

  c Work out Sophie's average speed in miles per hour for the whole run.

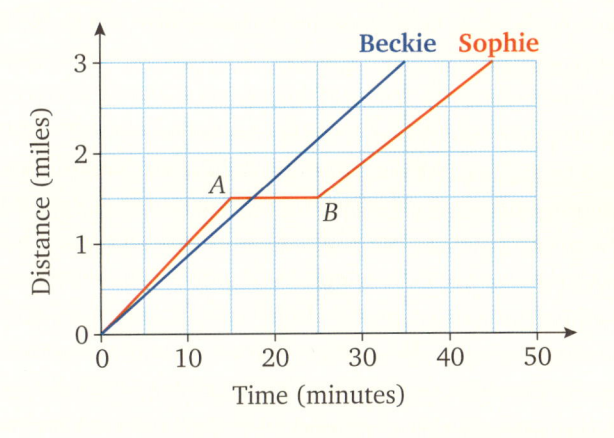

3 The graph shows the journey of a car as it accelerates and then slows down.

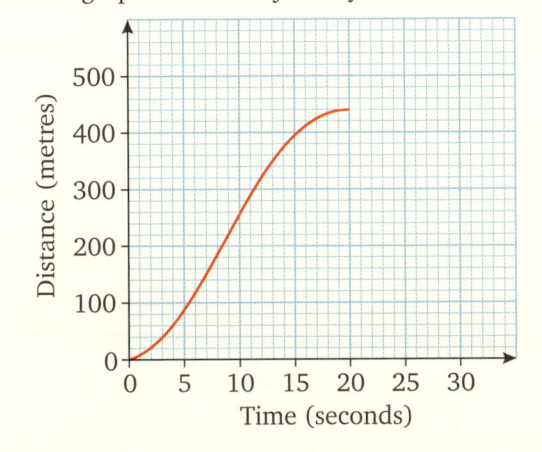

Calculate the average speed of the car for this journey.
State your units clearly.

4 Paul lives 10 miles from the nearest railway station. It takes him 30 minutes to drive to the station in his car. He travels at a constant speed.

a He sets off at 15:10 to meet his son at the station. Copy the axes and draw a distance–time graph to show his journey.

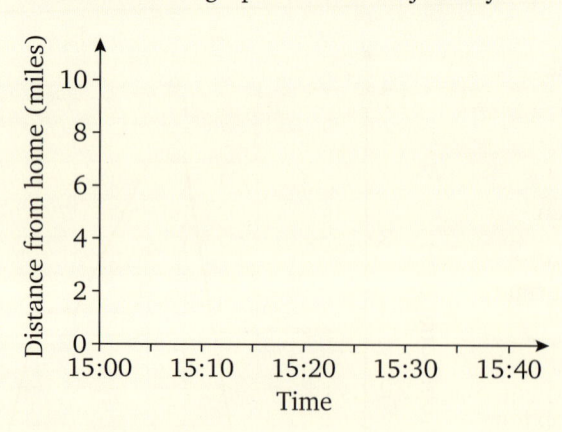

b Paul's son Sam arrives at the station at 15:00 and starts to walk home. He walks at a steady 4 mph.
Add a graph of his walk to your distance–time graph.

c Assuming Paul and Sam take the same route:

i what time do they meet?

ii how far has Sam walked when they meet?

5 The graph shows the path of a cricket ball through the air when thrown.

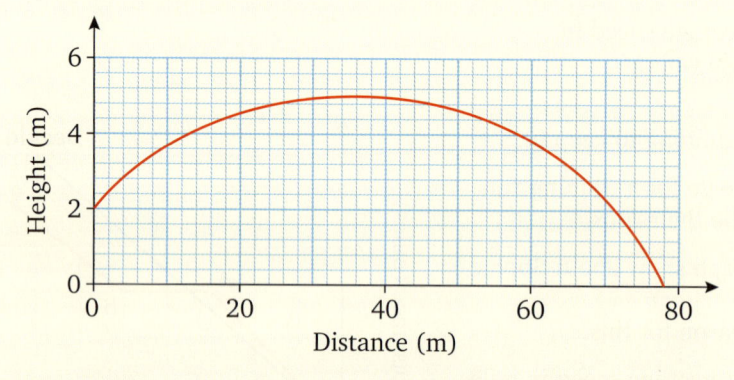

a What was the total distance thrown?

b What was the maximum height reached by the ball?

c What horizontal distance had been travelled when the ball was at its highest?

d Give a possible reason why the height of the ball started at 2 metres.

AQA Examination-style questions

1 This is part of a train timetable.

Train		A	B	C	D
Eastville	depart	0915	0948	1021	1054
Fraize	arrive	0927	1000	↓	1109
	depart	0930	1003		
Gamstone	arrive	1025	1058	↓	
	depart	1028			
Hunby	arrive	1055		1140	

a Which train, A, B, C or D, is shown in this distance–time graph?

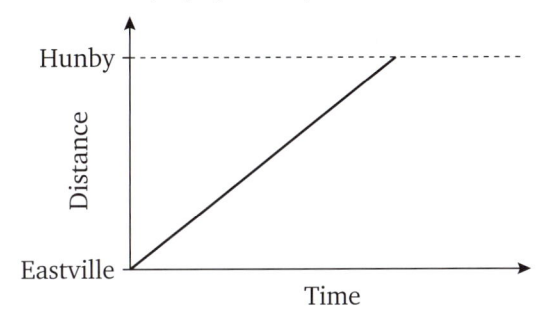

(1 mark)

b Which train is shown this distance–time graph?

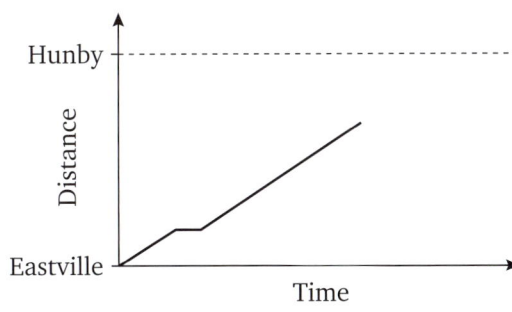

(1 mark)

c Here is the timetable for the next train.

Train		E
Eastville	depart	1135
Fraize	arrive	1147
	depart	1150
Gamstone	arrive	↓
	depart	
Hunby	arrive	1310

Copy the axes below. Sketch the distance–time graph for train E.

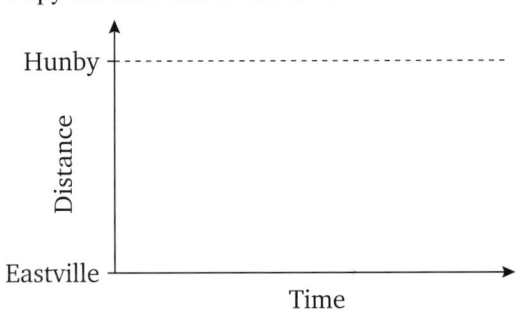

(2 marks)

AQA 2006

2   Viki has a mobile phone contract.
    It has a basic monthly charge and some free minutes.
    The graph shows how the total monthly charge is calculated for her mobile phone contract for up to 500 minutes of calls.

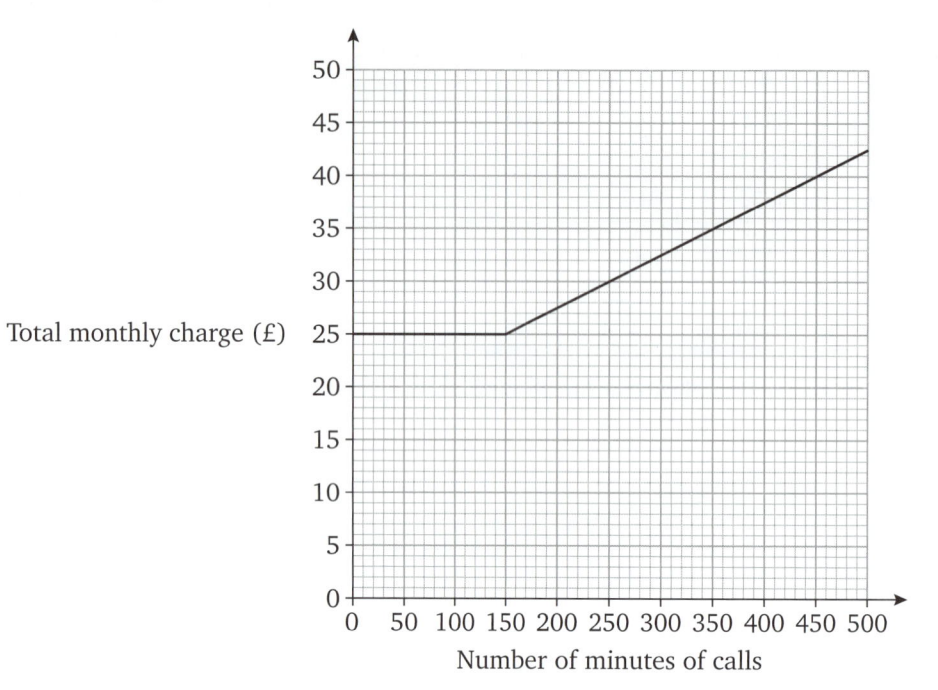

    a   Write down the number of free minutes of calls. *(1 mark)*
    b   Work out the charge per minute for the other calls. *(3 marks)*

    AQA 2009

13 Indices and standard index form

Objectives

Examiners would normally expect students who get these grades to be able to:

D
use the terms square, positive square root, negative square root, cube and cube root

recall integer squares from 2 × 2 to 15 × 15 and the corresponding square roots

recall the cubes of 2, 3, 4, 5 and 10 and the corresponding cube roots

C
use index notation and index laws for positive powers

B
use index notation and index laws for negative powers

convert between ordinary and standard index form numbers

use standard index form for calculations involving multiplication and/or division

A
use index notation and index laws for fractional powers such as $16^{\frac{1}{2}}$ and $16^{0.5}$

A*
use index notation and index laws for fractional powers such as $8^{\frac{2}{3}}$ and $8^{-\frac{2}{3}}$

Key terms
index (indices)
power
standard index form

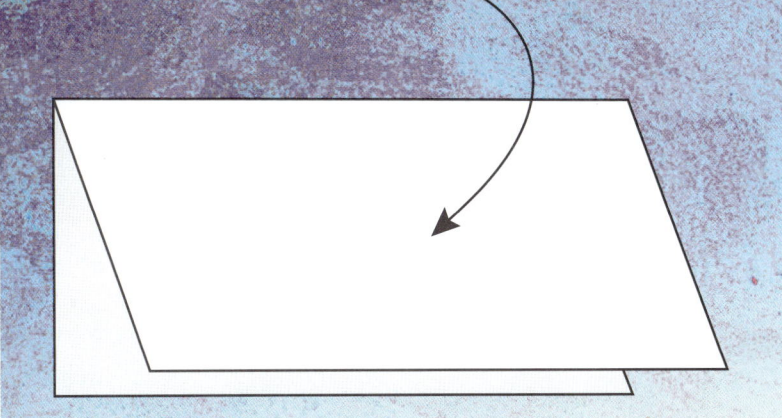

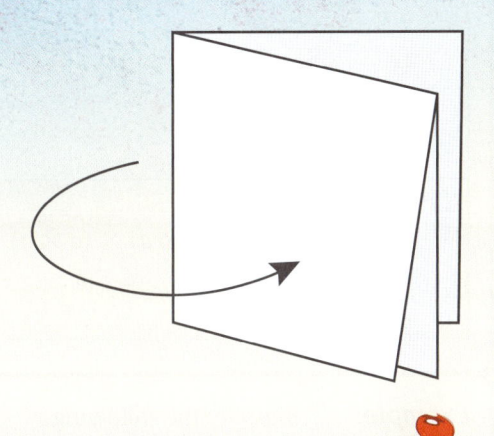

Did you know?

Folding paper

Did you know that it is impossible to fold a piece of paper more than 12 times?

If you fold the paper in half your paper is two sheets thick.

If you fold it in half again your paper is four sheets thick.

If you fold it in half again your paper is eight sheets thick.

How thick would your paper be after 12 folds?

Use the fact that paper is 0.1 millimetre or $\frac{1}{2540}$ inch thick.

You should already know:

✓ how to multiply numbers
✓ how to calculate squares and square roots
✓ how to calculate cubes and cube roots
✓ how to use algebra
✓ how to use reciprocals
✓ how to use function keys on a calculator.

Learn... 13.1 Rules of indices

The **index** (or **power**) tells you how many times the base number is to be multiplied by itself. This means that 5^3 tells you that 5 (the base number) is to be multiplied by itself 3 times (the index or power).

So $5^3 = 5 \times 5 \times 5 = 125$

5^3 — index (or power), base

Rules of indices

$a^3 \times a^5 = (a \times a \times a) \times (a \times a \times a \times a \times a)$ $= a \times a \times a \times a \times a \times a \times a \times a$ $= a^8$	So $a^3 \times a^5 = a^8$ In general $a^m \times a^n = a^{m+n}$
$a^7 \div a^3 = \dfrac{a^7}{a^3}$ $= \dfrac{a \times a \times a \times a \times a \times a \times a}{a \times a \times a}$ $= \dfrac{\cancel{a} \times \cancel{a} \times \cancel{a} \times a \times a \times a \times a}{\cancel{a} \times \cancel{a} \times \cancel{a}}$ $= a \times a \times a \times a$ $= a^4$	So $a^7 \div a^3 = a^4$ In general $a^m \div a^n = a^{m-n}$
$(a^2)^3 = a^2 \times a^2 \times a^2$ $= (a \times a) \times (a \times a) \times (a \times a)$ $= a \times a \times a \times a \times a \times a$ $= a^6$	So $(a^2)^3 = a^6$ In general $(a^m)^n = a^{m \times n}$

Example: Simplify the following.

	Number	Algebra	Higher algebra
a	$6^3 \times 6^2$	$a^3 \times a^2$	$6a^3 \times 3a^2$
b	$\dfrac{2^5}{2^2}$	$\dfrac{a^5}{a^2}$	$\dfrac{15a^5}{3a^2}$
c	$(3^5)^2$	$(a^3)^2$	$(6a^2)^3$

Solution:

a $6^3 \times 6^2$ $a^3 \times a^2$ $6a^3 \times 3a^2$
    $= 6^{(3+2)}$ $= a^{(3+2)}$ $= 6 \times a^3 \times 3 \times a^2$
    $= 6^5$ $= a^5$ $= 6 \times 3 \times a^3 \times a^2$
            $= 18 \times a^{(3+2)}$
            $= 18a^5$

b $\dfrac{2^5}{2^2}$ $\dfrac{a^5}{a^2}$ $\dfrac{15a^5}{3a^2}$
    $= 2^5 \div 2^2$ $= a^5 \div a^2$ $= \dfrac{15}{3} \times \dfrac{a^5}{a^2}$
    $= 2^{(5-2)}$ $= a^{(5-2)}$ $= 5 \times a^{(5-2)}$
    $= 2^3$ $= a^3$ $= 5a^3$

c $(3^5)^2$ $(a^3)^2$ $(6a^2)^3$
    $= 3^{3 \times 2}$ $= a^{3 \times 2}$ $= (6)^3 \times (a^2)^3$
    $= 3^6$ $= a^6$ $= 216 \times a^{2 \times 3}$
            $= 216 \times a^6$
            $= 216a^6$

Negative indices

$$a^2 \div a^5 = \frac{a \times a}{a \times a \times a \times a \times a}$$

$$= \frac{\cancel{a} \times \cancel{a}}{\cancel{a} \times \cancel{a} \times a \times a \times a}$$

$$= \frac{1}{a \times a \times a}$$

$$= \frac{1}{a^3}$$

$$a^2 \div a^5 = \frac{a^2}{a^5}$$

$$= a^{(2-5)}$$

$$= a^{-3}$$

So $\quad a^{-3} = \frac{1}{a^3}$

In general: $\quad a^{-n} = \frac{1}{a^n}$

Zero indices

$$a^3 \div a^3 = \frac{a \times a \times a}{a \times a \times a}$$

$$= \frac{\cancel{a}^1 \times \cancel{a}^1 \times \cancel{a}^1}{\cancel{a}^1 \times \cancel{a}^1 \times \cancel{a}^1}$$

$$= \frac{1}{1}$$

$$= 1$$

$$a^3 \div a^3 = \frac{a^3}{a^3}$$

$$= a^{(3-3)}$$

$$= a^0$$

So $\quad a^0 = 1$

Hint

You can use the $\boxed{x^{\blacksquare}}$ button on your calculator.

$\boxed{1}\,\boxed{0}\,\boxed{x^{\blacksquare}}\,\boxed{3}\,\boxed{=}\;125$

In general: $\quad a^0 = 1$

Fractional indices

$a^{\frac{1}{2}} \times a^{\frac{1}{2}} = a^{\frac{1}{2} + \frac{1}{2}} = a^1 = a \quad$ so $a^{\frac{1}{2}} = \sqrt{a}$ (since $\sqrt{a} \times \sqrt{a} = a$)

$a^{\frac{1}{3}} \times a^{\frac{1}{3}} \times a^{\frac{1}{3}} = a^{\frac{1}{3} + \frac{1}{3} + \frac{1}{3}} = a^1 = a \quad$ so $a^{\frac{1}{3}} = \sqrt[3]{a}$ (since $\sqrt[3]{a} \times \sqrt[3]{a} \times \sqrt[3]{a} = a$)

In general: $\quad a^{\frac{1}{n}} = \sqrt[n]{a}$

Summary of rules of indices

$a^m \times a^n = a^{m+n}$	$a^m \div a^n = a^{m-n}$	$(a^m)^n = a^{m \times n}$
$a^{-m} = \frac{1}{a^m}$	$a^0 = 1$	$a^{\frac{1}{n}} = \sqrt[n]{a}$

Bump up your grade

You will need to use index notation and index laws for positive and negative powers for an award of Grade C.

Example: Work out:

  a 3^{-2} **b** 999^0 **c** $100^{\frac{1}{2}}$ **d** $(-27)^{\frac{1}{3}}$ **e** $8^{\frac{2}{3}}$

Solution:

a $3^{-2} = \frac{1}{3^2}$ using negative indices

$\quad\quad = \frac{1}{9}$

b $999^0 = 1$ using zero indices

c $100^{\frac{1}{2}} = \sqrt{100}$ using fractional indices

$\quad\quad = 10$ -10 is also an acceptable answer

AQA Examiner's tip

Remember that for square roots there are always two possible answers (one is positive and the other negative. You can write this using the $\pm$ symbol.

d $(-27)^{\frac{1}{3}} = \sqrt[3]{(-27)}$ using fractional indices

$\quad\quad = -3$

e $8^{\frac{2}{3}} = (8^2)^{\frac{1}{3}}$ or $(8^{\frac{1}{3}})^2$ using $(a^m)^n = a^{m \times n}$

$(8^2)^{\frac{1}{3}} = (64)^{\frac{1}{3}} = 4$

$(8^{\frac{1}{3}})^2 = (2)^2 = 4$

AQA Examiner's tip

It does not matter which way you answer this question although $(8^{\frac{1}{3}})^2$ is probably easier. Try to plan your work to make the mathematics easier.

AQA GCSE Mathematics

Practise... 13.1 Rules of indices

1 Work out:

a $3^2 + 4^2$
b $2^3 \times 3^2$
c $10^3 - \sqrt{100}$
d $\sqrt{225} - \sqrt[3]{125}$
e $\sqrt{5^2 + 12^2}$
f $\sqrt{3^2 \times 5^2}$

2 Find the value of each of the following.

a 7^2
b 4^2
c 11^2
d $(-3)^2$
e 2^3
f 10^4
g 1^5
h 2^5
i 3^4
j 4^3
k $(-10)^6$
l $(-2)^7$

3 Work out the value of each of the following.

a 9^2
b -2^5
c -3^4
d 5^1
e 4^6
f 12^0
g 1^2
h 1^{100}
i 3^{-1}
j 2^{-3}
k 4^{-6}
l 100^{-1}
m $2^{11} - 5^3$
n $2^6 + 6^2$
o $5^3 \times 10^{-4}$
p $10^8 - 10^6$

4 Simplify the following, leaving your answer in index form.

a $5^6 \times 5^2$
b $12^8 \times 12^3$
c $\dfrac{4^7}{4^3}$
d $7^{10} \div 7^5$
e $3^7 \div 3^{10}$
f $(9^2)^5$
g $\dfrac{4^2 \times 4^3}{4^6}$

5 Are the following statements true or false? Give a reason for your answer.

a $6^2 = 12$
b $1^3 = 1$
c $1^{-\frac{1}{2}} = -1$
d $16^{-\frac{1}{2}} = -4$
e $\dfrac{2^{10}}{4^5} = 1$
f $3^4 + 3^5 = 3^9$
g $10^{50} \times 10^{50} = 10^{100}$
h $(-216)^{\frac{1}{3}} = -6$
i $1\,000\,000^0 = 0$

6 Work out:

a $49^{\frac{1}{2}}$
b $121^{\frac{1}{2}}$
c $64^{\frac{1}{3}}$
d $8^{\frac{2}{3}}$
e $32^{\frac{2}{5}}$
f $4^{-\frac{1}{2}}$
g $1^{\frac{1}{3}}$
h $1^{-\frac{1}{3}}$

7 Put the following in order, starting with the smallest.

$64^{\frac{1}{3}}$ $64^{\frac{1}{4}}$ $\left(\dfrac{1}{64}\right)^{\frac{1}{2}}$ $64^{-\frac{1}{3}}$

8 Simplify the following.

> **Hint**
> Write $2x^2 \times 3x^5$ as $2 \times x^2 \times 3 \times x^5$
> $= 2 \times 3 \times x^2 \times x^5$
> $= 6 \times x^2 \times x^5$

a $2x^2 \times 3x^5$
b $\dfrac{3a^6}{6a^2}$
c $5c^2 \times 2c^7$
d $(4b^2)^3$
e $\dfrac{c^6 \times c^9}{c^5}$
f $\dfrac{5c^2 \times 2c^7}{c^6}$

Chapter 13   Indices and standard index form   **175**

9 Work out:

a $8^{\frac{2}{3}}$ b $-8^{\frac{2}{3}}$ c $(-8)^{\frac{2}{3}}$ d $32^{\frac{2}{5}}$ e $(-125)^{\frac{2}{3}}$

10 Simplify $\dfrac{15a^7b^6c^3}{3a^4b^9c^{-2}}$

11 4^{3^2} can be ordered as $(4^3)^2$ or $4^{(3^2)}$

Marc says they are the same.

Is Marc correct?

Give a reason for your answer.

12 The number 64 can be written as 8^2 in index form.

Write down five other ways that it can be written in index form.

13 a Find the product of $7xy^2$ and $3x^4y^3$.

Hint
Write $7xy^2$ as $7 \times x \times y^2$

b Write down five other expressions which give the same product as your answer in part **a**.

14 Amy notices that $\sqrt{4} \times \sqrt{9} = \sqrt{4 \times 9}$

Does this always work?

Give some examples.

What happens if you divide the two numbers?

Learn... 13.2 Standard index form

Standard index form is a shorthand way of writing very large and very small numbers.

Standard index form numbers are always written as follows.

n is a positive or negative integer

$$A \times 10^n$$

A is a number between 1 and 10 ($1 \leq A < 10$)

Converting from standard index form

To convert from standard index form to ordinary form use the following information.

$10^1 = 10$

$10^2 = 10 \times 10 = 100$

$10^3 = 10 \times 10 \times 10 = 1000$

$10^4 = 10 \times 10 \times 10 \times 10 = 10\,000$

$10^5 = 10 \times 10 \times 10 \times 10 \times 10 = 100\,000$

$10^6 = 10 \times 10 \times 10 \times 10 \times 10 \times 10 = 1\,000\,000$ (1 million)

$10^{-1} = \dfrac{1}{10^1} = \dfrac{1}{10} = 0.1$

$10^{-2} = \dfrac{1}{10^2} = \dfrac{1}{100} = 0.01$

$10^{-3} = \dfrac{1}{10^3} = \dfrac{1}{1000} = 0.001$

$10^{-4} = \dfrac{1}{10^4} = \dfrac{1}{10\,000} = 0.0001$

$10^{-5} = \dfrac{1}{10^5} = \dfrac{1}{100\,000} = 0.00001$

$10^{-6} = \dfrac{1}{10^6} = \dfrac{1}{1\,000\,000} = 0.000001$

AQA Examiner's tip
Remember that multiplying by 10^{-1} is the same as dividing by 10, multiplying by 10^{-2} is the same as dividing by 10^2, etc.

Example: Write in ordinary form:

    a **i** 5×10^6 **b** **i** 4×10^{-3}

        ii 6.225×10^5 **ii** 7.295×10^{-6}

Solution:

  a **i** $5 \times 10^6 = 5 \times 1\,000\,000 = 5\,000\,000$

      ii $6.225 \times 10^5 = 6.225 \times 100\,000 = 622\,500$

  b **i** $4 \times 10^{-3} = 4 \times 0.001 = 0.004$

      ii $7.295 \times 10^{-6} = 7.295 \times 0.000001 = 0.000007295$

You can work these out by counting how many places the decimal point has to move.

5.0000000 (move the decimal point 6 places to the right) gives 5 000 000.0

0004. (move the point 3 places to the left) gives 0.004

Converting to standard index form

To convert to standard index form write your number in the form $A \times 10^n$

    where A is a number between 1 and 10

    and n is a positive or negative integer.

Example: Convert these ordinary form numbers into standard index form.

  a 701 000

  b 0.00000000153

Solution:

  a 701 000

      $A = 7.01$, so $701\,000 = 7.01 \times 100\,000 = 7.01 \times 10^5$

  b 0.00000000153

      $A = 1.53$, so $0.00000000153 = 1.53 \times 0.000000001 = 1.53 \times 10^{-9}$

Adding, subtracting, multiplying and dividing standard index form numbers

Use the rules of indices to multiply and divide standard index form numbers.

    $a^m \times a^n = a^{m+n}$

    $a^m \div a^n = a^{m-n}$

    $(a^m)^n = a^{m \times n}$

    $a^{-m} = \dfrac{1}{a^m}$

    $a^0 = 1$

Example: Work out the following, leaving your answer in standard index form.

  a $6 \times 10^8 \times 8 \times 10^{-3}$

  b $\dfrac{6 \times 10^8}{8 \times 10^{-3}}$

  c $5 \times 10^3 + 7 \times 10^4$

  d $7.3 \times 10^5 - 2.4 \times 10^5$

Solution:

a $6 \times 10^8 \times 8 \times 10^{-3} = 6 \times 8 \times 10^8 \times 10^{-3}$ rearranging the order

$\qquad\qquad\qquad\qquad\quad = 48 \times 10^8 \times 10^{-3}$

$\qquad\qquad\qquad\qquad\quad = 48 \times 10^{8-3}$ using the rules of indices for $10^8 \times 10^{-3}$

$\qquad\qquad\qquad\qquad\quad = 48 \times 10^5$ this is not yet in standard index form

$\qquad\qquad\qquad\qquad\quad = 4.8 \times 10^1 \times 10^5$ writing 48 as 4.8×10^1

$\qquad\qquad\qquad\qquad\quad = 4.8 \times 10^{1+5}$ using the rules of indices for $10^1 \times 10^5$

$\qquad\qquad\qquad\qquad\quad = 4.8 \times 10^6$

b $\dfrac{6 \times 10^8}{8 \times 10^{-3}} = \dfrac{6}{8} \times \dfrac{10^8}{10^{-3}}$

$\qquad\qquad\quad\; = 0.75 \times 10^{8--3}$ using the rules of indices for $10^8 \div 10^{-3}$

$\qquad\qquad\quad\; = 0.75 \times 10^{11}$ remembering that $8 - -3 = 11$

$\qquad\qquad\quad\; = 7.5 \times 10^{-1} \times 10^{11}$ writing 0.75 in standard index form as 7.5×10^{-1}

$\qquad\qquad\quad\; = 7.5 \times 10^{-1+11}$ using the rules of indices for $10^{-1} \times 10^{11}$

$\qquad\qquad\quad\; = 7.5 \times 10^{10}$

c $5 \times 10^3 + 7 \times 10^4 = 5000 + 70\,000$ writing numbers in ordinary form

$\qquad\qquad\qquad\qquad\;\; = 75\,000$ adding

$\qquad\qquad\qquad\qquad\;\; = 7.5 \times 10^4$ converting back to standard index form

d $7.3 \times 10^5 - 2.4 \times 10^5$

$\quad\; = (7.3 - 2.4) \times 10^5$ since the powers of 10 are the same

$\quad\; = 4.9 \times 10^5$

> **AQA Examiner's tip**
>
> Watch out for shortcuts when adding and subtracting numbers that have the same power of 10.

Practise... 13.2 Standard index form

1 Write the following ordinary form numbers in standard index form.

   a   4200   **c**   700 100   **e**   15   **g**   0.013

   b   590 000 000   **d**   8 600 000 000   **f**   0.0008   **h**   0.000000178

2 Write the following numbers in ordinary form.

   a 4×10^5 **c** 7.005×10^3 **e** 9×10^{-1} **g** 9.99×10^{-10}

   b 6.0×10^2 **d** 3.401×10^1 **f** 4.75×10^{-4}

3 The mass of an electron is approximately 0.00000000000000000000000000000910938 kilograms.

Write this number as a standard index form number.

4 Write the number 60^3 in standard index form.

5 Work out the following.

   a $(4 \times 10^4) \times (2 \times 10^7)$

   b $(3.3 \times 10^6) \times (3 \times 10^4)$

   c $(4.5 \times 10^5) \times (2 \times 10^{11})$

   d $(5 \times 10^5) \times (3 \times 10^9)$

   e $(2.5 \times 10^8) \times (5 \times 10^{-3})$

   f $(1.5 \times 10^7)^2$

   g $(5 \times 10^{-4})^2$

   h $\dfrac{4 \times 10^4}{2 \times 10^3}$

   i $\dfrac{3.9 \times 10^5}{1.3 \times 10^8}$

   j $\dfrac{2.2 \times 10^1}{5.5 \times 10^{-6}}$

   k $(2.2 \times 10^6) \div (4.4 \times 10^4)$

6 Use your calculator to calculate the following.

   a $(3 \times 10^5) \times (3 \times 10^7)$

   b $(5 \times 10^5) \times (3.2 \times 10^9)$

   c $(2.4 \times 10^5) \times (3.5 \times 10^7)$

   d $(4.55 \times 10^5) \times (6.2 \times 10^7)$

   e $(1.5 \times 10^7)^2$

   f $(5 \times 10^{-4})^2$

   g $\dfrac{8 \times 10^{11}}{4 \times 10^3}$

   h $\dfrac{3.9 \times 10^8}{1.3 \times 10^{-5}}$

   i $(2.2 \times 10^2) \div (4.4 \times 10^{11})$

   j $1 \div (2.5 \times 10^8)$

   k $(5 \times 10^5) + (3 \times 10^6)$

   l $(8 \times 10^2) + (8 \times 10^4)$

   m $(5.2 \times 10^4) - (5.2 \times 10^3)$

7 Given that $p = 4 \times 10^2$ and $q = 2 \times 10^{-1}$, work out:

   a $p \times q$ **c** $p + q$ **e** p^2

   b $p \div q$ **d** $p - q$

8 The distance to the edge of the observable universe is approximately 4.6×10^{26} metres.

Express this distance in kilometres, giving your answer in standard index form.

9 The speed of light is approximately 3.0×10^8 m/s.

How far will light travel in one week?

Give your answer in standard index form.

10 The mass of the Sun is approximately 2×10^{30} kg and the mass of the Earth is approximately 6×10^{24} kg.

How many times heavier is the Sun than the Earth?

11 The following table shows the diameters of the planets of the solar system.

Planet	Diameter (km)
Mercury	4.9×10^3
Venus	1.2×10^4
Earth	1.3×10^4
Mars	6.8×10^3
Jupiter	1.4×10^5
Saturn	1.2×10^5
Uranus	5.2×10^4
Neptune	4.9×10^4

Place the planets in order of size, starting with the smallest first.

12 Ali says that $(4 \times 10^4) + (2 \times 10^4) = (6 \times 10^4)$

Brian says that $(4 \times 10^4) + (2 \times 10^4) = (6 \times 10^8)$

Who is correct?

Give a reason for your answer.

13 Anil saves some images onto a memory stick. Each image requires 32 000 bytes of memory. How many images can he save if the memory stick has a memory of 1.36×10^8 bytes?

Give your answer in standard index form.

14 The thickness of a ream of paper (500 sheets) is 4.8 cm.

Work out the thickness of one sheet of paper in millimetres.

Give your answer in standard index form.

13 Assess

1 **a** Sam says all numbers have two square roots.
Gareth says some numbers have no square roots.

Who is right? Give a reason for your answer.

   b Livia joins in the conversation and says that all numbers have two cube roots.

Is she right? Give a reason for your answer.

2 Work out the following, leaving your answers as single powers.

   a $4^6 \times 4^2$ **e** $6^4 \times 6^2 \times 6^3$ **i** $5^8 \div 5^7$

   b $11^5 \times 11^3$ **f** $10^4 \div 10^2$ **j** $2^3 \div 2^3$

   c $(5^3)^2$ **g** $21^7 \div 21^5$

   d $7^5 \times 7$ **h** $16^{10} \div 16^9$

3 Find the value of:
  a $3^2 \times 4^2$
  b $5^4 \div 5^2$
  c $6^5 \times 6^3 \div 6^4$
  d $\dfrac{(10^8 \times 10^7)}{10^7 \times 10^6}$

4 Which is greater:
  a 3^5 or 5^3
  b 11^2 or 2^{11}
  c 2^4 or 4^2?

5 Which of the following statements is true?

  The sum of the squares of two odd numbers is always odd.
  The sum of the squares of two odd numbers is always even.
  The sum of the squares of two odd numbers could be odd or even.

  Give a reason for your answer.

6 The diameter of the dwarf planet Pluto is 2.27×10^3 km.

  The diameter of Neptune is 4.86×10^4 km.

  Express the diameter of Pluto to the diameter of Neptune as a ratio in the form $1:n$
  Give your answer to a suitable degree of accuracy.

7 Find the values of the following, leaving your answers as fractions where appropriate.
  a 5^{-1}
  b 23^0
  c $12^3 \div 12^4$
  d 3^{-2}
  e $2^6 \div 2^8$
  f $(\tfrac{1}{4})^0$
  g $(\tfrac{1}{2})^{-3}$

8 Work out:
  a $81^{\frac{1}{2}}$
  b $225^{\frac{1}{2}}$
  c $27^{-\frac{1}{3}}$
  d $1^{\frac{2}{3}}$
  e $-64^{\frac{2}{3}}$
  f $(-64)^{\frac{2}{3}}$
  g $32^{\frac{3}{5}}$
  h $9^{-\frac{1}{2}}$
  i $(-125)^{-\frac{2}{3}}$

AQA Examination-style questions

1 $x^a \times x^b = x^7$
   $(x^a)^b = x^{10}$
   Work out the values of a and b. *(3 marks)*
   AQA 2008

2 a Explain why 36×10^{18} is **not** in standard index form. *(1 mark)*

   b The mass of Saturn is 5.7×10^{26} kilograms.
      The mass of Uranus is 8.7×10^{25} kilograms.
      Saturn is heavier than Uranus.

      How many times heavier?
      Give your answer to an appropriate degree of accuracy. *(3 marks)*
      AQA 2008

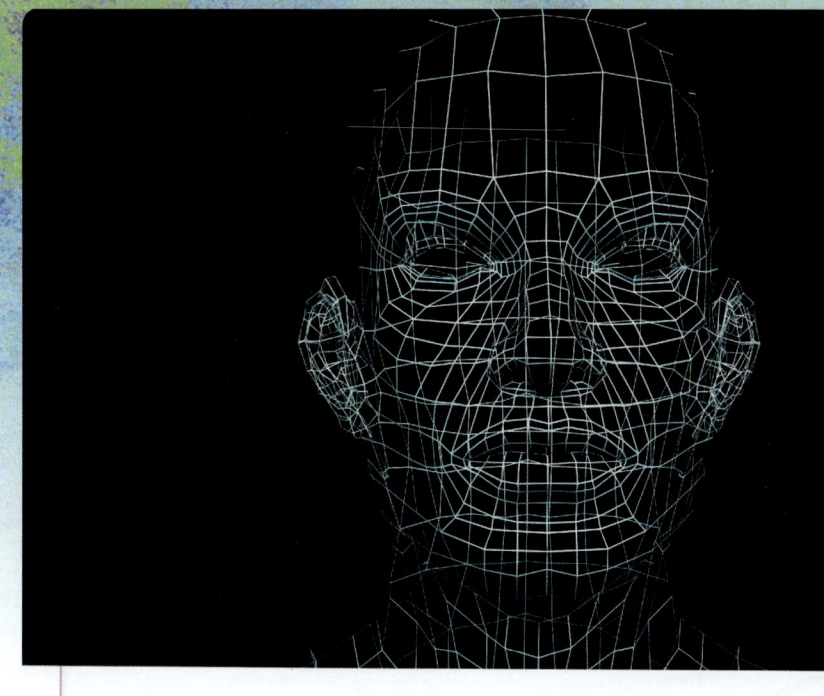

14 Properties of polygons

Objectives

Examiners would normally expect students who get these grades to be able to:

D
classify a quadrilateral using geometric properties

C
calculate exterior and interior angles of a regular polygon.

Key terms

quadrilateral
polygon
diagonal
bisect
perpendicular
exterior angle
interior angle
triangle
pentagon
hexagon
regular
octagon
decagon
nonagon

Did you know?

Polygons and video games

Objects in video games are made up of lots of polygons. Pictures are made up of a series of polygons such as triangles, squares, rectangles, parallelograms and rhombuses. The more polygons there are, the better the picture looks.

The polygons are all given coordinates. The computer changes and rotates the coordinates to match your position in the game. This gives the impression of movement.

For example, if you move away, the computer shrinks all the coordinates of the polygons. This makes the polygons appear smaller on the screen so they look further away.

You should already know:

✔ how to use properties of angles at a point, angles on a straight line, perpendicular lines, and opposite angles at a vertex
✔ the difference between between acute, obtuse, reflex and right angles
✔ how to use parallel lines, alternate angles and corresponding angles
✔ how to prove that the angle sum of a triangle is 180°
✔ how to prove that the exterior angle of a triangle is equal to the sum of the interior opposite angles
✔ how to use angle properties of equilateral, isosceles and right-angled triangles
✔ how to use angle properties of quadrilaterals.

Learn... 14.1 Properties of quadrilaterals

A **quadrilateral** is a **polygon** with four sides.

You need to know the names and properties of the following special quadrilaterals.

Square – a quadrilateral with four equal sides and four right angles.

Trapezium – a quadrilateral with one pair of parallel sides.

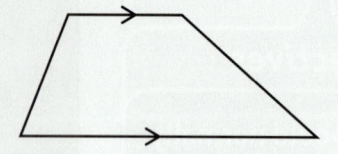

Rectangle – a quadrilateral with four right angles and opposite sides equal in length.

Parallelogram – a quadrilateral with opposite sides equal and parallel.

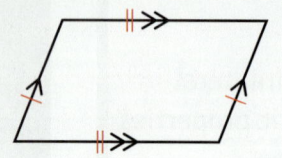

Kite – a quadrilateral with two pairs of equal adjacent sides.

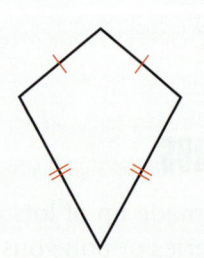

Rhombus – a quadrilateral with four equal sides and opposite sides parallel.

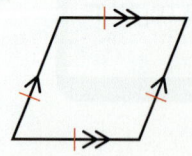

Isosceles trapezium – a trapezium where the non-parallel sides are equal in length.

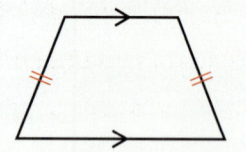

All quadrilaterals have four sides and four angles.
A quadrilateral can be split into two triangles.

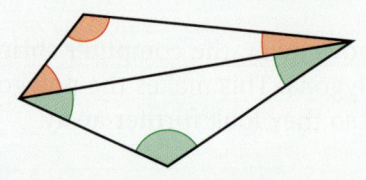

The angles in a triangle add up to 180°.
The quadrilateral is made up of two triangles.
The angles in a quadrilateral add up to 2 × 180° = 360°

The diagonals of a quadrilateral

A diagonal is a line joining one corner of a quadrilateral to another.

All quadrilaterals have two **diagonals**.

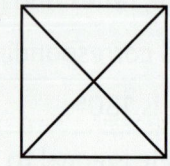

The square has two diagonals.

The diagonals are the same length.

The diagonals **bisect** one another.   Bisect means they cut one another in half.

The diagonals are **perpendicular**.   Perpendicular means at right angles.

Chapter 14 Properties of polygons 183

Example: Calculate the angles marked with letters in the shape below.

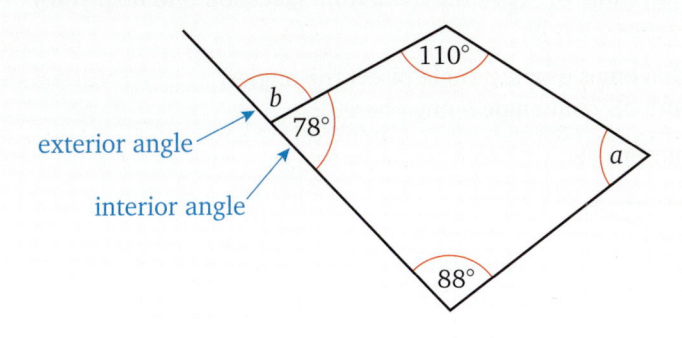

Not drawn accurately

Solution: The angles in the quadrilateral add up to 360°, so
$a = 360° - (78° + 88° + 110°)$
$= 360° - 276°$
$= 84°$

The **exterior** and **interior angles** add up to 180°, so
$b = 180° - 78°$
$= 102°$

AQA Examiner's tip
Always make sure that your answer is reasonable. Angle b is an obtuse angle so the answer calculated here is reasonable.

Practise... 14.1 Properties of quadrilaterals D C B A A*

1
square   rectangle   parallelogram   rhombus   kite   trapezium

a Which of these quadrilaterals have all four sides equal?
b Which of these quadrilaterals have opposite sides that are parallel?
c Which of these quadrilaterals have adjacent sides that are equal?
d Which of these quadrilaterals has only one pair of parallel sides?

2 Barry measures the angles of a quadrilateral. He says that three of the angles are 82° and the other one is 124°.

Could he be right? Explain your answer.

3 Make an accurate drawing of each quadrilateral listed in the table, then draw the diagonals.
Use your diagrams to complete a copy of the table.

Shape	Are the diagonals equal? (Yes/No)	Do the diagonals bisect each other? (Yes/No/Sometimes)	Do the diagonals cross at right angles? (Yes/No)	Do the diagonals bisect the angles of the quadrilateral? (Yes/No/Sometimes)
Square				
Kite				
Parallelogram				
Trapezium				
Isosceles trapezium				
Rectangle				
Rhombus				

4 Rajesh says that he has drawn a quadrilateral. Its diagonals are equal.

What shapes might he have drawn? (Use the table from Question 3 to help you.)

5 Michelle says that the diagonals of a rectangle bisect the angles.
So angles *a* and *c* are both 45° and angle *b* must be 90°.

Is she right? Explain your answer.

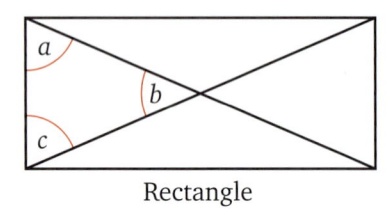

Rectangle

Not drawn accurately

6 The diagram shows a rhombus *ABCD*.
AC and *BD* are the diagonals.
Angle *ADB* = 32°

Calculate angle *DAC*.

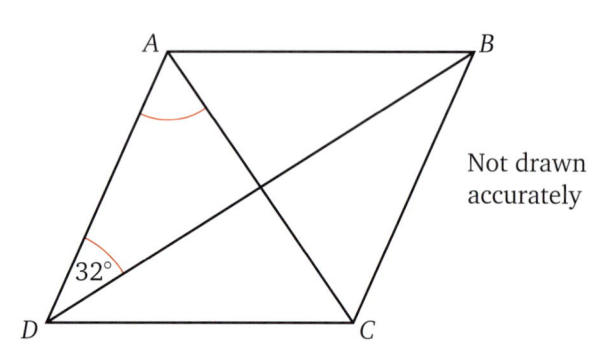

Not drawn accurately

7 Calculate the angles marked with letters in the diagrams. You will need to use parallel line facts and the properties of diagonals. Explain how you know the size of the angles.

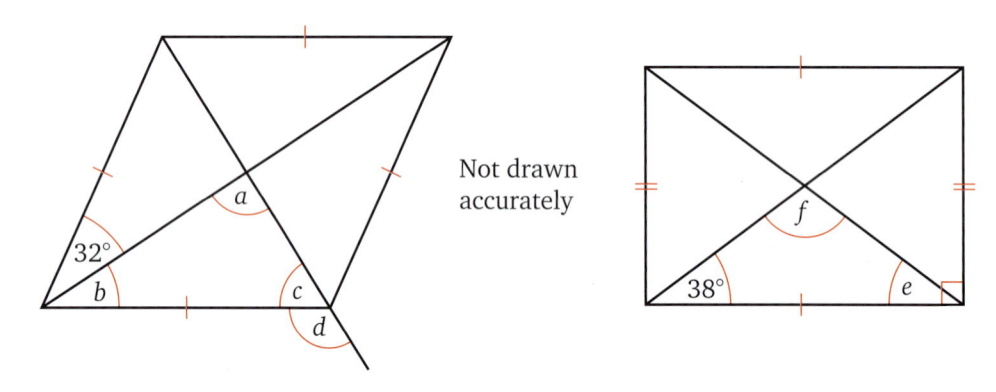

Not drawn accurately

8 In the diagram, *EF* is parallel to *GH*, and *AB* is parallel to *CD*.

IJ is perpendicular to *AB*, and *IK* is equal to *JK*.

Calculate the angles *a* to *f*, giving reasons for your answers.

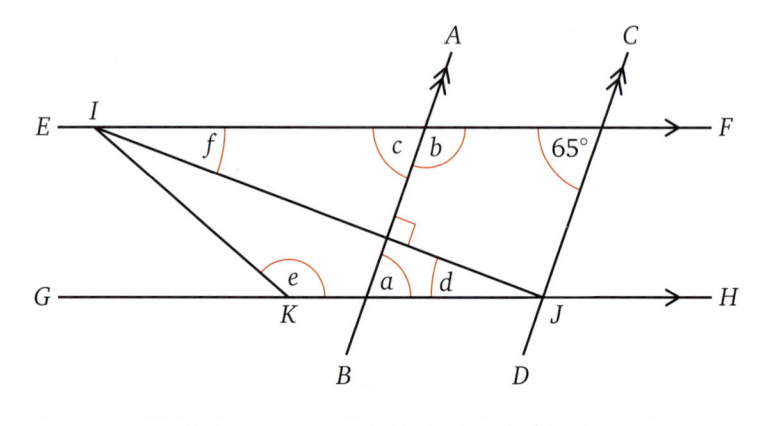

Not drawn accurately

Chapter 14 Properties of polygons   185

9 Matt, Tess and Sam all draw kites with one angle of 76° and one angle of 60°. All three kites are different. Matt's kite has two obtuse angles. Sam's kite has a larger angle than the other two kites.

What are the angles of each kite? Draw diagrams to help.

10 EDC is a straight line and angle DAB = angle ABC

Work out the angle ABC.

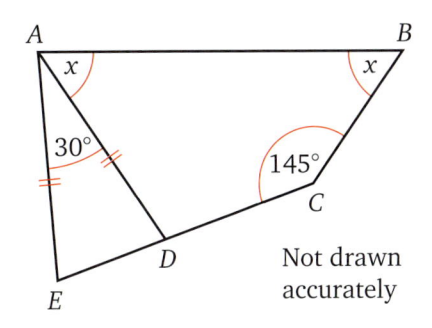

Not drawn accurately

Learn... 14.2 Angle properties of polygons

The interior angles of a **triangle** add up to 180°.

A quadrilateral has four sides and can be split into two triangles by drawing diagonals from a point.

The sum of the angles is 2 × 180° = 360°

A **pentagon** has five sides and can be split into three triangles by drawing diagonals from a point.

The sum of the angles is 3 × 180° = 540°

A **hexagon** has six sides and can be split into four triangles by drawing diagonals from a point.

The sum of the angles is 4 × 180° = 720°

In general, a polygon with n sides can be split into $(n - 2)$ triangles.

The sum of the angles is $(n - 2) \times 180°$

The interior angles of a polygon are the angles inside the polygon.

In a **convex** polygon all the internal angles are less than 180°

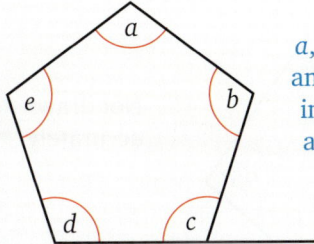

a, b, c, d and e are interior angles.

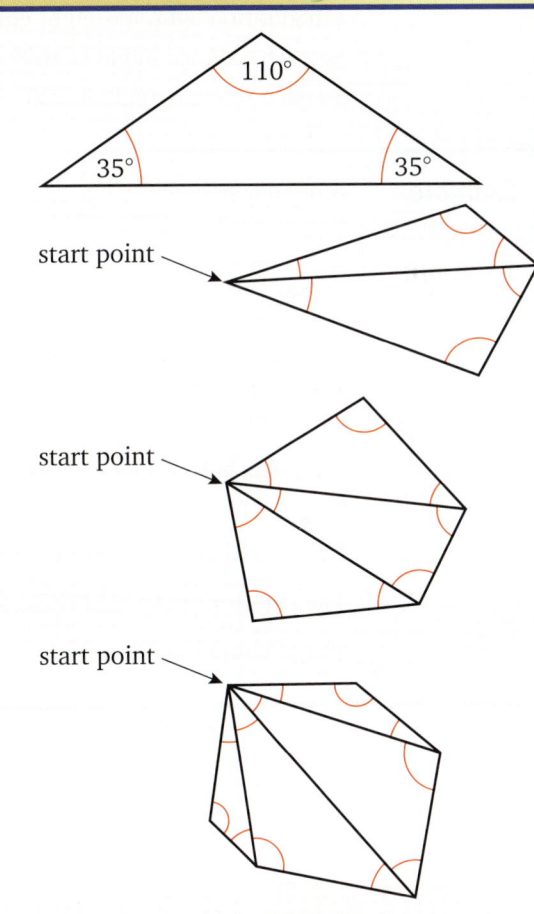

The exterior angles of a polygon are the angles between one side and the extension of the side.

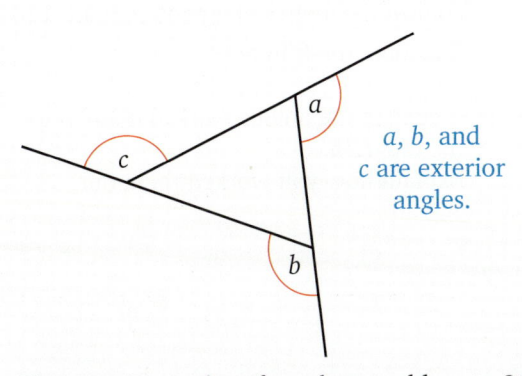

$a, b,$ and c are exterior angles.

The exterior angles of a polygon add up to 360°.

Example: Find the interior angle of a **regular octagon**.

Solution: **Either:**

An octagon has eight sides.

So the sum of the interior angles is $(8 - 2) \times 180° = 1080°$

A regular octagon has all angles equal, so each interior angle is $1080° \div 8 = 135°$

start point

Or:

A regular octagon has eight equal exterior angles.
So each exterior angle is $360° \div 8 = 45°$
So each interior angle is $180° - 45° = 135°$

Bump up your grade

You need to know how to calculate interior and exterior angles of any polygon for a Grade C.

Example: A regular polygon has interior angles of 144°. How many sides does it have?

Solution:

interior angle — exterior angle   144°

The exterior angles of a convex polygon add up to 360°.

A regular polygon has all sides equal and all angles equal.

Each exterior angle must be $180° - 144° = 36°$

The exterior angles add up to 360°, so there must be $360° \div 36° = 10$ exterior angles

The polygon has 10 sides.

AQA Examiner's tip

Always draw a diagram to help answer the questions.

You can then label the diagram to keep track of what you know.

Practise... 14.2 Angle properties of polygons   D C B A A*

1 Four of the angles of a pentagon are 110°, 130°, 102° and 97°.
Calculate the fifth angle.

2 Calculate the angles marked a and b in the diagram.
Explain how you worked them out.

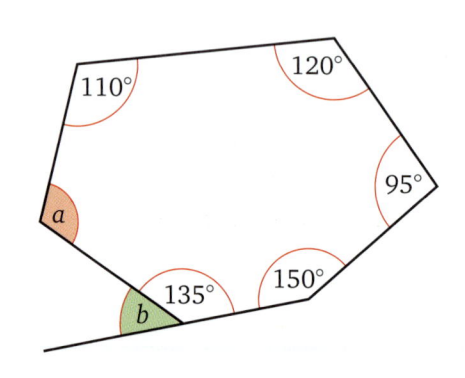

110°, 120°, 95°, 150°, 135°, a, b

Not drawn accurately

Chapter 14 Properties of polygons

3 A regular polygon has an exterior angle of 60°.

How many sides does it have?

4 Calculate the difference between the interior angle of a regular **decagon** (ten-sided shape) and the interior angle of a regular **nonagon** (nine-sided shape).

5 James divides a regular hexagon into six triangles as shown.

He says the angle sum of a regular hexagon is 6 × 180°.

Is he correct? Give a reason for your answer.

6 Lisa says that a regular octagon can be split into two trapeziums and a rectangle as shown.

She says the angle sum of the octagon is 3 × 360°.

Show that Lisa is correct.

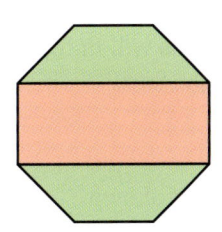

7 The diagrams show how you draw an equilateral triangle and a regular pentagon inside a circle. You do this by dividing the angle at the centre equally.

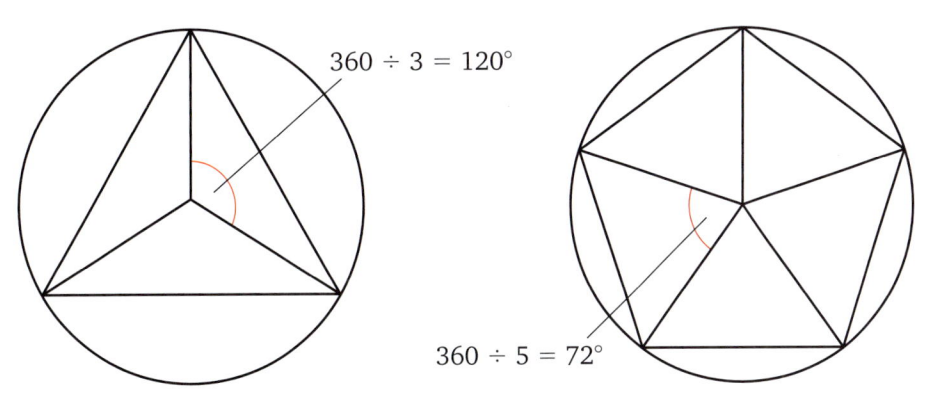

360 ÷ 3 = 120°

360 ÷ 5 = 72°

Use the same method to draw a regular hexagon and a regular nonagon (nine-sided shape) inside a circle.

8 The diagram shows a regular pentagon ABCDE and a regular hexagon DEFGHI.

Calculate:

a angle EDC
b angle EDI
c obtuse angle CDI
d angle BAC
e angle CAE
f angle HIG
g angle DIG.

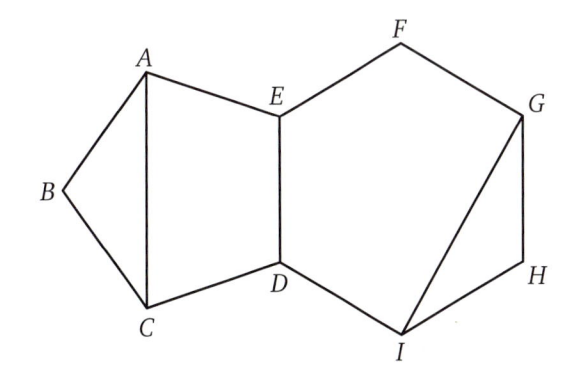

9 A badge is in the shape of a regular pentagon. The letter V is written on the badge.

What is the size of the angle marked x?

10 A convex polygon is one where all the interior angles are less than 180°.

Show that a convex polygon cannot have more than three acute angles.

Hint
Think about the sum of the exterior angles.

11 Show that if a convex polygon has more than six sides, then at least one of the sides has an obtuse angle at both ends.

12 Penny fits regular pentagons together in a circular arrangement.
Part of the arrangement is shown in the diagram.

Show that exactly ten pentagons will fit together in this way before meeting up.

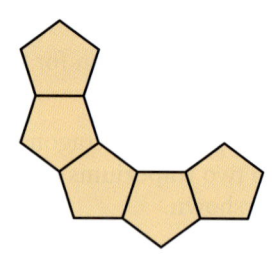

13 A company makes containers as shown.
The top is in the shape of a regular octagon.

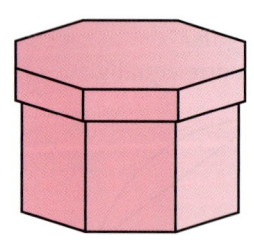

a What is the size of each interior angle?

b When the company packs them into a box, will they tessellate? If not, what shape will be left between them?

14 Assess

1 Which of the following polygons are possible and which ones are not possible?
Make an accurate drawing of each one that is possible.

a a kite with a right angle
b a kite with two right angles
c a trapezium with two right angles
d a trapezium with only one right angle
e a triangle with a right angle
f a triangle with two right angles
g a pentagon with one right angle
h a pentagon with two right angles
i a pentagon with three right angles
j a pentagon with four right angles

Chapter 14   Properties of polygons   189

2 Find the values of the angles marked in these diagrams.

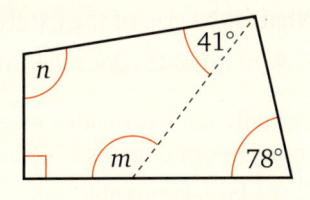

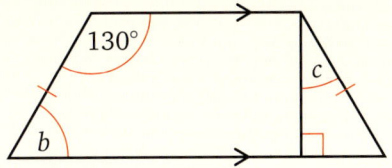

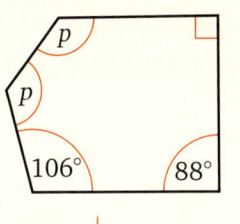

a [Quadrilateral with angles 48°, 110°, right angle, and a]

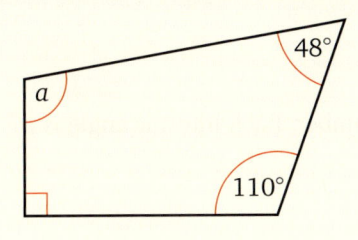

f [Quadrilateral with angles 41°, 78°, right angle, n, m, with a diagonal dashed line]

b [Trapezium with angles 130°, b, c, right angle]

g [Pentagon with angles p, p, 106°, 88°, right angle] Not drawn accurately

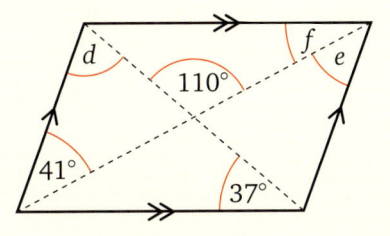

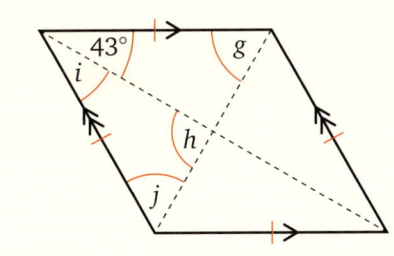

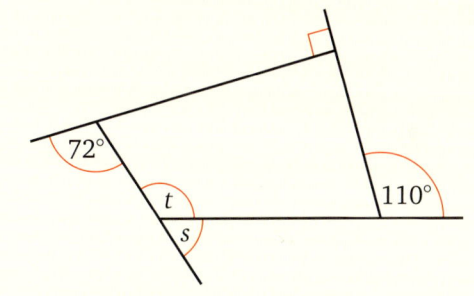

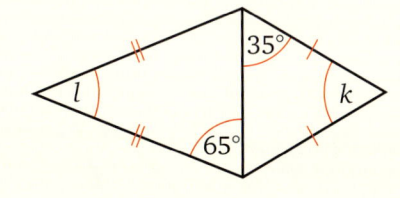

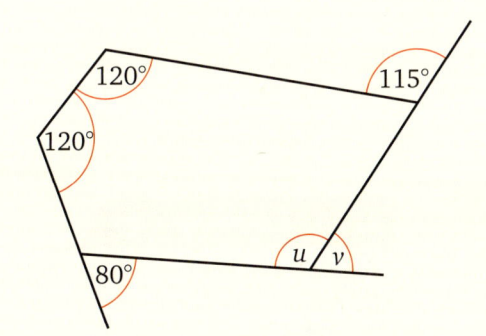

c [Parallelogram with angles d, 110°, f, e, 41°, 37°]

h [Pentagon with angles q, r, right angle, and tick marks]

d [Parallelogram with angles 43°, g, i, h, j]

i [Shape with angles 72°, t, s, 110°, right angle]

e [Kite/rhombus with angles 35°, 65°, l, k with tick marks]

j [Pentagon with angles 120°, 120°, 80°, 115°, u, v]

3 The only regular polygons that tessellate on their own are those whose interior angles divide exactly into 360°. Which ones are they?

4 Sophie says her regular polygon has an exterior angle of 40°.
Adam says that is not possible.

Who is correct? Give a reason for your answer.

5 The exterior angle of a regular polygon is 4°.

a How many sides does the polygon have?

b What is the size of each interior angle in the polygon?

c What is the sum of the interior angles of the polygon?

6 **a** A pentagon has angles of 110°, 155° and 75°.
The other two angles are equal. What size are they?

b A hexagon has three angles of 120°.
The remaining three angles are x, $2x$ and $3x$.
What is the size of the largest angle?

7 A regular polygon has an interior angle of 144°.

   a What is the size of the exterior angles.

   b How many sides does the polygon have?

8 A regular polygon has *n* sides where *n* is an odd number. Each interior angle is a whole numbers of degrees.

What is the largest possible value for *n*?

9 *ABCDE* is a regular pentagon.

DEG, *DCF* and *GABF* are straight lines.

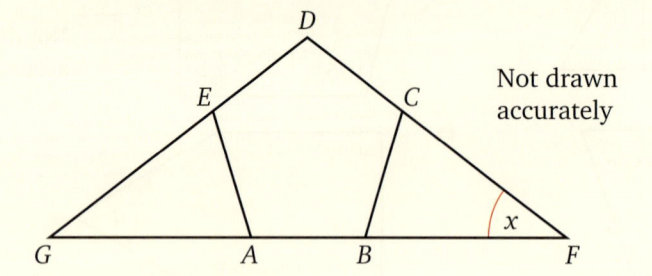

Not drawn accurately

Work out the size of angle *x*.

10 *ABCDEFGH* is a regular octagon.

Work out the value of *x*.

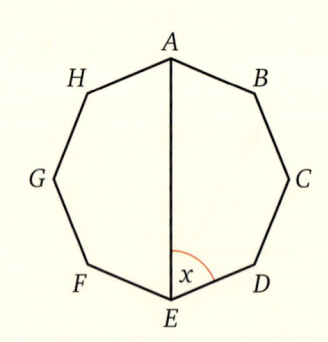

Not drawn accurately

11 *ABCD* is a rhombus. *CDE* is an isosceles triangle. *BCE* is a straight line.

Prove that angle *BAD* = 2*x*

Not drawn accurately

AQA Examiner's tip

A proof must use the general angle *x*. Do not use an example for *x* like 70°. Work round the diagram using geometrical facts to show angle *BAD* = 2*x*

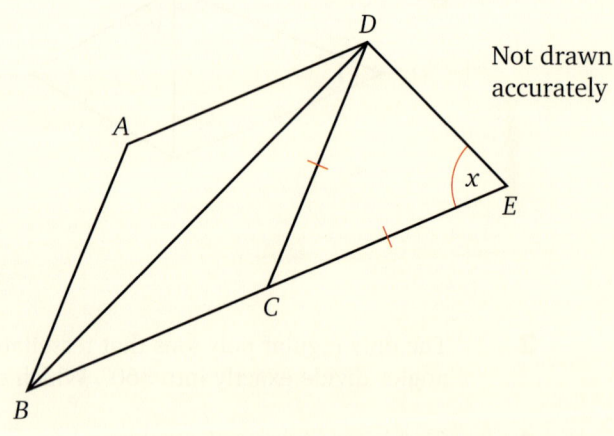

12 *ABCDEF* is a regular hexagon.

AFGH and *AJKB* are squares.

Prove that triangle *AHJ* is equilateral.

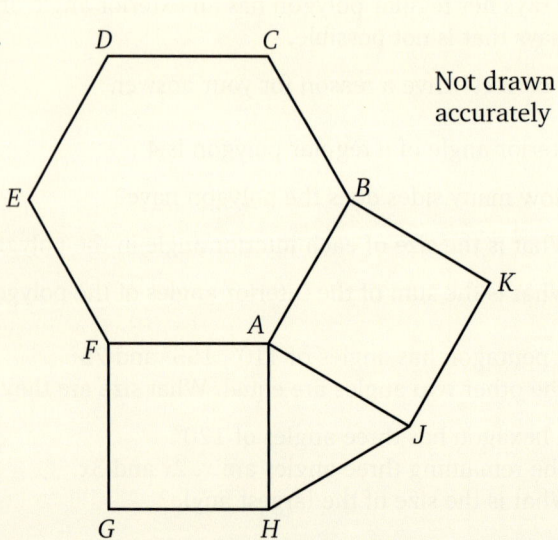

Not drawn accurately

AQA Examination-style questions

1 The diagram shows a regular pentagon and a regular decagon joined at side *XY*.

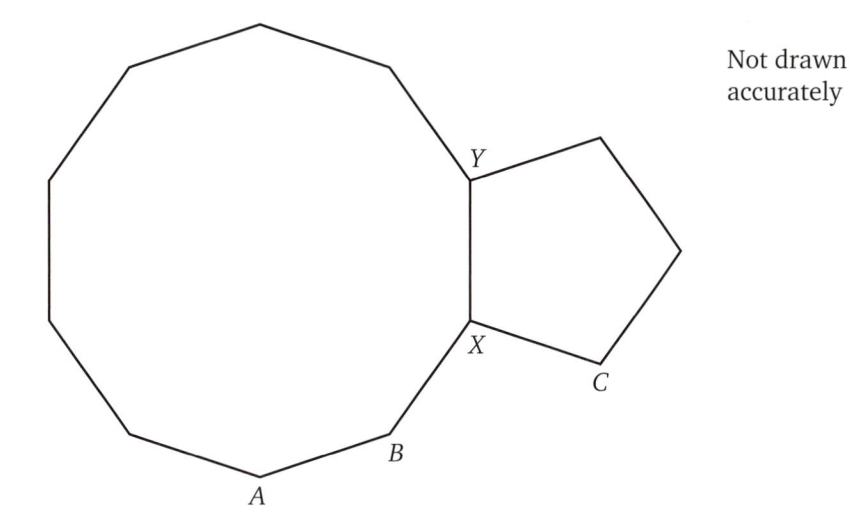

Not drawn accurately

Show that the points *A*, *B* and *C* lie on a straight line. *(5 marks)*

AQA 2009

15 Equations and inequalties

Objectives

Examiners would normally expect students who get these grades to be able to:

D

solve an equation such as $3x + 2 = 6 - x$ or $4(2x - 1) = 20$

represent and interpret inequalities on a number line

C

solve an equation such as $4x + 5 = 3(x + 4)$ or $\dfrac{x}{2} - \dfrac{x}{8} = 9$ or $\dfrac{2x - 7}{4} = 1$

solve an inequality such as $2x - 7 < 9$

find the integer solutions of an inequality such as $-8 < 2n \leqslant 5$

B

solve an equation such as $\dfrac{2x - 1}{6} + \dfrac{x + 3}{3} = \dfrac{5}{2}$

solve an inequality such as $3x + 2 \leqslant 4 - x$

represent linear inequalities in two variables, such as $x + y < 7$, as a region on a graph.

Did you know?

'Ink blots to space rockets'

🔵 $+ 3 = 21$

What is the number under the blob?

You can guess the answer without knowing any algebra.

You can't design a space rocket by guesswork but this chapter will show you how to take the first steps in solving complicated equations.

Then you might end up designing the next space rocket.

Key terms

solve
unknown
brackets
denominator
inequality
integer
inverse operation
region

You should already know:

✔ how to collect like terms
✔ how to use substitution
✔ how to multiply out brackets by a single term, such as $3x(x + 2)$
✔ how to cancel fractions
✔ how to add and subtract fractions
✔ how to solve equations such as $2x + 3 = 11$
✔ how to draw graphs of linear equations.

15.1 Equations where the unknown (x) appears on both sides

Learn...

Follow these steps to **solve** the equation.
- Collect together on one side all the terms that contain the **unknown** letter (x).
- Collect together on the other side all the other terms.
- Remember signs belong with the term **after** them.

Example: Solve:

a $\quad 2x + 3 = 18 - x$

b $\quad 3y + 9 = 5y - 8$

Solution:

a
$$2x + 3 = 18 - x$$
$$2x + x + 3 = 18 - x + x \quad$$ Add x to both sides (this collects all the x terms together on the left-hand side).

$$3x + 3 - 3 = 18 - 3 \quad$$ Take 3 from both sides (this collects all the numbers on right-hand side).

$$3x = 18 - 3$$
$$\frac{3x}{3} = \frac{15}{3} \quad$$ Divide both sides by 3.
$$x = 5$$

b
$$3y + 9 = 5y - 8$$
$$3y - 3y + 9 = 5y - 3y - 8 \quad$$ Take $3y$ from both sides (this collects all the y terms on the right-hand side). You could take $5y$ from both sides. You would get $-2y = -17$

$$9 = 2y - 8$$
$$9 + 8 = 2y - 8 + 8 \quad$$ Add 8 to both sides (this collects all the numbers on the left-hand side).

$$17 = 2y$$
$$\frac{17}{2} = \frac{2y}{2} \quad$$ Divide both sides by 2.
$$8.5 = y$$
$$y = 8.5 \quad$$ Write the equation with y on the left.

Practise...

15.1 Equations where the unknown (x) appears on both sides

D C B A A*

1 Solve these equations.

a $\quad 4x + 1 = 2x + 13$
b $\quad 2y - 3 = y + 4$
c $\quad 5z - 2 = 8 + 3z$
d $\quad 9 - 3t = t + 3$
e $\quad 6p + 2 = 9 + 4p$
f $\quad 17 - 6q = 3 + q$
g $\quad 2 - 3a = 7 + 2a$
h $\quad 8b - 3 = 2b - 15$
i $\quad 7c - 1 = 3 - c$
j $\quad 25 + 2d = 5d + 4$
k $\quad 6 - 7e = 3 - 6e$
l $\quad 5f + 10 = 2 + f$

2 Jared solves the equation $9x - 2 = 5 - 4x$
He writes down $5x - 2 = 5$

Is this correct?
Explain your answer.

AQA Examiner's tip

Set out each line of your working clearly so you can earn method marks even if your answer is wrong.

D

3 Ella solves the equation $5y + 6 = 2 - y$
She writes down $4y = 4$

Is this correct?
Explain your answer.

4 Dean solves the equation $3x - 11 = 4 + 2x$
He gets the answer $x = 7$

Can you find Dean's mistake?

5 Rick solves the equation $2y + 5 = 3 - 3y$
He gets the answer $y = -2$

Can you find Rick's mistake?

6 $4z - 3 = \boxed{} - 2z$
The answer to this equation is $z = 5$

What is the number under the rectangle?

7 $2a + \boxed{} = 5 - 7a$
The answer to this equation is $a = -1$

What is the number under the rectangle?

8 If $b = 11$, find the value of $3b - 8$

Hence explain why $b = 11$ is not the solution of the equation $3b - 8 = 19 - 2b$

9 If $c = -4$, find the value of $9 - 5c$

Hence explain why $c = -4$ is not the solution of the equation $6c + 13 = 9 - 5c$

Learn... 15.2 Equations with brackets

Your first step is usually to multiply out the **brackets**.

After this, you follow the rules for solving equations.

Example: Solve:

a $4(3x - 1) = 32$

b $7 - 3(y + 2) = 5 - 4y$

Solution: **a** $4(3x - 1) = 32$

$12x - 4 = 32$ Remember to multiply **both** terms in the bracket by 4.
$12x - 4 + 4 = 32 + 4$ Add 4 to both sides.
$12x = 36$ Divide both sides by 12.
$x = 3$

Alternative method:

$4(3x - 1) = 32$
$3x - 1 = 8$ Divide both sides by 4.
$3x - 1 + 1 = 8 + 1$ Add 1 to both sides.
$3x = 8 + 1$
$3x = 9$ Divide both sides by 3.
$x = 3$

This alternative method works because 4 is a factor of 32.
It cannot be used for all equations with brackets, as the next example shows.

b $7 - 3(y + 2) = 5 - 4y$

Multiply out the brackets first, then follow the rules for solving equations.

$7 - 3y - 6 = 5 - 4y$ Note: $-3 \times +2 = -6$

$1 - 3y = 5 - 4y$ The numbers on the left-hand side have been collected.

$1 - 3y - 1 = 5 - 4y - 1$ Subtract 1 from both sides.

$-3y = 4 - 4y$

$-3y + 4y = 4 - 4y + 4y$ Add $4y$ to both sides.

$-3y + 4y = 4$

$y = 4$

AQA Examiner's tip

Don't try to do two steps at once – most students make mistakes if they rush their working.

Bump up your grade

You need to be able to solve equations which have brackets **and** the unknown occurring twice to get a Grade C.

Practise... 15.2 Equations with brackets   k!   D C B A A*

1 Solve these equations.

    a $5(x + 3) = 55$ **d** $7(b - 2) = 7$

    b $2(y - 4) = 16$ **e** $13 = 2(c + 5)$

    c $9 = 3(z - 7)$

2 Solve these equations.

    a $4(p + 2) = 2p + 9$ **g** $11d - 1 = 3(d + 1)$

    b $6(q - 3) = 17 - q$ **h** $2(1 - 2e) = 5 - 3e$

    c $2(5t - 1) = 13$ **i** $2 - 5f = 3(2 - f)$

    d $5a + 3 = 4(a - 2)$ **j** $6(2 + 3x) = 11x + 5$

    e $3(2b - 3) = 1 + 7b$ **k** $3(y - 4) + 2(4y - 2) = 6$

    f $8 + c = 5(c - 2)$

3 Solve the equation $10 - 3(z + 2) = 7 - z$

4 Solve the equation $23 = 6 - 5(t - 4)$

5 Solve the equation $4(p - 3) - 3(p - 4) = 14$

6 Solve the equation $2(q - 9) - (7q - 3) + 25 = 0$

7 Natalie thinks of a number, adds 7 and then doubles the result.
Her answer is 46.
Write this as an equation.
Solve the equation to find Natalie's number.

8 Rob thinks of a number, subtracts 8 and then multiplies the result by 5.
His answer is 65.
Write this as an equation.
Solve the equation to find Rob's number.

Learn... 15.3 Equations with fractions

There are many methods of solving equations with fractions.
At some stage in solving an equation with a fraction, you have to clear the fraction by multiplying both sides by the **denominator.**

For example, if the equation contains $\frac{x}{3}$, you will need to multiply by 3.

If there is more than one fraction, say $\frac{3x}{5}$ and $\frac{x}{2}$, you will need to multiply by both denominators. In this case, this is $5 \times 2 = 10$

Harder equations have more than one term on the top of the fraction.
There are 'invisible brackets' around the terms on top of an algebraic fraction.

Example: Solve these equations.

a $\frac{x}{3} - 2 = 5$

b $\frac{5x}{6} - \frac{3x}{4} = 1$

c $\frac{5x + 2}{4} = 3$

d $\frac{2x - 1}{6} + \frac{x + 3}{3} = \frac{5}{2}$

Solution: a $\frac{x}{3} - 2 = 5$

Start by isolating the fraction.

$\frac{x}{3} - 2 + 2 = 5 + 2$ Add 2 to both sides so the fraction is on its own on the left-hand side.

$\frac{x}{3} = 7$

$x = 7 \times 3$ Multiply both sides by 3.

$x = 21$

b $\frac{5x}{6} - \frac{3x}{4} = 1$

This equation has more than one fraction term.

The lowest common **denominator** is 12.

Multiply **each term** by 12 and then cancel. This should remove all the fractions.

$\cancel{12}^2 \times \frac{5x}{\cancel{6}_1} - \cancel{12}^3 \times \frac{3x}{\cancel{4}_1} = 12 \times 1$ Don't forget to multiply the right-hand side as well as the left-hand side.

$2 \times 5x - 3 \times 3x = 12 \times 1$

$10x - 9x = 12$

$x = 12$

c $\frac{5x + 2}{4} = 3$ ⟵ This is the same as $\frac{1}{4}(5x + 2) = 3$

This equation has two terms on the top of the fraction.

There are 'invisible brackets' around these terms.   You should put in the invisible brackets before you start your working.

$\cancel{4}^1 \times \frac{(5x + 2)}{\cancel{4}_1} = 4 \times 3$ Multiply **both** sides by 4 and cancel.

$5x + 2 = 12$ Subtract 2 from both sides.

$5x = 12 - 2$

$5x = 10$ Divide both sides by 5.

$x = 2$

Chapter 15 Equations and inequalities 197

d $\dfrac{2x-1}{6} + \dfrac{x+3}{3} = \dfrac{5}{2}$

This equation shows you how to handle a complex equation with three fractions.

The lowest common denominator of 6, 3 and 2 is 6. (You could use larger common denominators like 18 or 24 but that would give you larger numbers to deal with.)

Put in the 'invisible brackets' to help you.

$\cancel{6}^1 \times \dfrac{(2x-1)}{\cancel{6}_1} + \cancel{6}^2 \times \dfrac{(x+3)}{\cancel{3}_1} = \cancel{6}^3 \times \dfrac{5}{\cancel{2}_1}$ Multiply both sides of the equation by 6 and cancel.

$(2x - 1) + 2(x + 3) = 3 \times 5$ Multiply out the brackets.
$2x - 1 + 2x + 6 = 15$ Collect like terms.
$4x + 5 = 15$ Subtract 5 from both sides.
$4x = 10$ Divide both sides by 4.
$x = 2.5$

Practise... 15.3 Equations with fractions D C B A A*

1 Solve these equations.

a $\dfrac{x}{2} - 5 = 4$ f $\dfrac{p}{3} + 1 = 5 - p$ k $\dfrac{1}{4}(p + 3) = 5$

b $\dfrac{y}{5} + 3 = 7$ g $\dfrac{q}{5} + 3 = 6 - q$ l $\dfrac{1}{2}(3q + 8) = 13$

c $5 = 1 + \dfrac{z}{3}$ h $\dfrac{4x+1}{3} = 11$ m $\dfrac{x}{5} + \dfrac{x}{3} = 4$

d $9 - \dfrac{b}{2} = 2$ i $\dfrac{2y-7}{5} = 3$ n $\dfrac{y}{2} - \dfrac{y}{8} = 3$

e $\dfrac{c}{6} + 5 = 2$ j $1 = \dfrac{9-z}{3}$

2 Ed and Gary solve the equation $\dfrac{4y-3}{5} = 2y + 3$

Ed gets the answer $y = -2$ and Gary gets $y = -3$

Check their answers to see which of them is correct.

3 Solve these equations.

a $\dfrac{x+1}{2} + \dfrac{x+2}{3} = 2$ d $\dfrac{a-1}{5} - \dfrac{a+1}{6} = 0$

b $\dfrac{y+3}{6} + \dfrac{y-3}{2} = 10$ e $\dfrac{3b+11}{4} - \dfrac{5b-3}{3} = 1$

c $\dfrac{z+5}{2} - \dfrac{z+3}{4} = 4$ f $\dfrac{c}{7} - \dfrac{1-c}{14} = 1$

AQA Examiner's tip
Take care with signs when the fractions are subtracted. Insert brackets to help you.
$-(z + 3) = -z - 3$

4 Solve these equations.

a $\dfrac{1}{2}(5a - 1) = a - 5$ f $\dfrac{3t}{8} + \dfrac{1}{4} = \dfrac{2t}{5}$

b $\dfrac{1}{8}(2b - 5) = 5 - b$ g $\dfrac{d+10}{3} + \dfrac{d+1}{6} = \dfrac{3d+5}{2}$

c $c - 7 = \dfrac{1}{3}(11 - c)$ h $\dfrac{e-2}{2} - \dfrac{e+2}{9} = \dfrac{2e+3}{18}$

d $\dfrac{3p}{2} = 5 - \dfrac{p}{6}$ i $\dfrac{p+4}{5} - \dfrac{2p+3}{6} = \dfrac{p}{15}$

e $\dfrac{q}{3} - \dfrac{1}{4} = \dfrac{q}{6}$ j $\dfrac{3q-1}{3} - \dfrac{5q-3}{4} = \dfrac{7-q}{12}$

5 Explain why you cannot solve the equation $\dfrac{6p-5}{2} = 4 + 3p$

Learn... 15.4 Inequalities and the number line

The four **inequality** symbols are shown in the table.

<	≤	>	≥
less than	less than or equal to	greater than	greater than or equal to

A number line shows the range of values for x.

An **open** circle shows that the range does not include that end of the line.
e.g. $x > 1$ or $y < 5$

A **closed** circle shows that the range includes that end of the line.
e.g. $x \leq 3$ or $y \geq 5$

This is the number line for $x > 1$

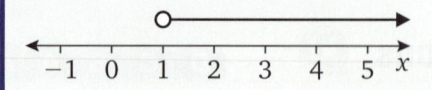

x could be any number greater than 1 **but not 1**.
The open circle shows that x can be close to 1 but not equal to 1.

This is the number line for $x \leq 3$

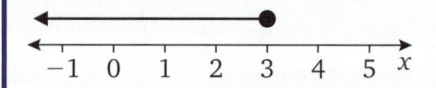

x could be any number less than or equal to 3.
The closed circle shows that x can be equal to 3.

This is the number line for $x < -1$ or $x \geq 2$

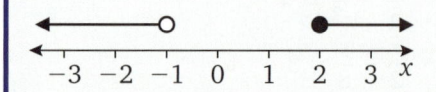

x could be any number less than -1 or it could be any number greater than or equal to 2.
x cannot be a number between -1 and 2.

Example: Show the inequality $-2 \leq x < 3$ on a number line.

Solution:

The open circle shows that x can be close to 3 but not equal to 3.
The closed circle shows that x can be equal to -2.

Practise... 15.4 Inequalities and the number line

D C B A A*

1 Write down the inequalities shown by these number lines.

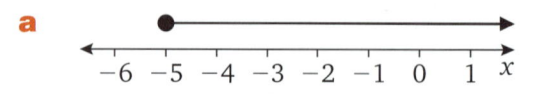

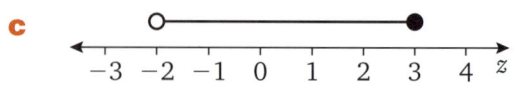

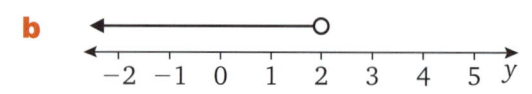

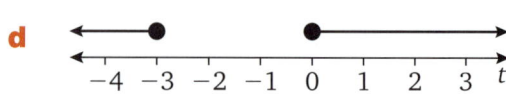

a

b

c

d

2 Show each of these inequalities on a number line.

a $x > 1$
b $x > -5$
c $x \geq 0$
d $x < 2$
e $x \leq -1$
f $-2 < x < 1$
g $-4 \leq x < 3$
h $x < 4$ or $x \geq 6$
i $x \leq -2$ or $x > 0$

3 Explain why it is incorrect to write $2 < x < -6$

4 Nic gets £10 a week in pocket money.
Nic asks Joe how much he gets each week.
Joe says 'I get more than £6 but less than you.'
Joe's pocket money is made up of pound coins and fifty pence pieces.

List the possible amounts Joe might get.

5 Natalie is five foot and six inches tall.
Olwen is five foot and two inches tall.
Pippa is taller than Olwen but not as tall as Natalie.

a Show Pippa's height on a number line.

b Explain why you cannot make a list of possible heights for Pippa.

Learn... 15.5 Solving inequalities

Some inequalities are very similar to equations.

The inequality $3x - 2 > 4$ is similar to the equation $3x - 2 = 4$

To solve this inequality, use **inverse operations** as you would with the equation.

$3x - 2 > 4$
$3x - 2 + 2 > 4 + 2$ Add 2 to both sides.
$3x > 6$ Divide both sides by 3.
$x > 2$

If you multiply or divide both sides of an inequality by a **negative number**, the inequality sign is **reversed**.

If $y > 5$, then $-y < -5$ Try this with a value for y, such as $y = 7$. 7 is greater than 5, but -7 is less than -5.

You may be asked to list **integer** values (whole numbers) that satisfy an inequality.

For example, the integers that satisfy $-3 \leq x < 5$ are $-3, -2, -1, 0, 1, 2, 3, 4$

Sometimes you have to combine these two skills, as in example **c** below.

Example:
a Solve the inequality $3x - 5 > 4$
b Solve the inequality $4 - 2x \leq 9 + 3x$
c List all the **integer** values of n such that $-5 < 2n \leq 6$

Solution:
a $3x - 5 > 4$ Add 5 to both sides.
$3x > 9$ Divide by 3.
$x > 3$

b $4 - 2x \leq 9 + 3x$ Subtract 4 from both sides.
$-2x \leq 5 + 3x$ Subtract $3x$ from both sides.
$-5x \leq 5$ Divide both sides by -5. (Remember to reverse the inequality sign.)
$x \geq -1$

c $-5 < 2n \leq 6$ Divide every term in the inequality by 2.
$-2.5 < n \leq 3$

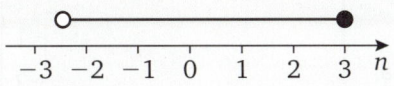

Integer values for n are: $-2, -1, 0, 1, 2, 3$

Practise... 15.5 Solving inequalities

1 Solve these inequalities.
   a $3x - 2 \geq 4$
   b $2y + 7 \leq 16$
   c $4z + 12 < 0$
   d $5 + 2p > 1$
   e $8 < 2 + 3q$
   f $5 > 13 - t$

2 Find the largest integer that satisfies the inequality $5 - 2x \geq 1$

3 Find the smallest integer that satisfies the inequality $7 < 3(2x + 9)$

4 List all the integer values of n such that:
   a $0 < 3n < 11$
   b $-4 < 2n \leq 6$
   c $-10 \leq 4n < 12$
   d $-5 \leq 5n \leq 8$

5 Solve these inequalities.
   a $7u - 5 > 3u - 1$
   b $8 - v < 2v + 11$
   c $5(w - 1) > 3(w + 2)$
   d $3x - 8 > 8x + 7$
   e $10 - 3y \geq 5 - y$
   f $7 - 2z \leq 4 + 3z$

6 List all the pairs of positive integers, x and y, such that $3x + 4y \leq 15$

7 Jiffa is 14 years old.
She says to her Uncle Asif 'How old are you?'
He says 'In 9 years' time I shall be more than twice as old as I was when you were born.'
Write down an inequality and solve it to find the greatest age Asif could be.

Learn... 15.6 Inequalities and graphs

You can represent an inequality such as $x > 1$ as an area, or **region**, on a graph.

The boundary of this region will be the line $x = 1$

The convention is that 'strict inequalities', such as $x > -1$ or $y < 5$, are shown with a dashed line at the boundary.

'Included inequalities' such as $x \geq 1$ or $y \leq 5$ are shown with a solid line at the boundary.

Example: Show the region defined by each of these inequalities.
   a $x \geq 3$
   b $y < -1$
   c $x + y > 2$

Solution:
   a The inequality is $\geq$ so draw the boundary, $x = 3$, with a solid line.
      Shade the region where $x \geq 3$

   AQA Examiner's tip
   Shade the region that is defined by the inequality.
   Write the inequality in this area.

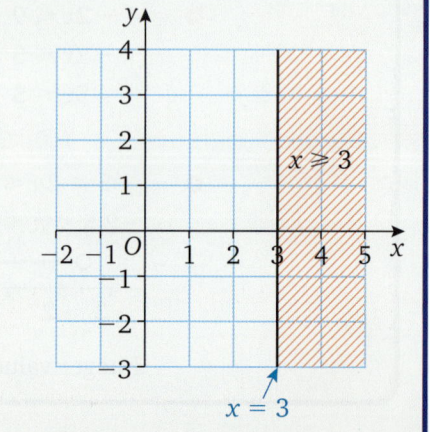

b The inequality is < so draw the boundary, $y = -1$, with a dashed line.

Shade the region where $y < -1$

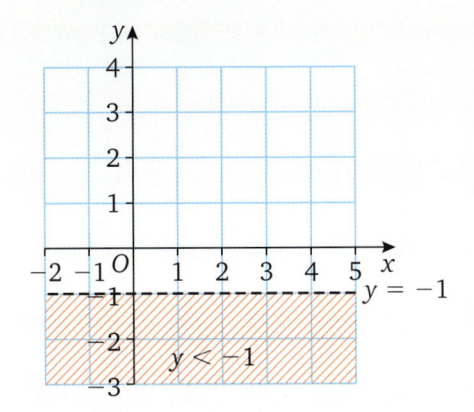

c The inequality is > so draw the boundary, $x + y = 2$, with a broken line.

Shade the region where $x + y > 2$

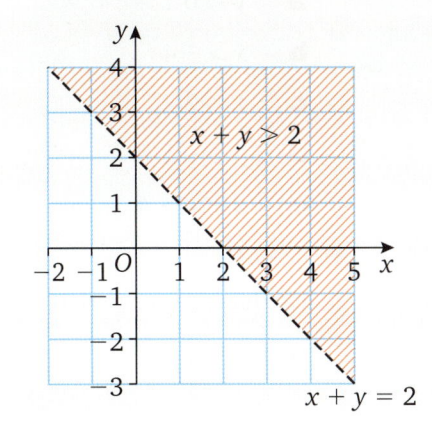

If you have a line that is not parallel to one of the axes, it is sometimes hard to decide which side of the line represents the inequality.

To help you decide:
- pick a point on one side of the line (use (0, 0) if the line does not go through the origin)
- check whether $x + y > 2$ is true for this point.

$0 + 0 > 2$ ✗ so this point is **not** on the side that represents the inequality.

If you represent a set of inequalities such as $x > 1$, $y \leqslant 2$ and $x + y < 5$ as regions on a graph, you can find number pairs that satisfy all the inequalities.

AQA Examiner's tip

If the line does not pass through the origin then test with (0, 0). This makes the working easier when substituting into the inequality.
If it does go through the origin, pick easy numbers like (1, 1).

Example: **a** Show the region defined by the inequalities $x + y \leqslant 5$, $x > 0$ and $y > 2$

b If x and y are integers, which points satisfy all three inequalities?

Solution: **a** Draw the three boundaries.

Shade above $y = 2$, to the right of $x = 0$ and below $x + y = 5$

To check your result, pick a point in the region such as (1, 3).

Checking that $x + y \leqslant 5$ $1 + 3 < 5$ ✓

Checking that $x > 0$ $1 > 0$ ✓

Checking that $y > 2$ $3 > 2$ ✓

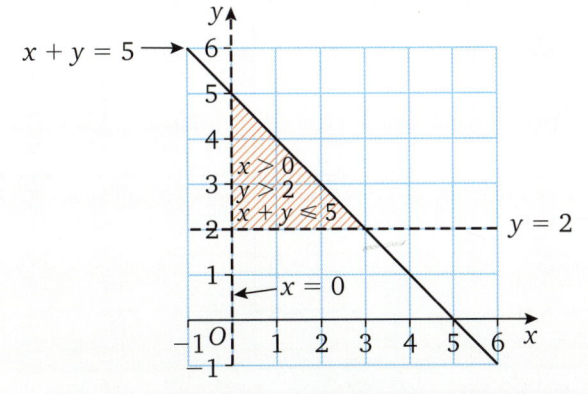

AQA Examiner's tip

In an exam, do not shade the region in colour as it often does not show up when your paper is scanned. Use hatching lines drawn with your pen instead.

b There are three points within this region that have integer coordinates.
They are (1, 3), (1, 4) and (2, 3).

Note: the points can lie on the solid line but not on the broken lines.

Practise... 15.6 Inequalities and graphs

1 On separate diagrams, draw the regions defined by these inequalities.
- **a** $y < 0$
- **b** $x > -4$
- **c** $x \leq 2$
- **d** $y \geq -1$
- **e** $x + y > 4$

2 Use inequalities to describe the shaded regions.

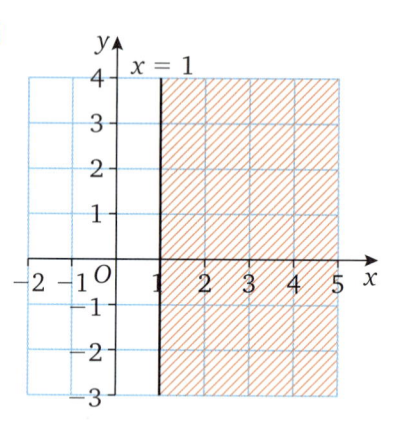

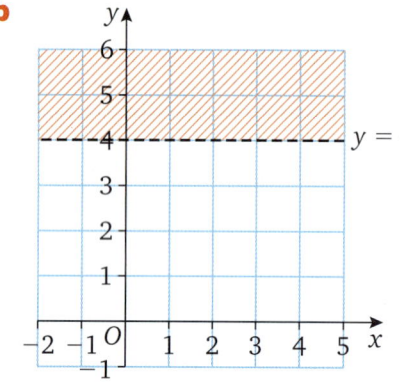

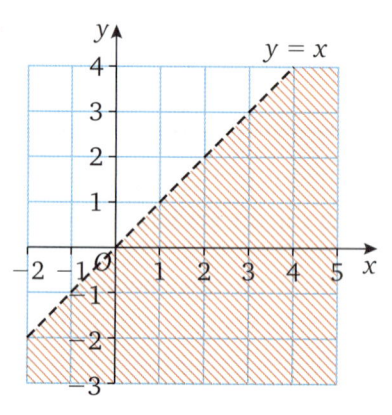

a (graph showing $x = 2$)

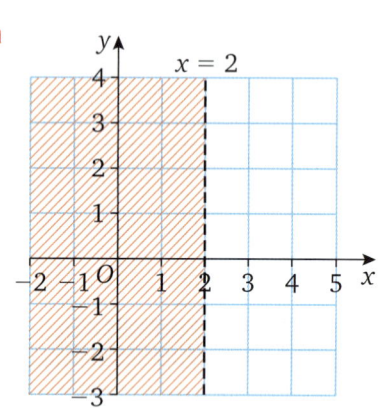

b (graph showing $y = 4$)

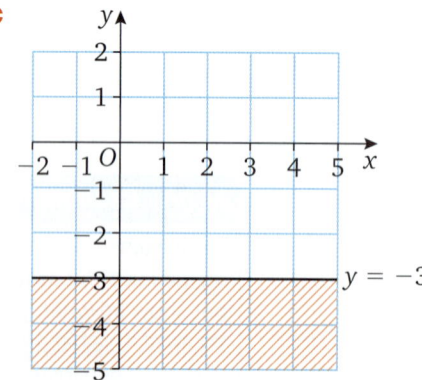

c (graph showing $y = -3$)

d (graph showing $x = 1$)

e (graph showing $y = x$)

f (graph showing $y + x = 3$)

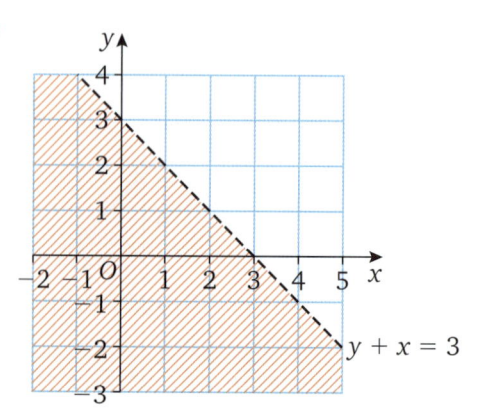

3 Draw x- and y-axes from 0 to 6.
- **a** Shade the region where $x < 5$, $y > 2$ and $y \leq x$
- **b** List the three points in the region whose coordinates are integers.

Chapter 15 Equations and inequalities **203**

4 **a** Find the equations of the straight lines on these graphs.

b Use inequalities to describe the shaded regions.

i

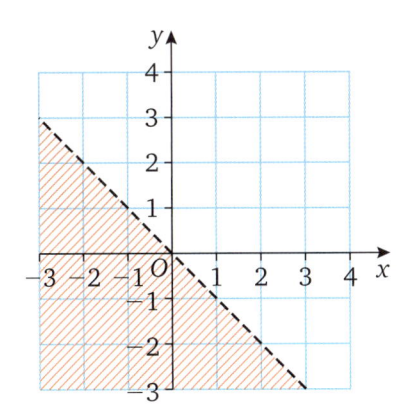

iii

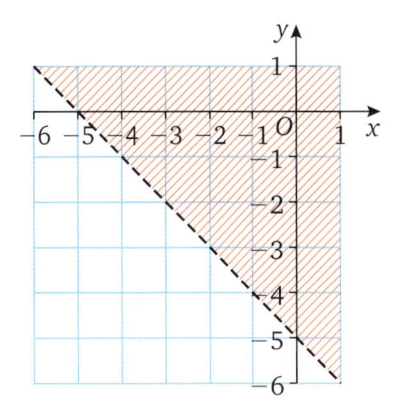

ii

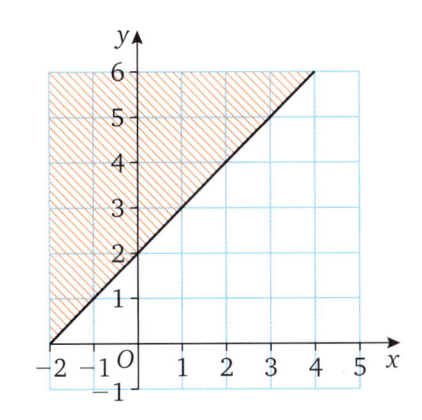

5 Draw x- and y-axes from 0 to 6.

a Shade the region where $y < 2x$, $y > \frac{1}{2}x$ and $x + y < 6$

b Dean says there are nine points in the region whose coordinates are integers.
Is he correct? Explain your answer.

6 Describe with inequalities these regions bounded by blue lines.

a A
b B
c E + F
d D
e C

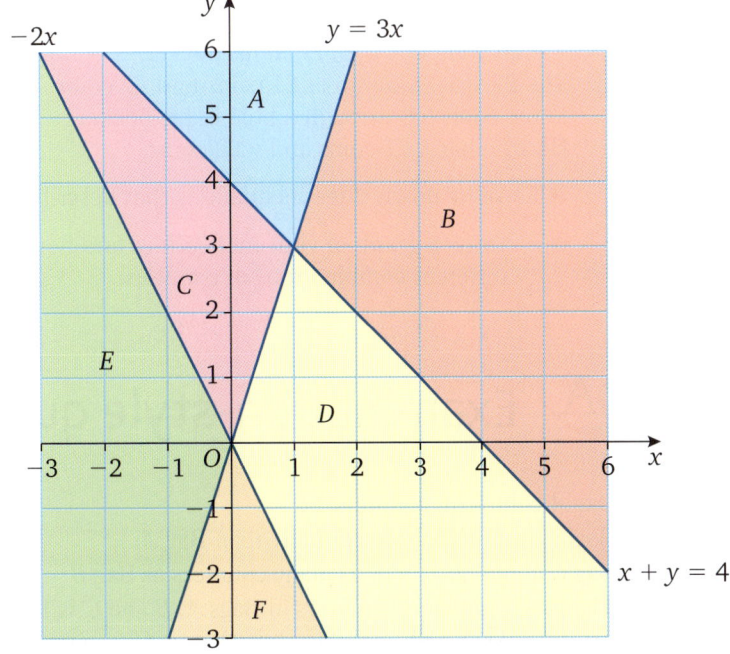

15 Assess

1 Solve these equations.
  a $p + 5 = 14 - 2p$
  b $2q - 1 = 5 - q$
  c $6m - 7 = 2m + 3$
  d $4 + 3n = n - 10$
  e $5(u + 1) = 35$
  f $49 = 7(3t - 2)$

2 Write down the inequalities shown by these number lines.
  a (number line from −5 to 3, open circle at −4, closed circle at 2)
  b (number line from −5 to 3, closed circle at −4, open circle at 2... showing arrow)

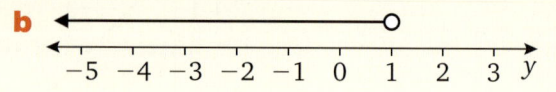

3 Solve these equations.
  a $3(v - 4) = 9 + 2v$
  b $4(w - 2) + 2(3w + 1) = 44$
  c $5(2x - 3) = 7 + 4(x - 1)$
  d $3(2t - 1) = 10 - 2(3t + 2)$

4 Solve these equations.
  a $\dfrac{y}{4} + 3 = 7$
  b $4 - \dfrac{z}{3} = 6$
  c $\dfrac{x}{5} + \dfrac{x}{10} = 6$

5 List all the integer solutions of the inequality $-8 < 3n \leq 9$

6 Solve these inequalities.
  a $6a - 7 \geq 5$
  b $3b + 10 < 4$

7 Find the largest integer that satisfies the inequality $2x + 3 < 17$

8 Solve the inequality $3(y - 1) > 5y + 7$

9 Solve these equations.
  a $\dfrac{7x - 2}{5} + \dfrac{4 - 3x}{3} = \dfrac{1}{3}$
  b $\dfrac{2 + 3y}{7} - \dfrac{y - 4}{3} = \dfrac{y}{2}$

10 Draw x- and y-axes from -3 to 5.
  a Shade the region where $y < 2x$, $x - 2y > 4$ and $x + 2y < 4$
  b List the five points in the region whose coordinates are integers.

11 Ramin went out with £7 in his pocket.
The £7 was made up of £1 coins and £2 coins.
Some coins fell through a hole in his pocket.
Now he has x £1 coins and y £2 coins.
  a Write down three inequalities that describe this.
  b Draw a graph of your inequalities and hence show that there are six possible different combinations of coins left.

AQA Examination-style questions

1 Bag A contains x counters.
Bag B contains 6 more counters than Bag A.
Bag C contains 4 times as many counters as Bag B.
The total number of counters in Bags A, B and C is 120.
Set up and solve an equation to work out the number of counters in Bag A. *(6 marks)*

AQA 2005

16 Trial and improvement

Objectives

Examiners would normally expect students who get these grades to be able to:

C

solve equations such as $x^3 + x = 12$ using systematic trial and improvement methods.

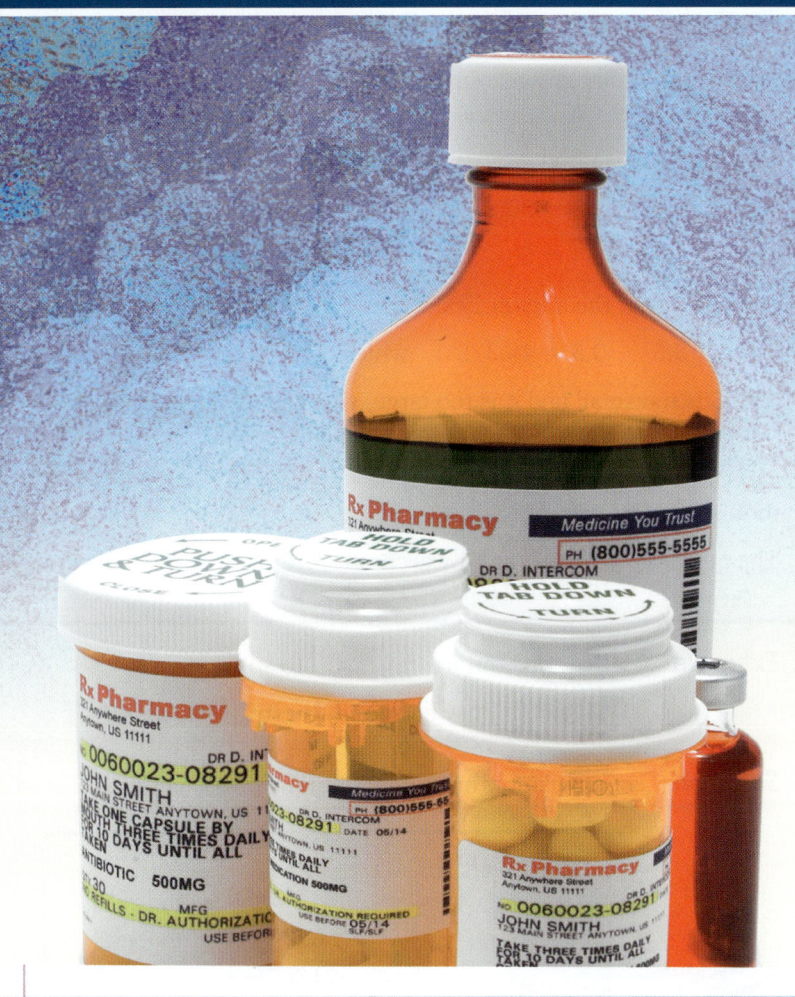

Did you know?

Trial and improvement

Trial and improvement (also known as trial and error) has many uses in the real world. It is often used by engineers when they develop complex equipment. For example, engineers will trial different fuel flow rates when determining the maximum thrust from a jet engine.

Also doctors may use trial and improvement to test different combinations of drugs for diabetes, epilepsy and high blood pressure. For the future, scientists are developing supercomputers which will act as 'virtual humans'. This will allow doctors to match different combinations of drugs to different patients.

You should already know:

✓ how to substitute into algebraic expressions
✓ how to rearrange formulae
✓ how to use the bracket and power buttons on your calculator.

Key terms

trial and improvement
decimal place

Learn... 16.1 Trial and improvement

Trial and improvement is a method for solving problems using estimations that get closer and closer to the actual answer. Trial and improvement is used where there is no exact answer, so you will be asked to give a rounded answer. On the examination paper, you will be told when to use a trial and improvement method.

If you are told that $x^3 + x = 50$ then you can work out that the answer lies between 3 and 4 because:

$3^3 + 3 = 30$ which is too small

and $4^3 + 4 = 68$ which is too large

You know that the answer lies between 3 and 4 so you might try 3.5:

$3.5^3 + 3.5 = 46.375$ which is too small

As 3.5 is too small and 4 is too large, you know that the answer lies between 3.5 and 4 so you might try 3.7 or 3.8…

You can keep going with this method to get an answer that is more and more accurate.

The question will tell you how accurate your answer should be.

> **AQA Examiner's tip**
> It is a good idea to lay your working out carefully. A table can be helpful.

Example: Use trial and improvement to solve $x^3 - x = 40$

Give your answer to one **decimal place**.

Solution: You can try out some different values to get you started.

Trial value of x	$x^3 - x$	Comment
1	0	too small
2	6	too small
3	24	too small
4	60 ← 40	too large

> **AQA Examiner's tip**
> On some examination questions you will be told where the answer lies. For example, you may be told that there is a solution between 2 and 3.

The answer 40 lies between 24 and 60.

This tells you that x lies between 3 and 4.

You might try 3.5

| 3.5 | 39.375 | too small |
| 3.6 | 43.056 | too large |

Again, you can see that 40 lies between 39.375 and 43.056

This tells you that x lies between 3.5 and 3.6

You should try 3.55

The answer to 1 d.p. is either 3.5 or 3.6

Work out the value for 3.55 to see whether it is larger than 40.

If it is too large, then 3.55 is too large and the answer to 1 d.p. is 3.5

If it is too small, then 3.55 is too small and the answer to 1 d.p. is 3.6

| 3.55 | 41.188875 | too large |

You know that x lies between 3.5 and 3.55

But any answer between 3.5 and 3.55 is the same as 3.5 to 1 d.p.

The required answer is 3.5 to 1 d.p.

Practise... 16.1 Trial and improvement

1 Find, using trial and improvement, a solution to the following equations.
Give your answers correct to one decimal place.
You **must** show all your working.

   a $x^3 + x = 10$
   c $x^3 - 5x = 400$
   b $x^3 + x = 520$
   d $x - x^3 = -336$

2 Use trial and improvement to solve the equation $x^3 + x = 75$
Give your answer to one decimal place.
The table has been started for you

Trial value of x	$x^3 + x$	Comment
2	10	too low
3	30	too low
4	68	too low
5	130	too high

So now we know that the value lies between 4 and 5.

4.5	95.625	Too high
?		
?		

3 Use trial and improvement to find solutions to the following equations.
Give your answer to two decimal places.

   a $a^3 - 10a = 50$ if the solution lies between 4 and 5
   b $x^3 - x = 100$ if the solution lies between 4 and 5
   c $5x - x^3 = 10$ if the solution lies between -2 and -3

4 Use trial and improvement to find solutions to the following.
Give your answer to two decimal places.

   a $t^3 - 5t = 10$ if t lies between 2 and 3
   b $x^3 - 5x = 60$ if x lies between 4 and 5
   c $x(x^2 + 1) = 60$ if x lies between 3 and 4
   d $p^3 + 6p = -50$ if p lies between -3 and -4

5 Use trial and improvement to find a negative solution of the equation $y^3 + 60 = 0$

6 The equation $x^3 - 4x^2 = -5$ has two solutions of x between 0 and 5.
Use trial and improvement to find these solutions.
Give your answer to three decimal places.

7 Use trial and improvement to find the value of $x^2 - \dfrac{1}{x} = 5$ where x lies between 2 and 3.
Give your answer to two decimal places.

8 Solve the following equations using trial and improvement.
Give your answer to two decimal places.
You must show your working.

   a $2^x = 20$
   c $x^3 - 2x^2 + x = 44$
   b $x^3 + \dfrac{1}{x^3} = 100$
   d $x^4 - 3x = 99$

9 The difference between the square of a number and the cube of a number is 100.
Find the number to one decimal place.

10 The following solid consists of a central square and four equal arms.
The volume of the solid is 100 cm³.
Find the value of x correct to two decimal places.

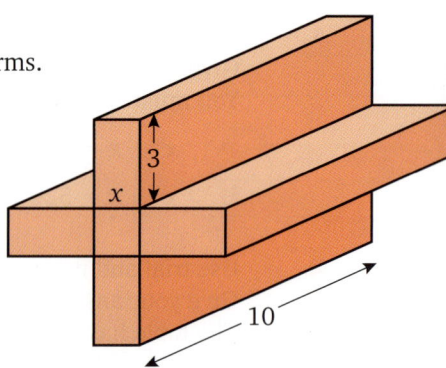

16 Assess k!

1 Use trial and improvement to solve the equation $x^3 - 4x = 100$
Give your answer to one decimal place.
The table has been started for you.

Trial value of x	$x^3 - 4x$	Comment
3	15	too small
4	48	too small
5	105	too large

2 The equation $x^3 + 8x^2 = 20$ has two negative solutions between 0 and −8.
Use trial and improvement to find these solutions.
Give your answer to two decimal places.

3 A cuboid measures $x \times x \times (x + 2)$.
The volume of the cuboid is 50 cm³.

Use trial and improvement to find x.
Give your answer to three decimal places.

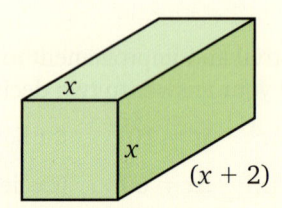

4 Use trial and improvement to find solutions to the following equations.
Give your answer to two decimal places.

a $x^3 + 5x = 50$ if the solution lies between 3 and 4
b $y^3 + 3y = 10$ if the solution lies between 1 and 2
c $x^3 - x = 100$ if the solution lies between 4 and 5
d $3x - x^3 = 25$ if the solution lies between −3 and −4

5 Use trial and improvement to find solutions to the following equations.
Give your answers to two decimal places.

a $x^3 + x = 60$ if x lies between 3 and 4
b $x^3 - 12x = 0$ if x lies between 2 and 6

6 Use trial and improvement to find the value of $8x - x^3 = 3$ where x is negative.
Give your answer to two decimal places.

7 Use trial and improvement to find the value of $t^3 + t^2 = 10$ where $1 \leq t \leq 2$
Give your answer to two decimal places.

Chapter 16 Trial and improvement

8 Solve the following using trial and improvement methods.
Give your answer to two decimal places. You must show your working.

 a $3^x = 15$
 b $x^4 + x = 40$

9 $\dfrac{x^2 + 1}{x} = 10$ has two solutions greater than zero.

Use trial and improvement to find these solutions.
Give your answer to two decimal places.

10 $x^2 + \dfrac{2}{x} = 10$ has one negative solution.

Use trial and improvement to find this solution.
Work out x to one decimal place.

AQA Examination-style questions

1 Kerry is using trial and improvement to find a solution to the equation $8x - x^3 = 5$
Her first two trials are shown in the table.

x	$8x - x^3$	Comment
2	8	too high
3	-3	too low

Copy and continue the table to find a solution to the equation.
Give your answer to one decimal place. *(3 marks)*

AQA 2007

2 The sketch shows the graph of $y = x^3 - 3x - 8$
The graph passes through the points $(2, -6)$ and $(3, 10)$.

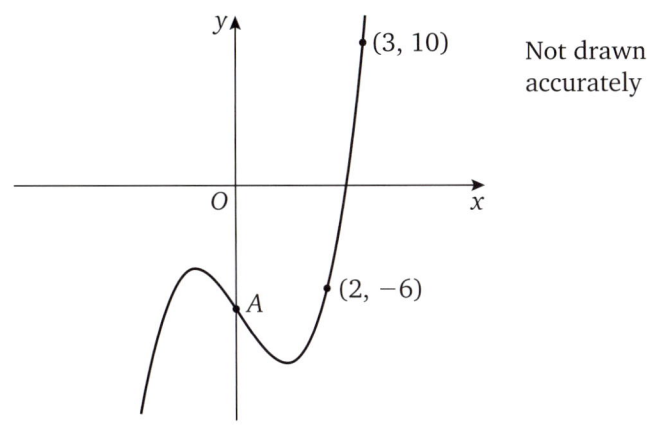

a The graph crosses the y-axis at the point A.
Write down the coordinates of point A. *(1 mark)*

b Use trial and improvement to find the solution of:
$x^3 - 3x - 8 = 0$
Give your answer to one decimal place. *(4 marks)*

AQA 2008

3 Use trial and improvement to find the solution to the equation
$x^3 + 2x = 60$
Give your answer to one decimal place. You **must** show your working *(4 marks)*

AQA 2007

17 Scatter graphs

Objectives

Examiners would normally expect students who get these grades to be able to:

D
draw a scatter graph by plotting points on a graph

interpret the scatter graph

C
draw a line of best fit on the scatter graph

interpret the line of best fit

identify the type and strength of the correlation.

Did you know?

Scatter graphs

Scatter graphs are frequently used in medical research to test for relationships. For example, a study of office workers found that those with a stressful job had higher blood pressure. Scatter graphs can also be used to test the effects of drugs on lowering blood pressure.

Key terms

coordinate
scatter graph
correlation
positive correlation
negative correlation
zero or no correlation
outlier
line of best fit

You should already know:

✓ how to use **coordinates** to plot points on a graph
✓ how to draw graphs including labelling axes and adding a title.

Chapter 17 Scatter graphs 211

Learn... 17.1 Interpreting scatter graphs

Scatter graphs (or scatter diagrams) are used to show the relationship between two sets of data.
Correlation measures the relationship between two sets of data.
It is measured in terms of **type** and **strength** of correlation.

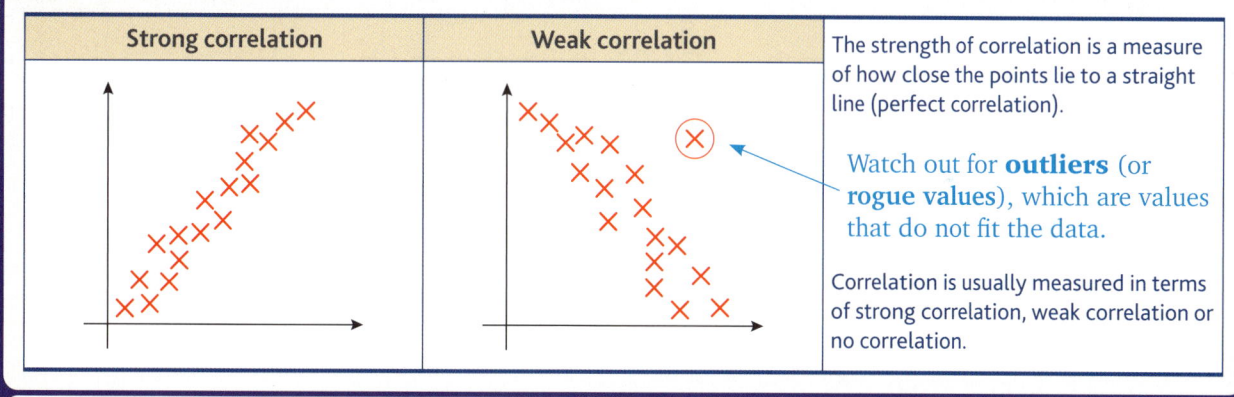

Type of correlation

Positive correlation	Negative correlation	Zero or no correlation
(scatter graph showing points trending upward)	(scatter graph showing points trending downward)	(scatter graph showing randomly scattered points)
Positive correlation As one set of data increases, the other set of data increases.	**Negative correlation** As one set of data increases, the other set of data decreases.	**Zero or no correlation** There is no obvious relationship between the two sets of data.

Example:
Temperature against ice cream sales. As the temperature increases, the number of ice cream sales increases.

Example:
Temperature against sales of coats. As the temperature increases, the sale of coats decreases.

Example:
Temperature against toothpaste sales. There is no obvious relationship between temperature and toothpaste sales.

Strength of correlation

Strong correlation	Weak correlation	
(scatter graph with tight trend)	(scatter graph with looser trend and outlier circled)	The strength of correlation is a measure of how close the points lie to a straight line (perfect correlation). Watch out for **outliers** (or **rogue values**), which are values that do not fit the data. Correlation is usually measured in terms of strong correlation, weak correlation or no correlation.

Example:
The graph shows the temperature and sales of ice cream.
Describe the relationship between the temperature and sales of ice cream.

> **Bump up your grade**
>
> You need to be able to describe the type and strength of the relationship between two sets of data to get a Grade C.

Solution:
You can see that there is a relationship between the temperature and sales of ice cream.
As the temperature increases, the sales of ice cream increase.
There is a **strong positive** correlation between the temperature and the sales of ice cream. This is probably because as the temperature goes up, people want to eat more ice cream.

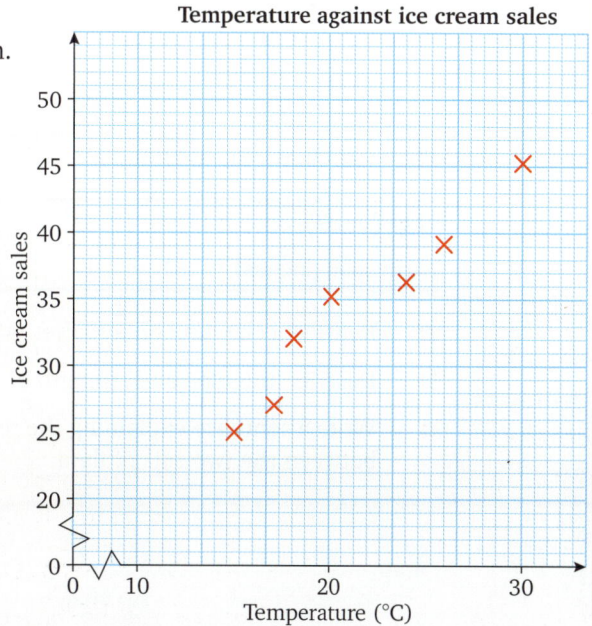

Temperature against ice cream sales
(scatter graph with Temperature (°C) on x-axis from 0 to 30, Ice cream sales on y-axis from 0 to 50)

Practise... 17.1 Interpreting scatter graphs

1 For each of the following:
  a describe the type and strength of correlation
  b write a sentence explaining the relationship between the two sets of data.

  i The hours of sunshine and the sales of iced drinks
  ii The number of cars on a road and the average speed
  iii The distance travelled and the amount of petrol used
  iv The cost of a house and the number of bedrooms
  v The amount of sunshine and the sale of umbrellas.

2 For each of these scatter graphs:
  a describe the type and strength of correlation
  b write a sentence explaining the relationship between the two sets of data (for example, the higher the rainfall, the heavier the weight of apples).

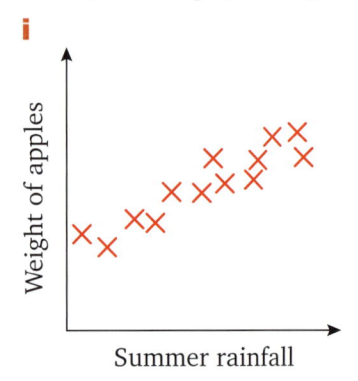

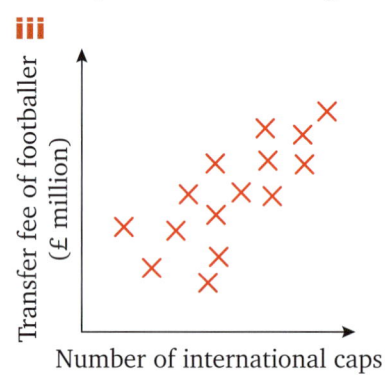

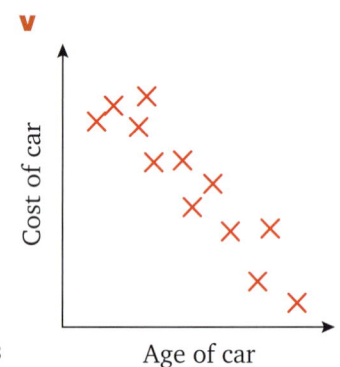

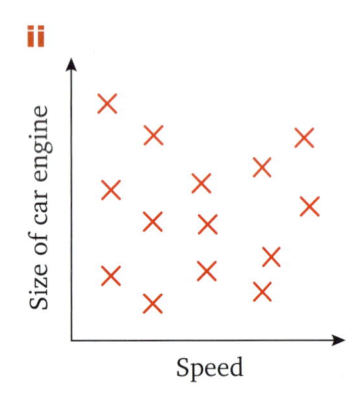

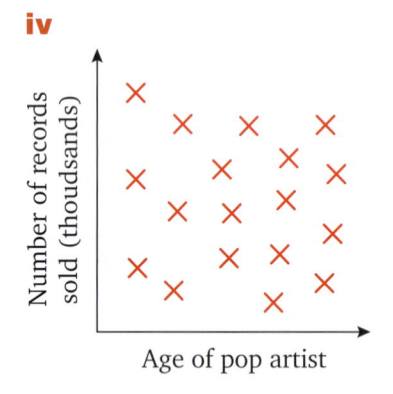

  i Weight of apples vs Summer rainfall
  ii Size of car engine vs Speed
  iii Transfer fee of footballer (£ million) vs Number of international caps
  iv Number of records sold (thousands) vs Age of pop artist
  v Cost of car vs Age of car

3 The table shows the ages and arm spans of seven students in a school.

Age (years)	16	13	13	10	18	10	15
Arm span (inches)	62	57	59	57	64	55	61

  a Represent the data on a scatter graph.
  b Describe the type and strength of correlation.
  c Write a sentence explaining the relationship between the two sets of data.

Chapter 17 Scatter graphs   213

4 The table shows the hours of sunshine and rainfall in 10 seaside towns.

Sunshine (hours)	Rainfall (mm)
650	11
400	30
530	28
640	11
520	24
550	20
480	26
600	15
550	16
525	23

a Represent the data on a scatter graph.

b Describe the type and strength of correlation.

c Write a sentence explaining the relationship between the two sets of data.

5 For each graph, write down two variables that might fit the relationship.

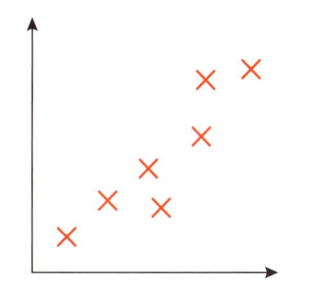

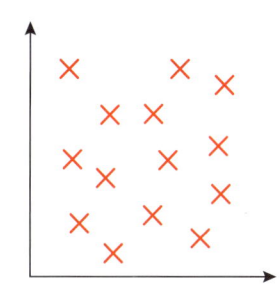

  a   **b**   **c**

6 The scatter graph shows the ages and shoe sizes of a group of people.

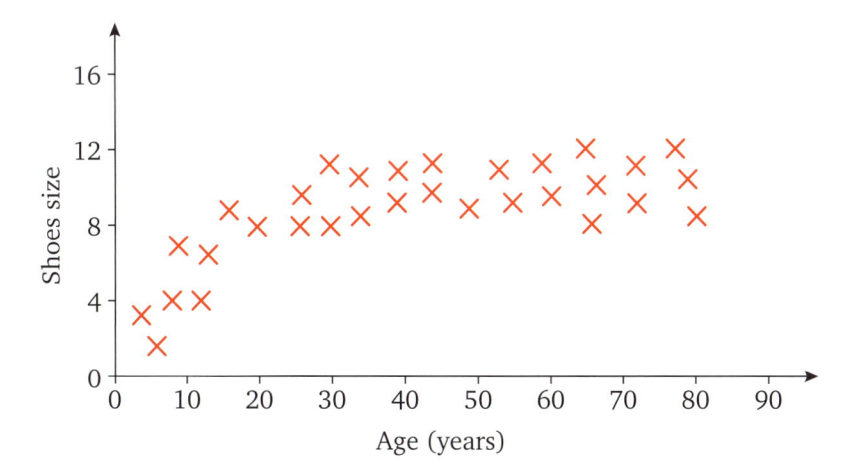

a Describe the type and strength of the correlation.

b Give a reason for your answer.

7 Ron is investigating the fat content and the calorie values of food at his local fast-food restaurant.

He collects the following information.

	Fat (g)	Calories
Hamburger	9	260
Cheeseburger	12	310
Chicken nuggets	24	420
Fish sandwich	18	400
Medium fries	16	350
Medium cola	0	210
Milkshake	26	1100
Breakfast	46	730

a   Describe the correlation between fat and calories.

b   Does the relationship hold for all the different foods? Give a reason for your answer.

Hint
If you are asked to describe correlation you should draw a scatter graph first, then describe the type and strength of correlation.

Learn... 17.2 Lines of best fit

A **line of best fit** is drawn to represent the relationship between two sets of data on a scatter graph.

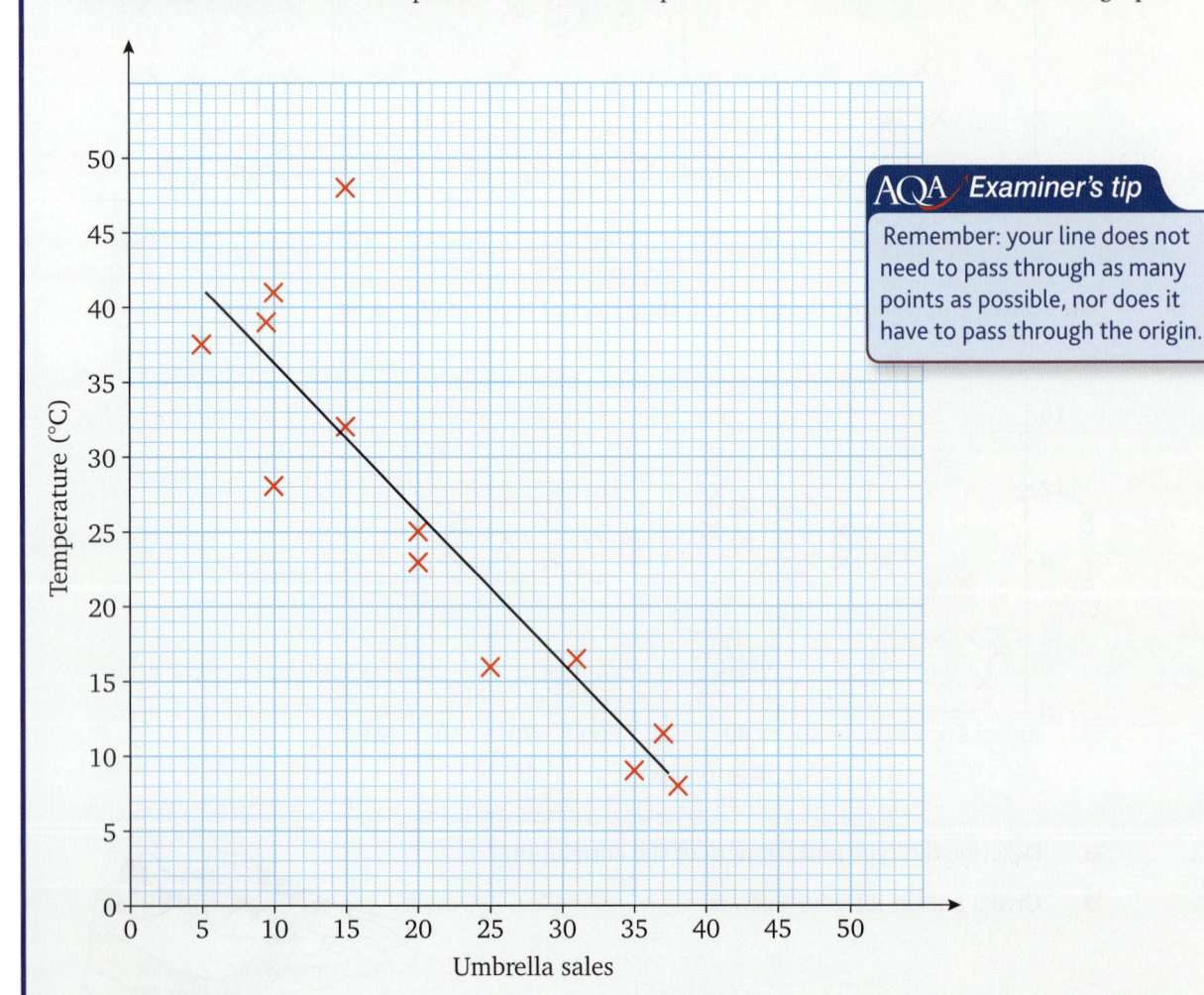

AQA Examiner's tip
Remember: your line does not need to pass through as many points as possible, nor does it have to pass through the origin.

In this example, one of the values does not seem to fit the rest of the data. This is called an **outlier** or rogue value. Ignore these values when drawing a line of best fit.

Chapter 17 Scatter graphs 215

You should draw the line of best fit so that:
- it gives a general trend for all of the data on the scatter graph
- it gives an idea of the strength and type of correlation
- there are roughly equal numbers of points above and below the line.

You can use the line of best fit to estimate missing data.

A line of best fit should only be drawn where the correlation is strong.

AQA Examiner's tip
The examiner will use a 'corridor of success' to check that your line of best fit is reasonable. This means that if your line is in a certain area on the graph, you will get the mark.

Example: The graph shows the number of hours revision and the number of GCSE passes for 10 students.

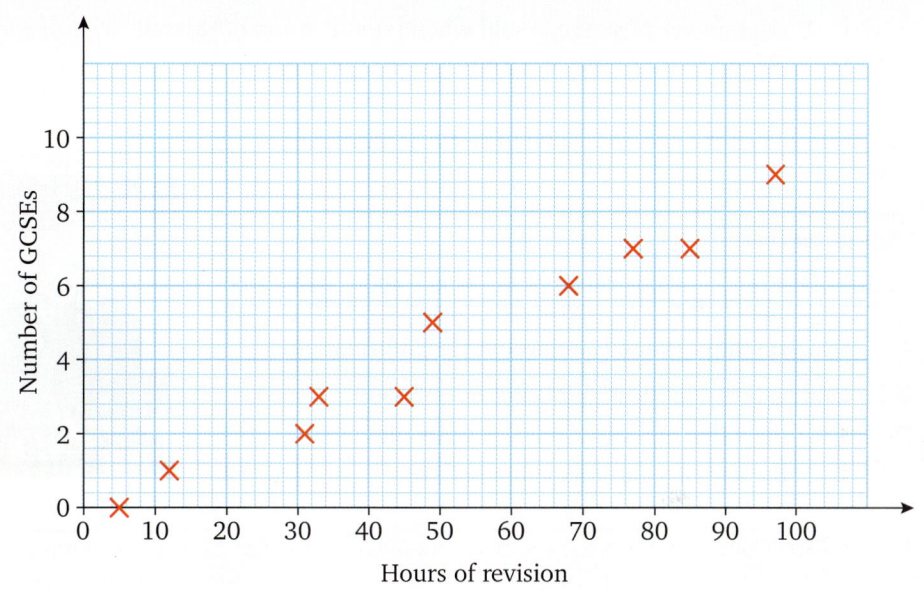

a Draw a line of best fit.

b Dinah studies for 60 hours. How many GCSE passes is she likely to get?

Solution: By drawing the line of best fit, you can use the graph to estimate the number of GCSE passes.

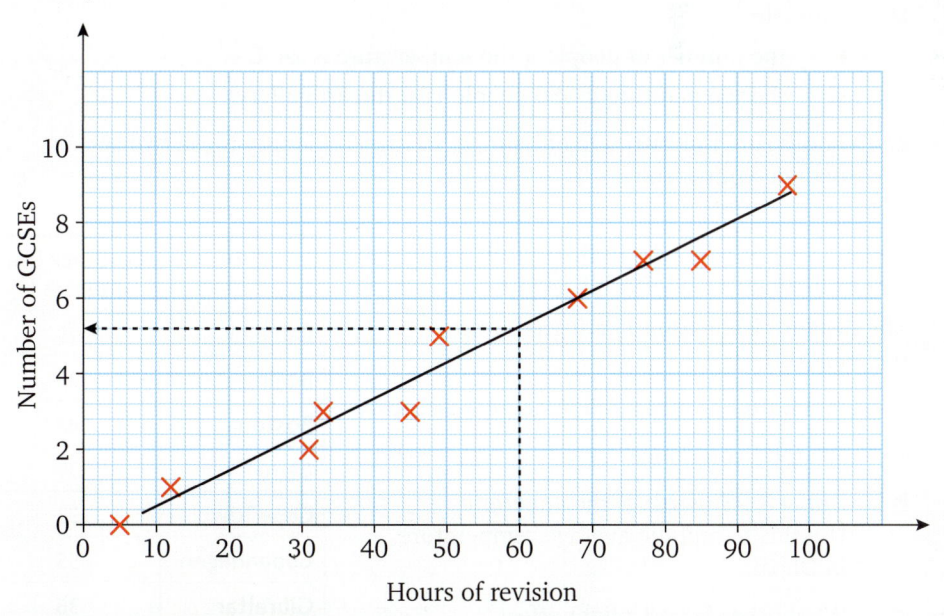

From the graph Dinah should expect to get five passes.

Bump up your grade
You will need to draw and interpret the line of best fit to get a Grade C.

Practise... 17.2 Lines of best fit

D C B A A*

1 The table shows the rainfall and the number of sunbeds sold in a day at a resort.

Amount of rainfall (mm)	0	1	2	5	6	9	11
Number of sunbeds sold	380	320	340	210	220	110	60

a Draw a scatter graph to represent this information.

b Draw a line of best fit and use it to estimate:
   i the number of sunbeds sold when there is 4 mm of rainfall
   ii the amount of rainfall if 100 sunbeds are sold.

2 The table shows the age and value of seven second-hand cars of the same model.

Age of car (years)	2	1	4	7	10	9	8
Value of car (£)	4200	4700	2800	1900	400	1100	2100

a Draw a scatter graph to represent this information.

b Draw a line of best fit and use it to estimate:
   i the value of a car if it is 7.5 years old
   ii the age of a car if its value is £3700.

3 Rob collects information on the temperature and the number of visitors to an art gallery.

Temperature (°C)	15	25	16	18	19	22	24	23	17	20	26	20
Number of visitors	720	180	160	620	510	400	310	670	720	530	180	420

a Draw a scatter graph to represent this information.

b Estimate:
   i the number of people if the temperature is 24 °C
   ii the temperature if 350 people visit the art gallery.

c Rob is sure that two sets of data are incorrect. Identify these two sets of data on your graph.

4 The table shows the distances from the equator and average temperatures for 12 cities.

The distance is measured in degrees from the equator.

The temperature is measured in degrees Celsius.

a What do you notice?

b Dubai is 25° north of the equator. Use this to find the average temperature in Dubai.

c What other factors might affect temperatures?

City	Distance from equator (°)	Average temp. (°C)
Bangkok	13	28
Beijing	39	12
Boston	42	9
Cairo	30	22
Cape Town	33	17
Copenhagen	55	8
Gibraltar	36	19
Istanbul	40	14
London	51	10
Moscow	55	4
Mumbai	18	27
Perth	32	18

Chapter 17 Scatter graphs   217

5 The graph shows the line for best fit for the relationship between house prices in 2006 and estimated house prices in 2020.

House prices

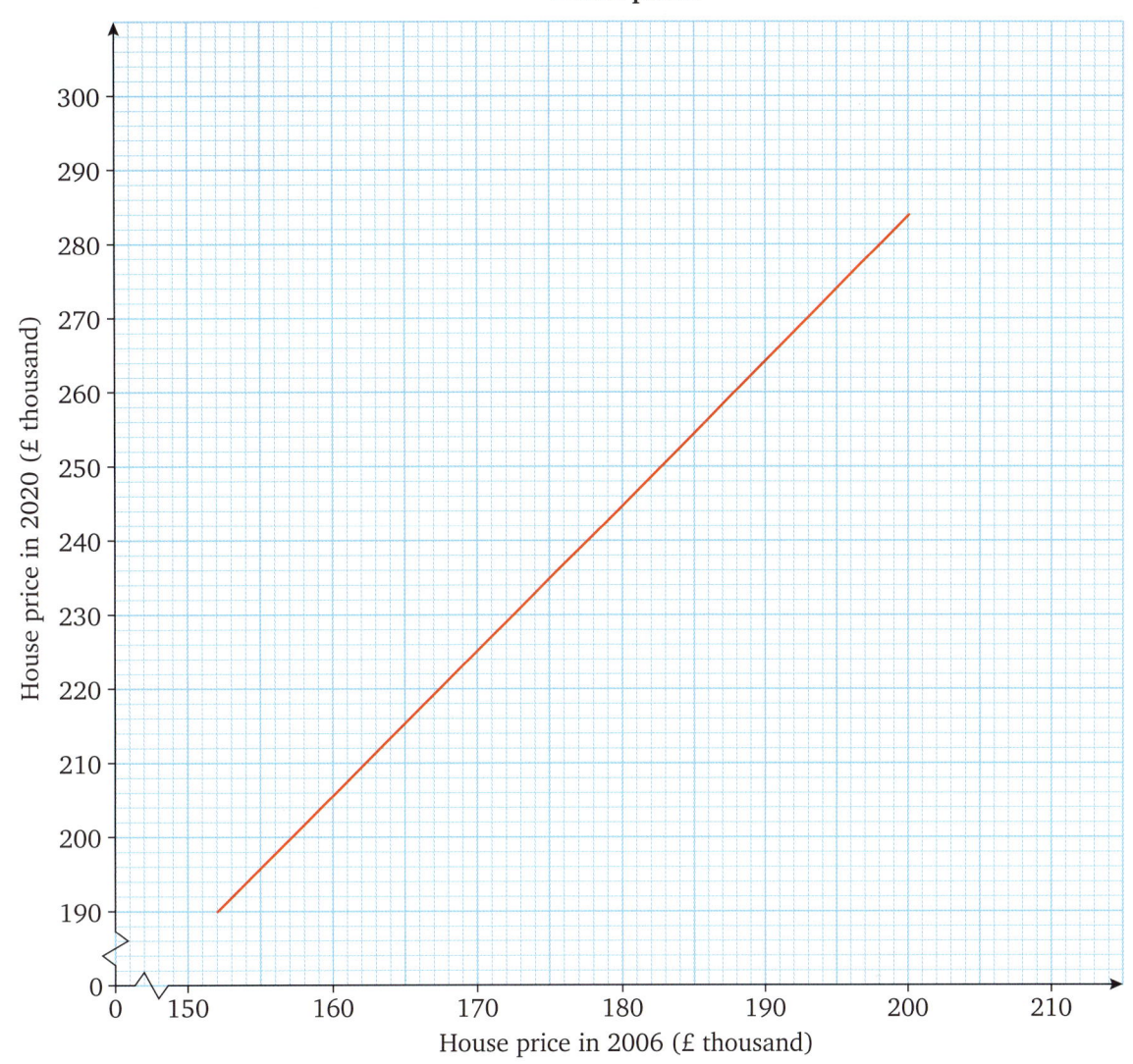

(Graph: x-axis "House price in 2006 (£ thousand)" from 150 to 210; y-axis "House price in 2020 (£ thousand)" from 0 then 190 to 300; line of best fit shown)

a Copy and complete the table, giving estimates for the missing values.

House price in 2006 (£ thousand)	170	175	190	200		
House price in 2020 (£ thousand)	225				305	355

b Rashid says his house price was £180 000 in 2006 and £270 000 in 2020. Is he correct? Give a reason for your answer.

c Find an estimate for the 2012 price of a house priced £155 000 in 2006.

d Find an estimate for the 2006 price of a house priced £280 000 in 2020.

e Which of these results is likely to be the most reliable? Give a reason for your answer.

6 Jenny collects information on the top speed and engine size of various motorbikes. Her results are shown in the table below.

Top speed (kph)	70	120	140	150	180	190	220	250	270	260	270	240
Engine size (cc)	50	250	350	270	400	440	600	800	950	900	1200	1000

a Draw a scatter graph of the results.

b What do you notice about the correlation between speed and engine size?

c Draw a curve of best fit and use this to estimate:

  i the engine size if the top speed is 170 kph

  ii the engine size if the top speed is 250 kph.

d Which of these results is likely to be the most reliable?

Give a reason for your answer.

17 Assess

1 The information below shows the marks of eight students in history and geography.

Student	A	B	C	D	E	F	G	H
History	25	35	28	30	36	44	15	21
Geography	27	40	29	32	41	48	17	20

Draw a scatter graph to represent this information and comment on the relationship between the history and geography marks.

2 The following table shows the hours of TV watched and test marks for 10 students.

Student	1	2	3	4	5	6	7	8	9	10
TV hours	4	7	9	10	13	14	15	20	21	25
Test mark	9	90	74	30	74	66	95	38	35	30

a Draw a scatter graph to represent this information and comment on the relationship between the figures.

b Two students do not seem to 'fit the trend'. Which ones are they? Explain why.

3 The table shows the relationship between the area (in thousands of km^2) of some European countries and their populations (in millions).

	Monaco	Malta	Jersey	Netherl.	UK	Germ.	Italy	Switz.	Andorra	Denm.
Area	0.002	0.3	0.1	41	245	357	294	41	0.5	43
Population	0.03	0.4	0.09	16	61	82	59	7	0.08	5

	France	Austria	Turkey	Greece	Spain	Ireland	Latvia	Sweden	Norway	Iceland
Area	551	84	783	130	504	84	65	450	323	100
Population	62	8	74	11	45	6	2	9	5	0.3

Draw a scatter graph of these data and comment on the graph.

Chapter 17 Scatter graphs   219

4 The table shows the distance jumped in long jump trials and the leg length of the jumpers.

Leg length (cm)	71	73	74	75	76	79	82
Distance jumped (m)	3.2	3.1	3.3	4.1	3.9	4	4.8

a Draw a scatter graph to represent this information.

b Use a line of best fit to estimate:
  i the leg length of an athlete who jumped a distance of 3.5 m.
  ii the distance jumped by an athlete with a leg length of 85 cm.

c Explain why one of those estimates is more reliable than the other.

5 The scatter graph shows the height and trunk diameter of eight trees.

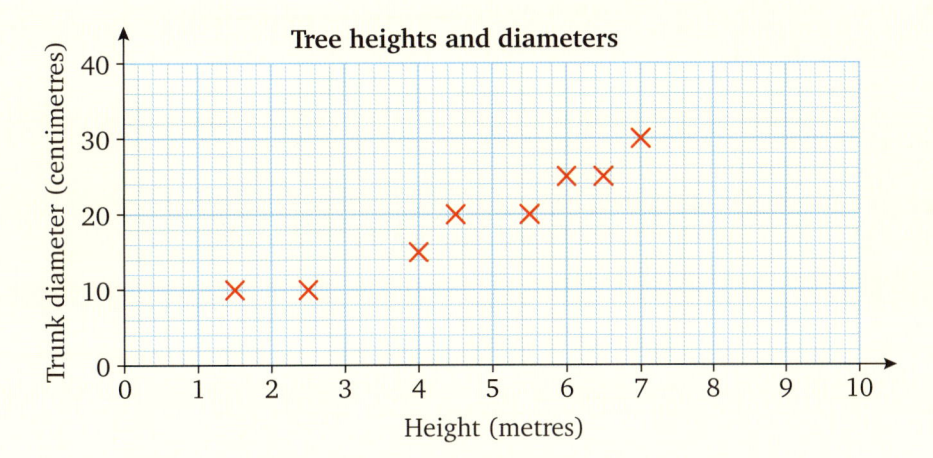

Tree heights and diameters

(scatter graph with Height (metres) on x-axis from 0 to 10 and Trunk diameter (centimetres) on y-axis from 0 to 40)

a What is the height of the tallest tree?

b Draw a line of best fit through the points on the scatter graph.

c Describe the relationship shown in the scatter graph.

d **i** Estimate the height of a tree with trunk diameter 35 cm.
  ii Comment on the reliability of your estimate.

6 Adnan is comparing A Level textbooks in order to test the hypothesis:
  'Books with more pages weigh more'.

He records the number of pages and then weighs each textbook.

His results are shown in the table below.

Number of pages	82	90	140	101	160	140	111	152	202
Weight (g)	165	155	210	192	245	96	190	231	280

a One of the readings is an outlier. Which reading is an outlier?
Give a reason why this might occur.

b Is Adnan's hypothesis true or false?
Show your working to justify your answer.

AQA Examination-style questions

1 The number of hours of sunshine and the maximum temperature at a seaside resort were measured on seven days in June.

Hours of sunshine	5	9	8	6	5	2	4
Temperature (°C)	26	30	29	26	24	19	23

   a Plot these data as a scatter graph. *(2 marks)*

   b Draw a line of best fit on your scatter graph. *(1 mark)*

   c Use your line of best fit to estimate the maximum temperature on a day in June when there are 7 hours of sunshine. *(1 mark)*

   d Describe the relationship shown by your scatter graph. *(1 mark)*

   e Explain why these data may not be representative of the maximum temperatures in June at this seaside resort. *(1 mark)*

AQA 2007

2 An investigation was carried out by 12 students.
They counted the number of books in their bags.
Each student weighed their bag with the books and recorded the total weight.
The results are shown on the scatter diagram.

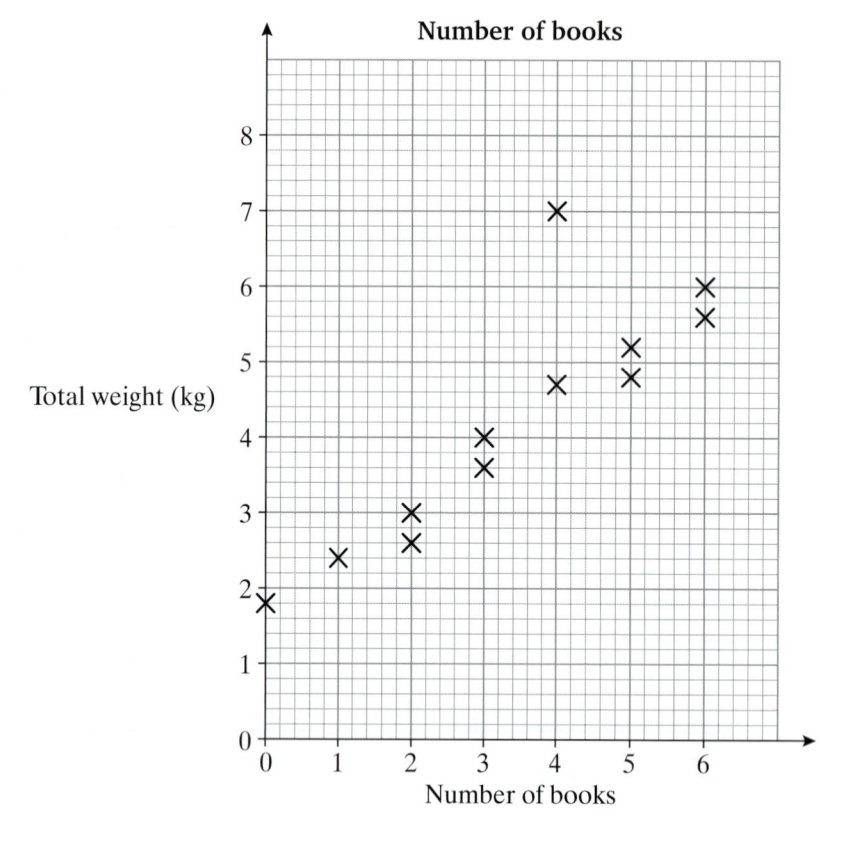

   a Describe the relationship between the number of books and the total weight. *(1 mark)*

   b **i** Which point does not fit the general pattern? *(1 mark)*

       ii If this point is removed from the scatter diagram what effect would this have on the correlation?

       Choose between: Weaker, No effect, Stronger

       Explain your answer. *(2 marks)*

AQA 2009

18 Reflections, rotations and translations

Objectives

Examiners would normally expect students who get these grades to be able to:

D

reflect shapes in lines parallel to the axes, such as $x = 2$ and $y = -1$

rotate shapes about the origin

describe fully reflections in a line and rotations about the origin

translate a shape using a description such as 4 units right and 3 units down

C

reflect shapes in lines such as $y = x$ and $y = -x$

rotate shapes about any point

describe fully reflections in any line parallel to the axes, $y = x$ or $y = -x$, and rotations about any point

find the centre of a rotation and describe it fully

transform shapes by a combination of translation, rotation and reflection

B

translate a shape by a vector such as $\begin{pmatrix} 4 \\ -3 \end{pmatrix}$

use congruence to show that translations, rotations and reflections preserve length and angle, so that any figure is congruent to its image under any of these transformations.

Did you know?

Looking for symmetry

Everywhere you look you can see symmetry: both in nature and in man-made constructions. This is the Compact Muon Solenoid, one of the detectors in the Large Hadron Collider. This is the world's largest and highest-energy particle accelerator. It is a symmetrical construction being used to advance science. It was built by scientists and engineers from over 100 countries. After initial problems, the collider has been in successful operation since November 2009.

You should already know:

✔ how to plot positive and negative coordinates

✔ equations of lines, such as $x = 3$, $y = -2$, $y = x$ and $y = -x$

✔ the names of 2-D and 3-D shapes

✔ how to draw all the lines of reflection on a 2-D shape and reflect shapes in the axes of a graph

✔ how to identify the order of rotational symmetry of a 2-D shape.

Key terms

reflection
image
coordinate
vertex, vertices
line of symmetry
rotation
centre of rotation
perpendicular bisector
translation
congruent
vector
transformation

Learn... 18.1 Reflection

This shape, P, has been **reflected** in the line $x = 2$

The image of an object is labelled with a dash symbol: '.

The **image** of P is P'.

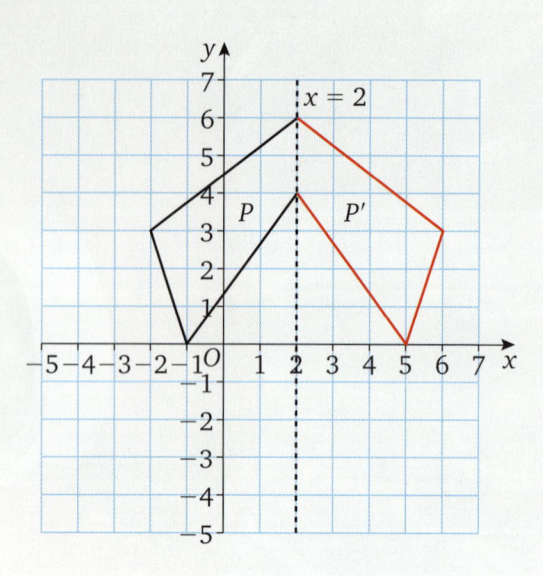

This shape, K, has been reflected in the line $y = x$

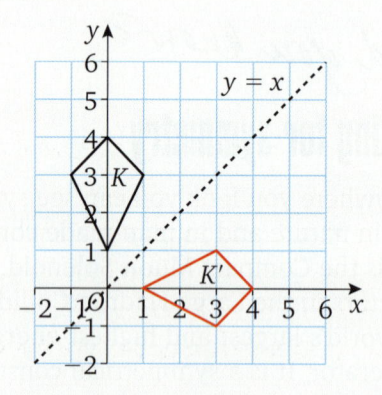

Coordinates of the vertices of K	Corresponding coordinates of the vertices of K'
(0, 1)	(1, 0)
(−1, 3)	(3, −1)
(0, 4)	(4, 0)
(1, 3)	(3, 1)

Notice the change in the coordinates of the vertices as K is mapped onto K'. The x-coordinate becomes the y-coordinate and the y-coordinate becomes the x-coordinate.

You can use tracing paper to check you have reflected a shape correctly. This method is particularly useful when the **line of symmetry** is diagonal because these are more difficult to visualise.

- Trace the shape.
- Draw in the line of symmetry.
- Fold the paper along the line of symmetry.
- You will then see clearly where the image should be.

Chapter 18 Reflections, rotations and translations 223

Example:
a Draw a pair of *x*- and *y*-axes from -8 to 8.
b Draw a polygon, *K*, by plotting and joining these points: $(-2, 1)$, $(2, 1)$, $(0, 4)$
c What is the name of this polygon?
d Reflect the polygon in the line $y = -2$. Label your reflected shape *K'*.
e Write down the coordinates of the vertices of the image, *K'*.

Solution: **a**, **b** and **d**

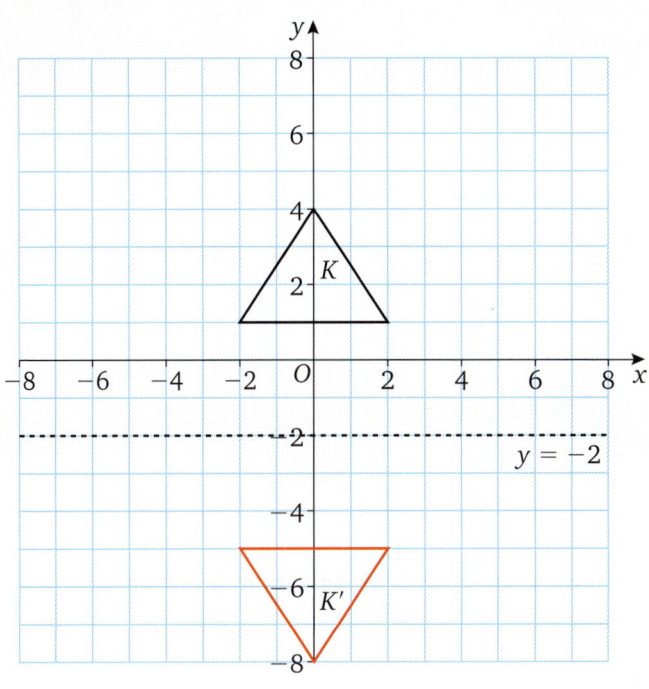

[Graph showing triangle K with vertices at (-2,1), (2,1), (0,4) and its reflection K' across the line y = -2, with vertices at (-2,-5), (2,-5), (0,-8)]

c The polygon is an isosceles triangle.   *You need to give the special name and not just answer 'triangle'.*

e The coordinates are: $(-2, -5)$, $(2, -5)$, $(0, -8)$ *Remember that a vertex is a corner, and the plural of vertex is vertices.*

Example: Find the coordinates of the image of the triangle, *T*, after a reflection in the line $y = -x$
The coordinates of *T* are: $(-1, 3)$, $(0, 2)$, $(2, 3)$

Solution: The coordinates of *T'* are: $(-3, 1)$, $(-2, 0)$, $(-3, -2)$

You can check your answer by sketching the triangle and its image under this **transformation**.

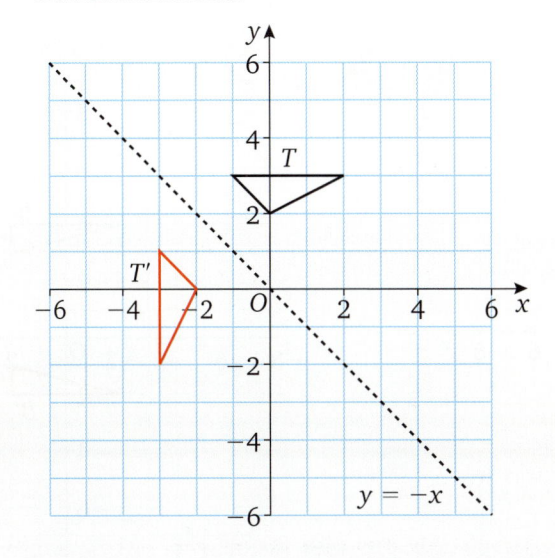

[Graph showing triangle T and its reflection T' across the line y = -x]

Practise... 18.1 Reflection

1 The diagram shows the triangle T.

   a Write down the coordinates of the vertices of T.

   b Use the diagram to find the coordinates of the vertices of the image of T after a reflection in each of the following lines.

   i $x = 1$
   ii $x = 2$
   iii $y = -1$
   iv $y = -2$

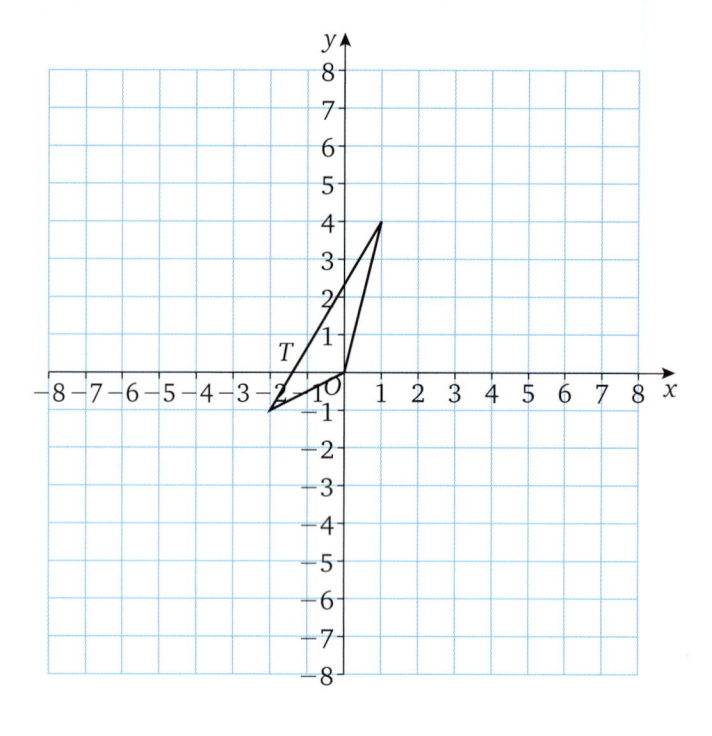

   Hint
   Remember that you can use tracing paper to help you with reflections.

2 Draw the following triangles on separate axes along with their image, a reflection in the given line.

   a A (3, 1), (0, 1), (0, −2) $y = -1$
   b B (−1, 0.5), (−1, 2), (1, 3) $y = -2$
   c C (0, 0), (3, 0), (2, 2) $y = 1$
   d D (0, 3.5), (−2, −2), (2, 2) $x = 1$
   e E (−2, −2), (−2, 2), (0, 0) $x = 2$
   f F (0, −1.5), (3, 1), (1, 4) $x = -1$

3 For each diagram, find the equation of the line of reflection.

   a

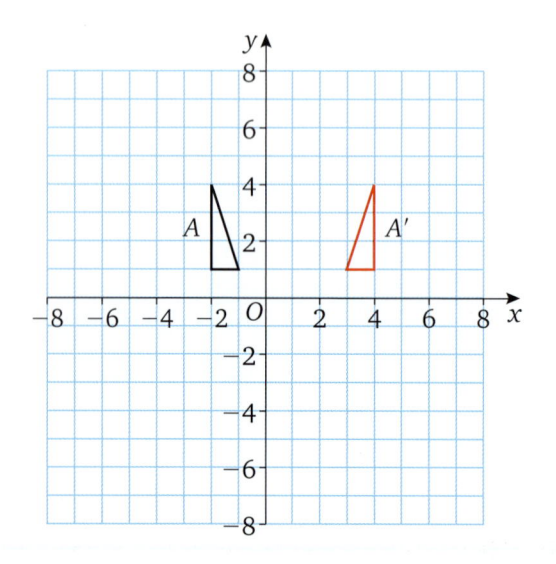

   b

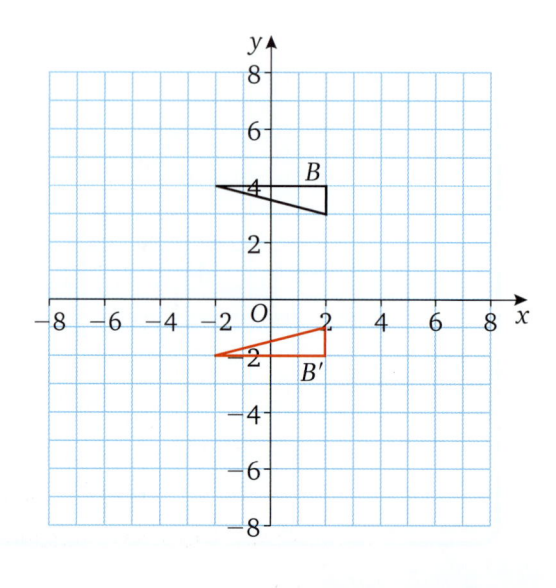

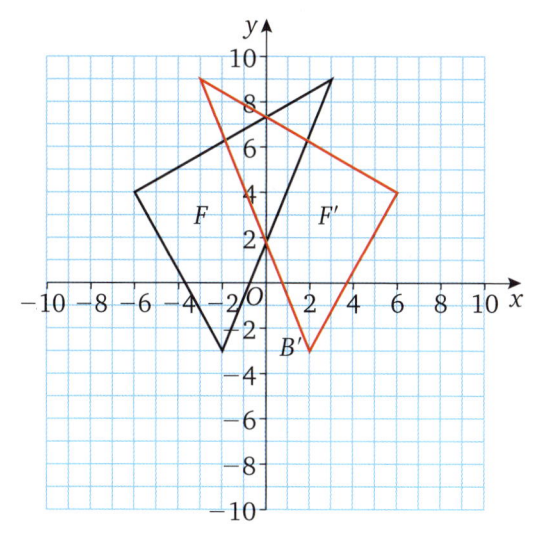

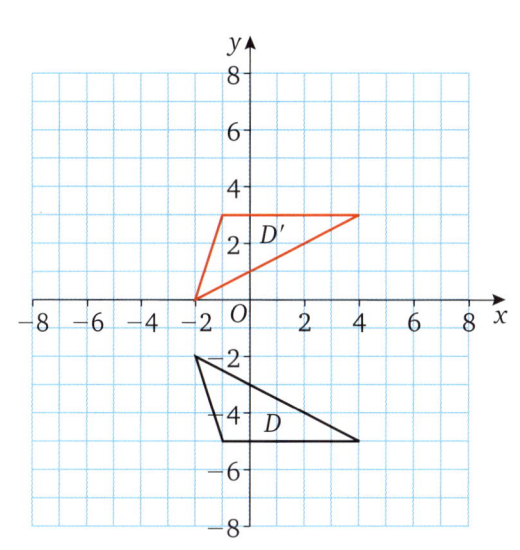

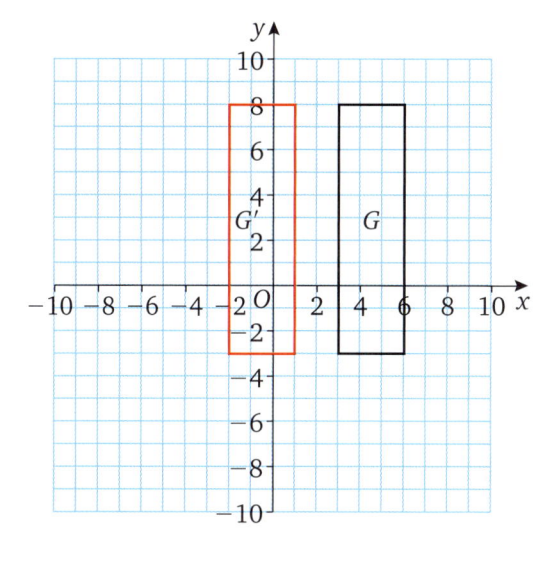

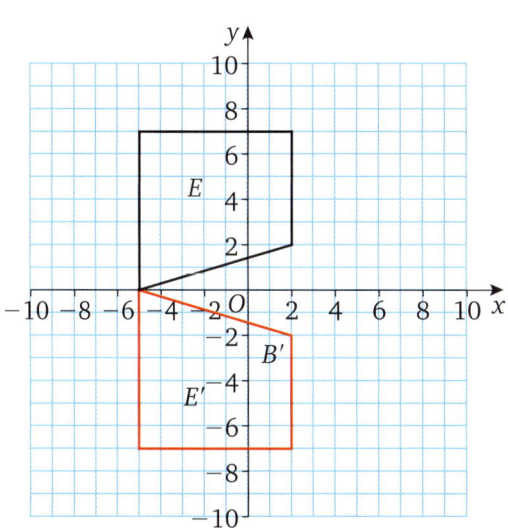

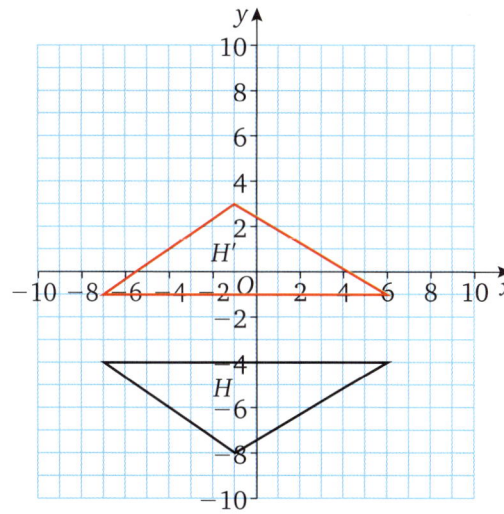

Chapter 18 Reflections, rotations and translations **225**

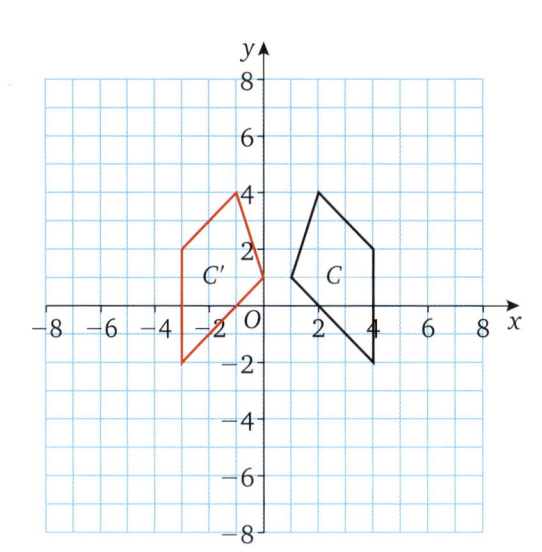

c, **d**, **e**, **f**, **g**, **h** (coordinate grid diagrams showing shapes C/C′, D/D′, E/E′ and B′, F/F′ and B′, G/G′, H/H′)

4 On isometric paper, draw a 3-D solid that has:
- **a** no planes of symmetry
- **b** one plane of symmetry
- **c** two planes of symmetry.

5
- **a** Draw a pair of x- and y-axes from −6 to 6.
- **b** Draw a polygon, R, by plotting and joining these points:
  (1, −1), (3, −1), (3, −2), (0, −3)
- **c** What is the mathematical name of the polygon?

d Reflect the polygon in the line $y = x$ and write down the coordinates of the corners of the image, R'.

e Reflect the polygon in the line $y = -x$ and write down the coordinates of the corners of the image, R''.

Hint
Two dashes are used after two transformations.

f Write down what you notice.

6 a Draw a polygon, P, by plotting and joining these points:
(0, 0), (4, 0), (1, 3), (2, 3)

b What is the mathematical name of the polygon, P?

c Find the coordinates of P', the image of P after a reflection in the line $y = x$

d Draw P' on the same pair of axes as P.

Bump up your grade
To get a Grade C you need to know how to reflect in the lines $y = x$ and $y = -x$ as well as horizontal and vertical lines.

7 The diagram shows a pentagon.

a Write down the coordinates of the vertices of the pentagon.

b The pentagon is reflected in the line $y = -x$. What are the coordinates of the vertices of the image of G?

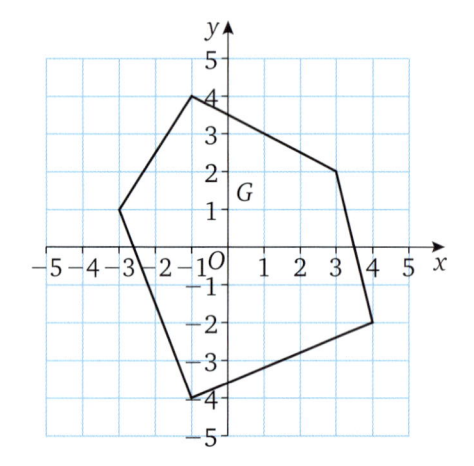

8 The diagram shows the line AB.

a What are the coordinates of the points A and B?

b Copy the diagram and draw the line BC, the image of AB after a reflection in the line $y = x$

c On the same diagram, draw the reflection of the lines AB and BC following a reflection in the line $y = -x$

d Describe the finished shape.

e Jason says that it doesn't matter which line you start with, you will always end up with this shape after a reflection in the line $y = x$ followed by a reflection in the line $y = -x$
Give an example that shows that Jason is wrong.

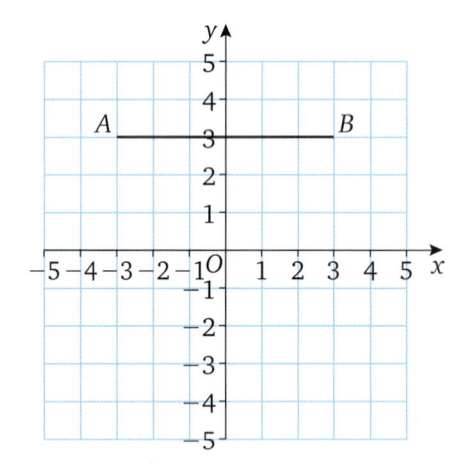

9 a Write down the coordinates of the vertices of these triangles after a reflection in the line $y = x$
  i (0, 2), (3, 4), (1, 5)
  ii (−2, −1), (−3, 4), (−2, 4)
  iii (−1.5, 2.5), (0.5, 3.5), (−1, 1)

b Write down the coordinates of the vertices of these triangles after a reflection in the line $y = -x$
  i (0, 2), (3, 4), (1, 5)
  ii (−2, −1), (−3, 4), (−2, 4)
  iii (−1.5, 2.5), (0.5, 3.5), (−1, 1)

10 This diagram shows a shape A and its reflection A′.

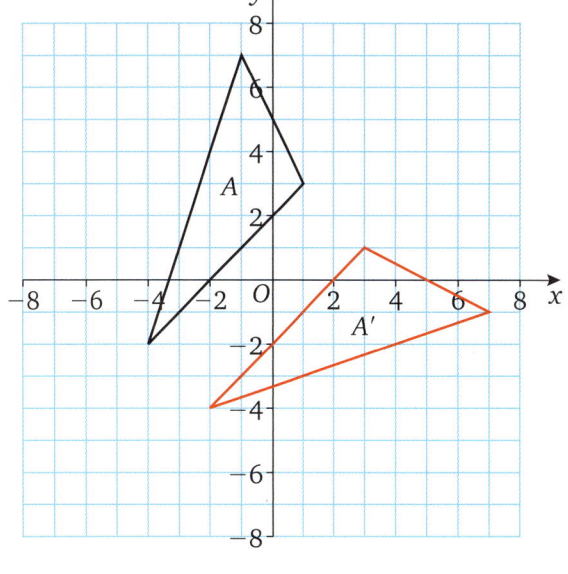

   a Describe the reflection that maps A onto A′.

   b Write down the coordinates of the vertices of both triangles.

   c Find a rule that connects the coordinates after the reflection.

   d A polygon has these coordinates: (2, 3), (−1, −2), (0, −4), (2, −2)
An image of this polygon is created by reflecting it in the same line of reflection as in part **a**.
Use your rule from part **c** to work out the coordinates of the vertices of this image.
Try to work out the coordinates by following your rule and not by drawing.

   e Can you find a rule for each of these lines of symmetry without drawing them?

      i $x = 0$ **ii** $y = 3$ **iii** $x = -5$

Learn... 18.2 Rotation

Shapes can be **rotated** on grids or axes.
- The amount the shape **rotates** is given as an angle or fraction of a complete turn, for example, 270° or $\frac{3}{4}$ turn.
- The **direction of rotation** is given as clockwise or anticlockwise.
- The **centre of rotation** is the fixed point around which the object is rotated. It is given using coordinates.

The shape is called the object and the rotation is called the image.

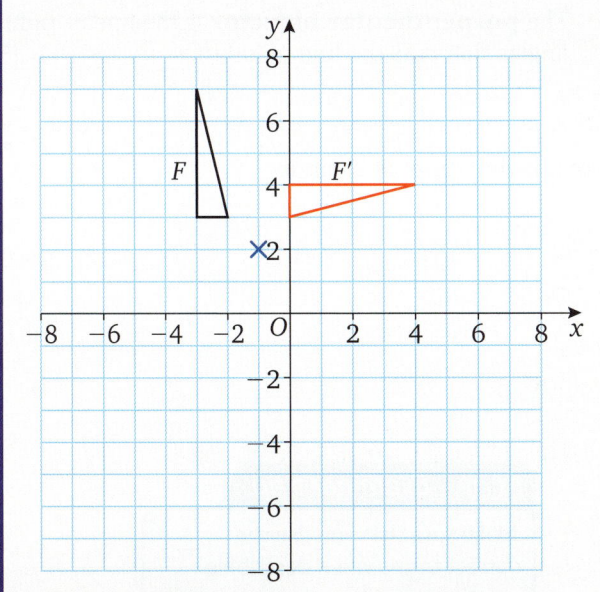

AQA Examiner's tip
In your exam you can ask for tracing paper to find the centre of rotation.

When describing a rotation you must give:
- angle or turn
- direction
- centre of rotation.

This shape has been rotated clockwise through 90°. The centre of rotation is the point (−1, 2).

If the object is labelled F then the image is usually labelled F′.

Angles of rotation can be any angle.

This shape has been rotated clockwise through 212°.

If you know or can work out the centre of rotation, you can use a protractor to measure the angle of rotation.

To describe a rotation fully, you must give the centre of rotation, the angle of rotation and the direction of rotation, either clockwise or anticlockwise.

To find the centre of rotation when you have the object and its image requires a number of constructions.

1   Draw a line joining corresponding vertices (blue line).

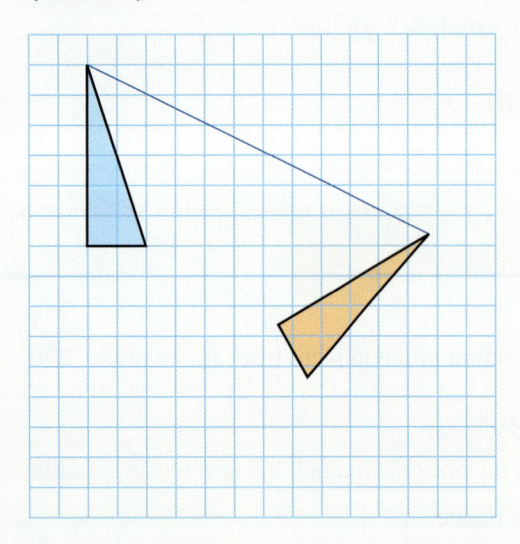

2   Draw the perpendicular bisector of this line (red line).

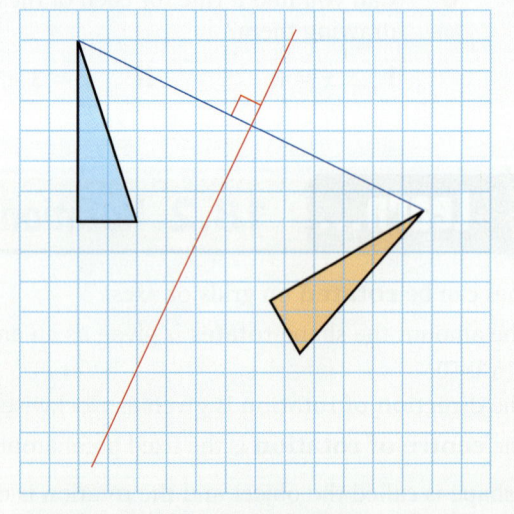

The **perpendicular bisector** is the line at right angles that cuts the line in half.

3   Repeat this for each vertex.

The point where the three perpendicular bisectors cross is the centre of rotation.

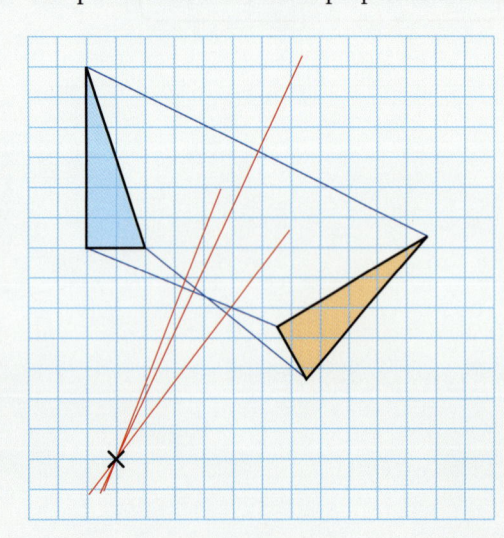

AQA Examiner's tip

Make sure that you use the correct terms when describing rotations. Use 'rotation' not 'turn'.

Chapter 18 Reflections, rotations and translations

Example: In this diagram the right-angled triangle, A, has been rotated clockwise by 270° about the origin.

The image of A following this rotation is B.

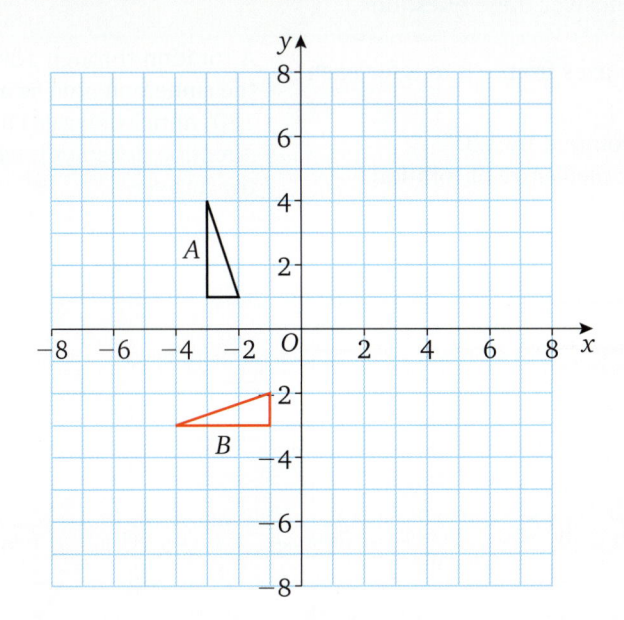

a Write down the anticlockwise rotation that also maps A onto B.

b Draw a diagram showing the image of A after a rotation of 90° clockwise about the point (−1, 0).

c Label the image C and write down the coordinates of the vertices of C.

Solution:

a An anticlockwise rotation of 90° gives the same image as a clockwise rotation of 270°.

b

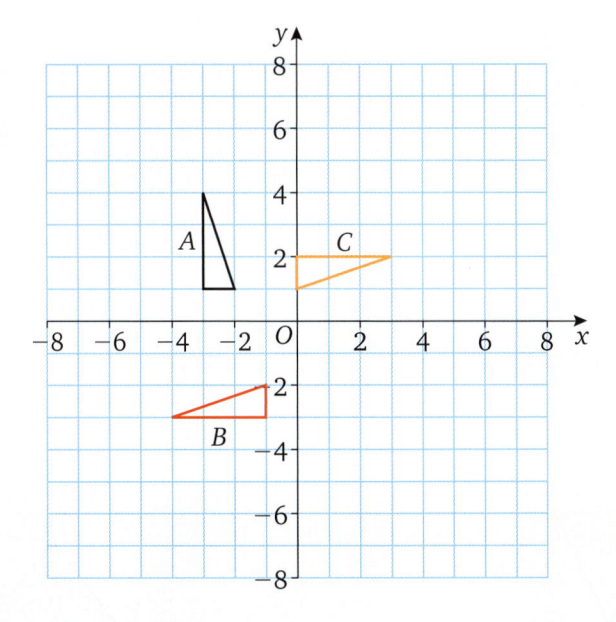

c The coordinates of the vertices of C are: (0, 1), (0, 2), (3, 2).

230 AQA GCSE Mathematics

Practise... 18.2 Rotation

D C B A A*

Hint

You can use tracing paper to help you answer these questions.

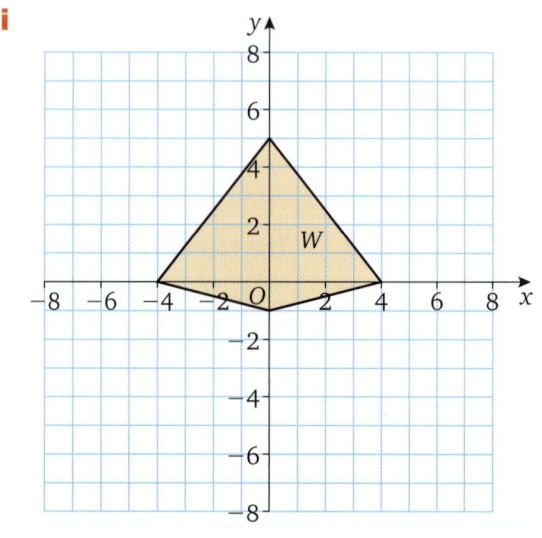

1 a Draw a pair of x- and y-axes from −8 to 8 for each question part.

Copy each object and rotate it by 180°.
Use the origin (0, 0) as the centre of rotation.
Label each image R′–W′.

A rotation through 180° clockwise has the same outcome as a rotation through 180° anticlockwise. This means that the direction does not have to be given in the answer.

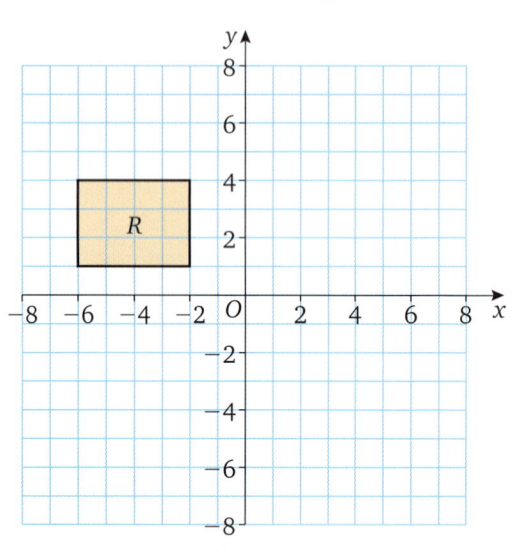

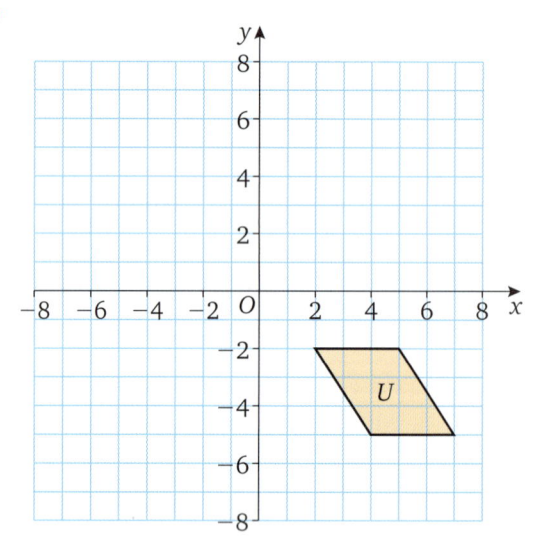

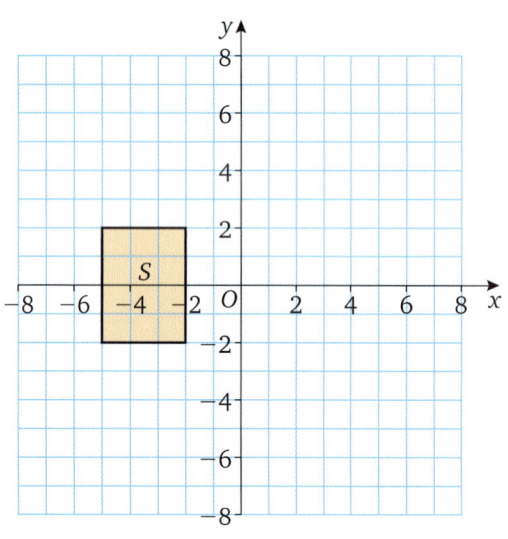

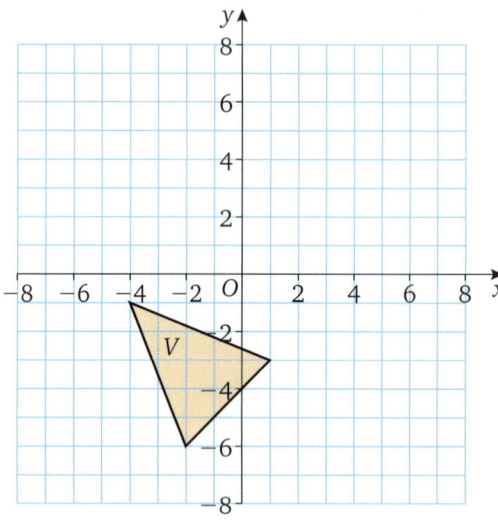

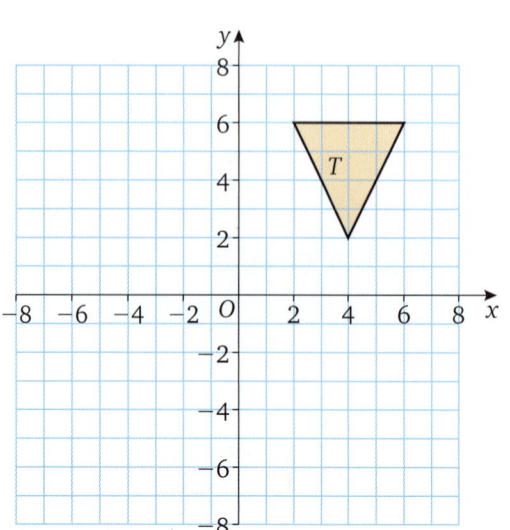

i — shape R
ii — shape S
iii — shape T
iv — shape U
v — shape V
vi — shape W

Chapter 18 Reflections, rotations and translations **231**

b Draw a pair of *x*- and *y*-axes from −8 to 8 for each question part.

Copy each object and rotate it by 90° clockwise.
Use the point (1, 2) as the centre of rotation.
Label each image A′–F′.

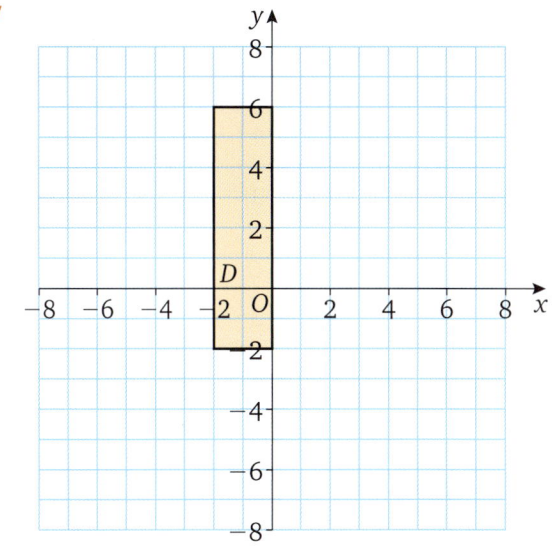

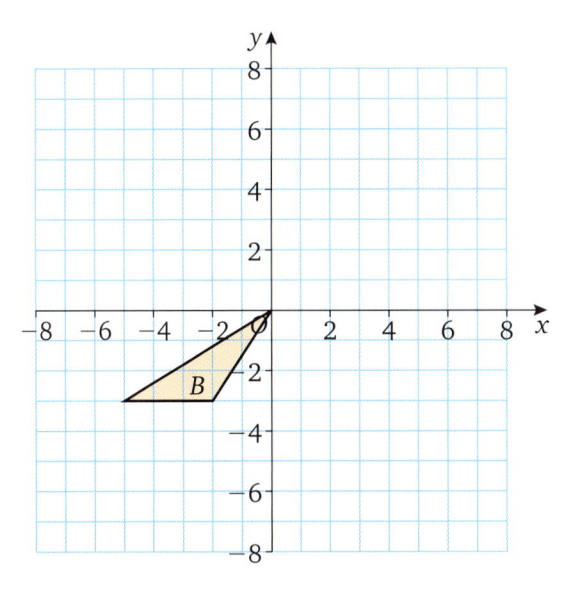

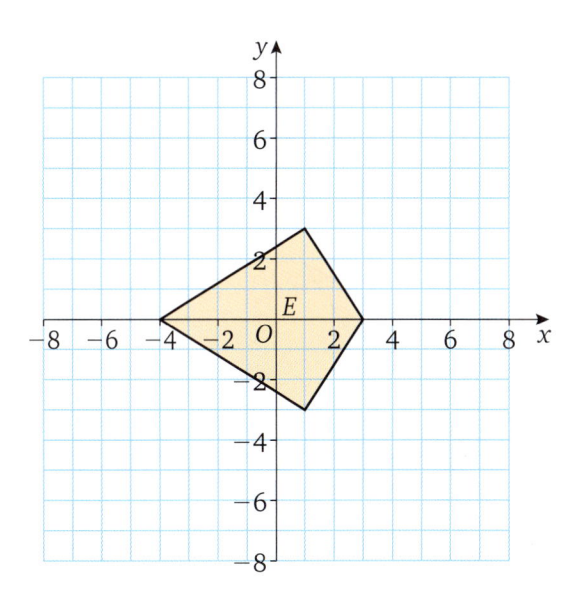

i, **ii**, **iii**, **iv**, **v**, **vi**

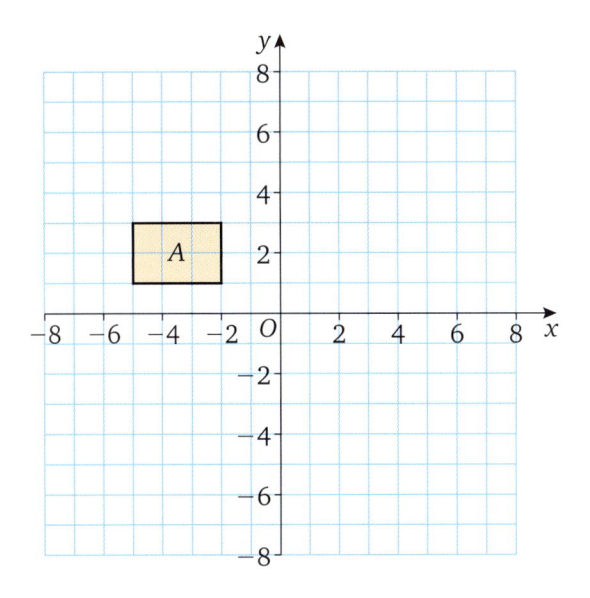

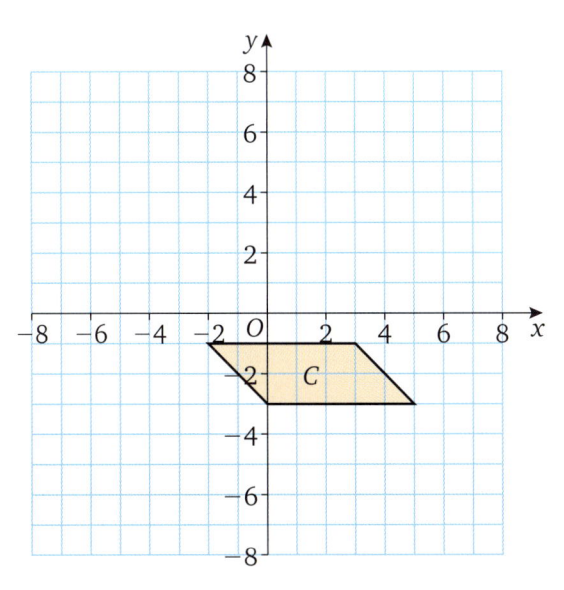

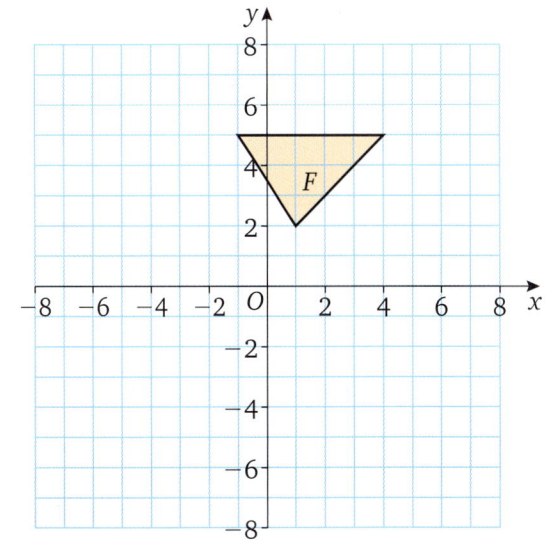

c Draw a pair of *x*- and *y*-axes from −8 to 8 for each question part.
Copy each object and rotate it by 270° clockwise.
Use the point (−1, −1) as the centre of rotation.
Label each image G′–L′.

i

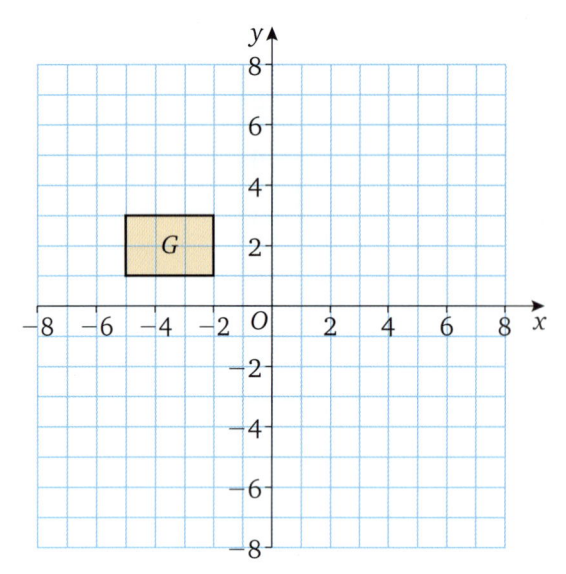

ii

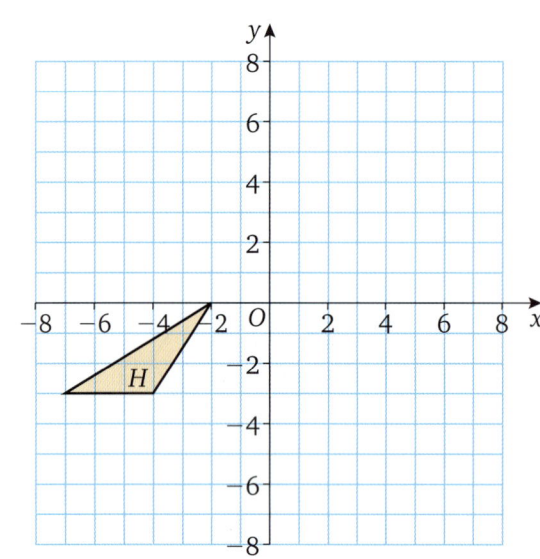

iii

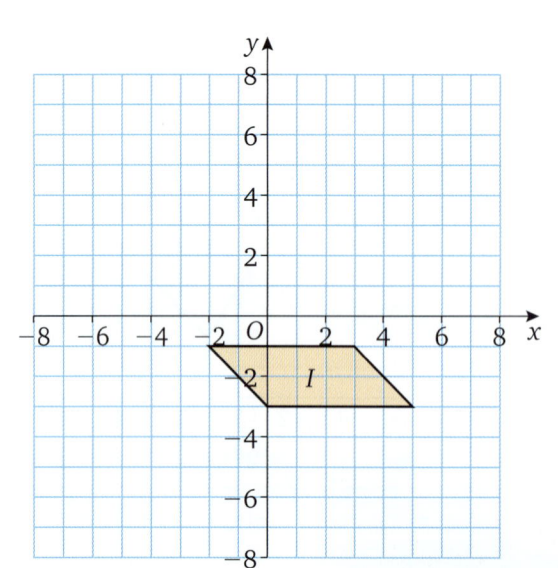

iv

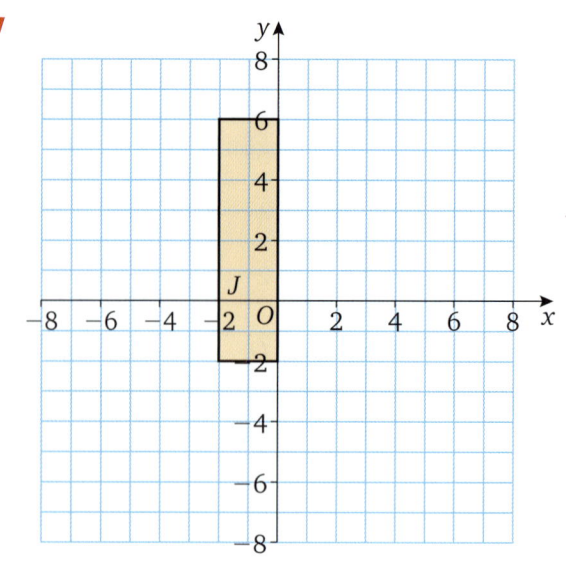

v

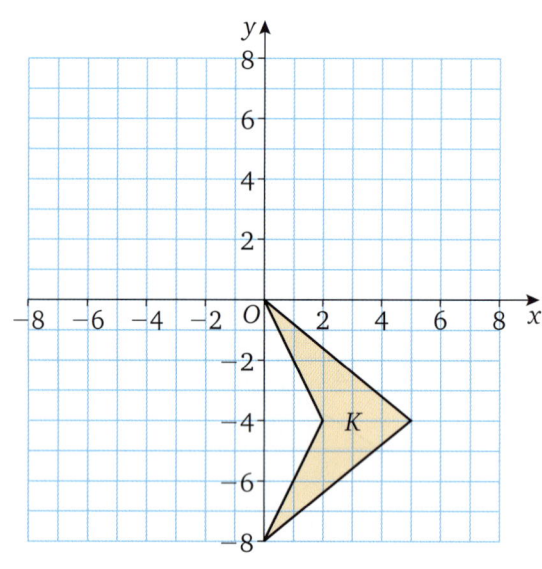

vi

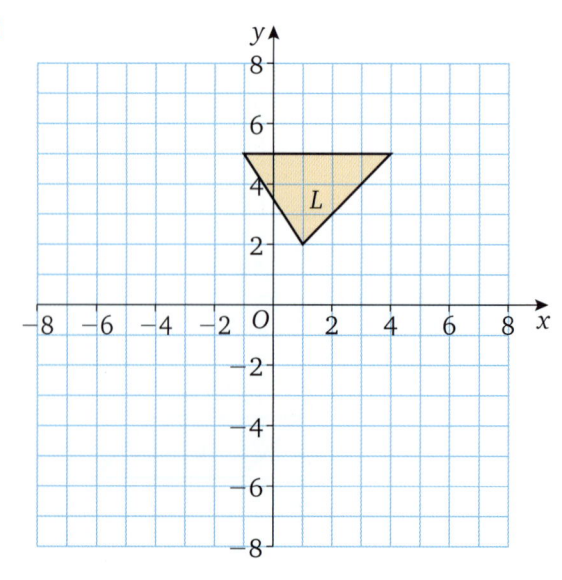

Bump up your grade

You need to be able to rotate objects around any point and not just the origin to get a Grade C.

Chapter 18 Reflections, rotations and translations | **233**

2 **a** Draw a pair of x- and y-axes from −7 to 7.
  b Draw a triangle T by plotting and joining these points: (0, 0), (−2, −1), (−1, −2)
  c Draw the image V by rotating T by 90° clockwise about (0, 0).
  d Draw the image W by rotating T by 180° about (0, 0).
  e Draw the image X by rotating T by 270° clockwise about (0, 0).

3 **a** Draw a pair of x- and y-axes from −7 to 7.
  b Draw a polygon Q by plotting and joining these points: (4, 1), (6, 1), (4, −1), (3, −1)
  c Draw the image Q' by rotating Q by 90° clockwise about (2, 3).

4 Use a protractor to find the angle of rotation for each shape.

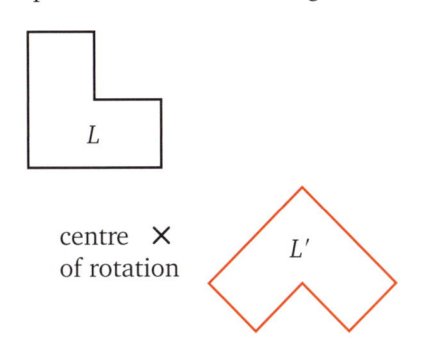

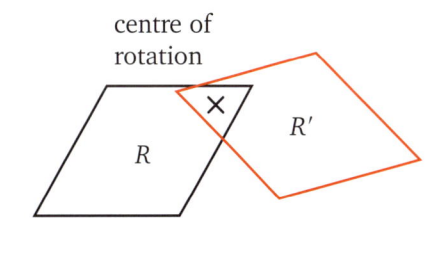

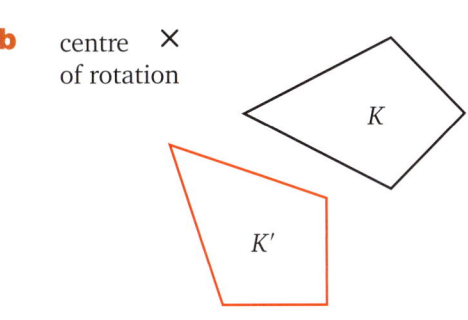

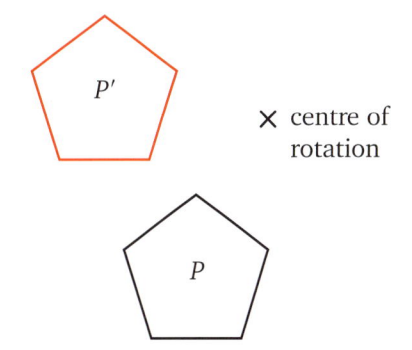

  a [L shape with L' image, centre of rotation marked]

  b [K shape with K' image, centre of rotation marked]

  c [R shape with R' image, centre of rotation marked]

  d [P shape with P' image, centre of rotation marked]

5 For each of the following mappings, give the angle of rotation, the direction of rotation and the centre of rotation.

  a A onto B
  b A onto C
  c A onto D
  d D onto B
  e B onto F
  f A onto E
  g C onto G
  h H onto A
  i B onto E
  j D onto C

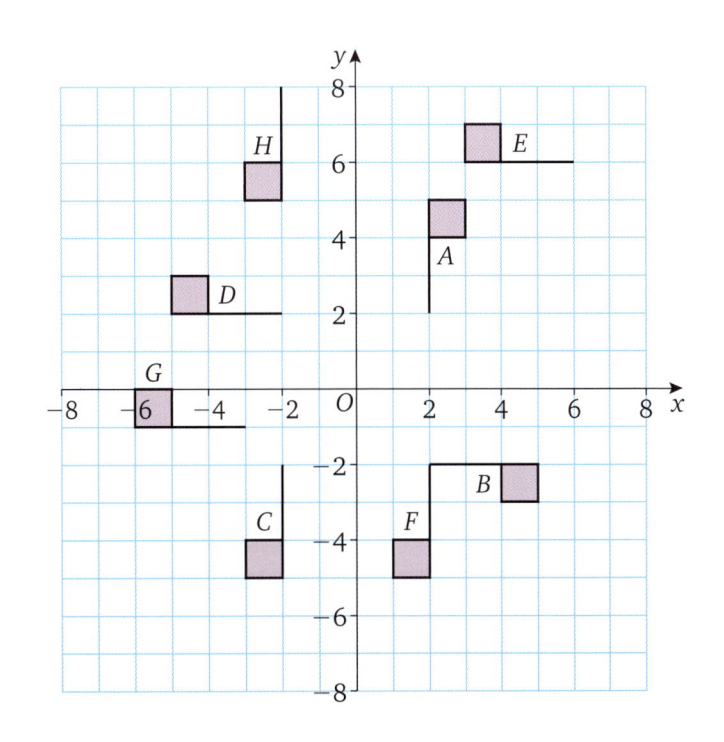

6. The pink triangle has been rotated clockwise through 90° to give its image, the blue triangle.

   Work out which of the points A, B, C or D is the centre of rotation.
   You can use tracing paper to help you.

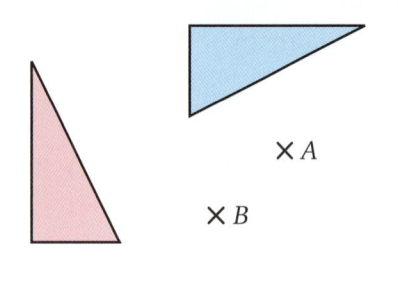

   × A

   × B

   × C   × D

7. This diagram shows two different images of a triangle, A, after two rotations by the same angle.

   Image B followed the first rotation clockwise about the point (1, 1).

   Image C followed the other rotation of A anticlockwise about the point (−1, 1).

   Find the position of triangle A.

   Hint
   Use tracing paper to try out both centres of rotation until you find a position for triangle A that works for both images.

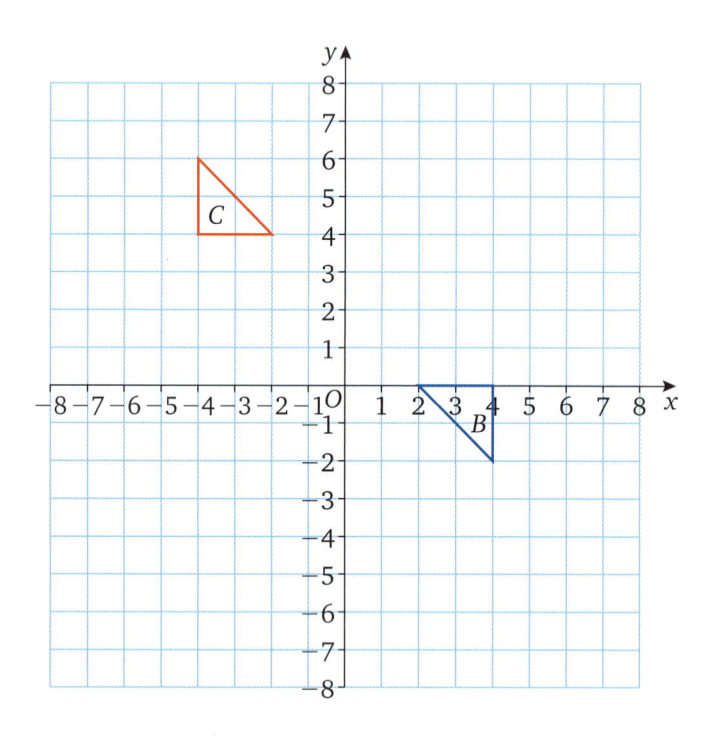

8. The yellow triangle has been rotated clockwise through 120° to give its image, the green triangle.

   Trace the diagram. Then find the centre of rotation by constructing appropriate perpendicular bisectors.

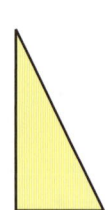

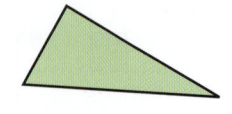

Chapter 18 Reflections, rotations and translations   235

9 Rotational symmetry is often used in the design of company logos.
The arrows on this logo make it look as if it has rotational symmetry order 2.

a Explain why this logo does not have rotational symmetry order 2.

b This logo uses arrows too.
  i What is the order of rotational symmetry of this logo?
  ii What is the angle of rotation of the logo?

c **i** Design your own company logo with rotational symmetry, order 5
  ii What is the angle of rotation of your logo?

Learn... 18.3 Translation

This shape has been **translated**.
Every point moves the same distance in the same direction.
The object and the image are **congruent**.
Two shapes are congruent if the lengths and angles stay the same when they are translated, rotated or reflected.
The distance and direction can be written as a **vector**.
Shape A has been mapped onto shape B by a translation of 2 to the right and 3 units up.

Written as a vector, this is $\begin{pmatrix} 2 \\ 3 \end{pmatrix}$ ← 2 units to the right
← 3 units up

The vector that maps shape C onto shape D is $\begin{pmatrix} 0 \\ -4 \end{pmatrix}$

The top number is the horizontal move.
- If the number is positive the shape moves to the right.
- If the number is negative the shape moves to the left.

The lower number is the vertical move.
- If the number is positive the shape moves up.
- If the number is negative the shape moves down.

Vectors can be used on any grid with or without a pair of axes.

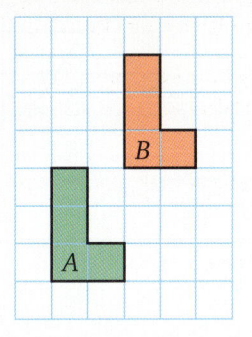

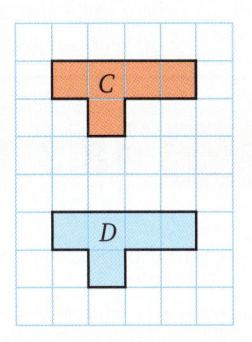

Example: Give the vector that translates shape A onto shape B.

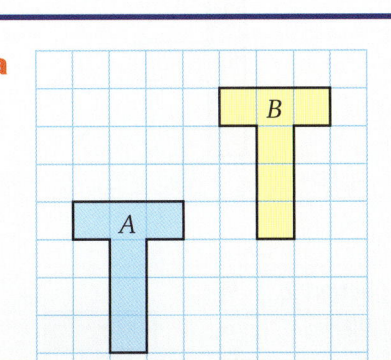

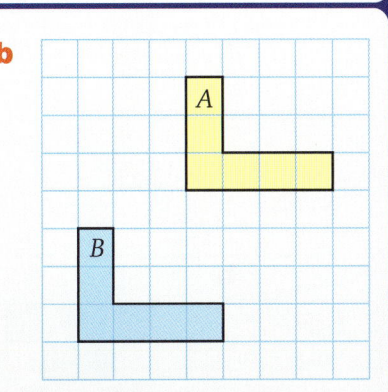

Solution: **a** A has moved 4 to the right and 3 up so the vector translation is $\begin{pmatrix} 4 \\ 3 \end{pmatrix}$

b A has moved 3 to the left and 4 down so the vector translation is $\begin{pmatrix} -3 \\ -4 \end{pmatrix}$

Example: Copy the diagram, drawing triangle *T* with the coordinates (2, 4), (4, 4) and (4, 1). Then answer the questions below.

a Draw the image of *T* after the vector translation $\begin{pmatrix} -5 \\ -3 \end{pmatrix}$. Label the image *R*.

b Write down the vector translation that maps *R* back onto *T*.

c What is the relationship between the coordinates of the vertices of *T* and the coordinates of *R*?

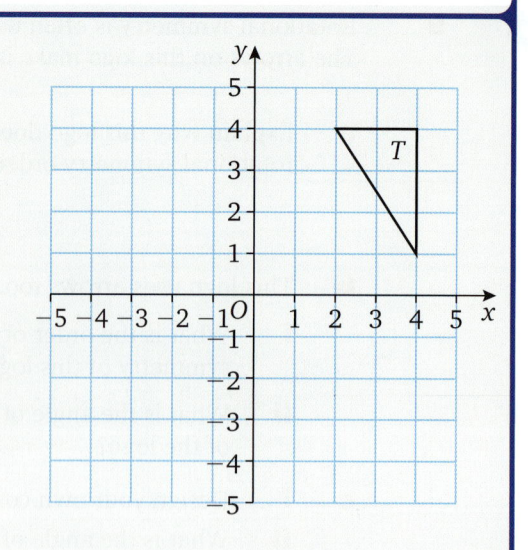

Solution: **a**

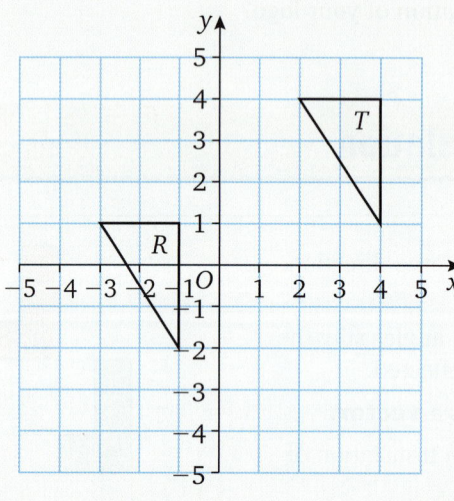

b The vector that maps *R* back onto *T* is $\begin{pmatrix} 5 \\ 3 \end{pmatrix}$

c The *x*-coordinates of *R* are all less than the *x*-coordinates of *T*. The *y*-coordinates of *R* are all less than the *y*-coordinates of *T*.

Practise... 18.3 Translation   D C B A A*

1 Using squared paper, copy these shapes and translate each one by the given amount.

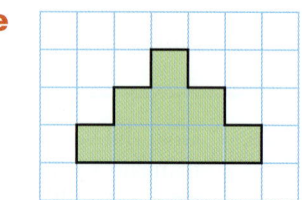

a across 3 down 3

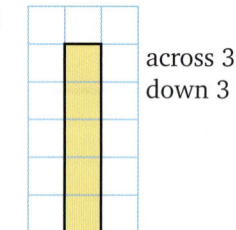

b across 2 up 4

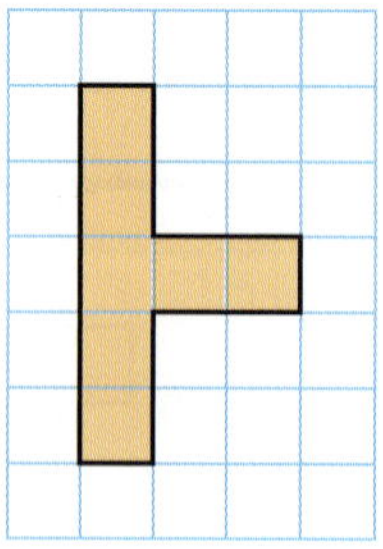

c across 4 down 1

d across 2 up 5

e across 5 up 0

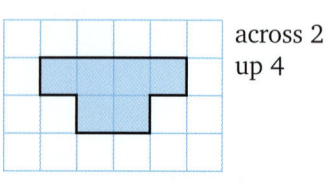

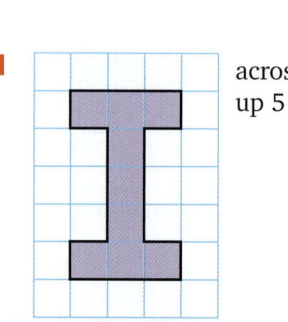

f across 0 up 5

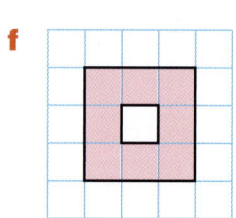

Chapter 18 Reflections, rotations and translations   237

2 Describe the translation that maps shape A onto shape B in each diagram.
Give your answers as vectors.

a

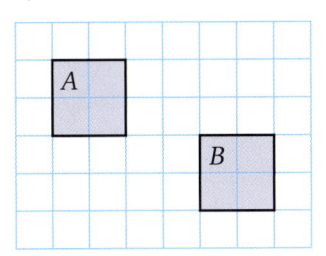

d

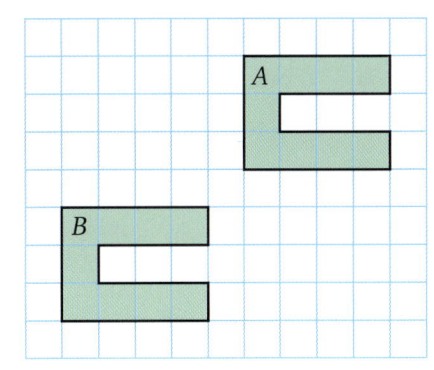

AQA Examiner's tip
Be careful not to mix up coordinates and vectors.
(x, y) are coordinates. $\begin{pmatrix} x \\ y \end{pmatrix}$ is a vector.

b

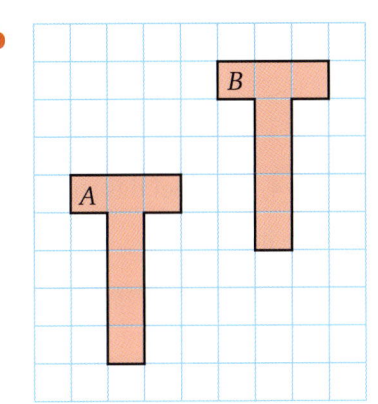

e

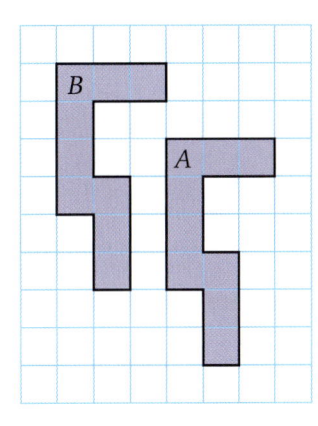

c

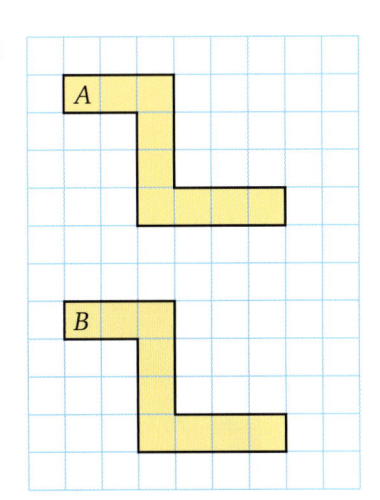

f

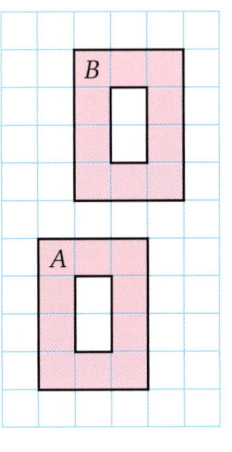

3 a Look at the diagram and write down the vector that translates:

  i A onto B

  ii A onto C

  iii B onto C

  iv C onto B.

b What is the relationship between the vector in part **a iii** and the vector in part **a iv**?

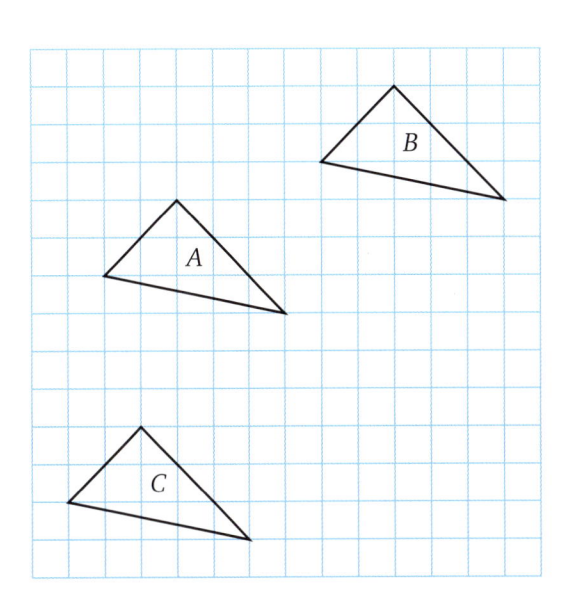

4 Look at the diagram to write down the vector that maps:

   a   A onto B

   b   C onto F

   c   E onto D

   d   B onto E.

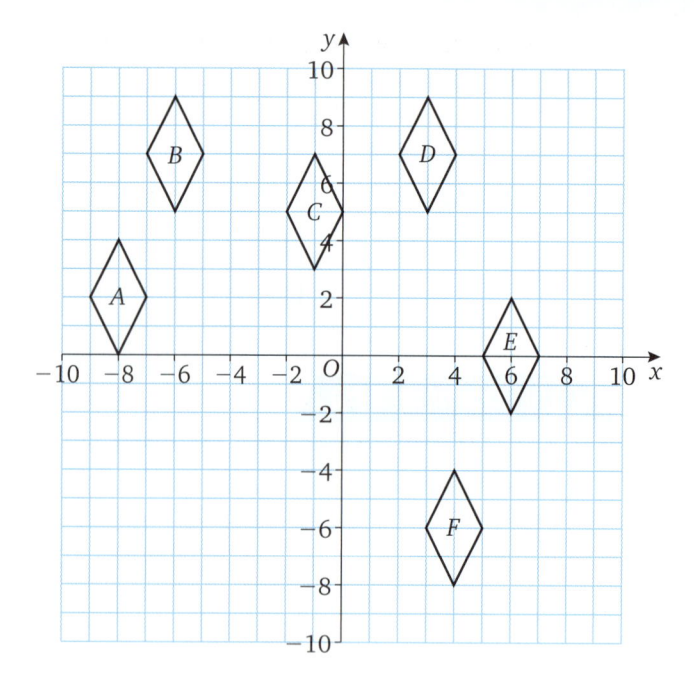

5 **a** **i** Draw a pair of x- and y-axes from −5 to 5.

       ii Plot and join the points (−4, −5), (−1, −5), (−4, 2). Label this shape T.

   b Translate T using the vector translation $\begin{pmatrix} 4 \\ 3 \end{pmatrix}$ to give the image U.

   c Translate U using the vector translation $\begin{pmatrix} -5 \\ 0 \end{pmatrix}$ to give the image V.

   d Translate V using the vector translation $\begin{pmatrix} 6 \\ -1 \end{pmatrix}$ to give the image W.

   e Describe fully the single translation that maps T directly onto W.

6 **a** Draw a pair of x- and y-axes from −5 to 5.

   b Begin at the origin as a starting point. After each of the following translations, put a cross.

      $\begin{pmatrix} 2 \\ 1 \end{pmatrix}$ $\begin{pmatrix} 1 \\ 1 \end{pmatrix}$ $\begin{pmatrix} 1 \\ 0 \end{pmatrix}$ $\begin{pmatrix} 1 \\ -1 \end{pmatrix}$ $\begin{pmatrix} 0 \\ -2 \end{pmatrix}$ $\begin{pmatrix} -5 \\ -4 \end{pmatrix}$

   c Join the crosses you have drawn in the order in which you drew them.

   d Reflect the shape in the y-axis.

7 Some wallpapers have translational symmetry. The design is made by repeatedly translating the feature design horizontally and vertically.

Emma is designing a wallpaper pattern on squared paper. She translates her design by the vector $\begin{pmatrix} 4 \\ 3 \end{pmatrix}$

She then repeats the pattern in a different colour.

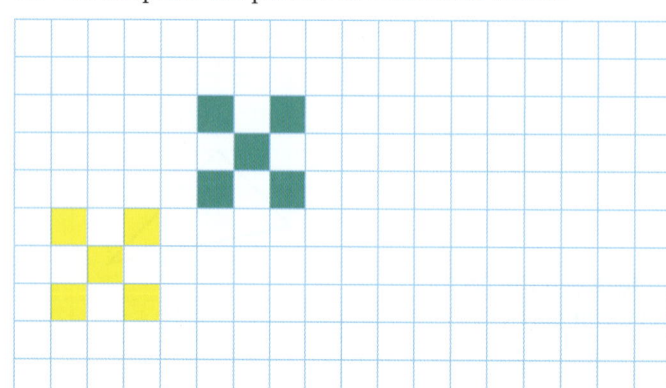

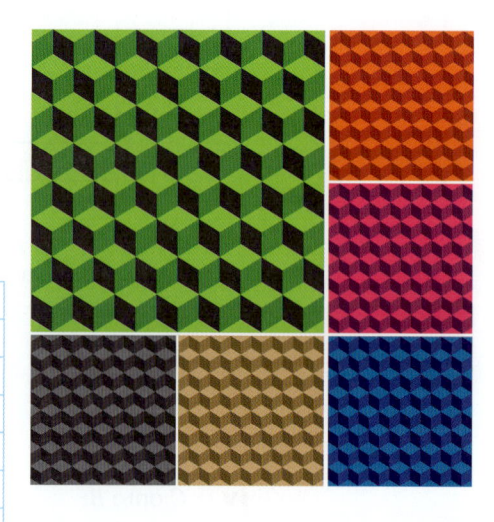

   a On squared or isometric paper, create a simple design.

   b Choose a translation vector. Repeat your pattern using your chosen translation vector to create your own wallpaper design.

Chapter 18　Reflections, rotations and translations　239

8 Sam and Holly designed this board for a vector game.
A **vector route** starts at X and lands on each of the other squares before returning to X.

a Holly wrote down this vector route.

$$\begin{pmatrix} 5 \\ -2 \end{pmatrix} \begin{pmatrix} -13 \\ 2 \end{pmatrix} \begin{pmatrix} -1 \\ 6 \end{pmatrix} \begin{pmatrix} 3 \\ -2 \end{pmatrix}$$

$$\begin{pmatrix} 5 \\ 4 \end{pmatrix} \begin{pmatrix} 3 \\ -2 \end{pmatrix} \begin{pmatrix} -2 \\ -6 \end{pmatrix}$$

Write down the order she landed on the squares.

b Sam chose to visit the triangles in this order: X F D C B A E X

Write down Sam's vector route.

c Create a vector route of your own and test it on a friend.

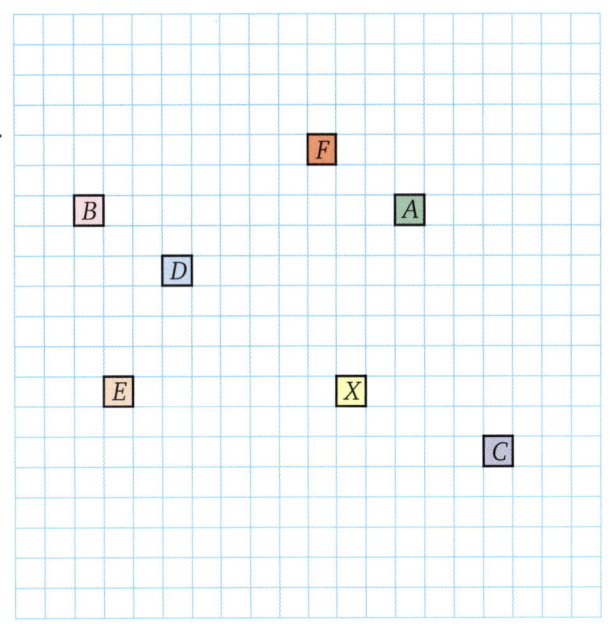

Learn... 18.4 Transformation and congruence

Reflections, rotations and translations can be combined into a single transformation.

A reflection in the y-axis, $x = 0$, followed by a reflection in the x-axis, $y = 0$, has the same effect as a rotation about the origin.

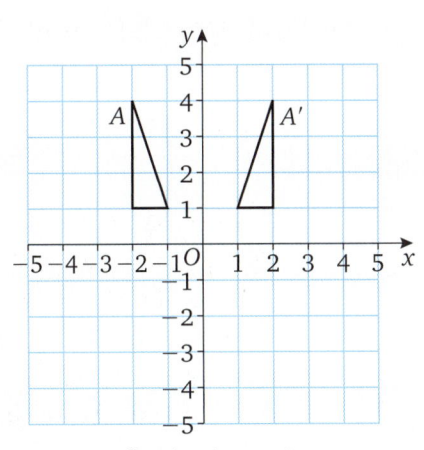

reflection in y-axis

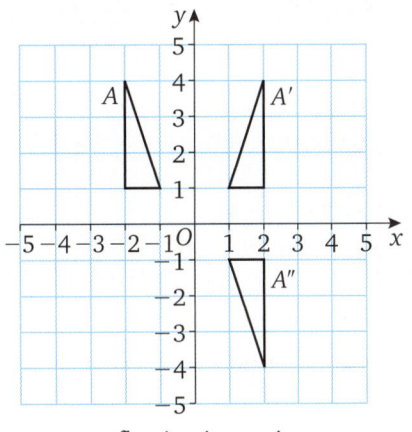

reflection in x-axis

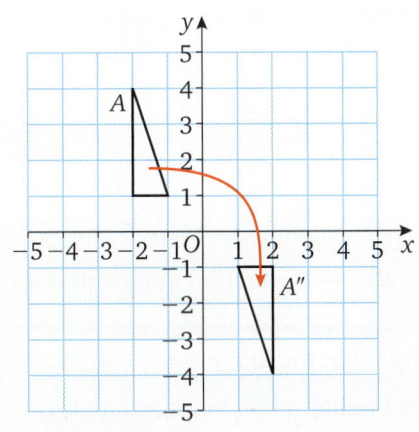

180° rotation about the origin

In the next diagram, the triangle A is mapped onto B by a 90° rotation clockwise about the origin.

The triangle B is mapped onto the triangle C by a reflection in the line $y = -1$

This can be described in one translation. Triangle A maps onto C by a vector translation $\begin{pmatrix} 8 \\ -10 \end{pmatrix}$

Rotation 90° clockwise about (0, 0)

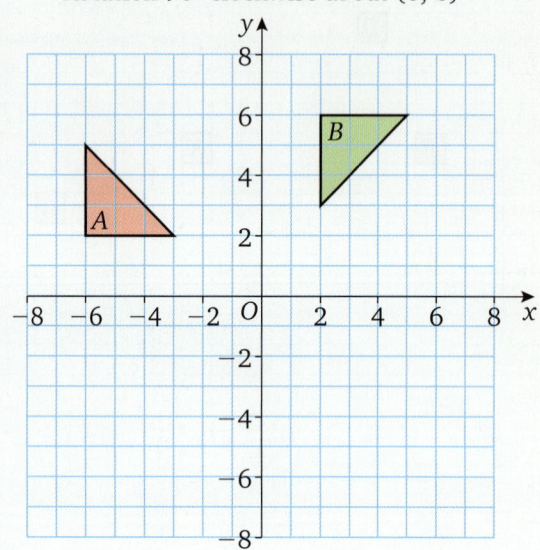

then reflection in the line $y = -1$

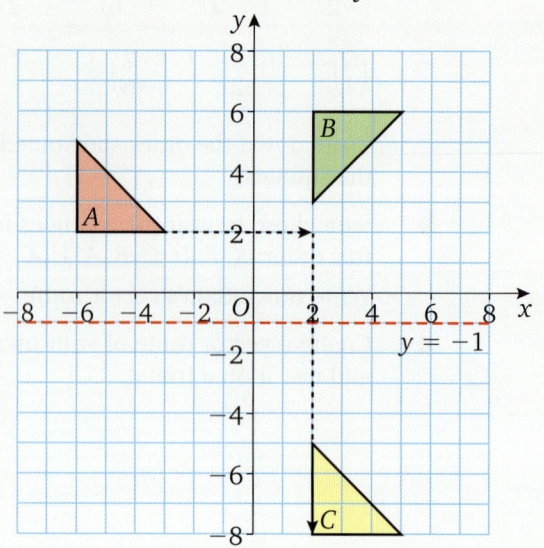

When a shape is transformed by a reflection, rotation, translation or combination of these, the shape and its image are said to be congruent. The size of the angles and lengths of the sides remain the same.

Example: In this diagram, A has been mapped onto B by a rotation clockwise by 90° about the origin.

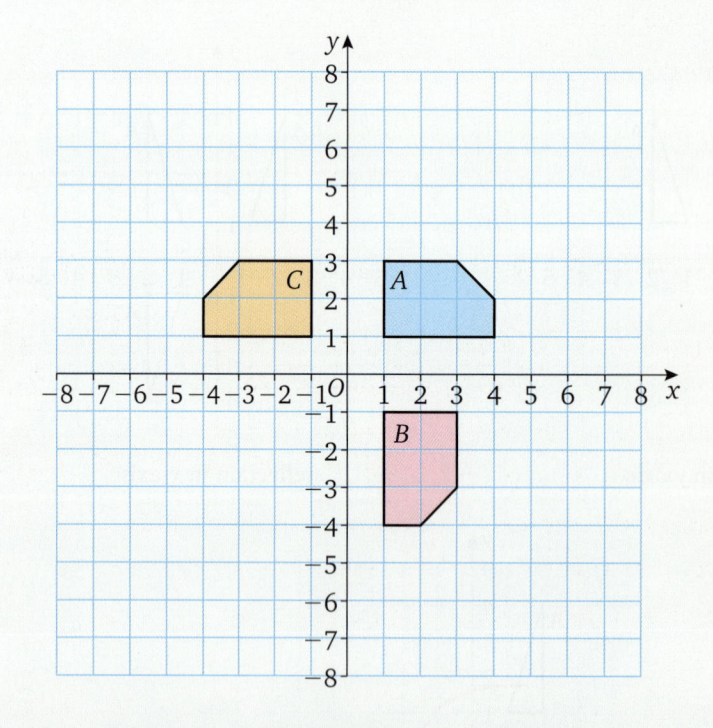

a Describe the transformation that maps B onto C.

b Describe the single transformation that maps A directly onto C.

Solution: **a** B has been reflected in the line $y = x$

b The single transformation that maps A onto C is a reflection in the y-axis ($x = 0$).

Chapter 18 Reflections, rotations and translations

Example: The diagram shows the shape A and its image after a number of transformations.

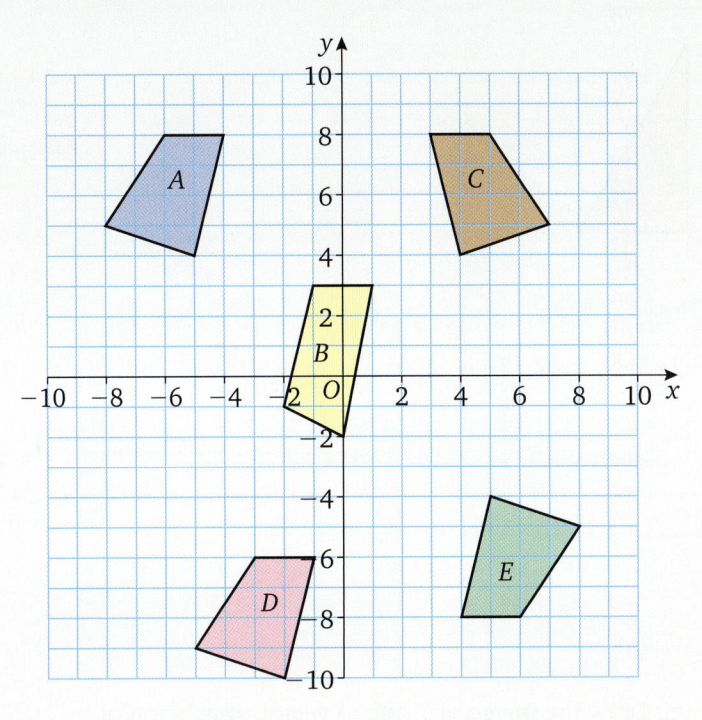

a Which of shapes B, C, D and E are congruent to A?

b Describe each single transformation that maps A onto each image.

Solution: **a** C, D and E are congruent to A.

B is not congruent because the length of each of its sides is not equal to the length of the corresponding side of A.

b C is a reflection in the y-axis.

D is a translation by vector $\begin{pmatrix} 3 \\ -14 \end{pmatrix}$

E is a rotation through 180° about the origin.

Practise... 18.4 Transformation and congruence

1
- **a**
  - **i** Draw a pair of x- and y-axes from −8 to 10.
  - **ii** Plot and join the points (0, 4), (2, 6), (5, 6), (4, 3) to create a quadrilateral Q.
- **b** Draw R, the image of Q, by reflecting Q in the line $y = 3$
- **c** Mark the sides and angles of Q and R that are equal.
- **d** Now rotate R 180° around the point (5, 3) to get S, the image of R.
- **e** Mark the sides and angles of R and S that are the same.
- **f** Describe the single transformation that maps Q onto S.
- **g** Copy and complete this sentence.
  Q, R and S are _____.

2
- **a**
  - **i** Draw a pair of x- and y-axes from −5 to 5.
  - **ii** Draw the quadrilateral M by plotting and joining the points (−3, 2), (−3, −1), (−2, −1), (−1, 2).
- **b** Draw the reflection of M in the line $y = -1$. Label the image M′.
- **c** Now rotate M′ 180° around the point (0, −1) and label the image M″.
- **d** Describe fully the single transformation that maps M onto M″.

3 This diagram shows the triangle, T.

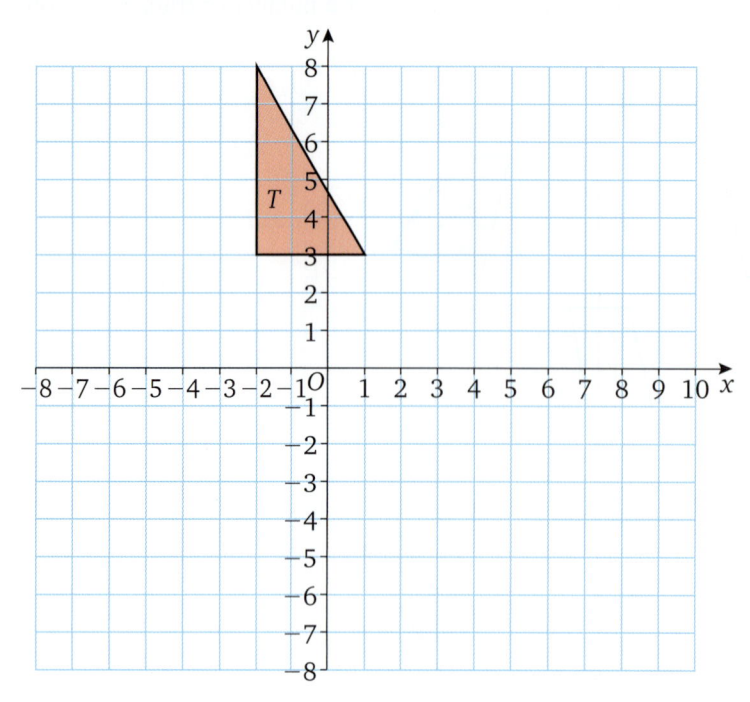

a Copy the diagram. Draw the image of T after a vector translation of $\begin{pmatrix}-4\\-9\end{pmatrix}$. Label this image U.

b Reflect U in the line $x = 2$ and label the image V.

c Reflect V in the line $y = -4.5$ and label the image W.

d Describe fully the single transformation that maps T onto W.

4 a Draw the triangle A with vertices (1, 4), (0, 0) and (0, 4) on x- and y-axes labelled −6 to 6.

b Rotate A by 180° around the point (−1, −1). Label the image B.

c Translate B by the vector $\begin{pmatrix}6\\0\end{pmatrix}$. Label the image C.

d Reflect C in the line $y = -1$. Label the image D.

e Describe the single transformation that maps A onto D.

5 In this diagram, the kite K has been transformed using a number of different transformations.

a Describe the transformation that maps K onto L.

b Describe the transformation that maps L onto M.

c Describe the transformation that maps M onto N.

d N can be mapped onto K with a clockwise rotation of 90°.

Find the coordinates of the centre of rotation.

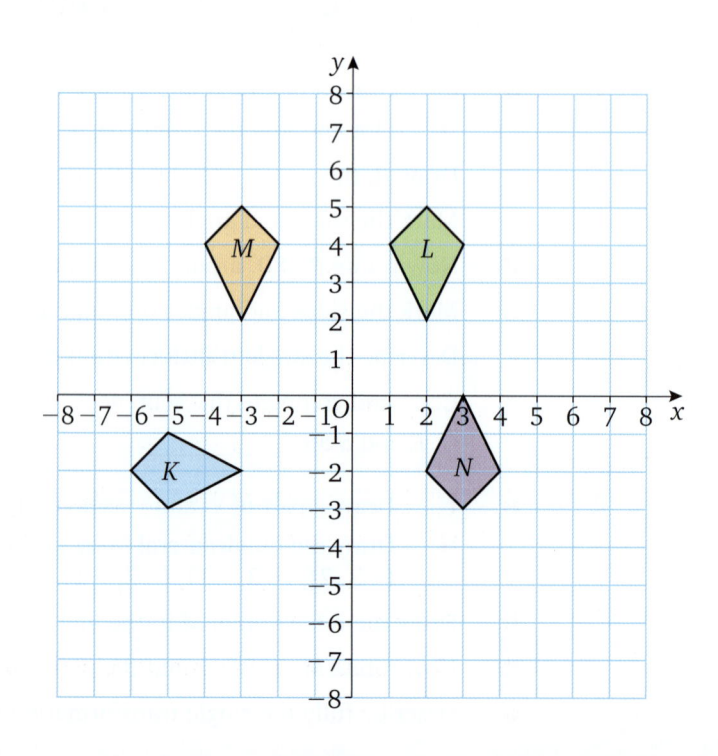

Chapter 18 Reflections, rotations and translations 243

6 Jake says that B is the image of A after a translation by the vector $\begin{pmatrix} 4 \\ -2 \end{pmatrix}$

Monique says Jake is wrong as A and B are not congruent.

Who is right, Jake or Monique?

Give an explanation for your answer.

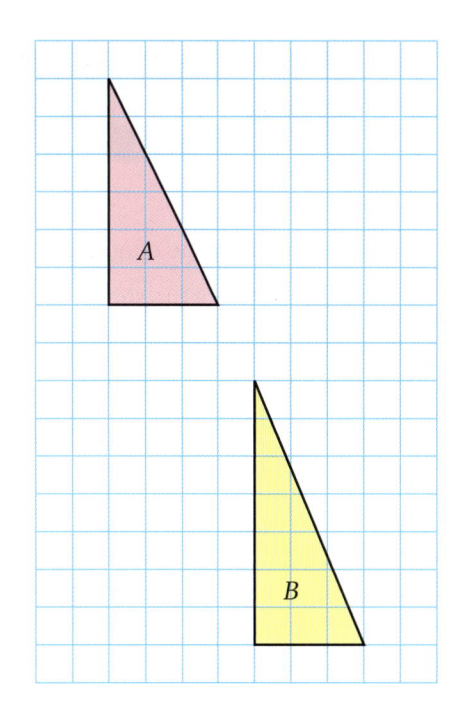

7 a Which of these shapes are congruent to P?
Give a reason for each answer.

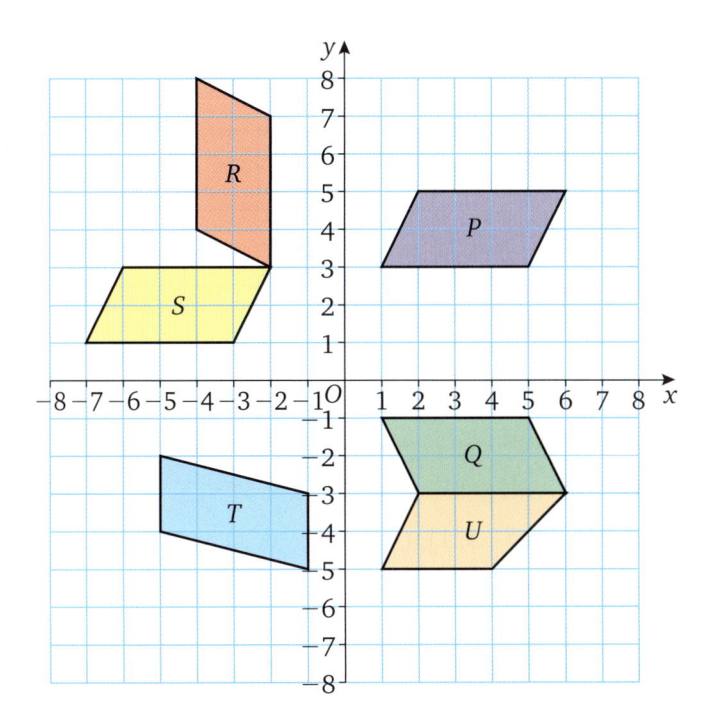

b Describe each single transformation that maps P onto each congruent image.

8 Josef is trying to answer these three questions.

- Does a reflection in the line $x = 2$, followed by a reflection in the line $y = 2$ have the same effect as a rotation around the point (2, 2)?
- Is this pattern true for negative values of x and y?
- Is this pattern true for all values of x and y?

a Draw some shapes and reflect and rotate them to help you answer all three questions.

b Draw at least three examples of each case to include in your answer.

18 Assess

1   **a**   Copy the diagram.

      b   Rotate the shape 90° clockwise about the origin.

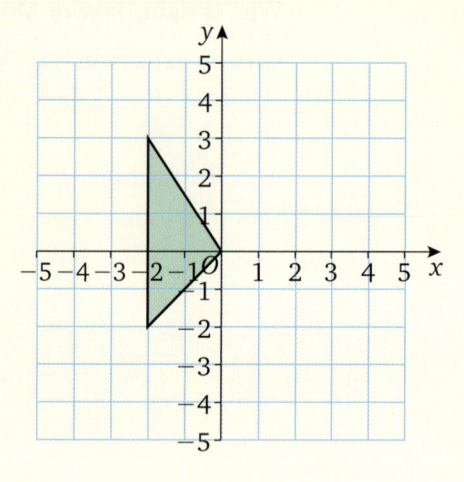

2   **a**   Write down the coordinates of the vertices of the triangle A.

      b   A is rotated 90° clockwise about the origin.

         Write down the coordinates of the vertices of the triangle after this rotation.

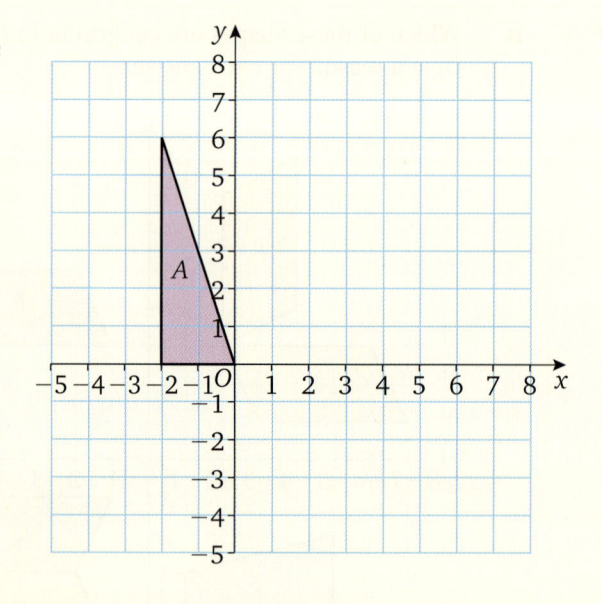

3   The coordinates of the triangle A are: $(-3, 1)$, $(-5, 3)$, $(-6, 1)$

      a   On suitable axes, draw the triangle A and it's image A' after a reflection in the line $x = -2$

      b   On the same axes, draw A'', the image of A after a rotation through 90° anticlockwise about the point $(-2, 1)$.

4   Write down the equation of the line of reflectional symmetry in this diagram.

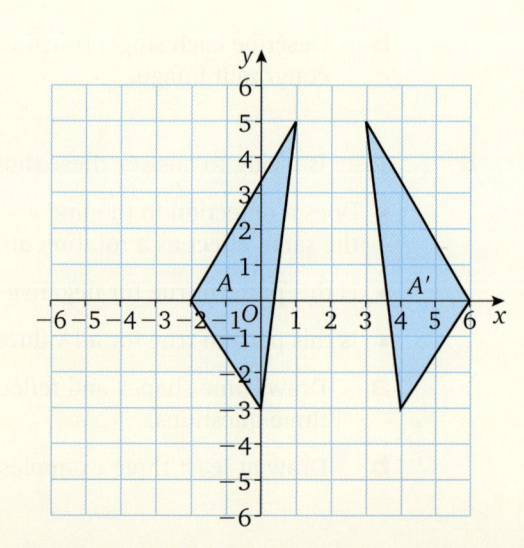

5
a Copy the diagram.
b Write down the coordinates of the vertices of the triangle.
c Reflect the triangle in the line $x = -y$
d Write down the coordinates of the vertices of the new triangle.

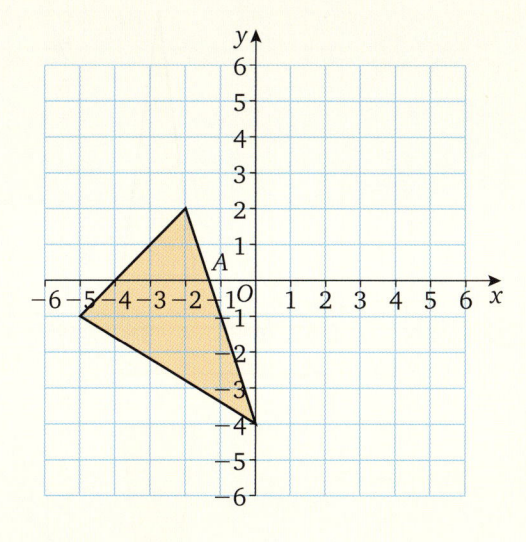

6
a Describe fully the single transformation that maps M onto N.
b Copy the diagram and rotate shape N 90° clockwise about the point (1, −1). Label the image P.
c Reflect P in the x-axis and label the image Q.
d Describe fully the single transformation that maps M onto Q.

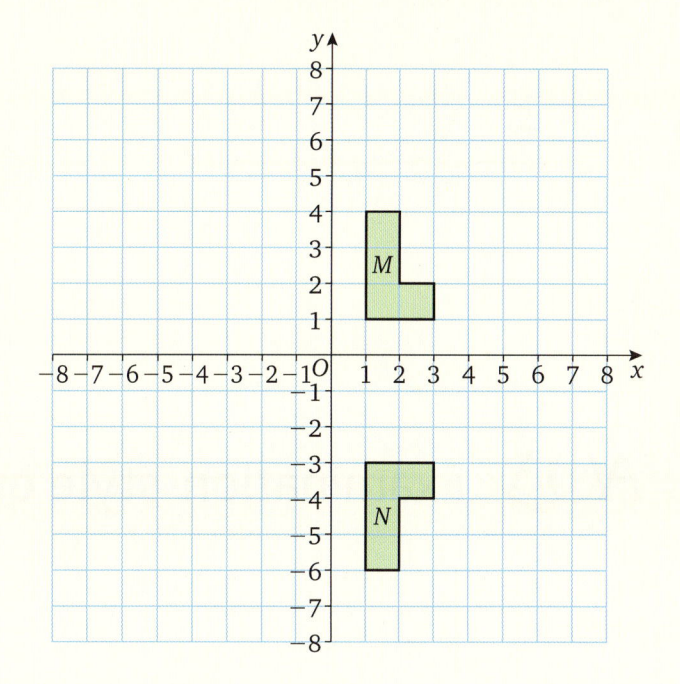

7 The shapes X and Y are congruent.
a Copy and complete the diagram of X and Y.
b Describe fully the **single** transformation that maps X onto Y.

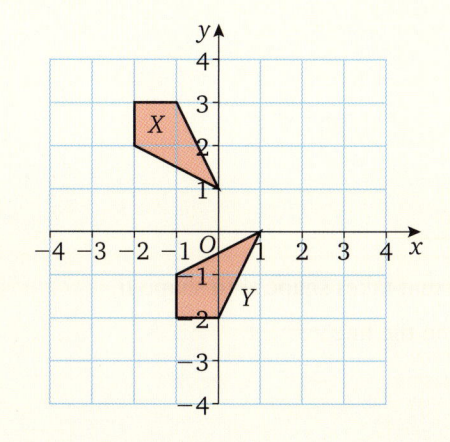

8 **a** Which of the shapes B, C and D are congruent to A?

b Which of the shapes B, C and D are a transformation of A?
Give an explanation for your answer.

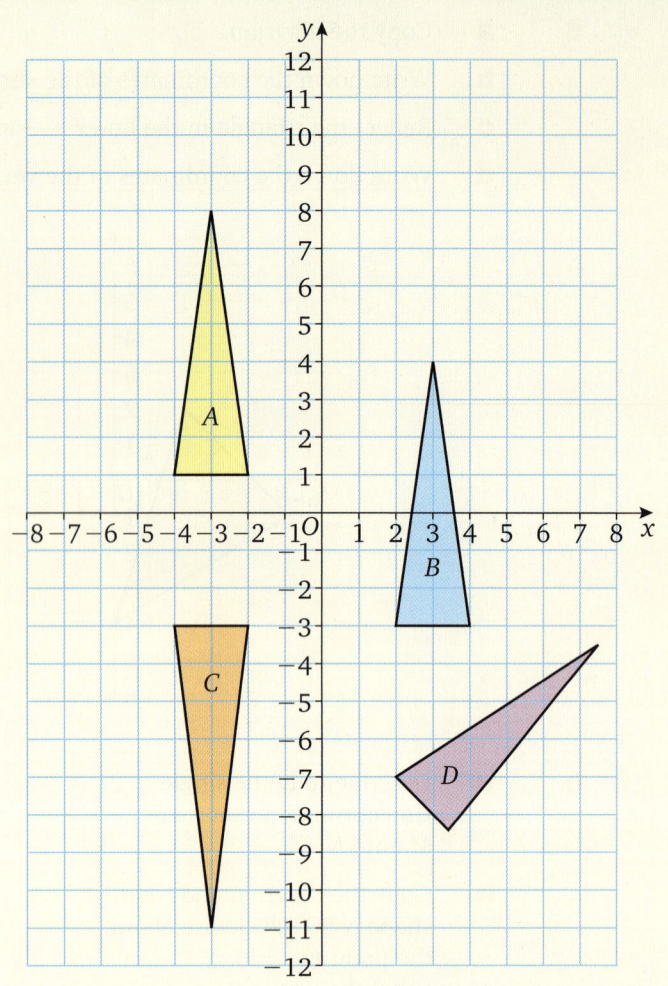

AQA Examination-style questions

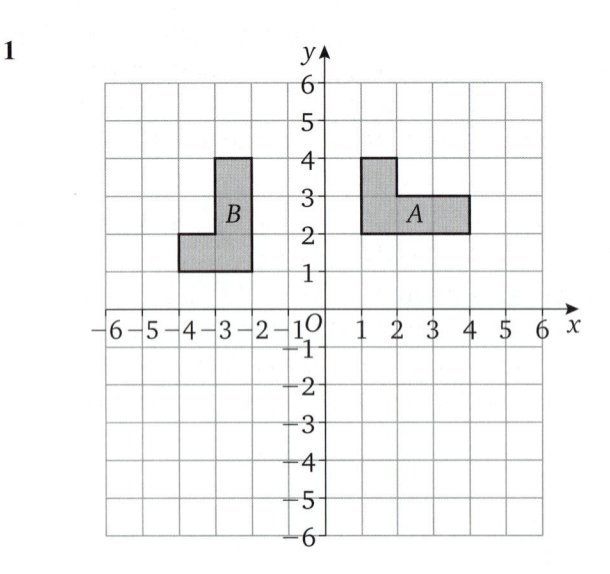

1

a Describe the single transformation that takes shape A to shape B. (3 marks)

b Copy the diagram. Reflect shape B in the line $y = -1$ (2 marks)

AQA 2008

19 Measures

Objectives

Examiners would normally expect students who get these grades to be able to:

D
calculate average speed

C
use compound measures such as speed

recognise that measurements to the nearest unit may be inaccurate by up to one half unit in either direction

B
use compound measures, such as density, for example find density given cross-sectional area, length and mass.

Did you know?

Archimedes

Part of Archimedes' fame comes from solving King Hiero's 'crown problem'. Legend has it that Hiero gave the goldsmith a quantity of gold to make a crown. The finished crown was the correct weight but Hiero suspected some silver had been substituted. The problem was brought to the attention of Archimedes.

Upon entering his bathtub, Archimedes noted that some water overflowed. This gave him an idea. A given weight of pure gold displaces a certain volume of water. The same weight of impure gold will displace a different volume of water. He could use this fact to tell whether the crown was made of impure gold. This proved bad news for the deceptive goldsmith.

Key terms

lower bound (or limit)
upper bound (or limit)
compound measures
density
mass

You should already know:

✓ how to convert between different units.

Learn... 19.1 Accuracy of measurement

When you measure to the nearest centimetre, any actual measurement, between 6.5 cm and up to but not including 7.5 cm, will round to 7 cm.

Any measurement in the shaded area of this scale rounds to 7.

The shaded area is from 6.5 up to 7.5

6.5 is the **lower bound**

7.5 is the **upper bound**

Notice: 'to the nearest centimetre' means that the actual distance could be any value from half a centimetre below to half a centimetre above.

Example: Zac measures the length of a shelf. He says it is 43 cm to the nearest cm.

What are the upper and lower bounds of Zac's measurement?

Solution: Zac's measurement rounds to 43 cm, so the actual length must be in the shaded area on the scale.

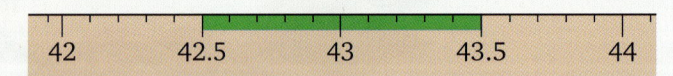

The shaded area is from 42.5 up to 43.5

The lower bound is 42.5 cm.

The upper bound is 43.5 cm.

Practise... 19.1 Accuracy of measurement

1 Round each of the following to the nearest unit.

a 12.9 cm
b 81.2 m
c 49.9 miles
d 6.5 g
e 43.56 kg
f 47.4999 litres

2 When rounded to the nearest centimetre each of these lengths rounds to 15 cm.

14.6 cm   15.4 cm   14.91 cm   15.49 cm

a Write down some other lengths that also round to 15 cm to the nearest centimetre.
b What is the minimum value that rounds up to 15 cm?
c What is the maximum value that rounds down to 15 cm?

3 George measured the length of a post for a washing line in his garden.
He found it was 3 metres to the nearest metre.

What are the upper and lower bounds for his measurement?

4 Faye measured some of the crayons in her pencil case.
She found they were all 8 cm to the nearest centimetre.

Does this mean they were all the same length? Explain your answer.

5 Beshar measured the distance from his home in Windermere to his school in Kendal. He found it was 18 km to the nearest kilometre.
   a What is the smallest distance that Beshar's measurement could be?
   b What is the largest distance that Beshar's measurement could be?

6 The weight of a letter is 43 g to the nearest gram.
What are the maximum and minimum values for the weight of the letter?

7 A bridge has a sign stating the maximum weight allowed on it is 2 tonnes.
A van driver knows his van weighs 2 tonnes to the nearest tonne.
Can the van driver be sure that it is safe for him to drive over the bridge?
Give a reason for your answer.

8 The contents of a packet of crisps weigh 33 g to the nearest gram.
Which of the following could be the weight of the crisps?
   a 33.2 g   **c** 33.49 g   **e** 32.5 g
   b 33.6 g   **d** 33.94 g   **f** 32.29 g

9 Rachel weighs the books in her school bag.
All of her textbooks together weigh 3 kg to the nearest kg.
All of her exercise books together weigh 1 kg to the nearest kg.
What is the maximum weight of the contents of her bag?

10 George, Mildred, Henrietta and Dan all get into a lift.
To the nearest 1 kg, George weighs 80 kg, Mildred weighs 70 kg and Henrietta weighs 60 kg.
The lift states: Maximum weight 250 kg.
What is Dan's maximum possible weight if it is to be safe to use the lift?

Learn... 19.2 Compound measures

Compound measures combine two different units.

For example, density = $\frac{\text{mass}}{\text{volume}}$ and average speed = $\frac{\text{total distance}}{\text{total time}}$, population density = $\frac{\text{number of people}}{\text{area of land}}$,

fuel consumption = $\frac{\text{number of miles}}{\text{number of gallons used}}$

The units give you clues about what to divide by.

Density is **mass** per unit volume, kg/m³ if the mass is in kg and the volume is in m³.

The units tell you the formula, density = mass ÷ volume.

Speed is measured in km/hour. This tells you the formula, speed = distance ÷ time.

Population density is measured in people per square kilometre.

Fuel consumption is measured in miles per gallon or kilometres per litre.

> **AQA Examiner's tip**
> Make sure that you have the correct units for the problem. You may need to convert some units before you use them.
> For km/h you need the distance to be in km and the time to be in hours.
> For g/cm³ you need the mass to be in grams and the volume to be in cm³.

Example: Jamie is a runner in a club. He runs 200 metres in 32 seconds. Find his speed in:

    i metres per second

    ii kilometres per hour.

Solution:

i Using the formula above:

$$\text{average speed} = \frac{\text{distance}}{\text{time}} = \frac{200}{32} \text{ m/s} = 6.25 \text{ m/s}$$

ii 6.25 m/s means 6.25 metres every second.

In 60 seconds he runs $60 \times 6.25 = 375$ metres

In 60 minutes he runs $60 \times 375 = 22\,500$ metres

To convert metres to kilometres, we need to divide by 1000 because there are 1000 metres in a kilometre, so:

$22\,500$ metres $= 22\,500 \div 1000 = 22.5$ km

Jamie runs at a speed of 22.5 km/h.

Example:

a Work out the average speed in mph of a train that takes $1\frac{1}{2}$ hours to travel 102 miles.

b Nazneen cycled at a steady speed of 8 km/h. How far did she travel in three and a half hours?

Solution:

a $\text{average speed} = \frac{\text{distance}}{\text{time}} = \frac{102}{1.5} = 68$ mph

b distance = average speed × time

distance = $8 \times 3.5 = 28$ km

> **AQA Examiner's tip**
>
> If time is in hours and minutes change it to hours and decimals of an hour before finding average speed. The unit for average speed is now mph or km/h.

Example: The density of lead is 11.4 g/cm^3.
A block of lead is 2 cm wide, 3 cm high and 6 cm long.

What is the mass of the lead in kilograms?

Solution: The volume of the block is $2 \times 3 \times 6 = 36$ cm^3

Density is mass per unit volume.

$$\text{density} = \frac{\text{mass}}{\text{volume}}$$

$$11.4 = \frac{\text{mass}}{36}$$

$11.4 \times 36 = 410.4 =$ mass in grams

The block has a mass of 0.41 kg.

> **AQA Examiner's tip**
>
> You will get decimals and fractions as answers when you work with compound measures. When your answer is a recurring decimal, it is important to make sure that the decimal is rounded correctly.
>
> Remember that $12\frac{2}{3} = 12.\dot{6} = 12.67$ (2 d.p.) and not 12.66

Chapter 19 Measures

Practise... 19.2 Compound measures D C B A A*

1 Work out the average speed for each of the following. State the units of your answer.
  a A car that travels 200 metres in 8 seconds
  b A man that takes 28 seconds to run 200 metres
  c A train that takes 2 hours to travel 230 miles

2 Write each of these times using decimals of an hour.
  a 30 minutes **b** 15 minutes **c** 4 hours 45 minutes

3 Write each of these times using hours and minutes.
  a 2.5 hours **b** 3.25 hours **c** 1.75 hours

4 Find the speed in mph of:
  a a car that travels 85 miles in 1 hour and a quarter
  b a lorry that travels 75 miles in 1 hour 25 minutes.

5 A snail crawls at a speed of 5 cm every minute.
  a How far does it crawl in one hour?
  b How long does it take to crawl one metre?

6 Work out the time taken for each of these journeys. Give your answer in hours and minutes.
  a A car travels at 50 km per hour for 40 km.
  b A bus travels at 30 km per hour for 20 km.
  c A cyclist travels 45 km at 25 km per hour.

7 Work out the distance travelled for each of these journeys.
  a A person walks at 4 km per hour for 75 minutes.
  b A train travels at 110 km per hour for 90 minutes.
  c A lorry travels for 45 minutes at 50 km per hour.

8 Jan drives her car 255 miles and uses 6 gallons of fuel.
  a What is her fuel consumption in miles per gallon?
  b How many gallons of fuel does Jan use for a journey of 400 miles?
  c The fuel tank in Jan's car contains 15 gallons of fuel when it is full.
  Is it possible for Jan to travel 600 miles on one full tank of fuel?

9 An island has an area of 680 km² and a population of 3100 people.
  What is the population density of the island?

10 A rock has a volume of 35 cm³ and a mass of 266 g.
  What is the density of the rock?

11 The density of gold is 19.3 g/cm³. A gold bar has a volume of 5 cm³.
  What is the mass of the gold?

12 Four blocks of metal are shown below.
Each length has been recorded to the nearest mm.
Each weight has been recorded to 1 d.p.
Each density has been given to 1 d.p.

Use the information given in the table and on the diagrams to identify what each block is made from.
Show working to justify your answers.

Metal	Density (g/cm³)
Copper	9.0
Iron	7.8
Lead	11.0
Gold	19.3

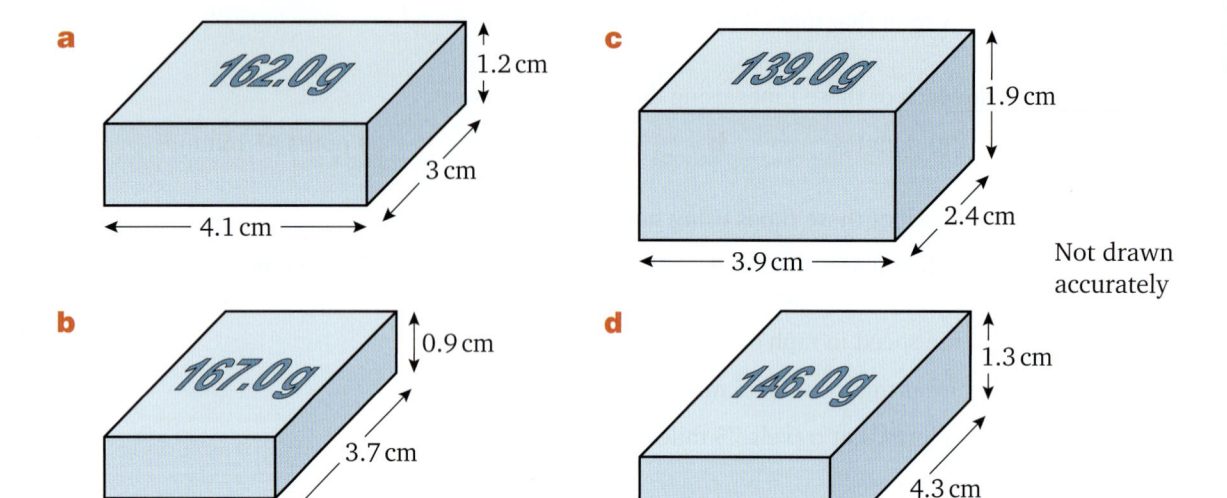

a 162.0 g, 1.2 cm, 3 cm, 4.1 cm

b 167.0 g, 0.9 cm, 3.7 cm, 2.6 cm

c 139.0 g, 1.9 cm, 2.4 cm, 3.9 cm

d 146.0 g, 1.3 cm, 4.3 cm, 2.9 cm

Not drawn accurately

AQA Examiner's tip

When you have a lot of steps to do in a calculation, take them one at a time. When you think you have finished answering a question, remember to check that you have completed your solution. Many candidates lose marks for stopping part-way through and not checking their work.

13 The diagram shows a prism with a trapezium as its cross-section.

a Find the volume of the prism.

b The prism is made of gold. Gold has a density of 19.3 g/cm³.
Find the mass of the gold.

c Gold is worth £38.90 per gram.
Find the value of the gold.

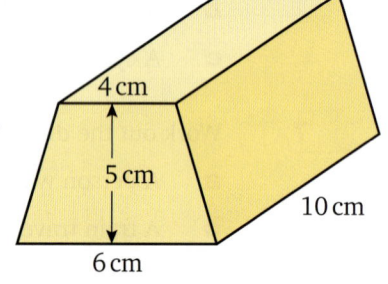

(4 cm, 5 cm, 6 cm, 10 cm)

14 Mary has a solid ball which has a mass of 540 g.
The ball is made from material which has a density of 6 g/cm³.
Mary's little brother drops the ball in their fish tank.
The fish tank is in the shape of a cuboid 30 cm by 20 cm and 50 cm deep.

By how much does the depth of water in the fish tank rise when the ball is dropped in the tank?

15 John runs at 9 km per hour for 40 minutes. He then walks 2.5 km in 30 minutes.

What is John's average speed in km per hour?

16 Sam drives 265 miles from Kendal to Bristol at an average of 50 miles per gallon (mpg).
He then drives 221 miles from Bristol to Norwich at an average of 48 mpg.
He drives from Norwich back to Kendal, a distance of 278 miles, at an average of 47 mpg.
His fuel tank contains 15 gallons of fuel when full.

a Is it possible for Sam to complete this journey on one tank of petrol?

b What if all the quantities of petrol found in part **a** had been given to the nearest whole number?

17 Mary jogs 2 miles at 5 mph, then runs 2 miles at 7 mph.

    a Explain why her average speed is not 6 mph.

    b Mary wants do training runs of about 4 miles jogging at 5 mph and running at 7 mph. How far does Mary go at each speed in order to have an average speed of 6 mph?

19 Assess

1 A van travels 230 miles in 7 hours. What is the average speed of the van?

2 A car takes 45 minutes to travel 17 miles. What is the average speed of the car?

3 The temperature in a classroom is 18 °C to the nearest degree. What are the maximum and minimum temperatures?

4 A bar of chocolate has a mass of 250 g and a volume of 60 cm^3. What is the density of the chocolate?

5 A log has a cross-sectional area of 70 cm^2 and a length of 25 cm. The density of the log is 0.63 g/cm^3.

What is the mass of the log?

6 Harry is replacing the carpet in his rectangular front room. It is 4.5 m by 3.6 m. He pays £526.50 for the new carpet.

What is the cost per square metre of his new carpet?

7 Hamish drives 23 miles to the nearest mile in his car. The car's computer says it has used 0.4 gallons of fuel.

Work out the fuel consumption in mpg of Hamish's car.

8 A car's fuel tank holds 60 litres of fuel when full. The density of the fuel is 925 kg/m^3.

    a Find the mass of the fuel in a full tank.

    b The car travels 375 miles at an average of 45 mph and 48 mpg.

        i How long does the car take to complete its journey?

        ii What is the mass of the fuel in the tank at the end of this journey?
(1 gallon = 4.546 litres)

9 Darren has a spherical ball of modelling clay. It has a mass of 462 g. The density of the clay is 2.3 g/cm^3. He reshapes the clay into a cubical block with base 3 cm by 6 cm.

Find the height of the block.

AQA Examination-style questions

1 Susan completes a journey in two stages.

In stage 1 of her journey, she drives at an average speed of 80 km/h and takes 1 hour 45 minutes.

    a How far does Susan travel in stage 1 of her journey? *(2 marks)*

    b Altogether, Susan drives 190 km and takes a total time of 2 hours 15 minutes. What is her average speed, in km/h, in **stage 2** of her journey? *(3 marks)*

AQA 2003

20 3-D shapes, coordinates and graphs

Objectives

Examiners would normally expect students who get these grades to be able to:

D
draw the elevations of a solid on squared paper

make simple interpretations of real-life graphs

C
further interpret real-life graphs, for example find the average speed in km/h from a distance–time graph over time in minutes

B
use 3-D coordinates

discuss and interpret graphs modelling real situations.

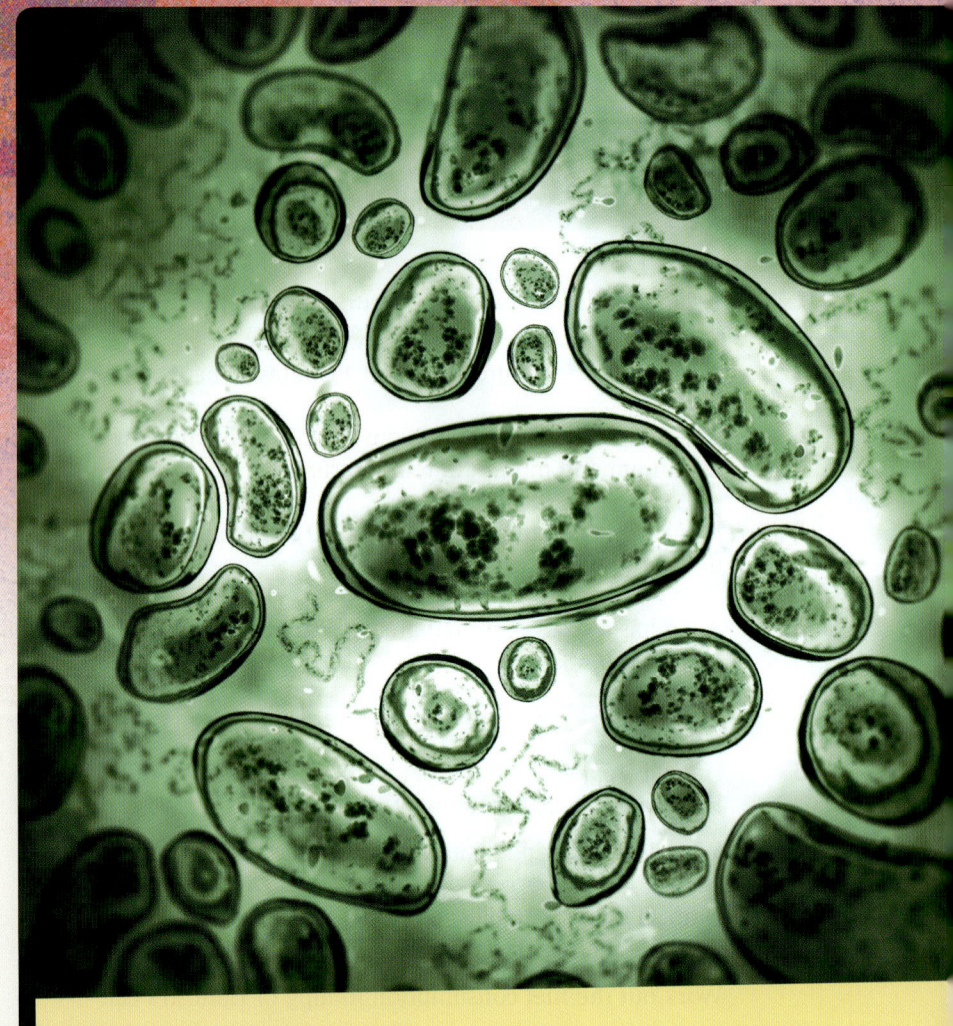

Did you know?

Modelling with graphs

Under laboratory conditions bacteria multiply rapidly, as rapidly as doubling their population every half hour. This type of growth is called exponential growth.

Graphs are used to plot experimental data. This can then be used for analysis to find relationships between variables.

Key terms
plan view
front elevation
side elevation
parabola

You should already know:
✓ what a plane is
✓ what a distance–time graph is
✓ coordinates in the x- and y-axes
✓ how to make nets of shapes.

Chapter 20 3-D shapes, coordinates and graphs

Learn... 20.1 Plans and elevations

3-D objects may be viewed from different directions.

The view from above is called the **plan view**.

The view from the front is called the **front elevation**.

The view from the side is called the **side elevation**.

Sometimes the front elevation will look the same as the side elevation.

Lines that cannot be seen are drawn using dotted lines.

Drawing 2-D representations of 3-D shapes

There are two ways to represent cubes and cuboids in 2-D.

Method 1
This uses special paper, either **isometric paper** (with lines) or **isometric dotty paper** (which just has dots and is sometimes called triangular dotty paper).

Using isometric dotty paper:
The dots are arranged in triangles 1 cm apart.
You need to make sure that the paper is the correct way round in order for your diagrams to work.

You should be able to draw triangles like these.

If you can only draw triangles like these then your paper is the wrong way round.

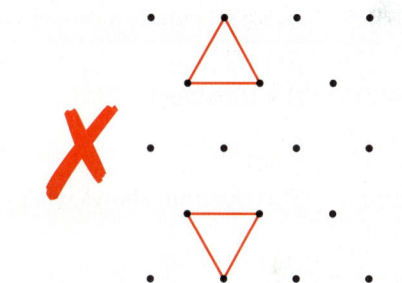

To draw a cube it is easiest to start with the top.
Join the dots to make a rhombus.
Then draw in the vertical edges.
Finally complete the edges on the base of the cube.

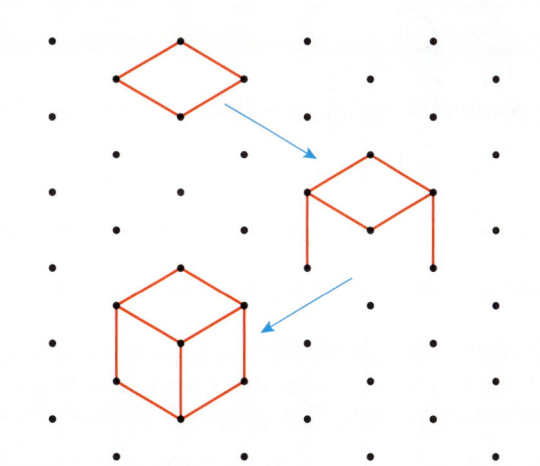

To draw shapes made of cuboids, start with the cube at the front, then work your way back.

Remember, you cannot see the front face of any cubes that are behind the cube at the front.

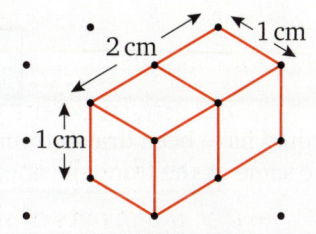

Using isometric paper.
This is just like the dotty paper, but the dots have all been joined up.

As with dotty paper, you need to make sure that it is the correct way round. You need to be able to draw the triangles the same way as for dotty paper. Another way to do this is to make sure that there are vertical lines on the page.

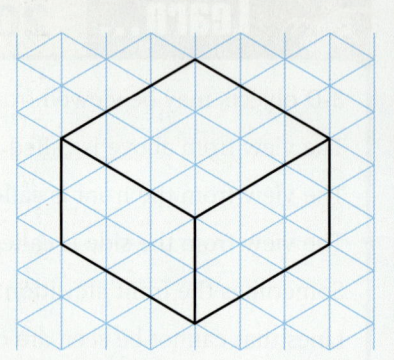

Method 2

This method can be used to sketch a cube when you don't have isometric paper or isometric dotty paper. Start with a square (this is the front).

Then draw three parallel lines going backwards like this (these are the edges going away from the front).
Any edges you cannot see need to be shown with dashed lines.

Add dashed edges to complete a square at the back and the fourth sloping line like this and you have sketched a cube.

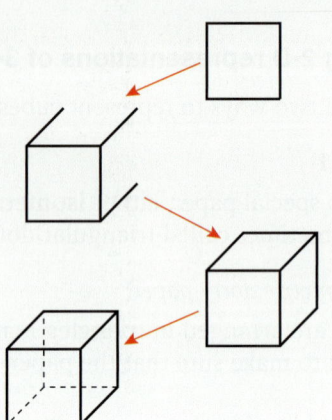

Example: Henri has made a model with five Multilink cubes.

Draw a plan view and front and side elevations of Henri's model.

Solution: This diagram shows where the views are from.

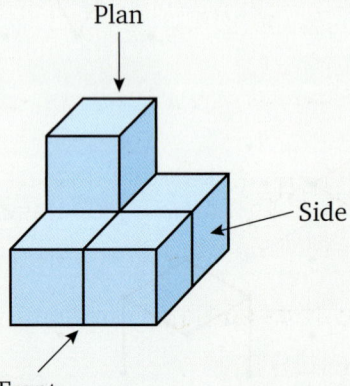

The plan view is from above:
All that can be seen from above are four squares.

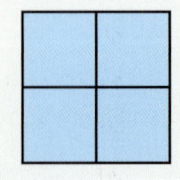

The front elevation is:

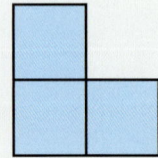

The side elevation is:

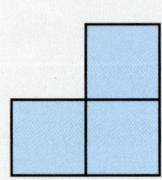

The side elevation could have been drawn from the 'other' side. If it had been, the side view would have been the same as the front elevation.

Chapter 20   3-D shapes, coordinates and graphs   **257**

Example: Jez makes this model using five Multilink cubes.

Draw the plan view and the front and side elevations of Jez's model.

Solution: From above only three cubes can be seen.
The plan view is:

Note that the two dotted lines show where the gap is underneath.

The front elevation is: The side elevation is:

The dotted line shows the top of the gap underneath.

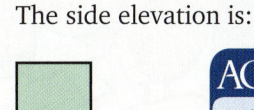

AQA Examiner's tip

When you use isometric paper, make sure you have the paper the right way round, otherwise you will not be able to draw 2-D representations of 3-D shapes on isometric or dotty paper.

Practise... 20.1 Plans and elevations   D C B A A*

1 Each of the following shapes is made using multilink cubes.

For each shape, draw the plan view and the elevations from the directions labelled F (front) and S (side).

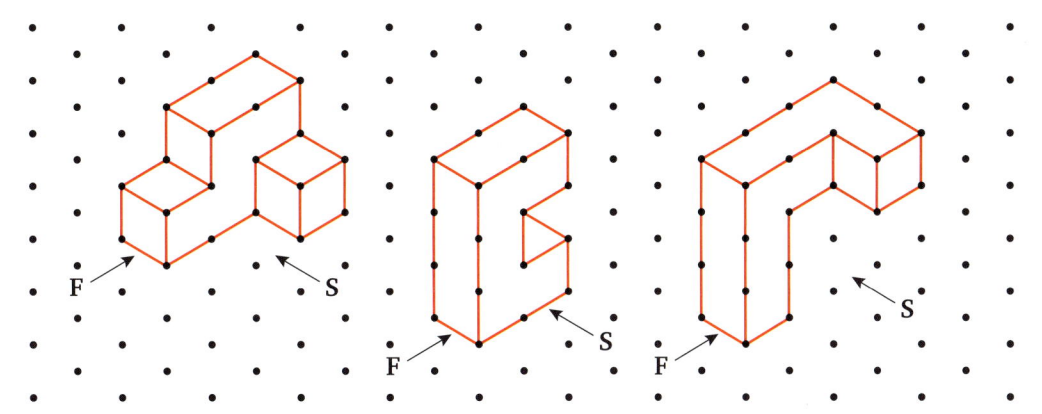

2 Here are the plan and elevations for an object made from multilink cubes.

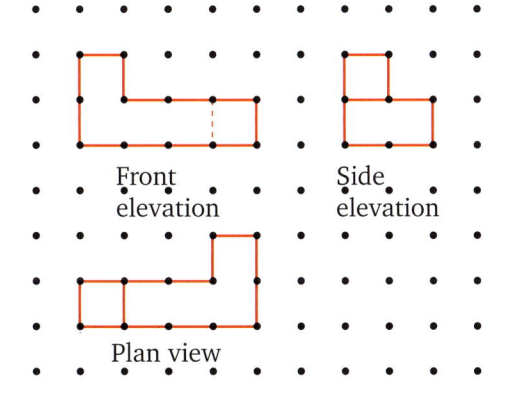

Front elevation   Side elevation

Plan view

Draw the object using isometric dotty paper.

3 Four mugs of coffee are on a table as shown.

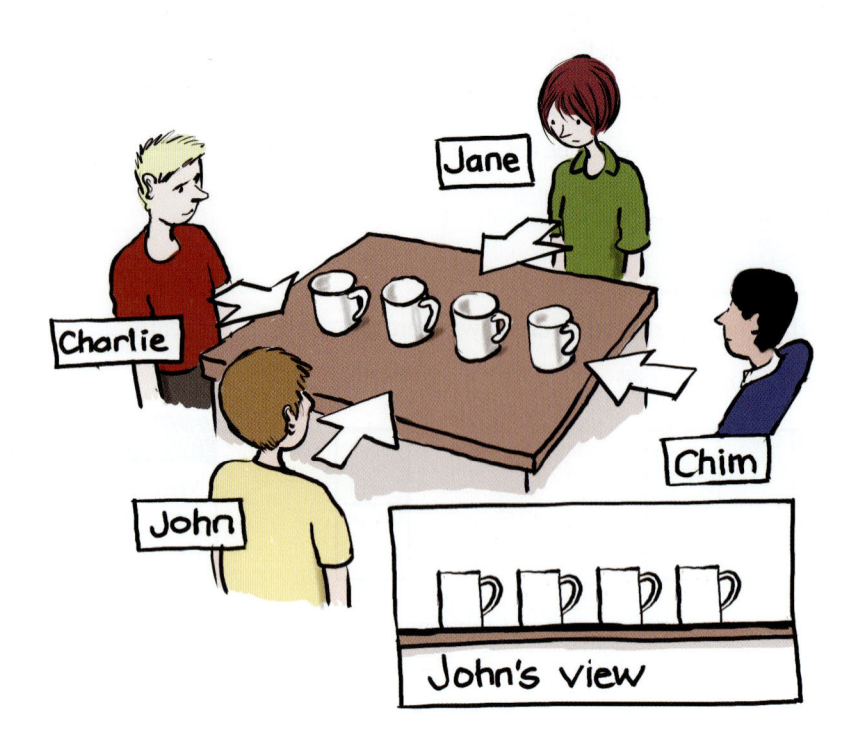

John sees the mugs as shown in the diagram.

a Sketch the mugs as Jane sees them.

b Sketch the view that Chim sees.

c Sketch the view that Charlie sees.

d Sketch the plan view.

4 The following diagrams show some pieces of furniture from a doll's house.

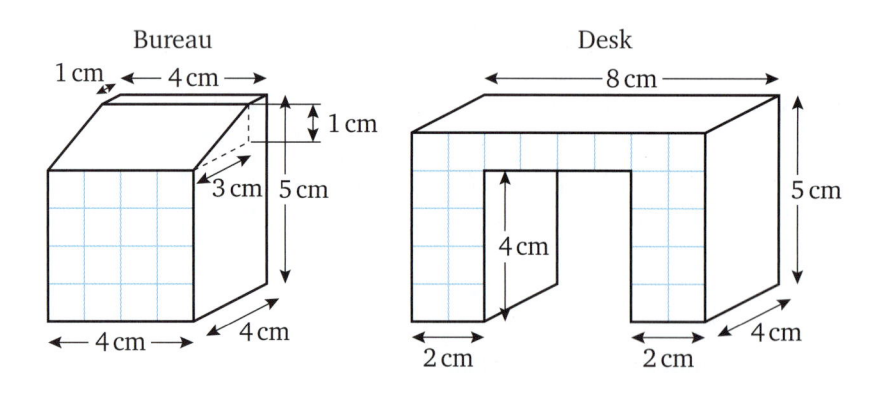

Bureau

Desk

Not drawn accurately

a Ian drew these plan views of the furniture.

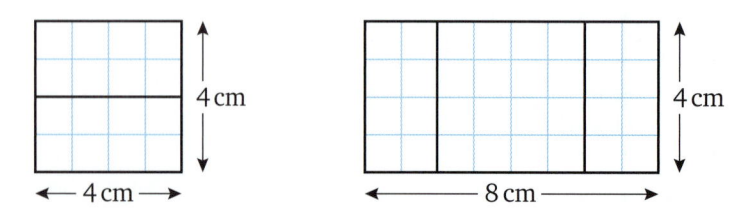

What mistakes has Ian made?

b Draw the plan views accurately.

Chapter 20 3-D shapes, coordinates and graphs 259

5 Alan, Bridgette, Charlotte, and Dan are doing some work on plans and elevations in a mathematics lesson.

They have arranged two matchboxes on the table. They are sitting around the table as shown in the diagram.

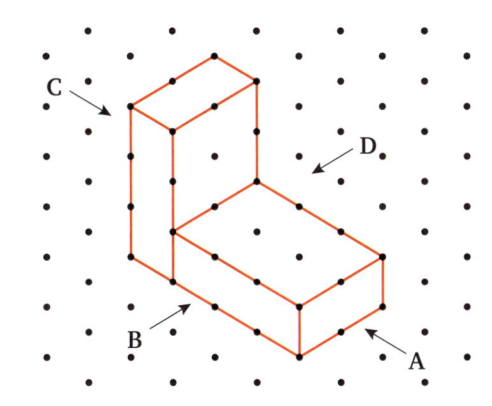

a They each draw the front elevation that they see. Which of the following does each draw?

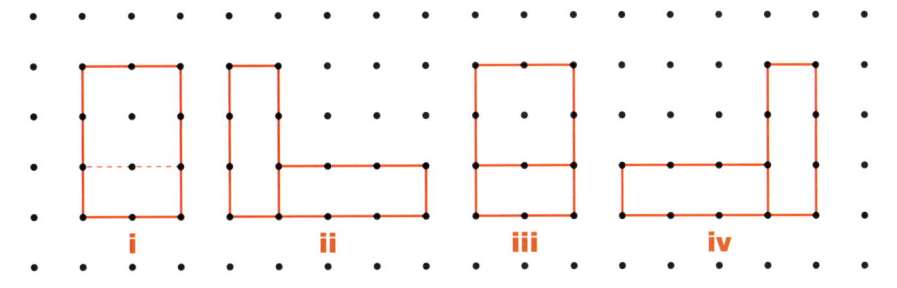

i　ii　iii　iv

b They rearrange the matchboxes as shown.

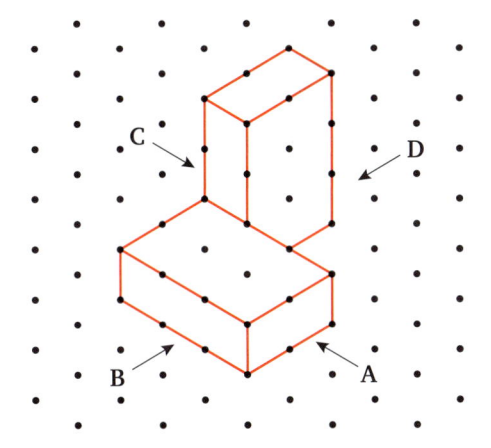

Draw the front elevation that each person sees. Label them clearly.

6 Jackie makes some models with multilink cubes. She draws a plan and elevations for each of her models.

Draw a representation of each model on triangular dotty paper.

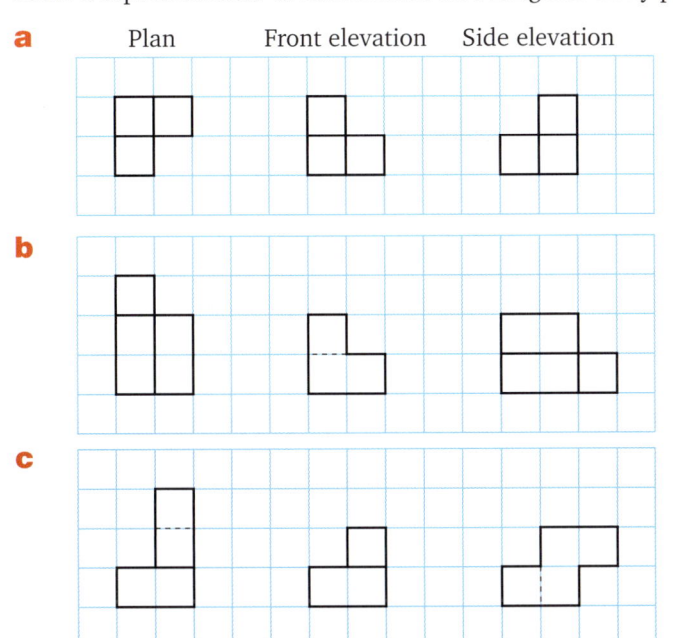

a　Plan　Front elevation　Side elevation

b

c

7 I have a shape. Both side elevations are a circle. The plan elevation is also a circle.

What shape have I got?

8 James is studying architecture and is doing a project on this building.

  a Draw the side elevation.

  b Draw the front elevation (don't forget the tree).

  c Draw the plan view.

Learn... 20.2 Coordinates in 3-D

You have already learned about coordinates in two dimensions.

Consider a classroom which has a floor in the shape of a rectangle. You can use x- and y-coordinates to specify where something is on the floor of the classroom. You need a third coordinate to say how high something is above any point on the floor.

This third coordinate is called the z-coordinate.

The z-axis is perpendicular to both the x- and y-axes.

You write the coordinates in alphabetical order (x, y, z).

Example: In the diagram of the cuboid $OA = 2$ units, $AB = 5$ units and $AD = 3$ units. O is the origin.

Write down the coordinates of A, B, C and D.

Solution: $A = (2, 0, 0)$
This is 2 units in the x-direction, 0 units in the y-direction and 0 units in the z-direction.

$B = (2, 5, 0)$
This is 2 units in the x-direction, 5 units in the y-direction and 0 units in the z-direction.

$C = (2, 5, 3)$
This is 2 units in the x-direction, 5 units in the y-direction and 3 units in the z-direction.

$D = (2, 0, 3)$
This is 2 units in the x-direction, 0 units in the y-direction and 3 units in the z-direction.

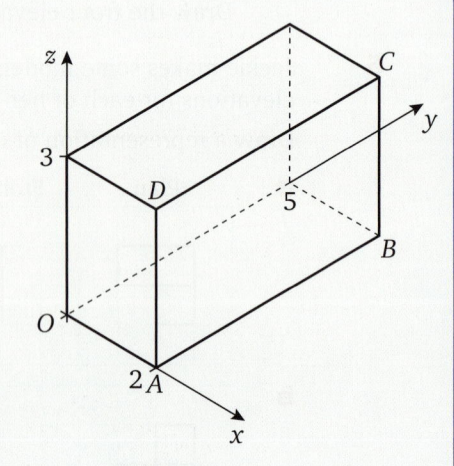

AQA Examiner's tip
Remember to get the coordinates in the correct order (x, y, z).
(x, y, z) is in alphabetical order.

Chapter 20 3-D shapes, coordinates and graphs 261

Practise... 20.2 Coordinates in 3-D

D C B A A*

1 The diagram shows a model made from 1 cm cubes.
The point A has coordinates (1, 1, 0).

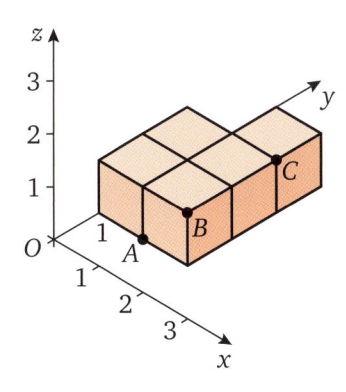

Write down the coordinates of points B and C.

2 The diagram shows a cube.

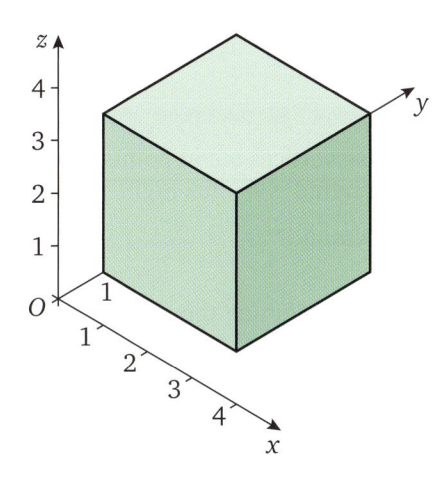

The coordinates of one vertex are (3, 1, 0). What are the coordinates of the other vertices?

3 The diagram shows a model made from 1 cm cubes.

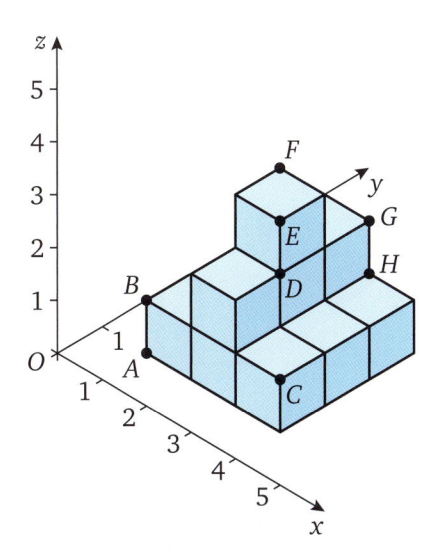

Write down the coordinates of the points labelled A to H in the diagram.

4 The diagram shows a cuboid.

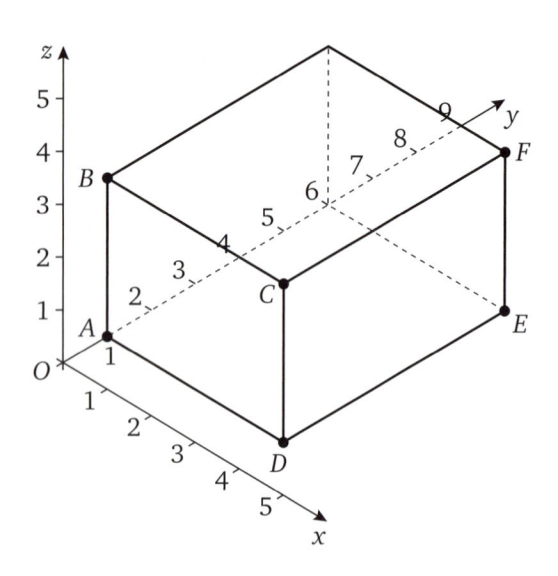

Write down the coordinates of the vertices labelled *A* to *F*.

5 A cube of side 3 cm has vertices at the points with coordinates (0, 0, 0), (0, 3, 0) and (3, 3, 0).

What are the coordinates of the other five vertices?

6 A square-based pyramid is placed so that three of the base vertices are at points with coordinates (0, 0, 0), (5, 5, 0) and (5, 0, 0). The pyramid is 4 units high.

What are the coordinates of the point at the top of the pyramid?

7 What are the coordinates of the midpoint of the line segment joining the points (2, 3, 4) and (8, 8, 10)?

Learn... 20.3 Graphs

Real-life graphs

Graphs are useful for tracking changes in a variable such as value, population size, height of a ball or temperature over time.

If you have ever been in a hospital you will have seen notes at the end of each bed. Included in these medical notes is a temperature chart. These record the temperature of patients over time.

You have already met distance–time graphs. Distance–time graphs tell you about a journey of some kind. They are used to compare **speeds**.

Examples of real-life graphs

A. Graph showing temperature of a cup of coffee from the time it is made.

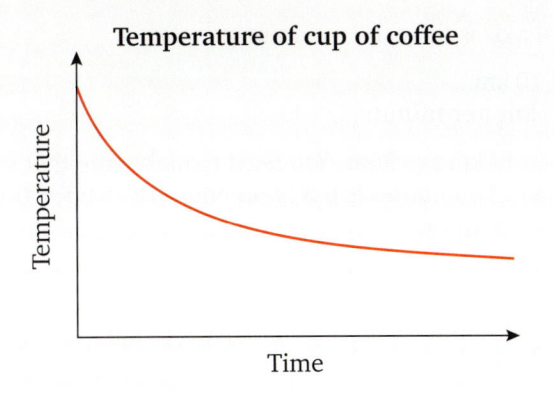

Temperature of cup of coffee

(Temperature vs Time graph showing exponential decay)

B. Graph showing height of a ball from the time it is thrown.

Height of a ball from the time it is thrown

(Height vs Time graph showing a parabolic curve)

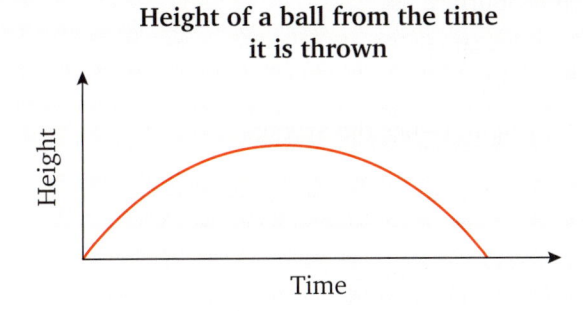

C. Graph showing population growth for a population.

Population growth for a population

(Population size vs Time graph showing S-shaped curve)

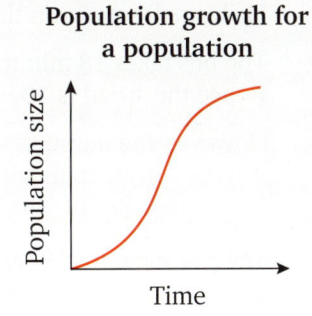

Graphs to help solve problems

Example: The distance–time graph shows the journey of the Year 10 football team in the school minibus to a nearby school for an after-school match.

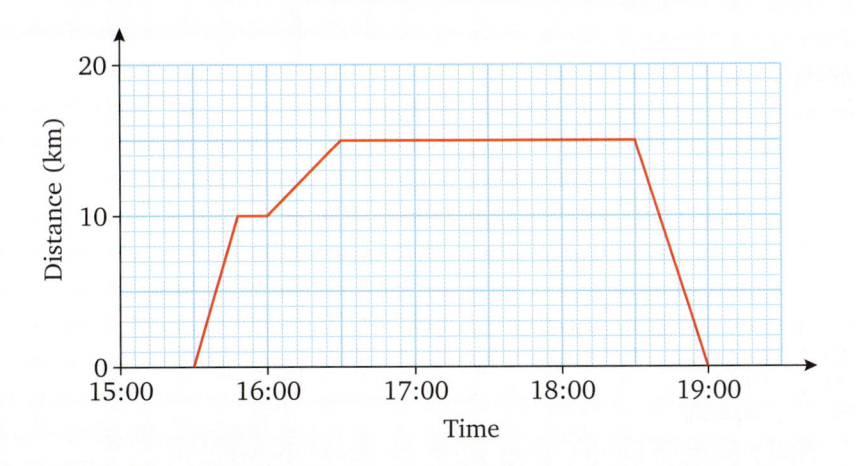

(Distance-time graph with Distance (km) on y-axis from 0 to 20, and Time on x-axis from 15:00 to 19:00)

a What is the speed for the first 10 km of the journey to the football match (in km per hour)?

b On the way to the football match, the bus stops for fuel. How long did it stop for?

c What was the speed of the minibus on the way home (in km per hour)?

d At which part of the journey did the minibus travel the fastest?

e What was the average speed for the journey to the football match?

Solution:

a speed = $\dfrac{\text{distance travelled}}{\text{time taken}}$

The **gradient** (steepness) of the line is a measure of speed. The steeper the line the faster the speed. A horizontal line represents a speed of zero (i.e. stopped).

Each small square on the horizontal axis is $60 \div 10 = 6$ minutes.

The bus takes 18 minutes to travel 10 km.
Hence the speed is $10 \div 18 = 0.55$ **km per minute**.

However, the question asks for speed in km per hour. You need to make sure that you use the correct units for your problem. 18 minutes is 0.3 of an hour ($18 \div 60 = 0.3$). So the speed is $10 \div 0.3 = 33.3$ **km per hour**.

b The bus stops for 12 minutes for fuel.

c On the way home the journey takes 30 minutes and the bus travels 15 km.
The speed is $15 \div 0.5 = 30$ km per hour.

d The graph has the steepest gradient for the first part of the journey to the football match. Therefore, this was the greatest speed and the bus travelled the fastest in this part of the journey.

e To find the average speed for a whole journey, use:

average speed = $\dfrac{\text{total distance travelled}}{\text{total time taken}}$

The distance is 15 km and this took 1 hour. Hence the average speed is 15 km per hour.

Example: A gardener is making a rectangular vegetable plot in her garden. She is enclosing it with a small hedge at one side of her garden. She has sufficient hedging plants for 10 metres of hedging.

The diagram shows the side of the garden shaded grey and the position of the hedge green. The side of the plot is labelled x. She wants to know how the area varies as x gets larger.

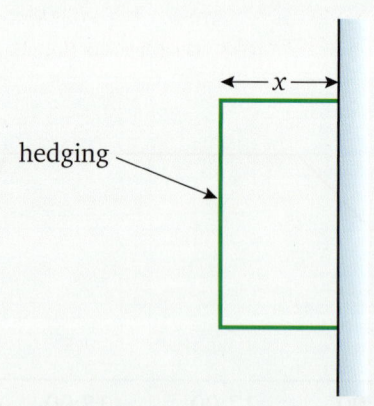

a Find a formula for the area y when you know the width x.

b Draw a table of values for different values of x.
Start with $x = 1$

c Draw a graph showing how the area changes.

d Find the largest possible area of the plot.

e Find the value of x when the area is 10 m².

Solution:

a Length = 10 − 2x
Area = length × width
= (10 − 2x) × x
y = x(10 − 2x)

b

x	1	2	3	4	5
(10 − 2x)	8	6	4	2	0
y	8	12	12	8	0

c

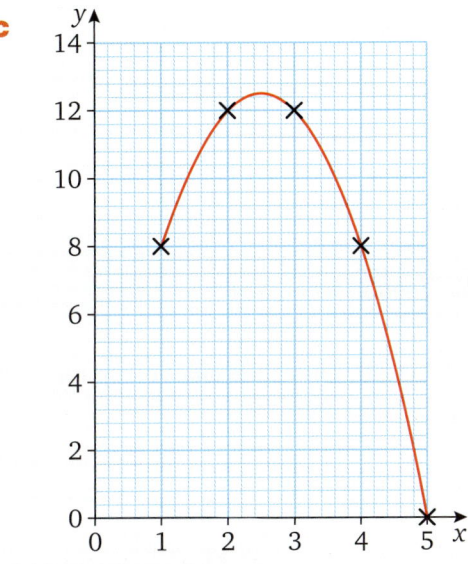

AQA Examiner's tip

Join the points with a smooth curve. Examiners do not give marks for using a ruler to join the points with straight lines.

d The largest possible area of the plot is when x is 2.5 (note the curve is a **parabola**, which is symmetrical) and you can read y is 12.5 m² from the graph.

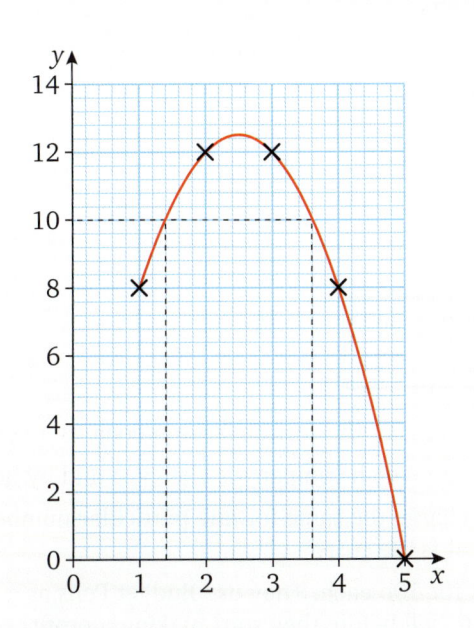

e Read across from 10 and down to the x-axis. x = 1.38 m and x = 3.62 m
When the width is 1.38 m or 3.62 m, the area is 10 m².

Practise... 20.3 Graphs

1 Ace-energy supply electricity. They have a standing charge of £8.50 each quarter. They then charge 10.5p per unit of electricity used.

  a Copy and complete the table for the cost of electricity from Ace-energy.

Units used	0	500	1000	1500	2000
Cost (£)	8.50	61			

  b Draw a graph showing this information using the scales shown on the axes below.

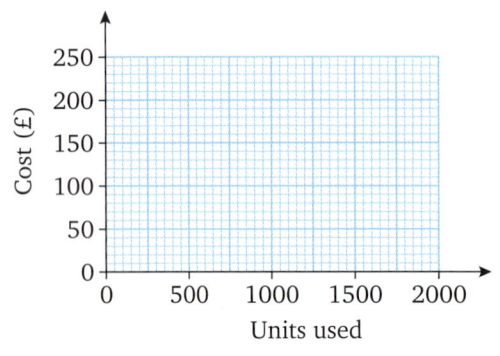

  Betta-supplies have a standing charge of £11.50. They then charge 10p for each unit of electricity used.

  c Add a line to your graph showing the cost of electricity from Betta-supplies.

  d Which of these electricity suppliers would you advise a new customer to use? Explain your answer.

2 Budget Pens supply pens to schools. Their charges are shown in the graph. Large orders get a discount.

  a What is the total cost of 80 pens from Budget Pens?

  b A school buys 80 pens. What is the cost of each pen?

  c What is the cost of 250 pens from Budget Pens?

  Cheapo Pens are a rival company who also supply pens to schools. They charge 9p for each pen, no matter how big the order.

  d Copy and complete the table for the cost of pens from Cheapo Pens.

Number of pens	100	200	300
Cost (£)	9		

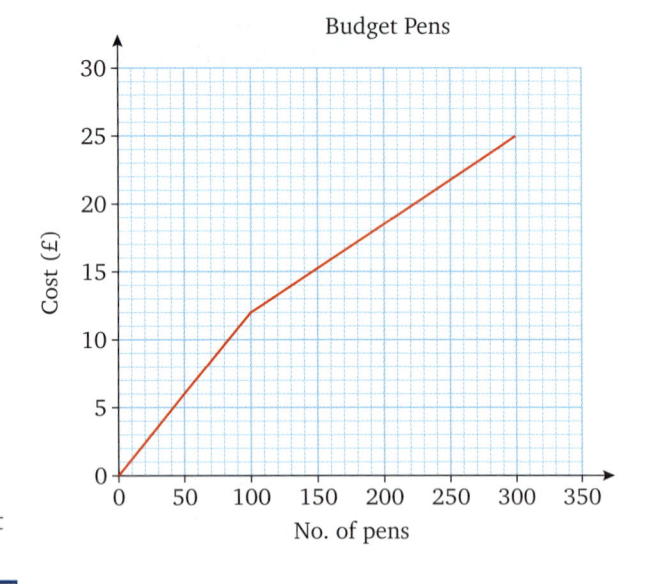

  e Copy the graph and add a line showing the cost of Cheapo Pens.

  f A school wants to order 150 pens. Which company is cheapest and by how much?

  g Budget Pens and Cheapo Pens charge the same for one particular number of pens. How many pens is this and what is the cost?

  h School A sells pens to students for 10p each. They use Budget Pens as a supplier. How many pens do they need to sell before they start making a profit?

  i School B buys 300 pens from Budget Pens. How much do they need to sell them for if they are not to make a loss? Give your answer to the nearest 1p. Will they make a profit? If so, how much?

Chapter 20 3-D shapes, coordinates and graphs **267**

3 The graph shows the distance of a train from Manchester in km.

Bump up your grade
To get a Grade C you need to be able to find the speed in km/h when the time is given in minutes. You need to remember to change the minutes to hours before dividing. Remember that there are 60 minutes in one hour.

a Find the speed of the train at 9.05am.

b What is the speed of the train between the points marked *B* and *C* on the graph?

c Adam says the train is travelling at a constant speed between *C* and *D*.
Is Adam correct? Explain your answer.

d Bev says that the train is going downhill until it gets to *C*.
Is Bev correct? Explain your answer.

e Calculate the average speed of the train between the points marked *A* and *C* on the graph.

4 'Go-Monkey' is a company that makes playground resources for teenagers. One of their products is a rope bridge.

The equation for the curve of the rope is:

$$y = \frac{x(x - 20)}{100}$$

y is the vertical height above the end *A* and *x* is the horizontal distance from *A*.

a Complete the table of values.

x	0	5	10	15	20
y	0	−0.75			

b Copy the axes below, plot the points from the table and draw a smooth curve through them.

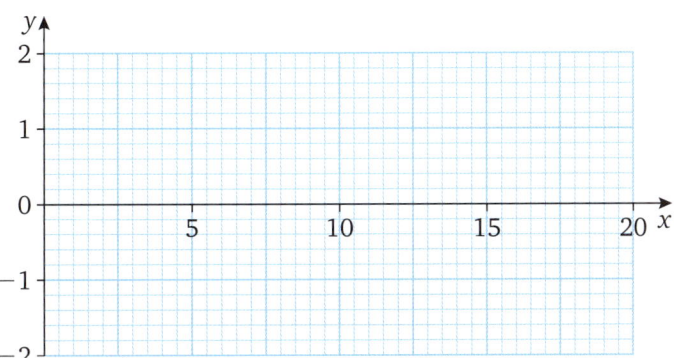

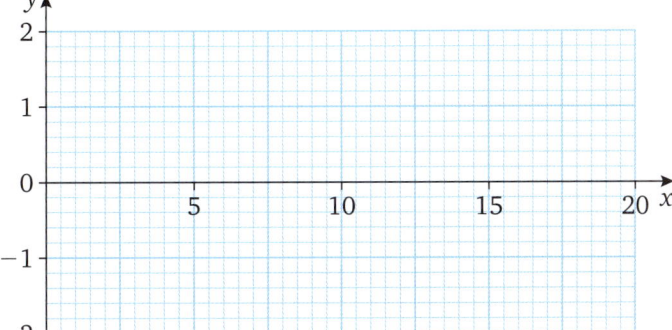

c Xavier says that the lowest point below the end is half way along and is 2 metres below the level of end *A*.
Is Xavier correct? Explain your answer.

5 Janet has a rectangular pond in her back garden.
It is 1 metre by 2 metres.
She wants to make a rectangular concrete border around the pond x metres wide. She wants to know how the area of concrete path changes as its width gets bigger.

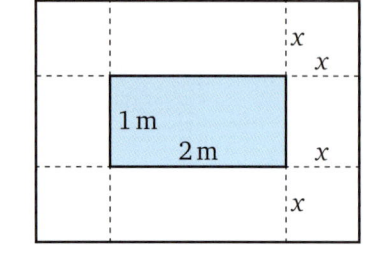

a Find a formula for the area of concrete y when you know the width x.

b Draw a table of values for values of x going from 0 to 5.

c Draw a graph showing how the area changes as the width gets larger.

d What is the area of concrete if the path is 1.5 metres wide?

e What is the width of the path when the area of concrete is 25 m²?

6 A caravan is bought new for £15 000. Each year the caravan loses 10% of its value at the start of the year.

a Draw a graph to show the depreciation of the value of the caravan.

b Use your graph to find:

    i when the caravan is worth half the price it had when new

    ii how much the caravan is worth after 10 years.

7 A rocket is launched vertically into the air. Its height, h metres, after t seconds is given by the formula $h = 96t - 16t^2$

a Draw a graph to show the height of the rocket after t seconds.

b How long does it take to reach a height of 144 metres?
Explain your answer.

8 James is researching different bridges on the internet.
He finds the following on one of the websites he visits.

The height above the water of the arch of a bridge is given by the formula

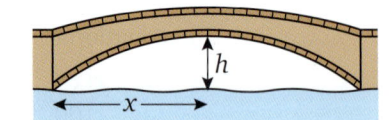

$$h = \frac{5x}{2} - \frac{1}{20}x^2$$

where h metres is the height at a distance x metres from the bank.

What width of water is available to a yacht with mast height 25 m?

9 Rachel is doing some history homework on the internet. She is researching journeys using different methods of transport. She finds the following formula giving the cost £C of ship's voyage at V km/h is given by the formula:

$$C = \frac{9900}{V} + \frac{V^2}{2}$$

a Plot the C–V curve for values of V from 10 to 30.

b What is the most economical speed for the voyage, and also the total cost at that speed?

10 A polygon with n sides has $\frac{n(n-3)}{2}$ diagonals.

How many sides does a polygon with 35 diagonals have?

11 A farmer has 70 metres of fencing with which to enclose three sides of a rectangular sheep pen. The 4th side is a wall.

If the area of the pen is 600 m², find the length of the shorter sides.

Chapter 20 3-D shapes, coordinates and graphs

20 Assess

1 Two matchboxes are arranged as shown.

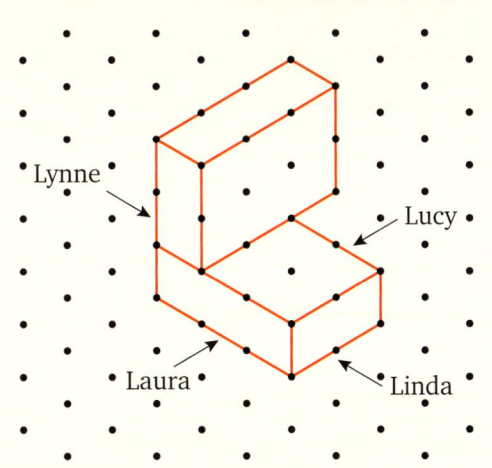

a Draw four diagrams showing the views that Linda, Laura, Lynne and Lucy see.

b Draw a plan view of the arrangement.

2 Rashid makes this object from four Multilink cubes.

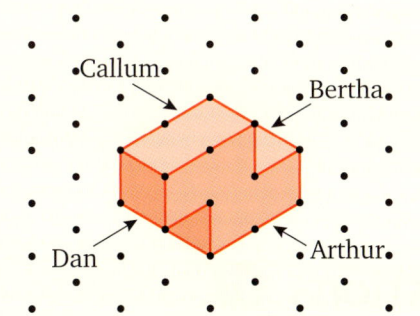

Draw the plan view of the object and the view each of his friends sees. Label your diagrams carefully.

3 The diagram shows a pile of 1 cm cubes.

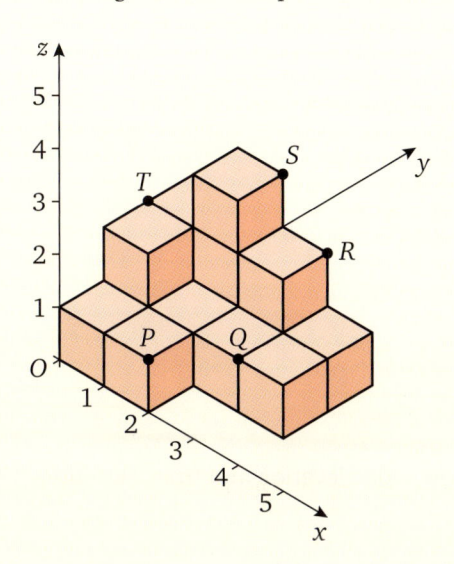

Write down the coordinates of the points P, Q, R, S and T.

4   The graph shows the path of a cricket ball through the air after it is thrown.

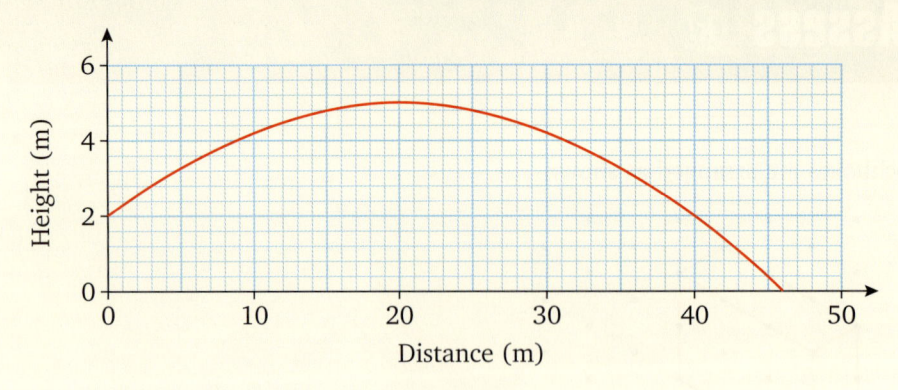

a   What was the total distance thrown?
b   What was the maximum height reached by the ball?
c   What horizontal distance had been travelled when the ball was at its highest?
d   Give a possible reason why the height of the ball started at 2 metres.

5   The area of a rectangle is $y\,m^2$. The length of the rectangle is 1 m greater than its width.

a   Find a formula for the area, y, in terms of x. Use x for the width of the rectangle.
b   Use values of x going from 0 to 5, draw a graph showing what happens to the area as the width changes.
c   What is the width when the area is $10\,m^2$?
d   What is the area when the length is 4.5 metres?
e   Find the length when the area is $4\,m^2$.

AQA Examination-style questions

1   The diagram shows a solid made from two cuboids.
The large cuboid is 5 cm by 4 cm by 3 cm.
The small cuboid is 3 cm by 1 cm by 1 cm.

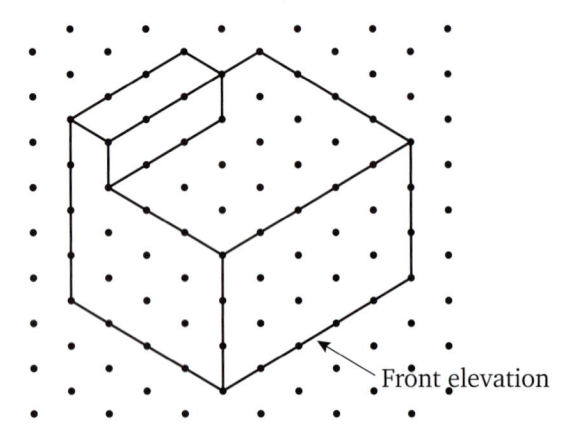

Copy the grids on the opposite page. Draw the plan view, side elevation and front elevation.

Plan view

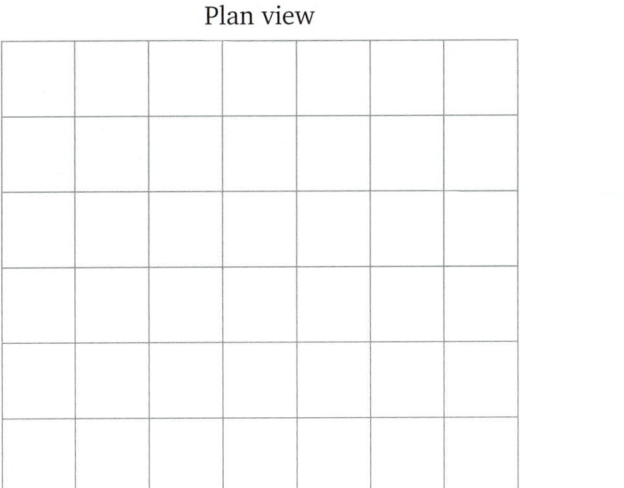

Side elevation

Front elevation

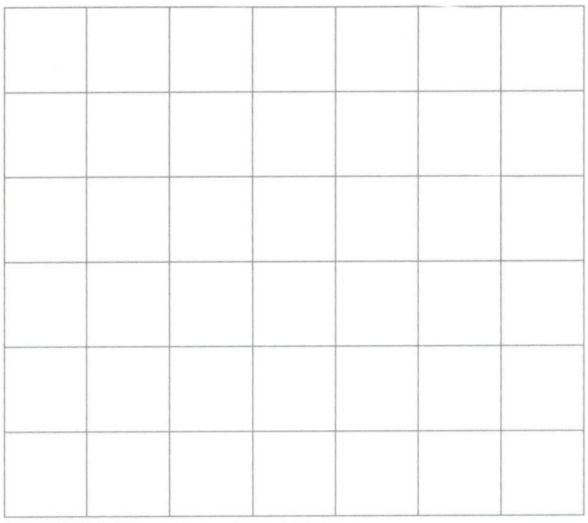

(3 marks)
AQA 2008

2   You may use graph paper to help you solve this question.

At 9am a man leaves point *P* and walks along a road at a steady speed of 6 kilometres per hour.

At 12 noon a cyclist leaves *P*, on the same road in the same direction, at a steady speed of 20 kilometres per hour.

After travelling for an hour, the cyclist gets a puncture, which delays her for 30 minutes.

She then continues at 20 kilometres per hour until she overtakes the walker.

a   At what time did the cyclist overtake the walker?   *(3 marks)*

b   A motorist leaves *P*, travelling at a steady speed of 50 kilometres per hour.
   The motorist overtakes the walker at the same time as the cyclist.
   At what time did the motorist leave *P*?   *(2 marks)*

AQA 2009

21 Pythagoras' theorem

Objectives

Examiners would normally expect students who get these grades to be able to:

C
use Pythagoras' theorem to find the third side of a right-angled triangle

use Pythagoras' theorem to prove that a triangle is right angled

B
find the distance between two points from their coordinates

A/A*
use Pythagoras' theorem in 3-D problems.

Key terms
hypotenuse
Pythagoras' theorem

Did you know?

Pythagoras

Pythagoras lived in the 5th century BCE, and was one of the first Greek mathematical thinkers.

Pythagoras is known to students of mathematics because of the theorem that bears his name:

'The square on the hypotenuse is equal to the sum of the squares on the other two sides.'

The Egyptians knew that a triangle with sides of length 3, 4 and 5 has a 90° angle.
They used a rope with 12 evenly spaced knots like this one, to make right angles.

However, they did not extend the idea to triangles with other dimensions.

Other people such as the Chinese and the Sumerians also already knew that it was generally true, and used it in their measurements. However, it was Pythagoras who is said to have proved that it is always true.

You should already know:

✓ how to find squares and square roots using a calculator
✓ the properties of triangles and quadrilaterals.

Chapter 21 Pythagoras' theorem

Learn... 21.1 Pythagoras' theorem

In any right-angled triangle the longest side is always opposite the right angle.

This side is called the **hypotenuse**.

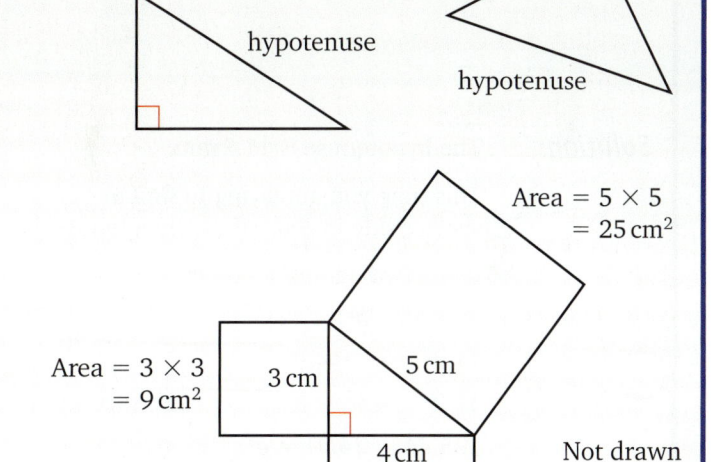

The sketch shows a right-angled triangle with sides of 3 cm, 4 cm and 5 cm.

Squares have been drawn on each side of the triangle and the area of each square is shown.

The area of the large square is equal to the sum of the areas of the two smaller squares:

$25 = 9 + 16$

This can be written as

$5^2 = 3^2 + 4^2$

This equation can be generalised for the sides of any right-angled triangle and is known as **Pythagoras' theorem**.

In general, in a right-angled triangle $c^2 = a^2 + b^2$

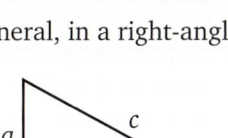

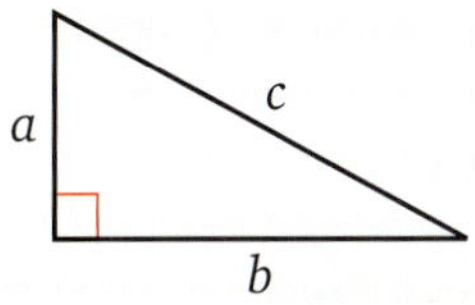

Area = 3 × 3 = 9 cm²
Area = 4 × 4 = 16 cm²
Area = 5 × 5 = 25 cm²

Not drawn accurately

AQA Examiner's tip

You will not be asked to prove Pythagoras' theorem in the exam. One example of a proof is given here to show how it can be done.

Proof of Pythagoras' theorem

There are many proofs, both geometric and algebraic. Here is one algebraic proof using area.

A square of side $(x + y)$ is divided up as shown.

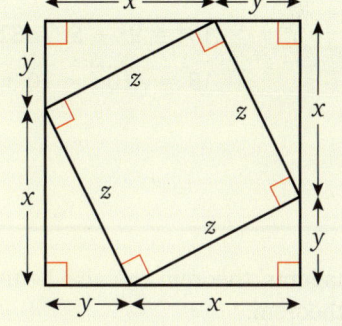

Each of the four right-angled triangles has area $\frac{1}{2}xy$.

The small square has area z^2.

Area of large square = $(x + y)^2 = (x + y)(x + y) = x^2 + 2xy + y^2$

This is also equal to the sum of the areas of the triangles and the small square.

So $x^2 + 2xy + y^2 = 4 \times \frac{1}{2}xy + z^2$

$x^2 + 2xy + y^2 = 2xy + z^2$ Take away 2xy from both sides.

Therefore $x^2 + y^2 = z^2$

Example: Calculate the length of the hypotenuse (labelled c) of this triangle.

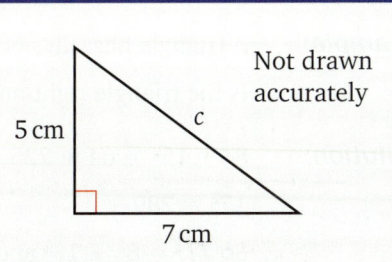

Not drawn accurately

Solution: Using Pythagoras' theorem:

$c^2 = a^2 + b^2$

$c^2 = 5^2 + 7^2 = 25 + 49 = 74$

$c = \sqrt{74} = 8.6$ cm (to 1 d.p.)   Take the square root of each side.

Example: Work out the length of side a.

Not drawn accurately

4.9 mm, 11.2 mm, a

Solution: The hypotenuse is 11.2 mm.

This time you are trying to find a shorter side instead of the hypotenuse.

Using Pythagoras' theorem:

$c^2 = a^2 + b^2$

$11.2^2 = a^2 + 4.9^2$

$11.2^2 - 4.9^2 = a^2$ Subtract 4.9^2 from both sides.

$125.44 - 24.01 = a^2$

So $a^2 = 101.43$

$a = \sqrt{101.43}$ Take the square root of both sides.

$a = 10.0712462...$ mm

$a = 10.1$ mm (to 1 d.p.)   Note the answer has been rounded to one decimal place as that is the same degree of accuracy as the question.

AQA Examiner's tip

When finding the hypotenuse you must **add** the squares of the other two sides.
When finding a shorter side you must **subtract** the square of the known short side from the square of the hypotenuse.

Example: A is the point $(2, 8)$ and B is the point $(7, -1)$. Find the distance between A and B.

Solution: Draw a sketch to show the positions of A and B.

The line AB is the hypotenuse of the right-angled triangle ACB so Pythagoras' theorem can be used.

The length of AC is $8 - -1 = 9$ units

The length of CB is $7 - 2 = 5$ units

$AB^2 = 9^2 + 5^2 = 81 + 25 = 106$

$AB = \sqrt{106} = 10.3$ units (to 1 d.p.)

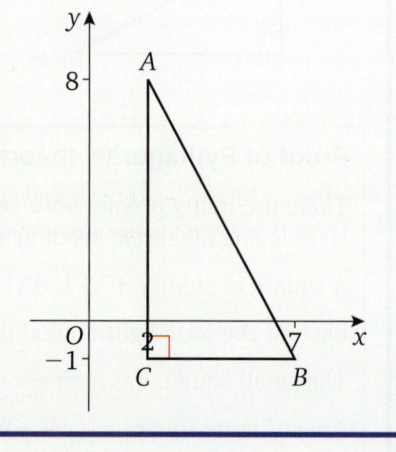

Pythagoras' theorem can also be used to test whether a triangle is right angled by showing that the sides fit the theorem.

To test for a right angle, first square the longest side.

Then add the squares of the two shorter sides.

If your results are equal, the triangle contains a right angle.

Example: A triangle has sides of 8 cm, 15 cm and 17 cm.

Is the triangle right-angled?

Solution: $8^2 + 15^2 = 64 + 225 = 289$

$17^2 = 289$

So $17^2 = 8^2 + 15^2$ and the sides of the triangle obey Pythagoras' theorem. Therefore, the triangle must be right-angled.

Chapter 21 Pythagoras' theorem

Right-angled triangles can be formed from other shapes. Some examples are shown below. Wherever a right-angled triangle is formed you can use Pythagoras' theorem to find the length of the third side.

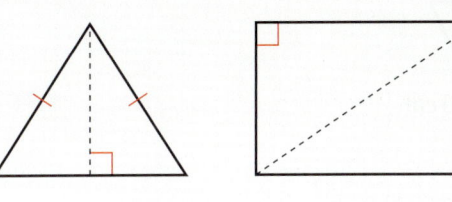

Isosceles triangle 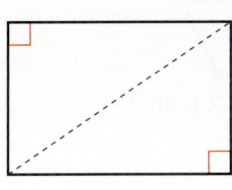   Rectangle 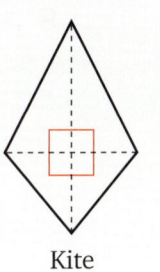   Kite

Bump up your grade

To get a Grade C make sure you understand Pythagoras' theorem and know how to apply it to solve problems.

Practise... 21.1 Pythagoras' theorem   D C B A A*

1 Find the length of the hypotenuse in each triangle.

a 5 cm, 12 cm

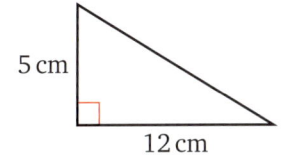

b 6 cm, 8 cm

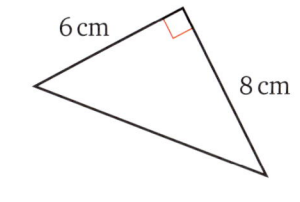

c 6 m, 1.1 m   Not drawn accurately

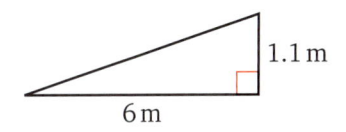

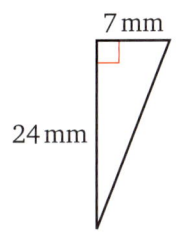

d 7 mm, 24 mm

2 Find the length of the diagonal in each of these rectangles. Give each answer correct to one decimal place.

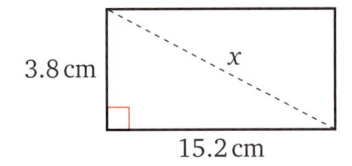

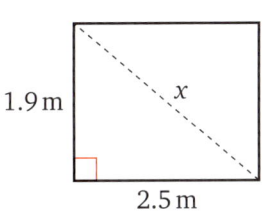

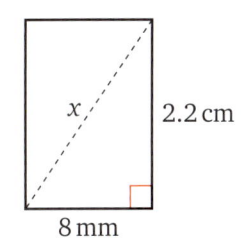

a 3.8 cm, 15.2 cm, x Not drawn accurately

b 1.9 m, 2.5 m, x

c 2.2 cm, 8 mm, x

3 Find the length of the missing side, marked x, in each of these triangles. Give each answer correct to one decimal place.

a x, 15 cm, 12 cm

b x, 38 cm, 14 cm   Not drawn accurately

c x, 4.2 m, 13.7 m   Not drawn accurately

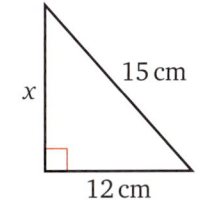

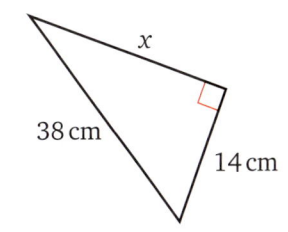

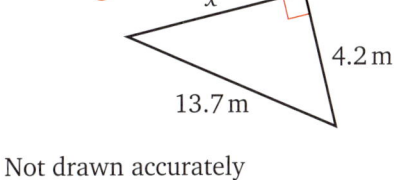

4 Check whether each of these triangles is right angled. Show your working.

a Side lengths: 13 cm, 84 cm and 85 cm

b Side lengths: 3.5 m, 5.8 m and 4.2 m

c Side lengths: 12 mm, 34 mm and 46 mm

d Side lengths: 26 cm, 24 cm and 10 cm

5 Find the length of the side marked x in each of these triangles.
Give each answer to one decimal place.

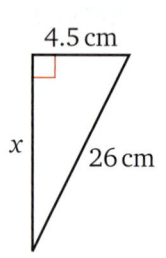

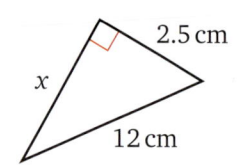

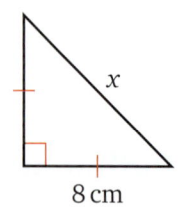

a 8.6 cm, 7.2 cm, x

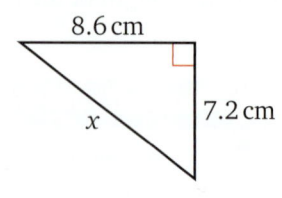

b 2.5 cm, 12 cm, x

c 4.5 cm, 26 cm, x

d 8 cm, x

6 Sarah and Ravi are working out the missing side in this triangle.

Sarah works out $7^2 + 22^2$ and says that $x = 23.1$ cm (to 1 d.p.).

Ravi works out $22^2 - 7^2$ and says that $x = 435$ cm.

Both of these answers are incorrect.

Explain each person's mistake and work out the correct value of x.

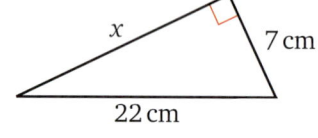

x, 7 cm, 22 cm

Not drawn accurately

7 An isosceles triangle has two sides of length 7.5 cm and one side of length 12 cm.

Calculate the height of the triangle.

Give your answer to one decimal place.

h, 7.5 cm, 12 cm

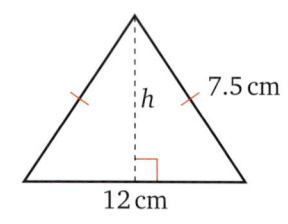

Not drawn accurately

8 Calculate the length of the chord AB of the circle.

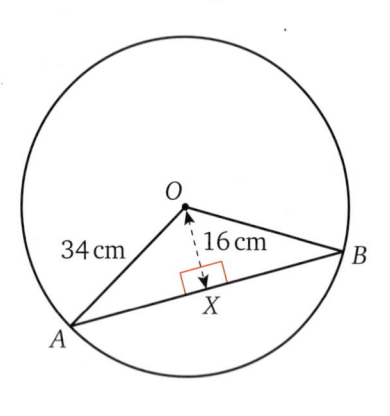

34 cm, 16 cm, O, A, B, X

Not drawn accurately

9 Find the length of the side marked x in each diagram.

a 2.3 cm, x, 11.6 cm, 10.5 cm

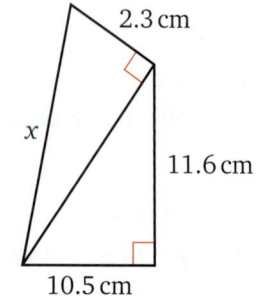

b 29 mm, x, 15.2 mm, 31.4 mm

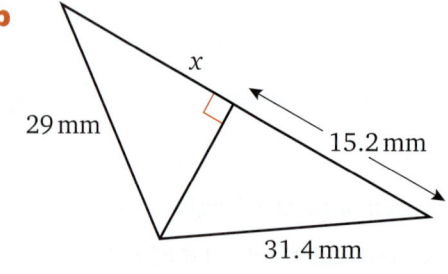

Not drawn accurately

Chapter 21 Pythagoras' theorem

10 **a** A is the point (2, 3) and B is the point (5, 7) as shown in the diagram.

Use Pythagoras' theorem to find the distance between points A and B.

b Sketch a diagram and use Pythagoras' theorem to find the distance between each of the following sets of points.

  i (3, 5) and (7, 8)
  ii (0, 4) and (5, 10)
  iii (−2, 3) and (1, 7)

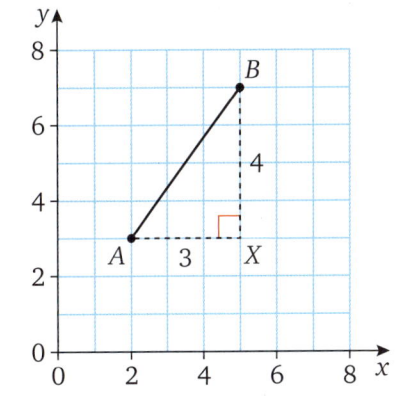

11 Leon walks 1.5 km due north from his house.

He then turns and walks 2 km due east.

How far is he now from his house?

12 A field is in the shape of a rectangle of length 45 metres and width 22 metres. A pipe runs from one corner of the field to the opposite corner.

How long is the pipe?

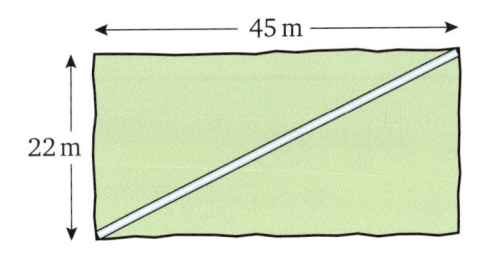

Not drawn accurately

13 A ladder is 6.5 metres long.

The safety instructions say that for a ladder of this length:
- the maximum safe distance of the foot of the ladder from the wall is 1.7 metres
- the minimum safe distance of the foot of the ladder from the wall is 1.5 metres.

What is the maximum vertical height that the ladder can safely reach?

Give your answer to the nearest centimetre.

14 Cath has designed a pendant, in the shape of a kite, for a necklace.

Work out the length, x, of the green line.

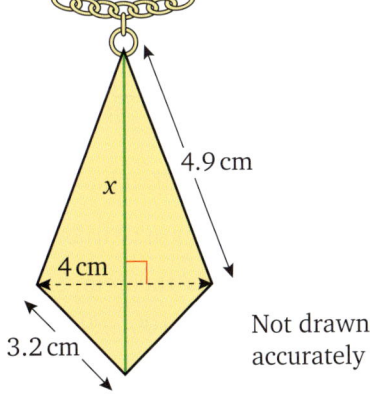

4.9 cm
x
4 cm
3.2 cm

Not drawn accurately

15 Pythagorean triples are sets of three integers that fit Pythagoras' theorem.

For example:

3, 4, 5   5, 12, 13   7, 24, 25

a Find other Pythagorean triples.

b What patterns can you see in the numbers?

c See whether you can find a rule to generate other triples.

16   **a**   Calculate the length x.

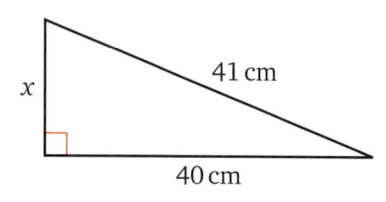

41 cm
x
40 cm

Not drawn accurately

b m and n are integers.

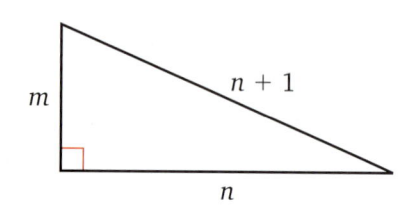

m
$n + 1$
n

Prove that m is an odd number.

Learn... 21.2 Pythagoras' theorem in three dimensions

When working in three dimensions, it is sometimes necessary to find the length of a line joining two points. Often this length will form the side of a right-angled triangle and so Pythagoras' theorem can be used. The triangles outlined in red are right-angled triangles.

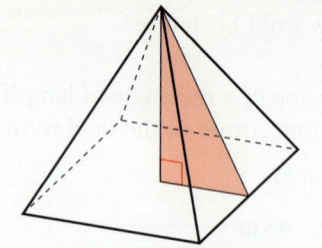

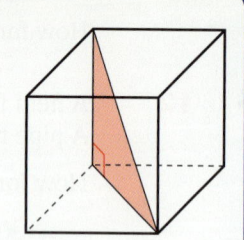

Example: Find the length of the diagonal AG in this cuboid. Give your answer to three significant figures.

Not drawn accurately

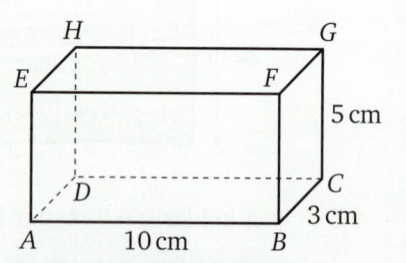

5 cm
3 cm
10 cm

Solution: Joining AG and AC gives the right-angled triangle ACG.

Make a sketch of this triangle so that you can see whether you are finding the length of the hypotenuse or a shorter side.

AQA Examiner's tip
Always draw out the right-angled triangle you are using.

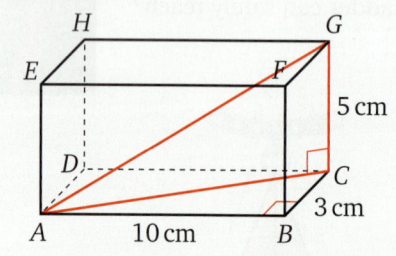

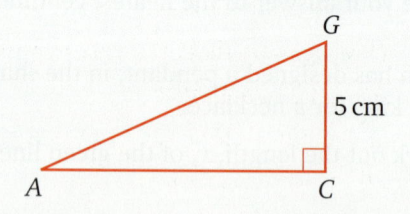

5 cm
3 cm
10 cm

5 cm

Not drawn accurately

To find AG you need to know the length AC.

AC is the hypotenuse of triangle ABC.

Using Pythagoras' theorem:
$AC^2 = 10^2 + 3^2 = 100 + 9 = 109$
$AC = \sqrt{109}$

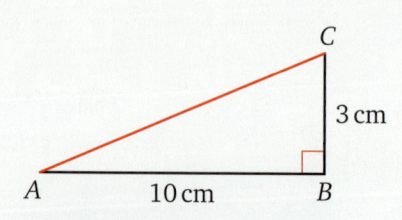

Now using triangle ACG:
$AG^2 = AC^2 + CG^2$
$= (\sqrt{109})^2 + 5^2$
$= 109 + 25 = 134$
$AG = \sqrt{134} = 11.5758369...$

$AG = 11.6$ cm (to 3 s.f.)

3 cm
10 cm

AQA Examiner's tip
Leave AC as $\sqrt{109}$ as you will be squaring it again in the next part of the solution.

Example: The square-based pyramid shown in the diagram has four triangular sides.

Each triangle is isosceles, with sides 13 cm, 13 cm and 10 cm.

Calculate the vertical height of the pyramid. Give your answer to three significant figures.

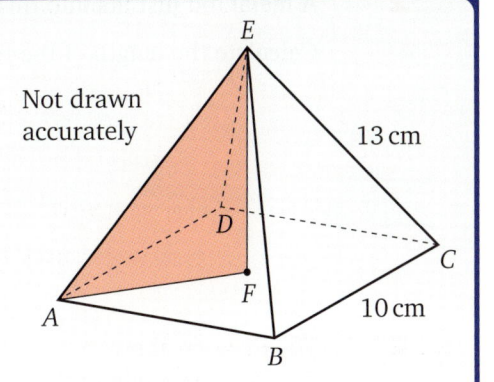

Solution: The vertical height is *EF*.

Triangle *AEF* is a right-angled triangle.

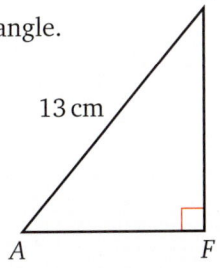

To find *EF* you first need to find the length of *AF*.

AF is $\frac{1}{2}AC$, where *AC* is the diagonal of the square base. So *ABC* is a right-angled triangle.

Using Pythagoras' theorem,
$AC^2 = 10^2 + 10^2$
$AC^2 = 200$
$AC = \sqrt{200} = 10\sqrt{2}$

So $AF = \frac{1}{2}AC$
$= 5\sqrt{2}$

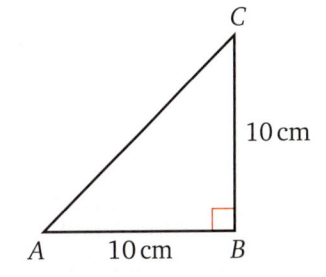

AQA Examiner's tip

You can leave the value of *AF* in surd form to avoid rounding until the end of the calculation.

Now using Pythagoras' theorem in the first triangle *AFE*:

AE is the hypotenuse.

$EF^2 = AE^2 - AF^2$.   As you want to find *EF* (a shorter side), you must subtract.

$EF^2 = 13^2 - (5\sqrt{2})^2$
$= 119$
$EF = \sqrt{119} = 10.9$ cm

21.2 Pythagoras' theorem in three dimensions

Practise...

D C B A A*

The shapes in these exercises are not drawn accurately.

1 The diagram shows a cuboid in which $AB = 11$ cm, $BC = 7$ cm and $CG = 4$ cm.

Calculate the length of:

a *AC*   **b** *BG*   **c** *CE*

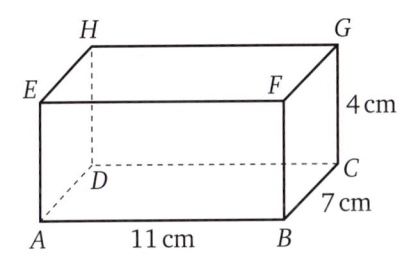

2 A metal rod just fits into this box as shown.

Calculate the length of the rod.

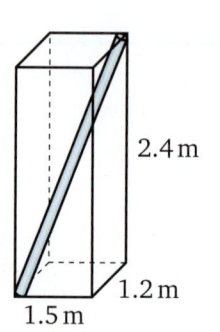

2.4 m
1.2 m
1.5 m

3 The diagram shows a pyramid with a square base of side 15 cm. The vertical height of the pyramid is 10 cm.

Calculate:

a the length of BD

b the length of YB.

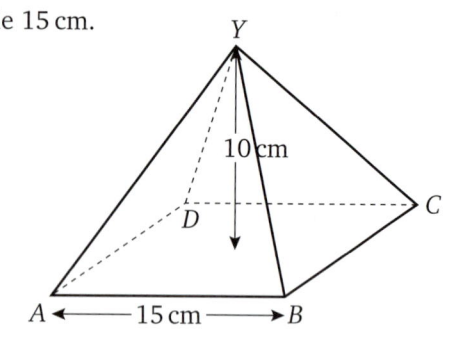

10 cm
15 cm

4 The diagram shows a cube of side 30 cm. X is the midpoint of CG.

Calculate the length of:

a DX

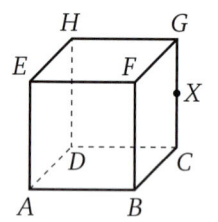

b AX

5 The diagram shows a pyramid with a rectangular base of length 15 cm and width 9 cm. Edges YA, YB, YC and YD are 20 cm long.

Work out the vertical height of the pyramid.

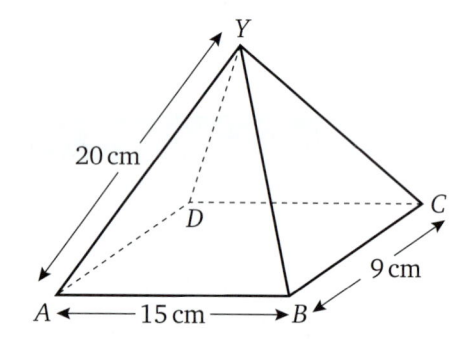

20 cm
15 cm
9 cm

6 The diagram shows a cube of side 8 cm. X, Y and Z are the midpoints of AE, BC and GH respectively.

Calculate the area of triangle XYZ.

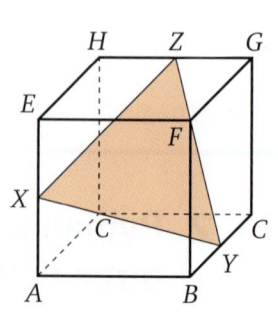

7 The diagram shows a skateboard ramp in a park. The ramp is a triangular prism. Jodie uses her skateboard to travel down the slope in a straight line from X to B. Kev uses his skateboard to travel down the slope in a straight line parallel to XA.

How much further does Jodie travel?

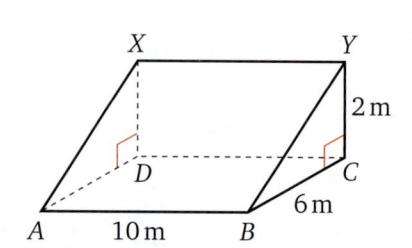

2 m
6 m
10 m

Chapter 21 Pythagoras' theorem 281

8 The great Pyramid of Giza in Egypt is built with a square base of side approximately 230 metres.
The slanting edges are approximately 214 m in length.

Calculate an estimate of the height of the pyramid.

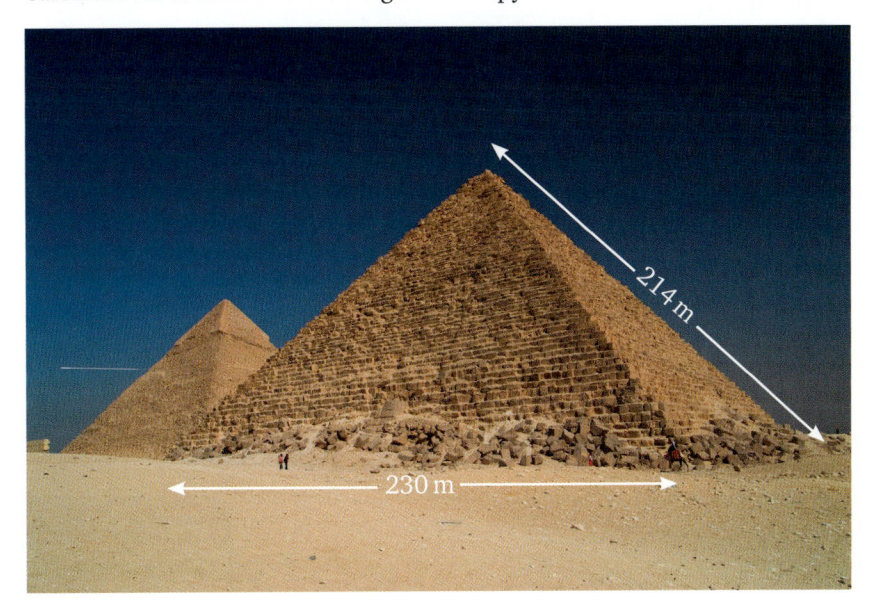

21 Assess k!

1 Find the length of side x in each triangle.

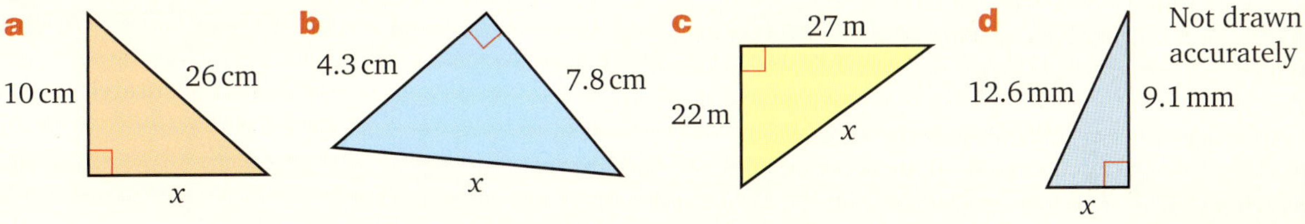

a 10 cm, 26 cm, x

b 4.3 cm, 7.8 cm, x

c 27 m, 22 m, x

d 12.6 mm, 9.1 mm, x Not drawn accurately

2 An equilateral triangle has sides of length 15 cm.

Work out the perpendicular height of the triangle.

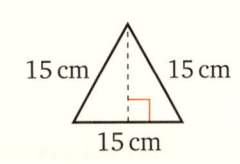

15 cm, 15 cm, 15 cm   Not drawn accurately

3 A field is in the shape of a rectangle of length 37 m and width 29 m.
A path runs diagonally from one corner of the field to the opposite corner.

What is the length of the path?

4 A telegraph pole is held vertically by wires of length 10 metres and x metres fixed to the ground.

Calculate:

a the height, h, of the telegraph pole

b the length, x, of the second wire.

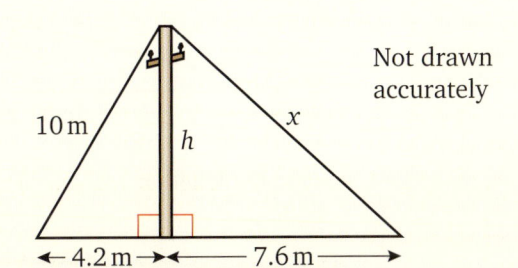

10 m, h, x, 4.2 m, 7.6 m   Not drawn accurately

5 Rob walks from his house 3 km due south then 2 km due west.

How far is Rob now from his house?

6 Find the distance between the following pairs of points.
Give each answer correct to one decimal place.

   a $A(3, 6)$ and $B(5, 9)$

   b $C(-2, 4)$ and $D(3, 1)$

   c $E(2, 1)$ and $F(15, 8)$

7 Work out the perimeter of this quadrilateral.

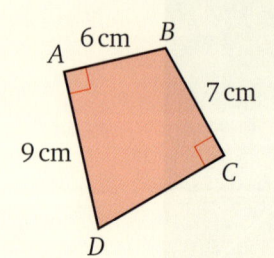

6 cm, 7 cm, 9 cm — A, B, C, D. Not drawn accurately

8 Work out the length of the longest straight rod that could fit into:

   a   a cube of side 6 cm

   b   a cuboid of length 12 cm, width 10 cm and height 8 cm.

AQA Examiner's tip
Draw a sketch of each solid.

9 A roof is 14 m long and 3.5 m wide (i.e. $AX = 3.5$ m).
The top ridge, XY, is 2.5 m above the base.
Calculate the length of:

   a AY **b** AC **c** BC

Give your answers to three significant figures.

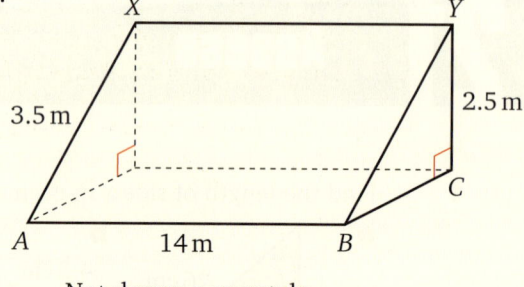

Not drawn accurately

AQA Examination-style questions

1 The diagram shows a right-angled triangle.

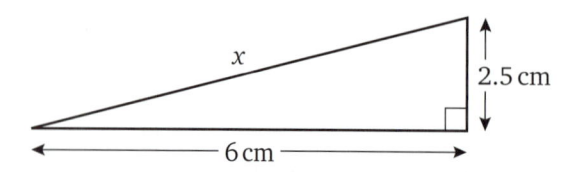

x, 2.5 cm, 6 cm. Not drawn accurately

Calculate the length x.

(3 marks)

AQA 2009

Chapter 21 Pythagoras' theorem 283

2 A ladder of length 5 m rests against a wall.
The foot of the ladder is 1.7 m from the base of the wall.

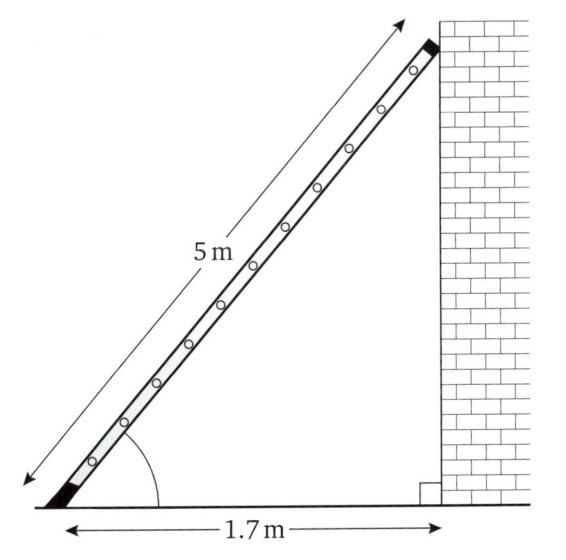

Not drawn accurately

How far up the wall does the ladder reach? *(3 marks)*
AQA 2008

3 Three circles fit inside a rectangle as shown.
Two of the circles are identical and the third is larger.
The circles have radii 9 cm, 9 cm and 25 cm.

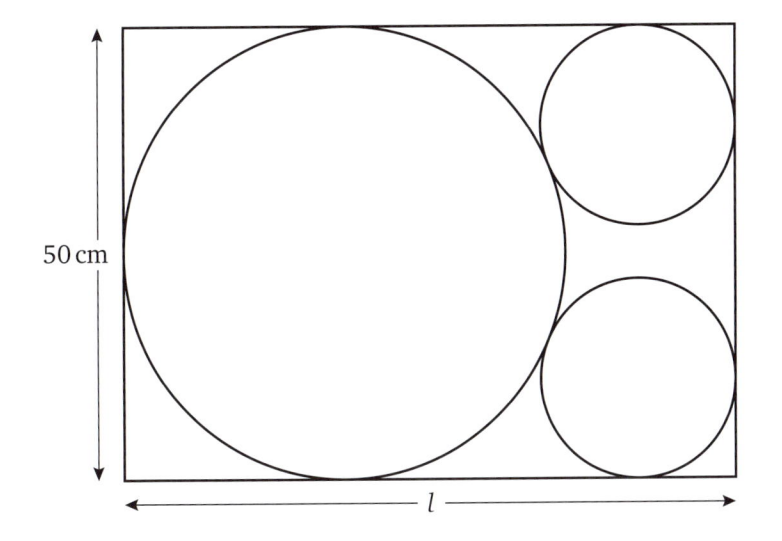

Not drawn accurately

Calculate the length, l, of the rectangle. *(6 marks)*
AQA 2009

4 The diagram shows an isosceles triangle *ABC*.

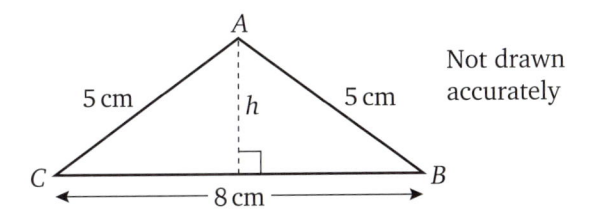

Not drawn accurately

Calculate the area of the triangle *ABC*.
Show your working.
State the units of your answer. *(6 marks)*
AQA 2007

22 Surds

Objectives

Examiners would normally expect students who get these grades to be able to:

A
rationalise the denominator of a surd

A*
simplify surds, such as write $(3 - \sqrt{5})^2$ in the form $a + b\sqrt{5}$

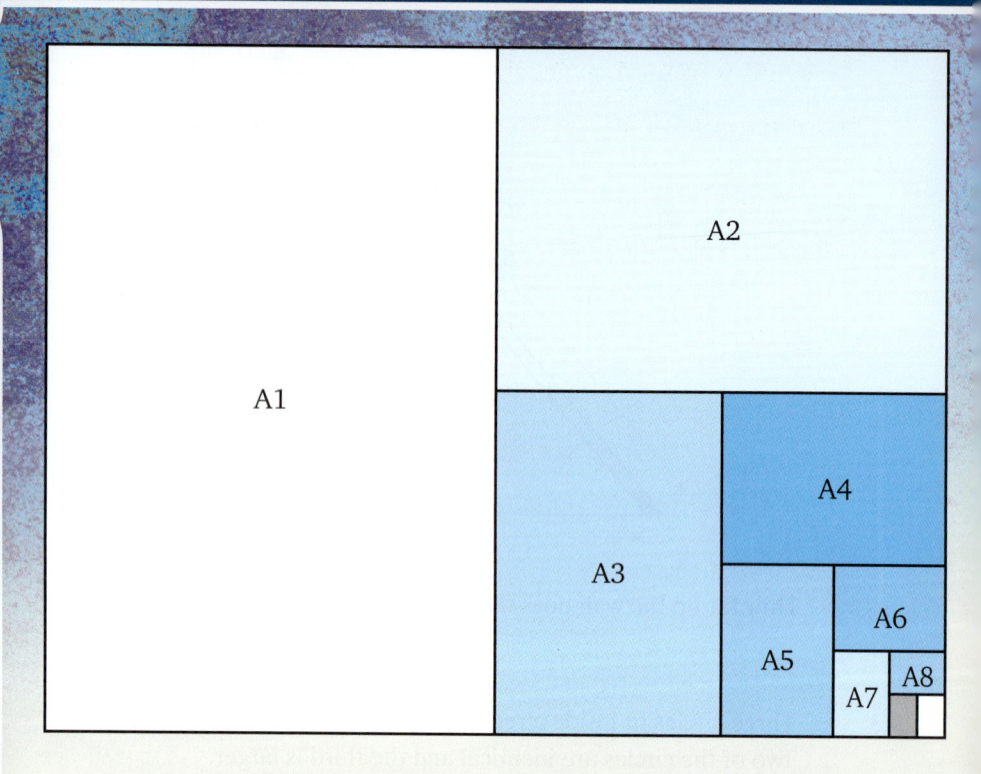

Key terms
rational number
irrational number
surd

Did you know?

Surds

Take a piece of A4 paper and carefully measure the length and the width. Use your answers to calculate the length ÷ width.

What do you notice?

What has this got to do with surds?

Try this out for a sheet of A3 paper or a sheet of A5 paper.

What do you notice?

What has this got to do with surds?

Does this work for all sizes of paper?

You should already know:

✔ how to multiply fractions, and convert fractions to decimals and vice versa
✔ the squares of numbers up to 15
✔ the meaning of $\sqrt{2}$
✔ how to find prime factors
✔ how to multiply out two brackets.

Chapter 22 Surds

Learn... 22.1 Simplifying surds

Irrational and rational numbers

Rational numbers are numbers that **can** be expressed in the form $\frac{p}{q}$ where p and q are both integers.

Irrational numbers are numbers that **cannot** be expressed in the form $\frac{p}{q}$ where p and q are both integers.

Rational numbers, written as decimals, either terminate or recur.

Irrational numbers, written as decimals, continue forever without recurring.

$\sqrt{2}, \sqrt{3}, \sqrt{5}, \sqrt{6}, \sqrt{7}, \sqrt{8}, \sqrt{10}, \sqrt{11}, \sqrt{12}, \sqrt{13}, \sqrt{14}, \sqrt{15}$ are all irrational numbers because they cannot be written as fractions. If you write them as decimals they continue forever without recurring.

π is another example of an irrational number because it cannot be written as a fraction. If you write π as a decimal it will continue forever without recurring.

$\sqrt{1}, \sqrt{4}, \sqrt{9}, \sqrt{16}$ are all rational numbers because they can be written as fractions:

$\sqrt{1} = \frac{1}{1}, \sqrt{4} = \frac{2}{1}, \sqrt{9} = \frac{3}{1}, \sqrt{16} = \frac{4}{1}$

Example: Decide whether these are rational or irrational.

    a $\sqrt{16}$ **b** $\sqrt{17}$ **c** $\sqrt{225}$ **d** $\frac{\pi}{2}$

Solution:
a $\sqrt{16} = 4$ so it is rational because 4 can be written $\frac{4}{1}$ All integers are rational.

b $\sqrt{17}$ is irrational because it cannot be written in the form $\frac{p}{q}$

c $\sqrt{225} = 15$ so it is rational because 15 can be written $\frac{15}{1}$

d $\frac{\pi}{2}$ is irrational because π is irrational and all multiples of irrational numbers are irrational.

> **AQA Examiner's tip**
>
> Remember that you must know your squares up to 15^2. This means you should also know the associated square roots.

Surds

A **surd** is a square root that cannot be written in the form $\frac{p}{q}$

The following rules apply to surds:

$\sqrt{ab} = \sqrt{a} \times \sqrt{b}$ $a\sqrt{c} + b\sqrt{c} = (a+b)\sqrt{c}$

$\sqrt{\frac{a}{b}} = \frac{\sqrt{a}}{\sqrt{b}}$ $a\sqrt{c} - b\sqrt{c} = (a-b)\sqrt{c}$

Example: Simplify:

    a $\sqrt{20}$ **b** $\sqrt{3} \times \sqrt{24}$ **c** $3\sqrt{3} + \sqrt{12}$ **d** $\frac{\sqrt{75}}{\sqrt{3}}$

Solution:
a To simplify $\sqrt{20}$ consider the factors of 20.

You need to find a factor which is a square number (but not 1).

$\sqrt{20} = \sqrt{1 \times 20}$
$\sqrt{20} = \sqrt{2 \times 10}$
$\sqrt{20} = \sqrt{4 \times 5}$

Choosing the pair of factors where one factor is a square number:

$\sqrt{20} = \sqrt{4 \times 5}$
$\quad\quad = \sqrt{4} \times \sqrt{5}$ ⟵ $\sqrt{ab} = \sqrt{a} \times \sqrt{b}$
$\quad\quad = 2 \times \sqrt{5}$
$\quad\quad = 2\sqrt{5}$

b $\sqrt{3} \times \sqrt{24} = \sqrt{3 \times 24}$ ← $\sqrt{ab} = \sqrt{a} \times \sqrt{b}$
$= \sqrt{72}$

To simplify $\sqrt{72}$ consider the factors of 72.

Again find a factor which is a square number (but not 1).
$\sqrt{72} = \sqrt{1 \times 72}$
$\sqrt{72} = \sqrt{2 \times 36}$
$\sqrt{72} = \sqrt{3 \times 24}$

Choosing the pair of factors where one factor is a square number:
$\sqrt{72} = \sqrt{2 \times 36}$
$= \sqrt{2} \times \sqrt{36}$
$= \sqrt{2} \times 6$
$= 6\sqrt{2}$

c $3\sqrt{3} + \sqrt{12} = 3\sqrt{3} + \sqrt{4 \times 3}$
$= 3\sqrt{3} + \sqrt{4} \times \sqrt{3}$
$= 3\sqrt{3} + 2\sqrt{3}$
$= 5\sqrt{3}$ ← $a\sqrt{c} + b\sqrt{c} = (a+b)\sqrt{c}$

d $\dfrac{\sqrt{75}}{\sqrt{3}} = \sqrt{\dfrac{75}{3}}$ ← $\sqrt{\dfrac{a}{b}} = \dfrac{\sqrt{a}}{\sqrt{b}}$
$= \sqrt{25}$
$= 5$

Practise... 22.1 Simplifying surds

1 Which of these numbers are irrational, and which are rational?

Give a reason for each answer.

a $\sqrt{32}$
b $\sqrt{16}$
c $\dfrac{3}{17}$
d $\dfrac{\sqrt{4}}{11}$
e $\dfrac{4}{\sqrt{11}}$
f $\sqrt{8}$
g $\sqrt{8} \times \sqrt{8}$
h $8 \times \sqrt{8}$
i $\sqrt{3}$
j $\sqrt{3} \times 3$
k $\sqrt{3} \times \sqrt{3}$
l $\sqrt{3} \times \sqrt{12}$
m $(\sqrt{7})^2$

2 Jill and Jack are having an argument about square roots.

Jill says that $\sqrt{90}$ must be irrational because all square roots are irrational.

Jack says she is wrong: $\sqrt{9} = 3$, so $\sqrt{90} = 30$

Who is wrong? How do you know?

3 Simplify the following.

a $\sqrt{40}$
b $\sqrt{90}$
c $\sqrt{98}$
d $5\sqrt{3} + 3\sqrt{3}$
e $7\sqrt{5} - 2\sqrt{5}$
f $\sqrt{20} + \sqrt{5}$
g $\sqrt{72} + \sqrt{18}$
h $\sqrt{8} + 3\sqrt{2} - \sqrt{50}$
i $\sqrt{3} \times \sqrt{27}$
j $4\sqrt{3} \times \sqrt{6}$
k $2\sqrt{5} \times \sqrt{10}$
l $\dfrac{\sqrt{27}}{\sqrt{3}}$
m $\dfrac{\sqrt{88}}{2}$
n $\dfrac{3\sqrt{12}}{\sqrt{3}}$

4 Marc says $\sqrt{10} + \sqrt{15} = \sqrt{25} = 5$

Tanya works it out differently, but gets the same answer.

She says $\sqrt{10} + \sqrt{15} = \sqrt{2} \times \sqrt{5} + \sqrt{3} \times \sqrt{5} = (\sqrt{2} + \sqrt{3}) \times \sqrt{5} = \sqrt{5} \times \sqrt{5} = 5$

a What did Marc do wrong?

b Where did Tanya go wrong?

5 Write down three irrational numbers between 1 and 2.

6 Show that:
$\sqrt{2} \times \sqrt{3} \times \sqrt{4} \times \sqrt{5} \times \sqrt{6} = 12\sqrt{5}$

7 A company makes wall tiles. The company makes two different sizes of square tile (purple and yellow) and one size rectangle (blue), to fit together as shown.
The yellow square tile has an area of 30 cm² and the purple square tile has an area of 15 cm².

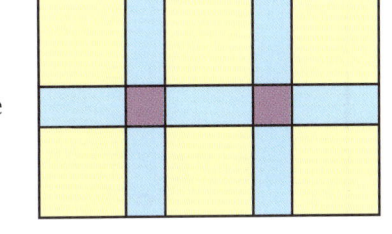

a What are the exact dimensions (length and width) of the rectangular blue tile?

b What is the area of the rectangular blue tile?

Give your answers as surds in their simplest form.

8 a Can you find two irrational numbers that multiply together to make a rational number?

b Can you find two irrational numbers that, when divided, give an answer of 2?

9 Write $\sqrt{5} \times \sqrt{35}$ in the form $p\sqrt{q}$, where p and q are both prime numbers.

10 a You are given that $A = \sqrt{a} + \sqrt{b}$ and $B = \sqrt{a} - \sqrt{b}$
Prove that $A^2 + B^2 = 30$ when $a = 12$ and $b = 3$.

b Find a different pair of values of a and b where $(\sqrt{a} + \sqrt{b})^2 + (\sqrt{a} - \sqrt{b})^2$ is a rational number.

Learn... 22.2 Rationalising the denominator

One way to simplify expressions involving surds is to rationalise the denominator.
This means removing the square root from the denominator.
Rationalising the denominator involves multiplying the numerator and denominator by fractions.

For example:
If the denominator is $\sqrt{a}$ then multiply the numerator and denominator by $\sqrt{a}$.
This leaves a in the denominator.

Using the fact that $\sqrt{a} \times \sqrt{a} = a$ since $\sqrt{a} \times \sqrt{a} = \sqrt{a \times a} = \sqrt{a^2} = a$

If the denominator is $b + \sqrt{c}$ then multiply the numerator and denominator by $b - \sqrt{c}$

Using the fact that $(b + \sqrt{c})(b - \sqrt{c}) = b^2 - c$ since $(b + \sqrt{c})(b - \sqrt{c}) = b^2 - b\sqrt{c} + b\sqrt{c} - c = b^2 - c$

Example: Rationalise the denominator of the following.

    a $\dfrac{\sqrt{3}}{\sqrt{5}}$ **b** $\dfrac{5}{2\sqrt{3}}$ **c** $\dfrac{2}{3+\sqrt{2}}$

Solution:

a $\dfrac{\sqrt{3}}{\sqrt{5}}$

$\dfrac{\sqrt{3}}{\sqrt{5}} = \dfrac{\sqrt{3} \times \sqrt{5}}{\sqrt{5} \times \sqrt{5}}$ If the denominator is $\sqrt{5}$ then multiply the numerator and denominator by $\sqrt{5}$

$= \dfrac{\sqrt{15}}{5}$

b $\dfrac{5}{2\sqrt{3}}$

$\dfrac{5}{2\sqrt{3}} = \dfrac{5 \times \sqrt{3}}{2\sqrt{3} \times \sqrt{3}}$ If the denominator is $\sqrt{3}$ (or a multiple of $\sqrt{3}$) then multiply the numerator and denominator by $\sqrt{3}$

$= \dfrac{5\sqrt{3}}{2 \times 3}$

$= \dfrac{5\sqrt{3}}{6}$

c $\dfrac{2}{3+\sqrt{2}}$

$\dfrac{2}{3+\sqrt{2}} = \dfrac{2(3-\sqrt{2})}{(3+\sqrt{2})(3-\sqrt{2})}$ If the denominator is $3+\sqrt{2}$ then multiply the numerator and denominator by $3-\sqrt{2}$

$= \dfrac{2(3-\sqrt{2})}{9 - 3\sqrt{2} + 3\sqrt{2} - 2}$

$= \dfrac{2(3-\sqrt{2})}{7}$

Practise... 22.2 Rationalising the denominator   D C B A A*

1 Rationalise the denominators of these fractions.

     a $\dfrac{\sqrt{7}}{\sqrt{3}}$ **d** $\dfrac{\sqrt{5}}{\sqrt{35}}$ **g** $\dfrac{5}{\sqrt{10}}$ **j** $\dfrac{30}{\sqrt{15}}$

     b $\dfrac{3}{2\sqrt{3}}$ **e** $\dfrac{7}{4\sqrt{7}}$ **h** $\dfrac{4}{2+\sqrt{3}}$ **k** $\dfrac{5}{2-\sqrt{3}}$

     c $\dfrac{7}{5+\sqrt{7}}$ **f** $\dfrac{3}{3-\sqrt{3}}$ **i** $\dfrac{\sqrt{3}}{3-\sqrt{3}}$ **l** $\dfrac{\sqrt{2}}{2+\sqrt{2}}$

2 Angela says $\sqrt{\dfrac{6}{18}} = \sqrt{\dfrac{1}{3}} = \sqrt{\dfrac{1 \times \sqrt{3}}{3 \times \sqrt{3}}} = \dfrac{\sqrt{3}}{3\sqrt{3}} = \dfrac{1}{3}$

Marco says $\sqrt{\dfrac{6}{18}} = \dfrac{\sqrt{6}}{\sqrt{18}} = \dfrac{\sqrt{6}}{\sqrt{9} \times \sqrt{2}} = \dfrac{\sqrt{6}}{3\sqrt{2}} = \dfrac{\sqrt{2}}{\sqrt{2}} = 1$

     a Find Angela's mistake.
     b Find Marco's mistake.
     c Work out the correct answer.

3 Show that $\dfrac{2}{3+\sqrt{5}} = \dfrac{3-\sqrt{5}}{2}$

4 A room has a length which is exactly $\sqrt{2}$ times its width. The length is 10 m.

     a What is the width? Give your answer as a surd (with a rational denominator).
     b What is the area of the room?

5 Simplify the following.

   a $\dfrac{1}{2} + \dfrac{3}{\sqrt{5}}$

   b $\dfrac{3}{2\sqrt{3}} - \dfrac{2}{3\sqrt{2}}$

6 Write $(3 - \sqrt{5})^2$ in the form $a + b\sqrt{5}$

7 If $x = \sqrt{2} + \sqrt{3}$

   a find x^2

   b show that $x^4 - 10x^2 + 1 = 0$

8 In his homework, Manesh had to rationalise the denominator of a fraction. He can remember that the denominator was $(2 - \sqrt{3})$, but he can't remember the numerator. He knows that the answer is $3(2 + \sqrt{3})$.

What was the numerator?

9 Prove that $\dfrac{\sqrt{20} - 10}{\sqrt{5}} = 2(1 - \sqrt{5})$

22 Assess

1 Which of the following numbers are rational and which are irrational? How can you tell?

   a $\sqrt{7}$
   b $\sqrt{16}$
   c $\dfrac{\sqrt{16}}{7}$
   d $\sqrt{\dfrac{16}{7}}$
   e $\dfrac{\sqrt{63}}{\sqrt{7}}$

2 Write these in their simplest form.

   a $\sqrt{8}$
   b $\sqrt{63}$
   c $\sqrt{98}$
   d $4\sqrt{27}$
   e $2\sqrt{50}$

3 Express each of these as a square root of a single number.

   a $2\sqrt{3}$
   b $4\sqrt{5}$
   c $5\sqrt{7}$
   d $2\sqrt{11}$
   e $10\sqrt{2}$

4 Rationalise the following expressions.

   a $\dfrac{2}{\sqrt{2}}$
   b $\dfrac{3}{\sqrt{7}}$
   c $\dfrac{4}{2\sqrt{5}}$
   d $\dfrac{5}{\sqrt{2} + 1}$
   e $\dfrac{7}{\sqrt{3} - \sqrt{2}}$
   f $\dfrac{\sqrt{2}}{\sqrt{3} + \sqrt{6}}$

5 Write the following in the form $a + b\sqrt{c}$

   a $(\sqrt{2} + 3)^2$
   b $(\sqrt{5} - 3)^2$
   c $(1 + \sqrt{2})(2 - \sqrt{2})$
   d $(\sqrt{3} + \sqrt{5})(\sqrt{3} - \sqrt{5})$
   e $(2\sqrt{5} + 3\sqrt{7})(2\sqrt{5} - 3\sqrt{7})$

6 Given that $a = \sqrt{2}$, $b = \sqrt{8}$ and $c = \sqrt{12}$, work out the value of $\dfrac{c}{a - b}$

Give your answer in its simplest form.

AQA Examination-style questions

1 The formula to find the volume of a cylinder is

   volume = $\pi \times$ radius$^2 \times$ height

   A cylinder has radius = $2\sqrt{3}$ metres and height = $\dfrac{1}{\sqrt{2}}$ metres.

   Work out the volume of the cylinder in terms of π.
   Rationalise the denominator and give your answer in its simplest form. *(5 marks)*

   AQA 2008

2 Find the value of x if $\dfrac{\sqrt{x} \times 50}{\sqrt{5}} = 4\sqrt{5}$ *(4 marks)*

   AQA 2008

Glossary

alternate angles – angles formed by parallel lines and a transversal that are on opposite sides of the transversal. For example, the angles marked a, which are on opposite sides of the transversal.

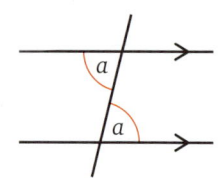

amount – the principal + the interest (i.e. the total you will have in the bank or the total you will owe the bank, at the end of the period of time).

average – the name given to a single value that represents a set of data.

balance – (i) how much money you have in your bank account (ii) how much you owe a shopkeeper after you have paid a deposit.

base – the lowest part of a 2-D or 3-D object (i.e. the side that it stands on).

bearing – an angle that denotes a direction. A bearing is measured clockwise from north.

bisect – to divide into two equal parts.

brackets – these show that the terms inside the brackets should be treated the same, for example, $3(2x + 1) = 3 \times 2x + 3 \times 1$

census – an official count or survey.

centre of rotation – the fixed point around which the object is rotated.

class interval – the range of values within a group (class) of grouped data.

closed questions – questions that control the responses allowed by using option boxes.

coefficient – the number (with its sign) in front of the letter representing the unknown, for example, in $4p - 5$, 4 is the coefficient of p. In $2 - 3p^2$, -3 is the coefficient of p^2.

common factor – factors that two or more numbers have in common, for example,
the factors of 10 are **1**, 2, **5**, 10
the factors of 15 are **1**, 3, **5**, 15
the common factors of 10 and 15 are **1** and **5**

compound interest – the interest paid is added to the amount in the account so that subsequently interest is calculated on the increased amount; the amount of money in the account grows exponentially.

compound measure – a measure formed from two or more measures. For example, speed $= \dfrac{\text{distance}}{\text{time}}$

congruent – exactly the same size and shape; one of the shapes might be rotated or flipped over.

constant – a number that does not change, for example, the formula $P = 4l$ states that the perimeter of a square is always four times the length of one side; 4 is a constant and P and l are variables. In the equation $y = 3x + 5$, $+5$ is the constant.

continuous data – quantitative data that are measured but must be rounded to be recorded such as heights, weights, times.

controlled experiment – data collection by a planned investigation of some type such as checking heart rates of runners.

coordinates – a system used to identify a point; an x-coordinate and a y-coordinate give the horizontal and vertical positions.

correlation – a measure of the relationship between two sets of data; correlation is measured in terms of type and strength.

corresponding angles – angles in the similar position between parallel lines and a transversal. For example, the angles marked b, which are on the same side of the transversal.

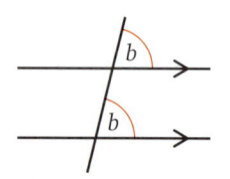

credit – when you buy goods 'on credit' you do not pay all the cost at once; instead you make a number of payments at regular intervals, often once a month. NB when your bank account is in 'credit', this means you have some money in it.

cross-section – a cut parallel to a face of, and usually at right angles to the length of, a prism.

data collection sheet – see **observation sheet**.

data logging – automatic collection of data by a 'dumb' machine, e.g. in a shop or car park entrance.

decagon – a polygon with ten sides.

decimal places – the number of digits after the decimal point. For example, the number 23.456 has three decimal places (4 tenths, 5 hundredths and 6 thousandths). Numbers can be rounded to different numbers of decimal places; 23.456 to 1 d.p. is 23.5

denominator – the bottom number of a fraction, indicating how many fractional parts the unit has been split into. In the fractions $\dfrac{4}{7}, \dfrac{23}{100}, \dfrac{6}{9}$ the denominators are 7 (indicating that the unit has been split into 7 parts, which are sevenths) 100 and 9

density – to find the density of an object, divide the mass by the volume. The units for density are usually grams per cubic centimetre (g/cm³) or kilograms per cubic metre (kg/m³).

deposit – an amount of money you pay towards the cost of an item; the rest of the cost is paid later.

depreciation – a reduction in value (of used cars, for example).

Glossary

diagonal – a line joining two vertices of a polygon (that are not next to each other).

dimension – the measurement between two points on the edge of a shape, for example length.

discount – a reduction in the price. Sometimes this is for paying in cash or paying early.

discrete data – quantitative data taking exact values such as frequencies, shoe size, dice scores.

equivalent fractions – two or more fractions that have the same value. Equivalent fractions can be made by multiplying or dividing the numerator and denominator of any fraction by the same number.

expand – to remove brackets to create an equivalent expression (expanding is the opposite of factorising).

expression – a mathematical statement written in symbols, for example, $3x + 1$ or $x^2 + 2x$.

exterior angle – the angle between one side of a polygon and the extension of the adjacent side.

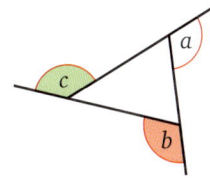

a, b and c are exterior angles

face – one of the flat surfaces of a solid. For example, a cube (such as a dice) has six flat faces.

factor – a natural number which divides exactly into another number with no remainder, for example, the factors of 18 are 1, 2, 3, 6, 9, 18

factorise – to include brackets by taking common factors (factorising is the opposite of expanding).

frequency distribution – shows the number of times particular values have occurred.

front elevation – this is the view of an object when viewed from the front or side. Sometimes called front elevation (view of the front), or side elevation (view of a side).

gradient – a measure of how steep a line is

$$\text{gradient} = \frac{\text{change in vertical distance}}{\text{change in horizontal distance}}$$

grouped data – data that are separated into data classes.

hexagon – a polygon with six sides.

highest common factor (HCF) – the highest factor that two or more numbers have in common, for example,
the factors of 12 are **1, 2**, 3, **4**, 6, 12
the factors of 20 are **1, 2, 4**, 5, 10, 20
the common factors are 1, 2, 4
the highest common factor is 4

hypotenuse – in a right-angled triangle, the longest side, opposite the right angle.

hypothesis – an idea that is put forward for investigation; for example, 'More girls are left handed than right handed'. Data would be collected and analysed in order to investigate whether the hypothesis might be true or not.

image – the shape following a transformation of the object, for example, reflection, rotation, translation or enlargement.

improper fraction – a fraction with a numerator greater than its denominator.

index (indices) – the index (or power or exponent) tells you how many times the base number is to be multiplied by itself.

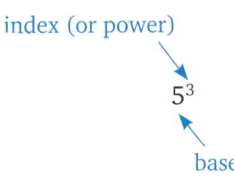

index (or power)

5^3

base

5^3 tells you that 5 (the base number) is to be multiplied by itself 3 times (the index or power). So $5^3 = 5 \times 5 \times 5$

inequality – statements such as $x < 5, y \geq -3$, are inequalities.

integer – any positive or negative whole number or zero, for example, $-2, -1, 0, 1, 2, \ldots$

intercept – the position where a graph crosses the y-axis.

interest – the money paid to you by a bank or building society when you save your money in an account with them.
NB It is also the money you pay for **borrowing** from a bank.

interior (or **allied**) – angles between two parallel lines and a transversal, which are on the same side of the transversal and between the parallel lines. For example, the angles marked a and b.

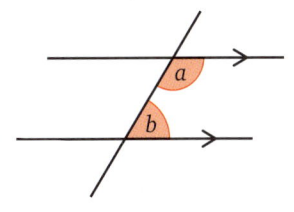

inter-quartile range – the upper quartile minus the lower quartile.

inverse operation – the operation that undoes a previous operation, for example, subtract is the inverse operation to add.

irrational number – a number that is not an integer and cannot be written as a fraction.
$\sqrt{2}, \sqrt{3}, \sqrt{5}, \sqrt{6}, \sqrt{7}, \sqrt{8}, \sqrt{10}, \sqrt{11}, \sqrt{12}, \sqrt{13}, \sqrt{14}, \sqrt{15}, \ldots$ are all irrational numbers,
but $\sqrt{1} = \frac{1}{1}$ or $\sqrt{4} = \frac{2}{1}$ or $\sqrt{9} = \frac{3}{1}$ or $\sqrt{16} = \frac{4}{1}, \ldots$ are all rational numbers. Roots of square numbers are all rational numbers.

least common multiple (LCM) – the least (or lowest) multiple that two or more numbers have in common, for example,
the multiples of 4 are 4, 8, **12**, 16, 20, **24**, 28, 32, **36** …
the multiples of 6 are 6, **12**, 18, **24**, 30, **36** …
the common multiples are 12, 24, 36 …
the least common multiple is 12

line of best fit – a line drawn to represent the relationship between two sets of data; ideally it should only be drawn where the correlation is strong, for example:

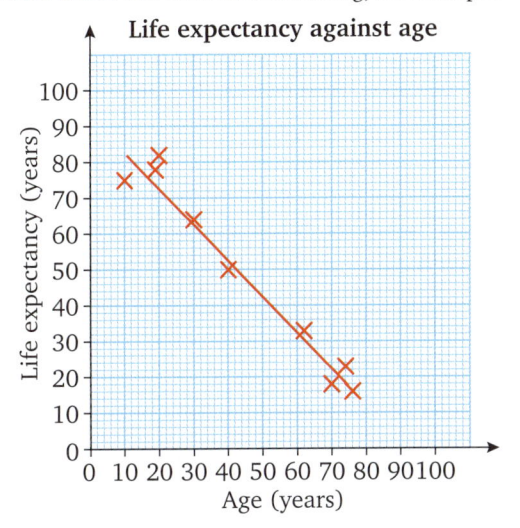

Life expectancy against age

line of symmetry – a shape has reflection symmetry about a line through its centre if reflecting it in that line gives an identical-looking shape.

line of symmetry

linear – describes an equation, expression, graph, etc. where the highest power of a variable is 1; for example, $3x + 2 = 7$ is a linear equation but $3x^2 + 2 = 7$ is not.

linear sequence – in a linear sequence, the differences are all the same.

This is a linear sequence

1st term	2nd term	3rd term	4th term
1,	8,	15,	22, …

+7   +7   +7

This is not a linear sequence

1st term	2nd term	3rd term	4th term
1,	4,	9,	16, …

+3   +5   +7

lower bound (or limit) – the value of a rounded quantity lies between two limits, the upper and lower bounds. The smallest possible value is called the lower bound (or limit).

mass – the weight of an object, measured in tonnes (t), kilograms (kg), grams (g) or milligrams (mg).

mean – the total of all the values divided by the number of values (also called the arithmetic mean).

$$\text{Mean} = \frac{\text{the total of (frequencies} \times \text{values)}}{\text{the total of frequencies}} = \frac{\Sigma fx}{\Sigma f}$$

median – the middle value when the data are listed in order.

mixed number – a fraction that has both a whole number and a fraction part.

modal class or modal group – the class or group within a frequency table that occurs most often.

mode – the value or item that occurs most often.

multiple – the multiples of a number are the products in its multiplication table, for example,
the multiples of 7 are 7, 14, 21, 28, 35, …

negative correlation – as one set of data increases, the other set of data decreases.

net – a net shows the faces and edges of an object. When the net is folded up it makes a 3-D object. For example, the net of a cube when folded up makes a cube.

nonagon – a polygon with nine sides.

nth term – this phrase is often used to describe a 'general' term in a sequence.

numerator – the top number of a fraction, indicating how many parts there are in the fraction.

observation – data collection by watching something happen.

observation sheet – prepared tables to record responses to questionnaires or outcomes for an observation such as noting car colours.

octagon – a polygon with eight sides.

open questions – allow for any response to be made by using an answer space.

outlier – a value that does not fit the general trend, for example:

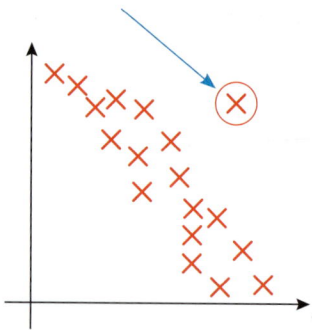

parabola – the locus of a point that moves so that it is always the same distance from a fixed point and a given line.

parallel – two lines that stay the same perpendicular distance apart.

pentagon – a polygon with five sides.

percentage – the number of parts per hundred. For example, 15% means $\frac{15}{100}$

perpendicular – at right angles to; two lines at right angles to each other are perpendicular lines.

perpendicular bisector – a line drawn at right angles to a line segment, cutting the segment into two equal parts.

perpendicular height – the height of a shape that is 90° to the base.

pilot survey – a small scale survey carried out before the main survey.

plan view – this is the view when an object is seen from above. Sometimes called the plan view.

polygon – a closed two-dimensional shape made from straight lines.

population – every possible item that could occur in a given situation.

positive correlation – as one set of data increases, the other set of data increases.

power – see **index**.

primary data – data that are collected specifically to answer the research question.

prime number – a natural number with exactly two factors. The first 7 prime numbers are:

2	3	5	7	11	13	17
Factors 1 & 2	Factors 1 & 3	Factors 1 & 5	Factors 1 & 7	Factors 1 & 11	Factors 1 & 13	Factors 1 & 17

1 is not a prime number because it has only one factor.
2 is the only even prime number.

prism – a solid that has the same cross-section all the way through.

product – the result of multiplying two or more numbers, for example, the product of 5 and 7 is 35.

proportion – compares one part with the whole, whereas a ratio compares one part with another. If a class has 10 boys and 15 girls, the proportion of boys in the class is $\frac{10}{25}$ (which simplifies to $\frac{2}{5}$). The proportion of girls in the class is $\frac{15}{25}$ (which simplifies to $\frac{3}{5}$).

Glossary

Pythagoras' theorem – in words 'the sum of squares on the two shorter sides of a right-angled triangle is equal to square on the hypotenuse' or $c^2 = a^2 + b^2$

quadratic expression – an expression containing terms where the highest power of the variable is 2.

quadrilateral – a polygon with four sides.

qualitative data – data that cannot be measured using numbers e.g. hair colour, sports, breeds of sheep.

quantitative data – data that can be measured such as heights, ages, times, frequencies.

questionnaire – data collection by a series of questions requiring responses.

random sampling – every member of the population has an equal chance of being in the sample.

range – the difference between the highest value and the lowest value in a distribution (a measure of spread, not a measure of average).

rate – the percentage at which interest is added.

ratio – a means of comparing numbers or quantities. A ratio shows how much bigger one number or quantity is than another. If two numbers or quantities are in the ratio 1 : 2, the second is always twice as big as the first. If two numbers or quantities are in the ratio 2 : 5, for every 2 parts of the first there are 5 parts of the second.

rational number – a number that can be expressed in the form $\frac{p}{q}$ where p and q are both integers. for example, $1 (= \frac{1}{1})$, $2\frac{1}{3} (= \frac{7}{3})$, $0.1 (= \frac{1}{10})$

raw data – data before they have been sorted in any way.

reciprocal – any number multiplied by its reciprocal equals 1. 1 divided by a number gives its reciprocal, for example, the reciprocal of 6 is $\frac{1}{6}$ because $6 \times \frac{1}{6} = 1$ or $1 \div 6 = \frac{1}{6}$

recurring decimal – a decimal whose digits after the point eventually form a repeating pattern. A dot over the digits indicates the repeating sequence, for example, $\frac{2}{7} = 0.\dot{2}8571\dot{4}$

reflection – a transformation involving a mirror line (or axis of symmetry), in which the line from the shape to its image is perpendicular to the mirror line. To describe a reflection fully, you must describe the position or give the equation of its mirror line, for example, the triangle A is reflected in the mirror line $y = 1$ to give the image B.

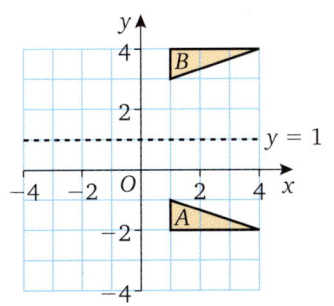

region – an area of a graph that has specific lines as its boundaries.

regular – a geometric shape where all internal angles are the same, e.g. a regular octagon has eight interior angles of 135°.

rotation – a transformation in which the shape is turned about a fixed point called the centre of rotation. To describe a rotation fully, you must give the centre, angle and direction (a positive angle is anticlockwise and a negative angle is clockwise), for example, the triangle A is rotated about the origin through 90° anticlockwise to give the image C.

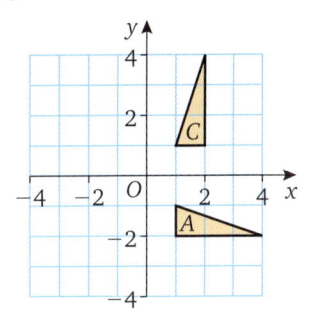

sample – a small part of a population from which information is taken.

sample size – the number of people or items in the sample.

scatter graph – a graph used to show the relationship between two sets of variables, for example, temperature and ice cream sales.

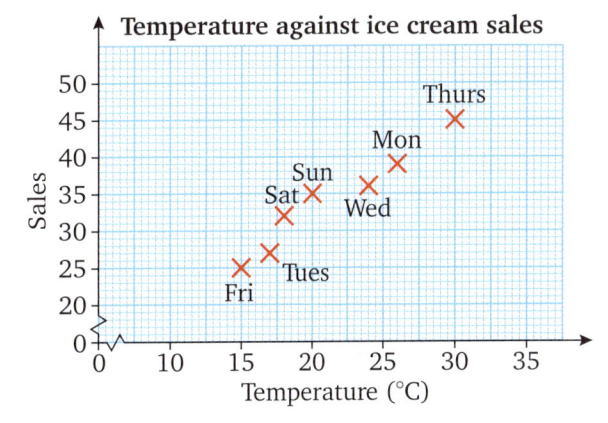

secondary data – data that others have collected; anything from newspapers, the internet and similar sources.

sequence – a sequence is a list of numbers or diagrams which are connected in some way.

side elevation – see **front elevation**.

significant figure – a digit in a number that is significant in the accuracy of the number. The closer the digit is to the beginning of the number the greater its significance. Zeros can be significant figures but are often in a number just to maintain the correct place value. Examples: The number 30 597 when rounded to three significant figures is 30 600; the first zero is significant but the final two are not. The number 3.0587 rounded to three significant figures is 3.06

simplify – (in algebra) to make simpler by collecting like terms.

solid – a three-dimensional shape.

solve – the instruction to find the value of the unknown, for example, $x = 3$, which is known as the solution of the equation.

speed – speed is the gradient of a line on a distance–time graph.

$$\text{Speed} = \frac{\text{distance travelled}}{\text{time taken}}$$

standard index form – standard index form is a shorthand way of writing very large and very small numbers.

stratified (random) sampling – if the population falls into a series of groups or 'strata' this ensures that the sample is representative of the population as a whole; for example, if the population has twice as many boys as girls, then the sample should have twice as many boys as girls (individuals within each strata are then chosen using random sampling).

surd – a number involving irrational numbers, for example, $\sqrt{2}, 3 + 2\sqrt{7}$

surface area – the exposed area of a solid object, often measured in square centimetres (cm^2) or square metres (m^2).

survey – general name for data collection using interviews or questionnaires.

terminating decimal – a decimal that has a finite number of digits after the decimal point for example, $\frac{1}{64} = 0.015625$

term-to-term – the rule which tells you how to move from one term to another.

1st term	2nd term	3rd term	4th term
5,	16,	27,	38, ...

+11 +11 +11

The rule to find the next number in the sequence is +11. The rule is called the term-to-term rule.

transformation – reflections, rotations, translations and enlargements are examples of transformations as they transform the position, orientation or size of a shape.

translation – a transformation where every point moves the same distance in the same direction so that the object and the image are congruent.

transversal – a line that crosses two or more parallel lines.

trial and improvement – a method for solving algebraic equations by making an informed guess, then refining this to get closer and closer to the solution.

triangle – a polygon with three sides.

two-way table – a table showing information about two sets of data at the same time.

unitary method – a method of calculating quantities that are in proportion by first finding one unit.

unitary ratio – a ratio in the form $1 : n$ or $n : 1$; this form of ratio is helpful for comparison, as it shows clearly how much of one quantity there is for one unit of the other.

unknown – in the equation $2x - 3 = 8$, x is the unknown.

upper bound (or limit) – the value of a rounded quantity lies between two limits, the upper and lower bounds. The upper limit is called the upper bound. The actual value of the quantity must lie below this bound.

variable – a symbol representing a quantity that can take different values, such as x, y or z.

VAT (Value Added Tax) – this tax is added on to the price of goods or services.

vector – a quantity with magnitude (size) and direction. In this diagram, the arrow represents the direction and the length of the line represents the magnitude.

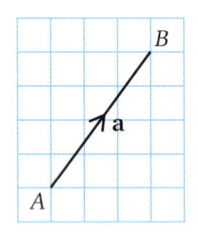

In print, this vector can be written as $\overrightarrow{AB}$ or **a**. In handwriting, this vector is usually written as $\overrightarrow{AB}$ or $\underline{a}$. The vector can also be described as a column vector:

where $\begin{pmatrix} x \\ y \end{pmatrix}$ ← x is the horizontal displacement
← y is the vertical displacement

vertex, vertices – the point where two or more edges meet.

vertically opposite angles – the opposite angles formed when two lines cross.

volume – the amount of space a solid takes up, often measured in cubic centimetres (cm^3) or cubic metres (m^3).

zero or no correlation – where there is no obvious relationship between the two sets of data.

Index

Key terms are given in **bold** and can be found in the glossary.

3-D shapes
    2-D representations 255–7
    coordinates 260–2
    Pythagoras' theorem 278–81
    surface area 152

addition
    decimals 63
    fractions 51–2, 90–1
    standard index form 176–7
algebra
    fractions 90–2
    indices 172
allied angles 8, 183
alternate angles 8
amounts
    compound interest 102
    percentages 97–9
angles 7–24
    bearings 11–12
    hexagons 185
    octagons 186
    parallel lines 8–10
    pentagons 185
    polygons 185–8
    quadrilaterals 182, 183
    triangles 185
Archimedes 247
area 7–24, 146–56
    circles 17–19
    compound shapes 20–2
    cubes 152
    cylinders 152
    parallelograms 13–16
    prisms 152–4
    trapeziums 13–16
    triangles 13–16
    triangular prisms 152
averages
    frequency distributions 115
    mean 115, 120
    median 116, 120
    mode 116, 120
    Vitruvian Man 114

balance 99
bases
    indices 172
    parallelograms 13
bearings 11–12
bisect 182
brackets
    equations 194–5
    expansion 82–6
    multiplication 89–90

cars, value of 162–3
census 43
centre of rotation 227
circles
    area 17–19
    circumference 17–19
class interval 120
closed questions 38
coefficients 71
collecting like terms 82–6
common factors 26
compound interest 102–4
compound measures 249–53
compound shapes 20–2
congruence 235, 239–43
constant (linear function) 71
continuing fractions 50
continuous data 35, 120
controlled experiments 39
convex polygons 185

coordinates 222, 260–2
correlation 211
corresponding angles 8
credit 99
credit card security 25
cross-section 147
cubes
    2-D representation 255–7
    surface area 152
    volume 148
cylinders
    surface area 152
    volume 147

data collection 34–49
    data-handling cycle 35
    methods 38–41
    organising data 41–2
    sampling 43–7
    sheets 41
    types of data 35–7
data collection sheets 41
data logging 39
decagons 187
decimal place 206–8
decimals 50–66
    addition 63
    calculations 63–5
    division 64
    fractions as 57–9
    multiplication 63
    percentages 94–7
    place 206–8
    rounding 61–2
    significant figures 62
    subtraction 63
denominators 51, 196, 197, 287–9
density 249, 250
deposit 99
depreciation 99, 162–3
diagonals 182
dimension 147
directions (bearings) 11–12
discount 98
discrete data 35, 115
distance-time graphs 158–61, 262, 263–4
division
    decimals 64
    fractions 53–5
    indices 172
    ratios 59–60
    standard index form 176–7
doctors 135

Egyptians 272, 281
email surveys 39
equations 192–204
    brackets 194–5
    fractions 196–7
    unknown on both sides 193–4
equivalent fractions 58, 64
expanding brackets 82–6
experiments 39
exponential growth 254
expressions
    bracket expansion 82
    factorisation 86–8
    quadratic expressions 89
exterior angles 183

face to face interviews 39
faces (3-D shapes) 152
factorising expressions 86–8
factors 26–8, 29, 86–8
Fibonacci sequence 128
fractions 50–66
    addition 51–2, 90–1
    algebraic 90–2
    comparing quantities 56–7

    decimal conversion 57–9
    division 53–5
    equations 196–7
    improper 51
    indices 173
    multiplication 53–5, 90
    percentages 94–7
    subtraction 51–2
frequency distributions 115–23
front elevation 255
fuel consumption 249

gradients
    distance-time graphs 158
    lines through two given points 76
    straight-line graphs 70–4
graphs 262–8
    distance-time graphs 158–61
    inequalities 200–3
    linear functions 67–80
    modelling 254
    real-life graphs 157–70, 262–5
    scatter graphs 210–20
    straight-line graphs 68–74
Great Fire of London 34
grouped data 120
grouped frequency distributions 120–3

HCF (highest common factor) 26
healthcare 135
hexagons 185
highest common factor (HCF) 26
house price graph 217
hypotenuse 273
hypothesis 35

image 222
improper fractions 51
index form 29
indices 171–80
    algebra 172
    division 172
    fractions 173
    multiplication 172
    negative indices 173
    notation 29
    rules 172–5
    simplification 172
    zero indices 173
inequalities 192–204
    graphs 200–3
    inverse operations 199
    number lines 198–9
    solving 199–200
integers 199
inter-quartile range 116–17, 120
intercepts 71, 76–8
interest 99, 102–4
interior (allied) angles 8, 183
internet shopping 25
interviews 39
inverse operations 199
irrational numbers 285
isometric paper 255
isosceles trapeziums 182
isosceles triangles 223, 275

kites 182, 275

Large Hadron Collider 221
least common multiple (LCM) 26
Leonardo da Vinci 114
like terms, collecting 82–6
line of best fit 214–18
line segment, midpoint 74–6
line of symmetry 222
line through two given points 76–8
linear equations 68
linear functions (graphs) 67–80

prime factors 25–33
prime numbers 25, 29–32
principal 103
prisms
    optical prisms 146
    surface area 152–4
    volume 147–51
products 25
proportion 135–45
proportional change, repeated 102
Pyramid of Giza 281
Pythagoras' theorem 272–83
    3-D shapes 278–81
    proof 273

quadratic expressions 89
quadrilaterals 182–5
qualitative data 35
quantitative data 35
questionnaires 38, 39
queuing theory 81

random sampling 43–4
range 116, 120
rate
    compound interest 102
    VAT 97
ratio 59–60, 135–45
    finding quantities 139–41
    simplification 136–9
    unitary method 141–3
rational numbers 285
rationalising the denominator 287–9
raw data 35
real-life graphs 157–70, 262–5
reciprocals 53
rectangles 182, 275
recurring decimals 57, 58
reflection 222–7, 239–40
region (graphs) 200
regular octagons 186
repeated proportional change 102
reverse percentages 110–11
rhombuses 182
rollercoasters 67
rotation 227–35, 239–40
rounding 60–3

sailing 7
sample 36
sample size 36
sampling methods 43–7
scatter graphs 210–20
    interpretation 211–14
    lines of best fit 214–18
secondary data 35
sequences 128–34
side elevation 255
significant figures 62
simplifying
    algebraic fractions 90–2
    indices 172
    like terms 82–6
    ratios 136–9
    surds 285–7
solids 147
solving equations 193–4
speed 158, 250, 262
square roots 173, 285
squares (shape) 182

standard index form 171–80
    addition 176–7
    conversions 175–6
    division 176–7
    multiplication 176–7
    subtraction 176–7
statistical measures 114–27
straight-line graphs
    drawing 68–70
    gradients 70–4
stratified (random) sampling 44
subtraction
    decimals 63
    fractions 51–2
    standard index form 176–7
successive percentages 100–2
supermarkets 81
surds 284–9
    rationalising the denominator 287–9
    simplification 285–7
surface area
    cubes 152
    cylinders 152
    prisms 152–4
    triangular prisms 152
surveys 38, 39
symbols 81–92

telephone surveys 39
temperature graphs 162, 211, 262
term-to-term rule 129
terminating decimals 57
time-distance graphs 158–61, 262, 263–4
transformation 223, 239–43
translation 235–9
transversal 8
trapeziums 13–16, 182
trial and improvement 205–9
triangles
    angles 185
    area 13–16
    Pythagoras' theorem 272–83
triangular dotty paper 255
triangular prisms
    surface area 152
    volume 147
two-way tables 41

unitary method 59
    ratios 141–3
    reverse percentages 110
unitary ratios 136, 141–3
unknowns (equations) 193–4
upper bound (or limit) 248

variables 71
VAT (Value Added Tax) 96, 97, 99
vectors 235
vertex/vertices 222
vertically opposite angles 8
video games 181
Vitruvian Man 114
volume 146–56
    cubes 148
    cylinders 147
    prisms 147–51
    triangular prisms 147

zero indices 173
zero or no correlation 211

...m 176–7

...on 211
...73
...s 199

...–32
...inequalities 198–9
...s 53

...tion 39
...ation sheets 41
...ons 186
...questions 38
...iers 211, 214

...aper folding 171
paper, isometric 255
parabolas 265
parallel lines 8–10, 76–8
parallelograms 13–16, 182
pentagons 185, 226
Pepys, Samuel 34
percentages 93–113
    comparing quantities 105–7
    compound interest 102–4
    as decimals 94–7
    decreases 97–9, 107–9
    as fractions 94–7
    increases 97–9, 107–9
    reverse percentages 110–11
    successive percentages 100–2
perpendicular 182
perpendicular bisector 228
perpendicular height 13
pi (π) 285
pilot surveys 38
plan view 255
plans 255–60
polygons 181–91
population 36, 162, 249
positive correlation 211
postal surveys 39
powers 172
primary data 35
prime factor decomposition 29